THE CREATION OF
FEMINIST CONSCIOUSNESS

WOMEN AND HISTORY
by GERDA LERNER

VOLUME ONE
The Creation of Patriarchy

VOLUME TWO
The Creation of Feminist Consciousness:
From the Middle Ages to Eighteen-seventy

THE CREATION
OF FEMINIST
CONSCIOUSNESS

*From the Middle Ages
to Eighteen-seventy*

GERDA LERNER

OXFORD UNIVERSITY PRESS
New York • Oxford • 1993

Oxford University Press

Oxford   New York   Toronto
Delhi   Bombay   Calcutta   Madras   Karachi
Kuala Lumpur   Singapore   Hong Kong   Tokyo
Nairobi   Dar es Salaam   Cape Town
Melbourne   Auckland   Madrid

and associated companies in
Berlin   Ibadan

Published by Oxford University Press, Inc.,
200 Madison Avenue, New York, New York 10016

Oxford is a registered trademark of Oxford University Press

Library of Congress Cataloging-in-Publication Data
Lerner, Gerda, 1920–
The creation of feminist consciousness:
From the Middle Ages to Eighteen-seventy
Gerda Lerner.
p. cm.   (Women and history ; v. 2)
Includes bibliographical references and index.
ISBN 0-19-506604-9
1. Women—History.   2. Feminist theory—History.
3. Women intellectuals—History.   4. Civilization, Western—History.
I. Title.   II. Series: Lerner, Gerda, 1920–   Women and history ; v. 2.
HQ1121.L47   1986 vol.2
305.42—dc20   92-20411

9 8 7 6 5 4 3 2 1

Printed in the United States of America
on acid-free paper

To my grandchildren
to whom the impossible will seem commonplace:

SOPHIA and JOSHUA
REED and CLAY

Preface and Acknowledgments

This two-volume work has been many years in the making. It began in 1977 with my hypothesis that it is the nature of the relationship of women to history which explains the long duration of their subordination and the slow development of the rise of feminist consciousness. The design for the present book was fairly clear in my mind when I began the work, but I soon found that I needed to know more about the origin and the causes of women's subordination which preceded the creation of written history, before I could adequately deal with women's relationship to that history. Thus, Volume One of this work, *The Creation of Patriarchy*, came to be written as a sort of grand detour. I have not regretted that detour, for it was indeed essential to sharpening my understanding of the interaction between access to resources (class), men's sexual and bodily control over women, and ideas about gender which spring from such material realities. But the most important thing I learned was the significance to women of their relationship to the Divine and the profound impact the severing of that relationship had on the history of women. Only after exploring the process of the "dethroning of the goddesses" in the various cultures of the Ancient Near East could I fully appreciate the depth and urgency of the search of Jewish and Christian women for connection to the Divine, which found expression in more than 1000 years of feminist Bible criticism and religious re-visioning. The insight that religion was the primary arena on which women fought for hundreds of years for feminist consciousness was not one I had previously had. It was won in work on Volume One; I listened to the voices of forgotten women and accepted what they told me.

Volume Two took another seven years of work. It would have taken far longer had it not been for the continuing support I received from the University of Wisconsin-Madison in the form of my appointment as Wisconsin Alumni Research Foundation Senior Distinguished Research Professor, 1984–91. This generous chair appointment gave me each year one semester free of teaching obligations, which permitted me to carry my research and writing forward without interruption. At my age, this kind of support and trust extended has more significance than in one's younger years. I am deeply grateful for it and hope the results will justify my colleagues' confidence in my work.

A resident fellowship at the Rockefeller Foundation's Study and Conference Center in Bellagio, Italy, in October–November 1991 helped me to complete the book and its bibliography in a beautiful environment and with stimulating company. I thank the Rockefeller Foundation for its generous support.

I presented a paper, "The Emergence of Feminist Consciousness: The Idea of Motherhood," based on what is now Chapter Six, at the Eighth Berkshire Conference on the History of Women, June 8–10, 1990, Douglass College. The comments and criticism of the panelists, Professors Eleanor McLaughlin (Mount Holyoke College), Clarissa Atkinson (Harvard Divinity School) and Sara Ruddick (New School for Social Research) were most helpful to me in rethinking this chapter.

Several other chapters of this book were the basis for lectures at the following institutions: Colorado College, January 1989; University of South Florida, November 1989; Walter E. Edge Lecture Series at Princeton University, April 1990; University of Wisconsin-Madison, September 1991; University of Pittsburgh, March 1991; Lewis and Clark College, April 1991; Victoria University, Wellington, New Zealand; Erasmus Universität, Rotterdam, Netherlands, 1991; Edgewood College, Madison, Wisconsin, 1992. In each case the lively and searching discussion following the lecture helped me to sharpen my argument and correct weaknesses.

My search for sources was greatly helped by the generosity of several scholars who shared their own work and knowledge with me and who led me to important sources: Professors Ursula Liebertz-Grün (Universität zu Köln); Kari Elizabeth Børressen (Research Professor, Oslo, Norway) and Suzanne Desan (University of Wisconsin-Madison). Chava Weissler (Princeton University) shared her own published and unpublished work and introduced me to many sources on Jewish women. Maryanne Horowitz (Occidental College) shared her thorough knowledge of Renaissance sources and argued passionately over my interpretations, much to my benefit.

In a work of this scope the criticism of experts in the various fields is indispensable. I benefited greatly from the generosity of many scholars who were willing to read and criticize parts of the manuscript which related to their particular expertise. My profound thanks go to: Clarissa Atkinson; Constance Berman; Maryanne Horowitz; Ruth Perry (Massachusetts Institute of Technology); Hilda Smith (University of Cincinnati); Nancy Isenberg (Commonwealth Center, Williamsburg); Virginia Brodine and my colleagues at the University of Wisconsin: Judy Leavitt (History of Medicine); Linda Gordon (History); Carl Kaestle (History of Education). Your sharing of knowledge and research resources made my "impossible" task less daunting.

A late draft of the entire book was read by Paul Boyer (University of Wisconsin-Madison); Kathleen Brown (Princeton University); Steven Feierman (University of Florida, Gainesville); Linda Kerber (University of Iowa); Ann Lane (University of Virginia); Lawrence Levine (University of California at Berkeley) and Elizabeth Minnich. The careful and detailed criticism I received from these scholars and friends enabled me to rewrite my work and find its final form. It also immensely encouraged and supported me during the most difficult periods.

This is the third book I am publishing with Sheldon Meyer and my appreciation for his style, his taste and perceptiveness has grown with each passing year. I cannot think of another editor who would tolerate a fifteen-year delay in completion of a manuscript without a murmur of disapproval and who would, on the contrary, encourage and approve of a grand detour like mine. His understanding of my thought and of my work process has been a constant source of surprise and delight to me. He has my warmest appreciation and gratitude.

Leona Capeless has done a superb job on this volume, as she did on the first one. Her knowledge and skills, enhanced by her seemingly boundless patience, make the technical work of producing a book quite tolerable, even interesting. I thank her sincerely.

A succession of project assistants have worked their way through the sources of the history of women and have in many ways facilitated and improved my work. Elizabeth Williams; Kathryn Tomasek, Samantha Langbaum and Jennifer Frost have my warmest thanks for their effort and support. Anita Olson, despite her many other taxing duties, always found time to improve the typing of this manuscript and of its difficult bibliography. Her interest in this work since its inception has gone far beyond the expert technical help she offered; she was often my first reader and sympathetic critic. I truly appreciate her help.

I am indebted for their knowledge and courteous help to archivists and librarians at the Wisconsin State Historical Society and Wisconsin University Memorial Libraries, both in Madison, Wisconsin; the University of California Library at Berkeley; the Schlesinger Library, Radcliffe College, Cambridge, Massachusetts, the British Library and the Fawcett Library, London, England. My special thanks to Sr. Angela Carlovaris, archivist of the Abtei St. Hildegard, Eibingen, Germany, who permitted me to see the Hildegard of Bingen manuscript at the abbey and who shared her extensive knowledge of sources and interpretations.

This work was done in years of solitary living; most likely, it could not have been done otherwise. It was the most difficult work I have ever done because the scope of women's difficulties, losses and disappointments, the horrifying tragedy of wasted talents and energy extending over centuries and millennia, became more visible to me than it had ever before. But in the end, I also sensed and experienced the strength of resistance, endurance and transcendence, the luminous thread of a common search for history, the insistence by women that we have a history and with it full humanity.

The ongoing work and continuing achievements of the Women's History community have provided for me what the women whose lives and struggles I described lacked so tragically—a supportive women's network. The many ways in which we have approached our enormous task with increasing awareness of differences among us have led to a solid foundation for our common enterprise. We no longer attempt to speak in one voice, but to appreciate and hear the many different voices. We no longer need to agree on one theory or one set of explanations and conflict, even among ourselves, no longer seems as threatening as it once did. Rather, it is a natural outgrowth of the breadth of our movement for cultural transformation.

On a personal level, the love of my family—Stephanie and Todd, Dan and Paula and the children—has nurtured and sustained me.

My close friends have given me love and friendship through the good times and the bad. And always, through these past decades, despite the geographical distance between us, my dear friend Eve Merriam has walked beside me, knowing and hearing and sharing. Now she is gone, but her poetry and thought and love live on. This book is for and of her.

Madison, Wisconsin   G.L.
August 1992

A NOTE ON STYLE

Generally, I follow the practice of citing all primary sources from the earliest available text in the language of origin. In instances of sources I cannot read due to my lack of language skills, I have tried to cite the earliest English version available. I have used the same principle in regard to authors' names, spelling them in the language of the author. (Thus—Vilemina for the leader of the movement known in English as "the Guglielmites.") Where I have had to deviate from this practice, I have indicated the reprint edition from which I drew my source in order to enable the reader to find the source easily and to know that I did not see the actual manuscript.

The terms of reference by which African-Americans have referred to themselves has changed in the course of history. At any given time there has usually been a range of differences among them in how they prefer to be designated. I have followed the practice of using the designation chosen by the author or by the group in question during a particular historical period. (Thus: "Negro Women's club movement," but "Black Liberation."). According to the same principle I refer to the 19th-century "woman's rights movement" and to the 20th century "women's rights movement." African-Americans have struggled for over a hundred years to have the term used to designate them be capitalized, as are the designations for other ethnic or racial groups. ("Italian, Spanish, Negro"). Thus, whenever the noun "Black" is used as a substitute for "African-American" or "Negro" it designates members of a racial group, therefore it should be spelled with a capital "B," a fact even the *New York Times* has finally recognized. There is a great deal of confusion about the spelling of the adjective "black." One can reason both ways—"Black women and Italian women"—both designating group adherence or "black and white women," both designating skin color, hence lower-case. I usually capitalize the noun and lower-case the adjective, but I recognize that this is a term in transition.

Because this book is organized thematically, it has been impossible to avoid the appearance of the same authors in several chapters. Thus, Christine de Pizan is discussed in different chapters regarding her writings on motherhood, education, the history of women. My practice is to give a biographical description of the author the first time she is mentioned. Readers can use the Index to find the other places on which each author is discussed.

The Bibliography is arranged with the needs of teachers in mind. Those wishing to gain quick access to the sources on one of the women featured in the book will find her listed with the pertinent sources under the appropriate chronological heading. A separate cross index of "Authors cited" will help locate sources and references on each author.

Contents

THE CREATION OF
FEMINIST CONSCIOUSNESS

ONE

Introduction

IN VOLUME ONE I DESCRIBED the creation of patriarchy, which took place prior to the formation of Western civilization. Patriarchal concepts are, therefore, built into all the mental constructs of that civilization in such a way as to remain largely invisible. Tracing the historical development by which patriarchy emerged as the dominant form of societal order, I have shown how it gradually institutionalized the rights of men to control and appropriate the sexual and reproductive services of women. Out of this form of dominance developed other forms of dominance, such as slavery. Once established as a functioning system of complex hierarchical relationships, patriarchy transformed sexual, social, economic relations and dominated all systems of ideas. In the course of the establishment of patriarchy and constantly reinforced as the result of it, the major idea systems which explain and order Western civilization incorporated a set of unstated assumptions about gender, which powerfully affected the development of history and of human thought.

I have shown how the metaphors of gender constructed the male as the norm and the female as deviant; the male as whole and powerful; the female as unfinished, physically mutilated and emotionally dependent.

Briefly summarized the major assumptions about gender in patriarchal society are these:

Men and women are essentially different creatures, not only in their biological equipment, but in their needs, capacities and functions. Men and women also differ in the way they were created and in the social function assigned to them by God.

Men are "naturally" superior, stronger and more rational, therefore designed to be dominant. From this follows that men are political citizens and responsible for and representing the polity. Women are "naturally" weaker, inferior in intellect and rational capacities, unstable emotionally and therefore incapable of political participation. They stand outside of the polity.

Men, by their rational minds, explain and order the world. Women by their nurturant function sustain daily life and the continuity of the species. While both functions are essential, that of men is superior to that of women. Another way of saying this is that men are engaged in "transcendent" activities, women—like lower-class people of both sexes—are engaged in "immanent" activities.

Men have an inherent right to control the sexuality and the reproductive functions of women, while women have no such right over men.

Men mediate between humans and God. Women reach God through the mediation of men.

These unproven, unprovable assumptions are not, of course, laws of either nature or society, although they have often been so regarded and have even been incorporated into human law. They are operative at different levels, in different forms and with different intensity during various periods of history. Changes in the way in which these patriarchal assumptions are acted upon describe in fact changes in the status and position of women in a given period in a given society. The development of concepts of gender should therefore be studied by any historian wishing to elicit information about women in any society.

In Volume One I concluded that women had a relationship to History and to historical process different from that of men. It is helpful to distinguish between history—events of the past—and recorded History—events of the past as interpreted by succeeding generations of historians. The latter is a cultural product, by which events of the past are selected, ordered and interpreted. It is in recorded history that women have been obliterated or marginalized. In this second volume, I attempt to define the nature of the difference between these two concepts more precisely and to show how the construction of recorded History has affected women.

The archaic states of the Ancient Near East which developed priesthood, kingship and militaristic elites did so in a context of developing male dominance over women and a structured system of slavery. It is not accidental that the time, leisure and education necessary for developing philosophy, religion and science was made available to an elite of priests, rulers and bureaucrats, whose domestic needs were met by the unpaid labor of women and slaves. In the second millennium B.C. this elite occasionally included female priestesses, queens and rulers, but by the time patriarchy was firmly established, approximately in the 6th century B.C., it was always male. (The appearance of an occasional queen to substitute for a missing male heir only confirms this rule.) In other words, it is patriarchal slave society which gives rise to the systems of ideas that explain and order the world for millennia thereafter. The twin mental constructs—the philosophical and the scientific systems of thought—explain and order the world in such a way as to confer and confirm power upon their adherents and deny power to those disputing them. Just as the distribution and allocation of resources give power to the rulers, so do the withholding of information and the denial of access to explanatory constructs give power to the system builders.

From the time of the establishment of patriarchy to the present, males of non-elite groups have struggled with increasing success for a share in this power of defining and naming. The history of the Western world can be viewed as the unfolding of that class-based struggle and the story of the process by which more and more non-elite males have gained access to economic and mental resources. But during this entire period, well into the middle of the 20th century, women have been excluded from all or part of that process and have been unable to gain access to it.

Not only have women been excluded through educational deprivation from the process of making mental constructs, it has also been the case that the mental constructs explaining the world have been androcentric, partial and distorted. Women have been defined out and marginalized in every philosophical system and have therefore had to struggle not only against exclusion but against a content which defines them as subhuman and deviant.[1] I argue that this dual deprivation has formed the female psyche over the centuries in such a way as to make women collude in creating and generationally re-creating the system which oppressed them.

I have shown in Volume One how gender became the dominant metaphor by which Aristotle defended and justified the system of slavery. At the time of Aristotle's writing of *Politics* the question of the moral rightness of slavery was still problematical. It was certainly questionable in light of the very system of ethics and morals Aristotle was constructing. Why should one man rule over another? Why should one man be master and another be slave? Aristotle reasoned that some men are born to rule, others to be ruled. He illustrated this principle by drawing an analogy between soul and body—the soul is superior to the body and therefore must rule it. Similarly, rational mind is superior to passion and so must rule it. And "the male is by nature superior, and the female inferior; and the one rules and the other is ruled; this principle, of necessity extends to all mankind."[2] The analogy extends also to men's rule over animals.

> And indeed the use made of slaves and of tame animals is equally not very different; for both with their bodies minister to the needs of life. . . . It is clear, then, that some men are by nature free, and others slaves, and that for these latter slavery is both expedient and right.[3]

The remarkable thing about this explanation is what is deemed in need of justification and what is assumed as a given. Aristotle admitted that there is some justification for a difference of opinion regarding the rightness of enslaving captive peoples in the event of an unjust war. But there is no difference of opinion regarding the inferiority of women. The subordination of women is assumed as a given, likened to a natural condition, and so the philosopher uses the marital relationship as an explanatory metaphor to justify slavery. By his efforts at justifying the moral rightness of slavery, Aristotle had indeed recognized the basic truth of the humanity of the slave. By denying and ignoring the need to explain the subordination of women, as well as by the kind of biological explanation Aristotle offered elsewhere, he had fixed women in a status of being less-than-human. The female is, in his words, "as it were, a mutilated male."[4]

More remarkable than Aristotle's misogynist construction is the fact that his assumptions remained virtually unchallenged and endlessly repeated for nearly two thousand years. They were reinforced by Old Testament restrictions on women and their exclusion from the covenant community, by the misogynist teachings of the Church fathers and by the continuing emphasis in the Christian era on charging Eve, and with her all women, with moral guilt for the Fall of humankind.

MORE THAN TWO THOUSAND years after Aristotle, the founding fathers of the American republic debated their Constitution. Once again, a group of revolutionary leaders, defining themselves as republicans and devoted to the creation of a democratic polity, was faced with the contradiction of the existence of slavery in their republic. The issue of how to deal with slavery was hotly contested and highly controversial. It ended in a pragmatic compromise which perpetuated a major social problem in the new republic.

The Declaration of Independence which states, "We hold these truths to be self-evident that all men are created equal and are endowed by their Creator with certain unalienable Rights, that among these are Life, Liberty and the pursuit of Happiness," implied that by natural right all human beings were endowed with the same rights. How were such principles to be upheld in the face of the existence of slavery in the Southern states? The issue surfaced in the constitutional debates on laws regulating the slave trade, assigning responsibility for the return of fugitive slaves and apportioning voting rights. The last issue proved to be the most difficult, the Northern states holding that slaves should be counted as property and not counted at all in voting apportionment. The Southern states wanted slaves to be counted as though they were citizens, with their votes being wielded by the men who owned them. What was at issue, more than the abstract principle of how to regard the Negro, was the relative regional strength in Congress. Since the Southern population including slaves was more numerous than the population of the free states, this would have given the Southerners predominance in the House of Representatives. The irony in the debate was that the proslavery forces argued the humanity of the slaves, while antislavery forces argued for their status as property. Definitions, in this case, were determined not by reason, logic or moral considerations, but by political/economic interest.

The compromise which was finally incorporated into the Constitution was couched in a language as devoid of concreteness and as abstract as possible. "Representatives and direct taxes" were to be apportioned by adding to the number of citizens in each of the states "including those bound to Service for a Term of Years, and excluding Indians not taxed, three fifths of all other Persons." In plain words, a slave was to be counted three-fifths of a man for purposes of voting apportionment. Implicit in both language and debate was the recognition that the Negro, although a chattel, was indeed human. The founders' uneasiness with the slavery issue was expressed in the outlawing of the external slave trade in 1808, which most men believed would doom slavery to wither of its own accord. It also found expression in the terms of the Northwest Ordinance of 1787, which explicitly stated that the territories then defined as the Northwest would remain free. This laid the basis for the constitutional argument of the antislavery campaigns of the antebellum period, that the power to keep slavery out of the territories lay with the Congress. Thus the Constitution in its unresolved contradiction over the slavery issue not only presaged the Civil War but set in motion the ideas and expectations that would fuel the struggle for the slaves' eventual emancipation and their admission to full citizenship.

It was different for women. There was no controversy or debate on the definition of a voter as a male. The American Constitution embodied the patriarchal assumption, shared by the entire society, that women were not members of the polity. It was felt necessary by the founders to define the status of indentured servants, persons "bound to Service for a Term of Years," and of Indians in regard to voting rights, but there was no need felt even to mention, much less to explain or justify, that while women were to be counted among "the whole number of free persons" in each state for purposes of representation, they had no right to vote and to be elected to public office (U.S. Constitution, Article I, 3). The issue of the civil and political status of women never entered the debate, just as it had not entered the debate in Aristotle's philosophy.

Yet women in large numbers had been involved in political actions in the American Revolution and had begun to define themselves differently than had their mothers and grandmothers in regard to the polity. At the very least, they had found ways of exerting influence on political events by fund-raising, tea boycotts and actions against profiteering merchants. Loyalist women made political claims when they argued for their property rights independent of those of their husbands or when they protested against various wartime atrocities. Several influential female members of elite families privately raised the issue of women's rights as citizens. Petitioners of various kinds thrust it into the public debate. Unbidden and without a recognized public forum and emboldened by the revolutionary rhetoric and the language of democracy, women began to reinterpret their own status. As did slaves, women took the preamble of the Declaration of Independence literally. But unlike slaves, they were not defined as being even problematic in the debate.[5]

The well-known exchange of private letters between John Adams and his wife Abigail sharply exemplifies the limits of consciousness on this issue. Here was a well-matched and loving couple, unusual in the wife's political interest and involvement, which would find active expression during her husband's later term as President when she handled some of his correspondence.[6] In 1776 Abigail Adams urged her husband in a letter to "remember the ladies" in his work on the legal code for the new republic, reminding him that wives needed protection against the "naturally tyrannical" tendencies of their husbands. Abigail's language was appropriate to women's subordinate status in marriage and society—she asked for men's chivalrous protection from the excesses of other men. John's reply was "As to your extraordinary code of laws, I cannot but laugh. . . ." He expressed astonishment that like children and disobedient servants, restless Indians and insolent Negroes "another tribe more numerous and powerful than all the rest [had] grown discontented." Chiding his wife for being "saucy," he trivialized her argument by claiming that men were, in practice "the subjects. We have only the name of masters."[7] A problem outside of definition and discourse could not be taken seriously. And yet, for an instant, John Adams allowed himself to think seriously on the subject—her code of laws, if enacted, would lead to social disorder: "Depend upon it, we know better than to repeal our Masculine systems."[8]

Here we see, in its extreme manifestation, the impact on History of men's power to define. Having established patriarchy as the foundation of the family and the state, it appeared immutable and became the very definition of social order. To challenge it was both ludicrous and profoundly threatening.

At the time Aristotle defined the rightness of slavery, the issue of the humanity of the slave was debatable but not yet political. By 1787 the founders of the new republic had to recognize the humanity of the slave and deal with its denial as a controversial political issue. The statement that the slave may be fully human yet for purposes of political power distribution (among the masters) may be counted as only three-fifths human and not at all as a citizen, was so profound a contradiction in a Christian nation founded on democratic principles that it made the end of slavery inevitable in less than a century. But for women nothing at all had changed in terms of the debate since the time of Aristotle. As far as the definition of humanity was concerned, they were still defined as incomplete and marginal, a sort of sub-species. As far as the polity was concerned, they were not even recognized sufficiently to be coddled with the sop of "virtual representation." The issue defined as a social problem can enter political debate and struggle. The issue defined out, remains silenced, outside the polity.

This ultimate consequence of men's power to define—the power to define what is a political issue and what is not—has had a profound effect on women's struggle for their own emancipation. Essentially, it has forced thinking women to waste much time and energy on defensive arguments; it has channeled their thinking into narrow fields; it has retarded their coming into consciousness as a collective entity and has literally aborted and distorted the intellectual talents of women for thousands of years.

In the literature dealing with the subject of women in history the emphasis has been on the various discriminations and disabilities under which women have lived. Structural, legal and economic inequalities between men and women have held the focus of attention, with educational deprivation seen mostly as yet another form of economic discrimination in that it restricted women's access to resources and self-support. I focus in this study on the educational disadvantaging of women as a major force in determining women's individual and collective consciousness and thus a major force in determining women's political behavior.

The systematic educational disadvantaging of women has affected women's self-perceptions, their ability to conceptualize their own situation and their ability to conceive of societal solutions to improve it. Not only has it affected women individually, but far more important, it has altered women's relationship to thought and to history. Women, for far longer than any other structured group in society, have lived in a condition of trained ignorance, alienated from their own collective experience through the denial of the existence of Women's History. Even more important, women have for millennia been forced to prove to themselves and to others their capacity for full humanity and their capacity for abstract thought. This has skewed the intellectual development of women as a group, since their major intellectual endeavor had to be to counteract the pervasive patriarchal assumptions of their inferiority and incompleteness as human beings. It is this basic fact about their condition which explains why women's major intellectual enterprise for more than a thousand years was to re-conceptualize religion in such a way as to allow for women's equal and central role in the Christian drama of the Fall and Redemption. Women's striving for emancipation was acted out in the arena of religion long before women could conceive of political solutions for their situation.

The next issue through which women's quest for equality found expression was the struggle for access to education. Here, again, women were forced for hundreds of years not only to argue for their right to equal education, but first to prove their capacity to be educated at all. This exhausted the energies of the most talented women and retarded their intellectual development. Further, up until the end of the 19th century in Europe and the United States, women in order to be educated had to forgo their sexual and reproductive lives—they had to choose between wifehood and motherhood on the one hand and education on the other. No group of men in history ever had to make such a choice or pay such a price for intellectual growth.

For many centuries the talents of women were directed not toward self-development but toward realizing themselves through the development of a man. Women, conditioned for millennia to accept the patriarchal definition of their role, have sexually and emotionally serviced men and nurtured them in a way that allowed men of talent a fuller development and a more intensive degree of specialization than women have ever had. The sexual division of labor which has allotted to women the major responsibility for domestic services and the nurturance of children has freed men from the cumbersome details of daily survival activities, while it disproportionately has burdened women with them. Women have had less spare time and above all less uninterrupted time in which to reflect, to think and to write. The psychological support from intimacy and love has been far more readily available to talented men than to talented women. Had there been a man behind each brilliant woman, there would have been women of achievement in history equal to the numbers of men of achievement.

On the other hand it can be argued that throughout the millennia of their subordination the kind of knowledge women acquired was more nearly correct and adequate than was the knowledge of men. It was knowledge not based on theoretical propositions and on works collected in books, but practical knowledge derived from essential social interaction with their families, their children, their neighbors.

Such knowledge was its own reward in making women aware of their essential role in maintaining life, family and community. Like men of subordinate castes, classes and races, women have all along had thorough knowledge of how the world works and how people work within it and with each other. This is survival knowledge for the oppressed, who must maneuver in a world in which they are excluded from structured power and who must know how to manipulate those in power to gain maximum protection for themselves and their children. The conditions under which they lived forced women to develop interpersonal skills and sensitivities, as have other oppressed groups. Their skill and knowledge were not made available to society as a whole because of patriarchal hegemony and instead found expression in what we now call women's culture. I will show in this book how women transformed the concepts and assumptions of male thought and subtly subverted male thought so as to incorporate women's cultural knowledge and viewpoint. This tension between patriarchal hegemony and women's re-definition is a feature of historical process we have hitherto neglected to describe and observe.

Women have also been deprived of "cultural prodding," the essential dialogue and encounter with persons of equal education and standing. Shut out of institutions of higher learning for centuries and treated with condescension or derision, educated women have had to develop their own social networks in order for their thoughts, ideas and work to find audiences and resonance. And finally, the fact that women were denied knowledge of the existence of Women's History decisively and negatively affected their intellectual development as a group. Women who did not know that others like them had made intellectual contributions to knowledge and to creative thought were overwhelmed by the sense of their own inferiority or, conversely, the sense of the dangers of their daring to be different. Without knowledge of women's past, no group of women could test their own ideas against those of their equals, those who had come out of similar conditions and similar life situations. Every thinking woman had to argue with the "great man" in her head, instead of being strengthened and encouraged by her foremothers. For thinking women, the absence of Women's History was perhaps the most serious obstacle of all to their intellectual growth.

THIS BOOK ATTEMPTS to trace the creation of feminist consciousness in Western Europe and the United States from approximately the

7th century A.D. to 1870. While we can assume that as long as patriarchy existed there must have been women who thought in opposition to it, we cannot verify that assumption by the use of primary sources until the Christian era. While we do have some primary sources for Classical Antiquity, such as the writings of Sappho and her school, these represent isolated voices that found neither echo nor response for centuries. For the purposes of this study I have based my inquiry on the extant written record of women's thought and that essentially, in Western civilization, begins in the 7th century A.D.

As for the cut-off date of my periodization, I am interested in the stages of development *prior* to the historic moment when in Europe and the United States significant numbers of women attained feminist consciousness, a moment marked by the appearance of organized movements for women's rights, roughly in the third quarter of the 19th century. I have included in my research the written evidence of women's thought from the early medieval period on up to the 1870s and I have left out of consideration all the writings of women in the organized feminist movement, with the exception of writings on religion and on Women's History, which seem to demand a different periodization. Admittedly, this is not a particularly neat periodization and it runs counter to the historiography on the subject, which has been much concerned with recording the immediate, short-range origins of the women's movement and the History of that movement.

It is a well established insight regarding Women's History that the customary periodization of traditional history is not appropriate to it and must be used with great caution. Since for so long in their history women were not active or visible in the public arena of warfare and politics most of them were affected differently than were men by the historical changes set up as signposts in the traditional historical narrative. The historiographic emphasis on the organized women's movement reflects traditional interest in organized political activity in the public realm. This is an important and useful subject for historical inquiry and interpretation, but it tends to obscure other aspects of Women's History: the continuity and tradition of women's long-range resistance to patriarchy and the factors which have brought about changes in women's consciousness of their own situation. It is these two themes that interest me and have determined the organization of this book.

This book is not an intellectual History of women nor is it a comprehensive synthesis of women's ideas. The latter is desperately needed and my hope is that the present work will inspire others to undertake it. I am focusing on certain basic themes in the development of women's consciousness of their own situation in society. Of necessity, the tracing out of these themes will lead to certain theoretical insights, chief among them the differences between men and women in their relationship to historical process and to the creation of mental constructs. It is my belief that once these differences are defined and recognized we will at last be able to construct a new recorded History based on a synthesis of traditional (men's) History and the History of women.

IT WAS UNDER patriarchal hegemony in thought, values, institutions and resources that women had to struggle to form their own feminist consciousness. I define feminist consciousness as the awareness of women that they belong to a subordinate group; that they have suffered wrongs as a group; that their condition of subordination is not natural, but is societally determined; that they must join with other women to remedy these wrongs; and finally, that they must and can provide an alternate vision of societal organization in which women as well as men will enjoy autonomy and self-determination.[9] Historians have traditionally located the development of feminist consciousness in the 19th century, coinciding with and manifested through the development of a political woman's rights movement. But historians of Women's History have begun to trace a much earlier development of feminist thought. Some have located it in the works of 17th-century English writers, such as Mary Astell, Bathsua Makin, Aphra Behn; others have claimed its origin in the work of the 15th-century French author Christine de Pizan.[10] By defining the term "feminist consciousness" the way I have, I can include the earliest stages of women's resistance to patriarchal ideas and show that this kind of feminist oppositional thought developed over a far longer period.

The development of women's feminist consciousness took place in different stages and over hundreds of years. This development for a long time took the form of isolated insights by individual women, which did not reverberate in their time and were lost to future generations. I will attempt to trace the different stages of the development of women's group consciousness and discuss the circumstances under which these stages occur.

Of necessity this combination of a thematic and a chronological approach will create problems for the reader. At times I will not be able to deal with the historical development of an idea, an intellectual or a social movement as fully as I would wish, since I am not so much writing a history as seeking to trace historical patterns. The subject will be covered over a vast span of time and space: nearly 1200 years of history (from A.D. 700 to 1870) in England, France, the German and Italian realms, and in its more limited time span, the United States of America. Inevitably, the selection of the countries to be studied is made on the basis of one's own training and knowledge of languages. And so, at the outset, I must admit that this book is centered on Western European cultures, not because I think that entirely desirable—I would consider a cross-culturally comparative approach to be more effective—but because I could not have written it otherwise. On the other hand, both in this and the preceding volume, I have been studying the origins of patriarchy and its development in *Western* civilization, and as such the countries and periods studied are quite appropriate.

I believe that what Mary Beard called "long history" is especially important for understanding the history of women. Only by looking at a long time-span and by comparing different histories and cultures can we begin to see major developmental patterns and essential differences in the way historical events affect women and men. It is by now evident that technological, economic and political innovations which decisively affected men had quite a different impact on women. Thus, only by studying the "long history" of women's educational disadvantaging can one see its long-range impact on women's ability to develop economic alternatives to support by marriage and understand why women's emancipation was so greatly retarded historically in comparison with the emancipation movements of other disadvantaged groups.

In a thematic survey of this sort it is difficult to strike the right balance between groups of subjects to be studied and individuals to be featured as "outstanding" or "typical." I have in each chapter tried to highlight and treat at some length the life and work of at least one woman, while including others with only a brief summary of their biographies. Since women's intellectual product has been so greatly influenced by constraints on the lives of all women, the life and the work of a woman need to be considered in close interrelation. For women, the decision to take up the life of the intellect has frequently meant giving up sexual or maternal lives. Conversely, certain intellectual insights and advances could be made by women only at life stages when they could be economically and emotionally independent of men. In the modern period, for some women, their choice of a liberated lifestyle has been used to discredit their intellectual work. Thought and life are inextricably connected for women; the form of this book attempts to express this connection.

Today, when historians and literary scholars are very much aware of the differences within large groups, that is, the factors of race, ethnicity, class, religion, any attempt at making generalizations is suspect and full of pitfalls. Still, in order to understand differences between men and women *as groups*, such generalizations need to be attempted. It is quite true that the group of women I am studying in this book is largely white, upper-class, wealthy or economically privileged, but that is precisely the problematic of women's intellectual history: for women, far longer than for men, education was a class privilege. I have, throughout, included whatever I could find of the lives and works of less privileged women, of middle- and lower-class women, of women of oppressed groups, such as African-Americans and Jews.

There is a strong connection here to the question of the "women of genius," and of "outstanding women" or "notables" and "worthies." The latter categories have long been suspect in Women's History because the bias of patriarchally framed selection has tended to make only those women "notable" and "worthy" who did what men did and what men recognize as important. I have tried to avoid this obvious pitfall in selecting the women to be discussed, by focusing only on what women wrote and thought about themselves and other women. But in dealing with the intellectual product of women these issues become a good deal more complex than when dealing with social history. The systematic long-range educational deprivation of women has guaranteed that for centuries the only women who could get an education and partake of any kind of tradition of learning were women of the nobility. Further, even after the invention of printing, access to printing (and with it to posterity or recorded History) was essentially a class privilege. The sources available for finding out what women thought and reasoned are the sources that survived. They are subject to the above-defined bias of selection well into the middle of the 17th century. I am assuming, that for every woman whose diary, letters, tracts or visions survived, there were many others with equal talent and reasoning ability whose records were lost or destroyed. Oppression brings with it the hegemony of the thought and ideas of the dominant; thus women's oppression has meant that much of their mental product and creation has been lost forever. The historian wishing to restore to the historical record the silenced voices and the obliterated traces has to accept severe limitations.

Why then use the term "women of genius" at all and why single out some of them for special attention? I have done so because the struggle for women's emancipation has historically always begun with a defense of women's intellectual equality. Even this late in the development of Women's History, contemporary women and men still doubt that some of the most outstanding intellectual achievements of Western civilization were made by women as well as by men. Why have there been no female system-builders, no Kant, no Marx, no Freud? Why have there been no great female intellectual innovators? I believe there have been such women, and we have not sufficiently respected them in the narrative of the past. I also believe, and will show, that women of great talent were kept from realizing their talents fully by the constraints patriarchy imposed on them. Last, I am assuming and demonstrating in this book that the terms of these constraints fell on *all* women in some measure, regardless of other determinants in their lives, and that this fact is what needed to be identified and named in developing feminist consciousness. The conditions under which women thought themselves free of patriarchy were conditions imposed upon them by patriarchy. In short, a woman of whatever talent had less chance of developing it than did her brother.

Which women to include in this study, out of the large numbers of women whose lives and works I have studied, presented a difficult problem. My subject is the rise of *feminist* consciousness, thus I excluded all women whose work was not concerned with the emancipation of women. On the other hand, I have included many women who would not have defined themselves as feminist in their own time, even allowing for the fact that the word itself did not appear until late in the 19th century. Such women would have denied that they were concerned with problems of women as such and several of them were explicitly opposed to women's rights movements. I have included some of them, such as some female mystics or early proponents of women's education, because their work and thought directly contributed to the development of feminist consciousness, whether they so intended or not.

THE LONG HISTORY of women's educational disadvantaging, seen as a structural and institutional problem, is synthesized in Chapter Two. The disadvantaging of women in gaining access to education and in participating in educational establishments has been a consistent feature of patriarchal power in every state for over two thousand years. I show the impact educational deprivation had on women's self-perceptions. The waste of female talent and its cost to individual women will be illustrated by three concrete examples.

In Chapter Three I discuss women's effort to authorize themselves to speak and write and to defend their authorship. The chapter focuses on the life and work of a woman of genius, Hildegard of Bingen, who felt authorized by divine inspiration to speak publicly. The chapter deals with her struggles to establish a new role for women in public life and to conceptualize an enhanced role for women in Christian theology.

Chapters Four and Five deal with mysticism as an alternative mode of thought for women. These chapters detail women's long struggle to establish their full and equal humanity by insisting on their ability to speak to God and to be heard by God. Not only did God speak to these female mystics, but they made their contemporaries believe that their ecstatic experiences were real. Mystical practice and discipline enabled women to proceed to another level of re-definition—in their visions, dreams and writings they asserted the female component of the Divine. Chapter Four offers a brief history of mysticism and discusses female mystics of the 11th through the 16th century.

Chapter Five discusses women mystics of the Protestant Reformation and women in heretical sects. It focuses on women who reconceptualized Christian theology so as to give women a more central role in redemption.

Chapter Six discusses the concept of motherhood, both as an idea authorizing women to write and as the unifying concept for women's solidarity. The cult of the Virgin Mary; the lone voices of women speaking as mothers; the impact of the Reformation on upgrading motherhood and allowing women to justify religious and secular thought through their duty as mothers—these are the themes here discussed. Finally, the concept of motherhood as the basis of women's collectivity, which long preceded the concept of sisterhood, is studied and analyzed.

In Chapter Seven I show the waste of talent and insight which was due to women's being deprived of knowledge of their own past and of the works of other women. Men develop ideas and systems of explanation by absorbing past knowledge and critiquing and superseding it. Women, ignorant of their own history, did not know what women before them had thought and taught. So, generation after generation, they struggled for insights others had already had before them. I illustrate this by surveying women's Bible criticism over a period of one thousand years and show the endless repetition of effort, the constant reinventing of the wheel.

Chapter Eight discusses how women authorized themselves to think and speak through creative talent. These were the innovators who simply by-passed patriarchal thought and created alternate worlds. The works of writers from Marie de France to Emily Dickinson are analyzed to show how they contributed to the development of feminist consciousness.

Chapter Nine deals with women's long struggle for equal education. Women's arguments for their right to learn and their theoretical approach to knowledge from the Renaissance through the 19th century are surveyed in this chapter. The development of the argument for education as it evolved into a feminist argument for equal rights is traced and interpreted.

In their struggle to think for themselves, women had first to define themselves as central, not as "Other." They did this, as did other oppressed groups, by orienting themselves to those like them, in this case other women. But women faced far greater obstacles than did other groups in this process of thinking their way out of oppression. In Chapter Ten I discuss the conditions out of which feminist consciousness arises historically and explore whether there are any patterns in its appearance. I trace the appearances of female clusters and female networks to explore their impact on the group consciousness of women. The particular problems of women thinkers in social spaces in which they are considered equal, but still under male hegemony, is discussed in the case of the women of the German Romantic movement.

The struggle for Women's History is the subject of Chapter Eleven. Like men's History, which begins with the kings' lists, Women's History features the making of lists, beginning in the Renaissance. Other aspects of it are biographies, autobiographies and the records of communities, movements and organizations. This is followed by actual historical work. The effort to find female role models, heroines and inspired leaders always included respect for practical accomplishments in the world, not only for abstract knowledge. The chapter ends with a discussion of the 19th-century woman's movement and its efforts at creating and preserving history and briefly touches upon the historic significance of the 20th-century Women's History movement.

In Chapter Twelve I synthesize the theoretical principles that distinguish men's relations to historical process from those of women and discuss the significance of my findings.

TWO

The Educational Disadvantaging of Women

IN THE 1850s SARAH GRIMKÉ (1792–1873), then sixty-two years old, left the household of her sister and brother-in-law, Angelina and Theodore Weld, and made an effort to pursue a career of her own. She corresponded with lawyers and doctors of her acquaintance and explored the possibility of getting professional training. She worked in public libraries, hoping to create a compilation of laws pertaining to women in the different states in order to expose their unfairness. All her inquiries resulted in discouragement. The study of law was still closed to women; the study of medicine was unthinkable for a woman her age. Sarah Grimké, having seventeen years earlier produced the first coherent argument for the emancipation of women penned by an American, felt deeply discouraged. "The powers of my mind have never been allowed expansion," she complained in a letter to a friend.[1]

Sarah Grimké summarized her sense of personal deprivation and attempted to generalize from it with a program for equal education outlined in an essay fragment which was never published:

> With me learning was a passion. . . . Had I received the education I craved and been bred to the profession of the law, I might have been a useful member of society, and instead of myself and my property being taken care of, I might have been a protector of the helpless. . . .
>
> Many a woman shudders . . . at the terrible eclipse of those intellectual powers which in early life seemed prophetic of usefulness and happiness. . . . It is because we feel we have powers which are crushed,

responsibilities which we are not permitted to exercise . . . rights vested in us as moral and intellectual beings which are utterly ignored and trampled upon . . . it is because we feel this so keenly we now demand an equal education with man.[2]

In this pathetic and futile outcry, Grimké gave voice to the suffering and deprivation of millions of women who had been denied an education, and identified that deprivation as a crucial problem of their condition as a group. The significance of that deprivation in determining the development of women's emancipation is even today still inadequately understood.

As we survey the history of women's education in Europe and later in the United States, we can make two generalizations: women are almost universally educationally disadvantaged in comparison with their brothers, and education is, for those few women able to obtain it, distinctly a class privilege.

Historically, education has served a utilitarian purpose by training persons in the specific skills needed by a given society. Such education was, for millennia, family-based in the form of apprenticeship. While resources and opportunities in family-based education were allocated according to a sexual division of labor and were designed to fit boys and girls into their gender-defined roles, girls could often acquire skills and knowledge equal to that of their brothers. Home-economy skills, while assigned according to ideas of gender division, did equip women with the knowledge necessary for survival in case of spinster- or widowhood. In the Middle Ages, for example, widows frequently carried on an artisan's trade and business and were granted guild privileges and status. The development of brewing, silk- and textile-making, embroidery and other such female trades as recognized crafts illustrates this point. Household-based education was informal, utilitarian and individualized; it was non-literate and offered in the vernacular. Mothers educated daughters and female servants; fathers educated sons and male servants. It must also be remembered, that, statistically, the number of people in any given population who were educated to the point of literacy remained very small until the 17th century. In the Middle Ages and during the Renaissance the vast majority of people were illiterate and had no formal schooling. Even later, when education became institutionalized and boys, after infancy, were sent outside the home to be educated, the early education of children of both sexes was still provided by their mothers. Thus the educational disadvantaging of girls did not become obvious for most of the populations of Europe until the 16th century and for the American colonies through the 18th century. Yet it was a reality, as can be seen when we analyze educational opportunities for the narrow segment of the population which had such opportunities, namely, the nobility and the wealthier urban middle class. With the establishment of universities, during the 13th and 14th centuries, education for these classes became institutionalized. The universities prepared young men for the ministry and for service in the state, and in order to attend universities they had to master Latin. When sons began to be prepared for university education in academies and preparatory schools, the educational disadvantaging of women became apparent and the gap in the education of boys and girls widened and became firmly institutionalized.

In general, education becomes institutionalized when elites—military, religious or political—need to assure their position in power by means of training a group to serve and perpetuate their interests. Whenever that has happened, historically, women were discriminated against and excluded from the very inception of each system. The earliest example is the exclusion of women from training in the newly discovered skills of writing and reading in Sumer and Babylon of the 2nd millennium B.C., which was discussed in Volume One. With a few notable exceptions, such as the education of girls in Sparta of Classical Antiquity and the monastic system of education in Europe, which will be more fully discussed below, girls were disadvantaged in every known society of the Western world in regard to the length of their training, the content they were taught and the skills of their teachers. This followed logically from the purposes of education: since women were excluded from military, religious and political elites, they were considered to have little need for formalized learning. On the other hand, daughters of the elites, such as princesses and noble women who might have to serve as stand-ins for sons or husbands, were as carefully tutored and trained as their brothers. During the Middle Ages the content of their learning was the same and they often shared tutors with their brothers. Education was a class privilege for both sexes and served kin and state interests. It is not surprising therefore to find that almost all the known educated women from Antiquity to the 16th century A.D. were members of the nobility.[3]

In the early Middle Ages formal learning could be acquired only through tutors or in religious institutions. For many centuries learned women appear only in convents, with the exception of a few noble women at certain courts. The spread of nunneries is therefore a rough indicator of the spread of learning among women.

In the first several centuries of the Christian era, when saints and missionaries spread Christianity to the heathen tribes of Europe, women's participation was welcomed and their active role was encouraged. They joined male missionaries in proselytizing and preaching and helped to convert members of their own families by holding religious observances in their homes. In the first three centuries of the Christian era, widows and unmarried women, known as canonesses, lived in communities ruled by deaconesses, devoting themselves to a life of common prayer and the preparation of other women for Christian baptism. Deaconesses and canonesses also tended the sick and ministered to the poor. This tradition was expanded and formalized in the early Middle Ages with the spread of monastic life.

In the 7th century more women entered monastic life than ever before. In France/Belgium and Britain this can be seen from the dramatic increase in the number of women's monastic houses being established. Whereas a century earlier about 10 percent of all monastic houses had been established for women, during the 7th century over 30 percent were women's houses.[4] This increased religious activity of women coincided with the process of converting the Franks and Anglo-Saxons to Christianity. The Church encouraged women's role as proselytizers within their own families. Noble families, in turn, derived not only religious but economic gains from founding religious houses as part of their landed estates. Such cloisters became refuges for unmarried daughters or widows, and often reverted to the donor's family after the death of the founding abbess.

The same period also saw the flourishing of dual monasteries in Britain and on the European continent. Many of these were organized so that the nuns could benefit from the protection, physical labor and spiritual guidance of male religious. Since most double monasteries were administered by abbesses, or jointly by an abbot and abbess, they fostered women's leadership. Laon, one of the largest Frankish double monasteries, housed three hundred nuns under the supervision of St. Salaberga. St. Gertrude of Nivelles shared the rule of the convent with St. Amand, but she retained supreme authority. Under Abbess Gertrude's guidance Nivelles developed into a center of learning. She herself was a collector of books and she encouraged her nuns to learn and read poetry. Queen Balthild founded the abbey of Chelles on the ruins of an abandoned convent around

658 and developed it into a famous institution, in which the nuns wrote the lives of several women saints. Its reputation for fostering learning attracted so many men that by the end of the century Chelles was a double monastery.[5] In Britain, Hilda (—d.680), the great-niece of King Edwin of Northumbria, entered the religious life in her thirties. She was called by Aidan of Lindisfarne to help him convert the Northumbrians. She founded several convents but is best known for becoming the abbess of Whitby, a double monastery famous for its learning. While she was abbess she hosted the Synod of Whitby in 664. She is outstanding among a number of learned nuns who worked and lived in dual monasteries.

A century later, Lioba, an English nun at Thanet, was taught by Abbess Eadburga to memorize divine laws as poetry. She later composed religious poetry herself and was a skilled classicist. At his request she followed St. Boniface to Germany in 748 and aided him in Christianizing it by setting up convents. She became abbess of Bischofsheim and served there twenty-eight years, combining manual labor with the study of Latin and patristic literature.[6]

Even after the waning of the double monasteries the tradition of powerful abbesses continued. In the 11th century, the abbess of Maubeuge had authority not only over her monasteries but over the city and territory owned by it. The abbesses of Regensburg were princesses of the Holy Roman Empire and sent their deputies to national assemblies. The abbesses of Herford and Quedlinburg furnished military contingents to the Emperor's army and were represented in diets of the Empire.[7]

In the early Middle Ages, when warfare was endemic and the sons of the nobility were mainly trained in martial skills, their sisters may, as a group, have had more formal learning than they did. Clothilde, the daughter of the Burgundian king, who lived in the 5th century and who converted her husband, the Frankish King Clovis, to Christianity, may have done so under the influence of her superior education. In the 6th century, Radegund, a Thuringian princess (c.530–587), was captured by Chlotar, the youngest son of Clovis, when she was still a child and brought to the French court, where she was raised to become Chlotar's queen. Educated at a French convent, she could read and write Latin with ease and composed an elegy in which she compared the fall of Thuringia, when her father and relatives had been killed by the invaders, to the fall of Troy. Like the Trojan women, she too was removed from her home by the victors to become the sexual property of her captor. Her married life was most unhappy, since Chlotar, like other Frankish kings, practiced polygamy and had five wives. He was brutal to her and resented her piety and the fact she bore him no children. When Chlotar murdered her brother, Radegund fled under the protection of Bishop Medard and became a nun. Later she founded the monastery of St. Croix, where she lived with two hundred nuns and which became an educational center with a poet in residence.

All through the Middle Ages, royal and noble women founded and endowed convents, in which the daughters of the nobility and some of the poor, at times boys and girls together, received education in religion, Latin, reading, writing, simple arithmetic and chants. All girls received domestic training and instruction in needlework, spinning and weaving. Certain nunneries specialized in the production of fine embroidery, others in transcribing and illuminating manuscripts. Some nuns were trained in these highly specialized skills, others were skilled in medicine and surgery.[8]

In the 10th and 11th centuries several famous canonical abbeys were founded in Saxony, among these Gandersheim and Quedlinburg. There a tradition of female scholarship developed which would give rise to outstanding achievement. Abbess Gerberga II of Gandersheim, herself the daughter of Henry, Duke of Bavaria, was the teacher of the nun Hrosvitha, one of the first outstanding female literary figures in Europe. In later centuries, religious houses would train not only their own novitiates but also the daughters of the nobility and rising bourgeoisie. An example of the way in which a convent could foster learning and scholarship was the Paraclete, founded in the 12th century by Abelard and left under the guidance of Héloïse, herself one of the most learned women of the age. Abelard encouraged the nuns of the Paraclete to study not only the Bible but to learn Latin, Greek and Hebrew in order to understand and instruct others in the biblical text. In the rule for the order he provided that there should be reading and instruction going on at the convent during all the daytime hours.[9]

It is arguable whether the gender-based privilege of formal education seriously disadvantaged women at least until the rise of universities. The vast majority of the population was, at any rate, illiterate and depended on informal, family-based skill training. For men, as well as for women, education was a class privilege. But there was an important difference—the Church educated poor boys for the ministry, while for centuries access to nunneries for girls depended on their families' ability to provide a dowry.

Until the 12th century, Latin was taught in most convents, which meant that the nuns could read not only the Bible and the Church fathers but Latin verse and secular literature. Coincident with the rise of the universities and the acceptance of Latin as the language of the university-educated male clergy, the use and teaching of Latin dramatically declined in the convents. One reason for this decline may have been the great increase in female religious expression and activities, starting with the 11th century, which encouraged the translation of the Bible and of religious literature into the vernacular. Many of the women mystics of the 11th–14th centuries wrote in the vernacular. (See Chapter Four.) Regardless of whether the causes for this educational decline were negative or positive for women, the effect was a widening of the gap of educational opportunity between males and females.

On the lowest level of educational access, urbanization brought the development of lay schools, taught by parish priests and lay scholars, in which boys of the poorest classes were offered the rudiments of learning—reading, writing and ciphering sufficient to qualify them for urban employments. There are also a few cases known of lay schools for girls run by schoolmistresses in the High Middle Ages.[10]

In the 15th century the founding of urban grammar schools for the poor in France opened up some educational opportunities to girls as well as boys. But in these schools, as in similar schools for the poor in Britain and the United States well into the 19th century, girls were taught only the rudiments of signing, reading, numbers and religion. Some talented boys, even of the poorer classes, could have access to higher education through scholarships; for girls education ended at the elementary level.[11]

In general then, the institutionalization of higher education in the universities led to increasing class divisions for men, in which access to education became one means of structuring permanent class differences. These differences also accentuated gender divisions and made them more rigid.

In this dreary landscape of educational discrimination against women, extending over more than a millennium, there appear several islands of privileged space for women. From these emerge groups of educated women, exceptional for their attainments only because of the abysmal ignorance out of which they appear and against which they are measured. Such privileged spaces were the double monasteries of the 7th and 8th centuries, the nunneries earlier discussed as centers of learning in the 8th–13th centuries, the urban centers of Holland and the Rhineland in which the beguinage movement flourished in the 12th century, the courts of some of the cities of Renaissance Italy and France, and centers of the Protestant Reformation. It is in these privileged spaces that the small number of learned women appear. While we will be dealing with them individually in later chapters, it might be well here to analyze what they had in common and what patterns seem to emerge from their lives.

We can generalize that up until the late 17th century a woman's chances for acquiring any education at all were best if she were the daughter of wealth or rank; a daughter in a family without sons; and if her father were enlightened on the subject of women's educability. Such combinations were rare, but they did exist. The educated princesses of the Carolingian court have often been noted. Charlemagne, himself an illiterate patron of learning, had all his daughters instructed by tutors, among them the great scholar Alcuin. The latter also instructed the Emperor's sister, Gisela, who was learned enough to read the works of Bede and to give criticism to Alcuin on his commentary on the Gospel of St. John. In later life, she retired to the abbey of Chelles. Judith, the second wife of Charlemagne's successor, Louis the Pious, was a patron of learning. Many writers dedicated their works to her and she commissioned Florus of Lyon to write a world history for her.[12]

Many learned women were instructed by their fathers, such as Christine de Pizan in the 14th century, the Renaissance scholars Laura Cereta, Caterina Caldiera, Alessandra Scala, Olimpia Morata and the daughters of Sir Thomas More. The few Jewish women known to us for their learning were educated by their fathers and sometimes by their husbands. The three daughters of the famous Hebrew scholar Rashi, who lived in France 1040–1105, were learned in Hebrew and wrote commentary on talmudic law to substitute for their father when he was sick. Miriam Luria was a rabbinic scholar in Italy in the 13th century, as was Paula Dei Mansi, who translated and edited a collection of Bible commentaries. Nothing is known of their background. Rebecca Tiktiner wrote and published a book of moral teachings, selections from the Talmud and poetry addressed to women. Eva Bacharach was an expert on biblical writings and commentary. Both women lived in Prague in the 16th century and were the daughters of learned rabbis.[13] The tradition of "educated daughters of educated men," to use Virgina Woolf's felicitous phrase, continued through the centuries, down to the children of Bronson Alcott and to Margaret Fuller in 19th-century America.

Other women were educated by private tutors they shared with their brothers, such as Isotta and Ginevra Nogarola, Cassandra Fedele, Ippolita Sforza. While a number of the great ruling families of the Italian Renaissance produced several learned women, only one, Cecilia Gonzaga, joined her brothers in the pioneering school, La Giocosa, founded by her father, the Marquis of Mantua, and led by the famous humanities scholar Vittorino da Feltre. It is not astonishing that among the noted learned women were a number of ruling queens, such as Eleanor of Aquitaine (12th century), Marguerite de Navarre, Elizabeth I of England. These were women who from infancy were trained to be stand-ins for ruling men, if the need should arise, and they were therefore trained to fulfill such roles as men would.

The fame and notoriety of "learned women" of the Middle Ages and the early Renaissance attest to their rarity—with a few exceptions, they were noted more for existing at all than for their accomplishments.[14] Up to the 17th century, learned women are extremely rare. We can identify perhaps thirty learned nuns in the period up to 1400, and some of the most accomplished of these, such as Hildegard of Bingen and Mechthild of Magdeburg, were unable to write in Latin. In the period 1350–1530, which is regarded by historians as a time when learned women are particularly numerous, a leading scholar on the subject, Margaret King, has identified no more than thirty-five such women in Italy. The medievalist Roland Bainton, in his three-volume work on women of the Reformation in Europe, adds no more than ten names of learned women to those mentioned by King. One can safely say that up to 1700 there are fewer than 300 learned women in Western Europe known to historians.[15]

We have seen that during the Middle Ages only women wealthy enough to afford the necessary dowry to enter a convent or those who were members of ruling families had access to education. Margaret King has found that all of the learned women of the Italian Renaissance came from wealthy families. With urbanization, from the 13th century onward we find small numbers of women from middle-class families among the educated. Until the end of the 16th century the generalization that, for women, education is a class privilege holds unchallenged. A law promulgated by King Henry VIII of England illustrates this dramatically. It "prohibited all women other than gentle- and noble-women together with artificers, journeymen, husbandmen, labourers and serving men . . . from reading the Bible in English either in private or to others."[16] While the purpose of the legislation was probably to discourage the spread of radical sectarianism, the fact that all women except noblewomen are classed with lower-class men shows how class is defined differently for women than for men.

Another generalization that can be made about these learned women is that they were mostly single, frequently cloistered or sequestered from society, or widowed. There is a general pattern of intellectual precociousness, which was encouraged in their youth, but severely discouraged later in life. Several of these women were forced into early marriages by their families and, inevitably, their intellectual life ceased with marriage. Others resisted such pressure by entering convents. Only a very few were able to resume their studies after raising families or upon widowhood. They were forced to choose between the life of a woman or the life of the mind. There was no accepted role for a woman to lead a "normal" woman's life and also to think. What the cost of such narrow choices was for individual women we can see in considering several concrete examples. What the cost was to society in general through the loss of talent and intellectual work of half the population cannot be estimated. But we might well ponder the fact that it was not until the first decades of the 20th century that in the United States and several other industrialized nations there existed the possibility for women to combine a sexual and reproductive life with the life of the intellect. To this day such choices do not exist for most women in the underdeveloped world.

One kind of cost for her daring to think and write was exacted from one Gaudairenca, wife of the troubadour Raimon de Miraval. According to an anecdote told about him, "Miraval . . . said to his wife, he did not want a wife who could write poetry; one troubadour in the house was sufficient; she should prepare to return to the house of her father, because he no longer considered her his wife." What became of the offending poet we do not know. What we do know is that none of her poems survived.[17]

Isotta Nogarola (1418–66) provides an example of a different kind of solution for the thinking woman faced with male disapproval and discouragement for her intellectual efforts. Known as the most learned woman of the century, she and her sister Ginevra had received an excellent education by a humanist tutor. At age eighteen she began to correspond with male humanists in the circle of Guarino of Verona, who had been her tutor's teacher. She hoped to enter into their circle by way of such intellectual correspondence and was encouraged when Guarino was shown her letters and praised them to a friend. Yet he did not answer the letters she addressed to him, which made her the subject of ridicule by her female friends for having dared to approach so great a man and expect a reply. Isotta wrote Guarino once again and said:

> There are already so many women in the world! Why then . . . was I born a woman, to be scorned by men in words and deeds. I ask myself this question in solitude. . . . For they jeer at me throughout the city, the women mock me . . .[18]

This letter finally drew an encouraging reply from Guarino. But other men with whom she corresponded told her that she must "become a man," if she wanted to continue writing. And one anonymous writer in Verona in 1438 accused Isotta of incest with her brother and linked this accusation with an attack on all learned women: "an eloquent woman is never chaste; and the behavior of many learned women also confirms this truth."[19] These attacks so discouraged Nogarola that she stopped writing for three years. Then she arrived at an unusual decision: she would neither marry nor become a nun but would live her life as a recluse in her own home shared with her mother and devote herself to religious studies. This role for a woman intellectual was approved by society because it continued the tradition of learned women religious. Nogarola lived that way for twenty-five years, producing an important theological tract in the brief interlude in which she engaged in an intellectual platonic friendship with the humanist Ludovico Foscarini. When, at age thirty-five, she unexpectedly received a proposal of marriage from another man, she asked Foscarini's advice. He urged her to keep the vow of chastity she had imposed on herself for the sake of her intellectual development. She accepted his advice, but from that time forward was repeatedly ill. The price paid by Isotta Nogarola for being a thinking woman and keeping her respectability was isolation from other intellectuals and lifelong chastity. It was a price no male intellectual has ever been forced to pay and it should not be confused with the choice of a religious life freely chosen by other men and women.

Isotta Nogarola's acceptance of the culturally approved gender role for a thinking woman was shared by her contemporaries Cecilia Gonzaga and Maddalena Scrovegni. Although this decision was greeted by praise for these women on the part of male intellectuals, it resulted in little or no intellectual productivity. These learned women and those others who had chosen marriage never repeated the intellectual feats of their adolescent years or fulfilled their intellectual promise. There simply was no acceptable social role during the Renaissance for a thinking woman who did not renounce her sexuality.[20] Their life stories tell of thwarted ambitions, aborted talents and long despairing silences.

THE PROTESTANT REFORMATION resulted in the spreading of schools in general and in particular in improved educational opportunities for girls. This was especially obvious in the German states, where Protestant reformers such as Philipp Melanchton, Martin Bucer, Andreas Muculus and Johann Agricola advocated the creation of elementary and secondary schools for both boys and girls. During the 17th century school attendance was made mandatory for children of both sexes in Thuringia, Württemberg and many other German territories. Still, after a century of spectacular growth, the educational disadvantaging of girls was firmly institutionalized. For example in 102 cities of Brandenburg, while schools for boys doubled in number and those for girls increased tenfold from 1539 to 1600, there were 100 schools for boys at the end of the period and only 45 for girls.[21] Many of the Protestant humanists wrote in favor of expanding schools for girls, but their plans were not fully carried out. And even these advanced reformers advocated a greatly simplified curriculum for girls as compared with that for boys, with heavy emphasis on religious instruction.

In France, parish schools, attached to the cathedrals and offering only the most rudimentary skills, provided education for boys and girls from the 16th century on. For girls, the monastic orders continued to offer more thorough training. From the 17th century on the new teaching orders, such as the Ursulines and the Filles de la Croix, provided expanded educational opportunities for girls of the upper and middle classes, but the emphasis was on moral and religious training and the recruitment of future nuns. For aristocratic women, education in the home, by tutors and with the use of private libraries, offset some of the disadvantages of gender indoctrination. For several centuries the most highly educated women came from such backgrounds, often strongly encouraged by their fathers.[22]

In England the founding of grammar schools in the 16th century made primary education available to most boys, while the education of girls remained wholly private in the hands of mothers or governesses. The disbanding of monastic orders and their schools during the Reformation seriously affected the educational opportunities of Englishwomen. For nearly a century there was no tradition of learning for them, and upper-class girls were trained only sufficiently to be competitive in the marriage market—that is, to acquire "accomplishments," such as embroidery, music and singing. Jonathan Swift lamented that "not one gentleman's daughter in a thousand can read or understand her own language or be the judge of the easiest books that are written in it . . . . They are not so much as taught to spell in their childhood, nor can ever attain to it in their whole lives." [23] Nevertheless, as will be seen below, English literacy rates were high compared to the rest of Europe, but more advanced learning was not readily available. In the 18th and 19th centuries missionary and Sunday schools raised literacy levels among the children of the lower classes, but here too, girls were strongly disadvantaged. It would take more than a hundred years of individual and organized effort on the part of women to improve their access to higher education (see Chapter Nine).

Yet throughout the centuries there appeared women of extraordinary talent who, despite all obstacles, acquired an education and produced intellectual work of great quality. Inevitably, their talents were stifled and their efforts were thwarted, as had been the case with the learned women of the Renaissance. This is exemplified by the life of Sor Juana Ines de la Cruz of Mexico (1651–95), who is remarkable not only for her genius and her life story but because she is one of the few women intellectuals of her time who was not upper class by birth.

She was born in a Mexican village, one of six illegitimate children of an illiterate mother. Sent to her grandfather's home in town, she early showed an unusual love of learning. At age three, she tricked her older sister's teacher into teaching her to read, which she learned to do in a short time. She then proceeded to read the books in her grandfather's library and by age six had mastered writing as well. She pleaded with her mother to allow her to dress as a boy so she could go to the University in Mexico City and study science, but such a wish could only be denied. However, she was sent to Mexico City at age eight and there given twenty lessons in Latin, after which she studied the language on her own. Her talents brought her to the attention of the Viceroy's wife, who brought her to court, made her a lady-in-waiting and later official court poet. She was exhibited to the court and visitors as an amazing prodigy and called upon to produce an unending series of occasional poems for various public events. In addition to the poems she wrote for the court, she also wrote comedies and a religious play. In one of her longer poems she strongly criticized men for their contemptuous attitude toward women. The demands of court life so interfered with her ability to pursue her studies that she decided to become a nun. She explains her reasons for this decision:

> . . . considering the total negative opinion that I had of matrimony, it was the least unsuitable and the most decent station that I was able to select in order to bring about my salvation . . . . I conquered all the stupidities of my disposition which included the desire to live alone and to have no obligatory occupations in order to enjoy complete freedom to study without communal obligations which would interrupt the peaceful silence of my books . . .[24]

Over and over again in history we find thinking women internalizing self-denial, so that this gifted woman can refer to her desire to be a scholar as a "stupidity of my disposition." She took her final vows in 1669 and, protected by her influence at court, she was allowed by her religious superiors to line her convent cell with books, to receive many visitors and to engage in an active literary life. Yet even during these relatively protected years, Sor Juana was under constant admonition and censure on the part of her confessor, Father Antonio Nuñez. Apparently, he censured her in public for writing poetry and for socializing with persons in authority and power. In a recently discovered letter to Father Nuñez, Sor Juana, then secure in the protection of the Viceroy and his wife, vigorously defended herself, her right to write poetry, since Heaven had bestowed the talent of writing on her, and her right to education. She stated that she had always kept her studies private, had not sought public acclaim and did not desire it. But, she continued forcefully:

> who has forbidden women to engage in private and individual studies? Have they not a rational soul as men do? Well, then, why cannot a woman profit by the privilege of enlightenment as they do? . . . What divine revelation, what rule of the Church, what reasonable judgement formulated such a severe law for us women? . . . I have this inclination [to study] and if it is evil I am not the one who formed me thus— I was born with it and with it I shall die.[25]

Apparently, despite this heated exchange of letters, Father Nuñez continued as her confessor and Sor Juana continued her studies and literary activities until 1686, when, after the death of the Marquesa and the departure of several of her patrons, her influence at court ceased. A few years later Sor Juana became involved in an ambiguous literary/theological quarrel which doomed her fate and writing.

In 1690 Sor Juana wrote an essay critical of a sermon delivered forty years earlier by an eminent Jesuit priest who was greatly admired in Spain and Mexico, especially by Archbishop Francisco Aguiar y Seijas. Her essay came to the attention of the Bishop of Puebla, Fernandez de Santa Cruz. He had her essay published at his own expense without her knowledge and sent her a copy accompanied by a letter in which he criticized her, but which he signed "Sor Philotea." Apparently, the Bishop considered it unseemly that she was writing on theological questions and urged her henceforth to give up all but religious reading. "It is a pity that so great a mind should stoop to lowly earthbound knowledge and not desire to probe what transpires in heaven. But since it does lower itself to ground level, may it not descend further still and ponder what goes on in hell."[26] Sor Juana apparently knew the identity of the author, yet she addressed her reply to "Sor Philotea" and maintained the conceit that she was writing to a nun. Her "Reply" is a brilliant defense of women's right to education. She recounts her life story to show that her love of learning could not be suppressed or thwarted and cites a long list of learned women from the Bible who have inspired her. She ends with a strong argument in favor of older women teaching younger women and of women's right to intellectual growth. There is no record of the Bishop's reply and Sor Juana's essay was not published until after her death.

The circumstances of this exchange of letters have puzzled historians and appear quite ambiguous. Did the Bishop simply use an occasion to censure Sor Juana? Octavio Paz speculates that the entire incident was due to the rivalry between the Archbishop and the Bishop, in which Sor Juana was merely a pawn. This explanation is plausible, but clearly Sor Juana intervened in the quarrel between the two churchmen and, as her earlier private letter shows, the ideas she advanced had been long gestating. She may have welcomed a chance to present them in a more public manner.[27] After Sor Juana wrote her "Reply," which may have been privately circulated, the pressure on her mounted. Her confessor, Father Nuñez, refused her confession and accused her of lacking humility. Shortly thereafter the Archbishop ordered her to sell her books in order to raise money for the poor. Sor Juana, humiliated, lonely and without support, complied and by 1693 had given away all her books except three religious texts. She then made an abject public confession, begged the forgiveness of the nuns in her order and in 1694 signed in her own blood a rededication to her religious vows and renounced all other aspirations. Possibly seeking death, she nursed other sick nuns during an epidemic and died in 1695.[28]

THE LAST EXAMPLE of the thwarting and forced neglect of extraordinary talent falls in a later century, when learned women no longer are quite such rarities. The story of the denial of opportunity to women of talent does not follow the usual chronology of educational progress, rather it seems to exemplify the principle that regardless of what advances women make toward education, the best of them will be thwarted and ultimately stopped before they can achieve what talent and effort should entitle them to achieve.

Elizabeth Elstob (1683–1756) was encouraged by her mother in her pursuit of education, but after her mother's death, when Elizabeth was eight, her guardian who disapproved of learned women denied her the education she craved. He refused even her request to study French with the comment that one language was enough for a woman, but she managed anyway to obtain a reading knowledge of the language.[29]

She acquired an education by sharing the books of her brother, William, a graduate of Oxford, who encouraged her intellectual development. She lived for thirteen years with him, first at Oxford, where he taught, and later in London, where he was rector of two parishes. It was he who enabled her to take up a life of serious scholarship. She knew eight languages fluently, among them Gothic, Frankish, old Teutonic, and became recognized as one of the foremost Saxon scholars of her time. She worked with her brother on his translation of King Alfred's Saxon version of Orosius' history. In 1708 she published a translation of Madeleine de Scudèry's *Essay on Glory* and in 1709 she published a translation of Aelfric's *An Anglo-Saxon Homily on the Birthday of St. Gregory.*[30] Typically, Elstob felt compelled to apologize for her undertaking in the Preface:

> I know it will be said, What has a Woman to do with learning? . . . Where is the Fault in Womens seeking after Learning? why are they not to be valu'd for acquiring to themselves the noblest ornaments? what hurt can this be to themselves? what Disadvantage to others? But

there are two things usually opposed against Womens Learning. That it makes them impertinent, and neglect their household affairs. Where this happens it is a Fault. . . . I do not observe it so frequently objected against Womens Diversions, that They take them off from Household Affairs. . . . [She then deplored the fact that not only men, but some women opposed female scholarship.] Admit a Woman may have Learning, is there no other kind of Learning to employ her time? What is this Saxon? What has she to do with this barbarous antiquated Stuff? so useless, so altogether out of the way?[31]

Elizabeth Elstob, posing these unanswerable questions, acknowledged the daring of her undertaking—unlike other learned women who simply displayed acquired knowledge or those who spoke from creative imagination, she laid claim to a woman's right to academic scholarship. Inevitably, she had to defend herself against the accusation that her work was not her own, but her brother's, but that was readily answered by him in showing that it was she who helped him with his work, not the other way around.

She proceeded, with general acclaim, to compile the first Anglo-Saxon grammar, *The Rudiments of Grammar,* in modern English, which was intended to make this work available to people, mostly women, who knew no Latin. Published by subscription in 1715, it became the standard work on the subject. The list of 250 subscribers included the most noted Anglo-Saxon scholars of the day who were her patrons; half of the subscribers were women.[32] Shortly before its publication her brother had died, and she was left without support and the indispensable means of access to academic life. She hoped to publish several volumes of Saxon homilies, but this work faltered on lack of money and academic support. Deprived of a livelihood in her chosen profession, Elizabeth Elstob disappeared from the circle of her friends for twenty years. Sarah Chapone, a minister's wife with literary interests and a friend of several writers, discovered her living in near destitution in Worcestershire and supporting herself by teaching in a small day school. Mrs. Chapone introduced her to one George Ballard, a tailor who was an amateur collector of "antiquities," with an interest in learning Anglo-Saxon, and who later, at Elstob's suggestion, published a book on "Learned Ladies." Her friendship with Ballard revived her intellectually and led to some years of fruitful collaboration between them on his project.[33]

Mrs. Chapone, determined to help Elstob to more suitable employment, circulated a letter in her behalf to women of the local gentry as a result of which Elstob was offered a job as mistress of a local charity school. Her acceptance letter was considered so remarkable it was shown to Queen Caroline, who was so moved by it she settled 100 pounds a year on Elstob, but the payments were never made. Again, through the intervention of women friends, Elstob was brought to the attention of the Duchess of Portland. This lady decided, after some hesitation, to offer her the job of governess to her children at 30 pounds a year. The hesitation was due to her husband's concern that Elstob was not adequately qualified, because she did not speak French. But the Duchess overcame these objections and defined her new governess's job as follows: " . . . she requires and hopes Mrs. Elstob . . . to instruct her children in the principles of religion and virtue, to teach them to speak, read, and understand English well, and to cultivate their minds as far as their capacity will allow, and to keep them company."[34] After twenty years of abject poverty, during which she had been unable to pursue scholarly work, Elizabeth Elstob, then fifty-four, by training and actual achievement one of the foremost scholars in the field of Anglo-Saxon languages and literature, accepted this offer with gratitude. She spent the remaining seventeen years of her life in the routine activities of governess in an aristocratic household.

The rarity of learned women, and the difficulty of their lives, is one way to measure the cost of the educational disadvantaging of women. Another is to look at the spread of literacy from the point of view of gender differences. While any study of literacy and illiteracy poses great methodological difficulties, all the available evidence from all parts of the world points to the same pattern: with some rare exceptions for certain elites, women everywhere reach literacy later and in smaller numbers than men.

The first historical example of widespread literacy is in Ptolemaic Alexandria. There, 60 percent of the male and 40 percent of the female middle-class population wrote Greek, with many more who only wrote Egyptian. In 4th-century Greece there was similarly high literacy. In parts of India in the 4th and 5th centuries A.D. and up into medieval times half the men and five-sixths of all women were illiterate.[35]

In the Middle Ages the term *litteratus* meant a person with a knowledge of literature (Latin) and became affixed to *clericus*, the clergy. It stood in contrast to *illitteratus*, which became affixed to *laicus*, the laity.[36] We have earlier discussed how that distinction along the lines of the knowledge of Latin tended to separate the sexes and eventually to increase the educational disabilities of women. The rise of literacy in the vernacular was connected to the ascendancy of the merchant class, with literacy widespread among Florentine merchants in the 11th century and merchants in the Hanseatic League in the 13th century. By 1400, English and German artisans were literate.[37] While there are no accurate figures available, we can assume that wives of those groups acquired the rudimentary literacy needed to help their husbands in business and trade, but all the while the majority of women remained illiterate.

The invention of the printing press by Johann Gutenberg in 1440, while it was the single most important technological advance making widespread literacy possible, did not immediately have that effect. The major advance of literacy in Europe begins with the Protestant Reformation. This is the earliest period from which historians can date detailed studies of literacy based on signatures of documents. All show the same trend. Male literacy everywhere is greater than female, but it varies by class and region and is tied to trade and occupation.[38] Thus a study of court records of the diocese of Norwich, England, 1530–1730, shows male illiteracy varying from zero (clergy) to 85 percent (laborers), while female illiteracy overall is 89 percent.[39] A study of illiteracy in Scotland, 1630–1760, shows male illiteracy rates of 28 percent against female of 80 percent. Here as elsewhere, literacy appears to be connected with the availability of schooling and is definitely class-related, but age and location also seem to matter, with older women and urban women more likely to be literate than younger and rural women.[40]

The methodological difficulty in assessing the literacy studies based on ability to sign is that there is a built-in bias toward middle- and upper-class people. Reading was taught first (between ages 2–6), usually at home, and writing later (age 6 on), usually at school. Even where schools were available, the poor could not afford to send their children to school, since their labor was needed at home or, later, in the factories. Thus people who could sign their names were apt to be better off than those not considered in a survey based on signatures. A few studies attempt to get around this difficulty. A study of 17th-century English spiritual autobiographers showed that many more lower-class people could read than write. This study also offered some interesting insights into the way semi-literate women could and did foster the spread of literacy. A survey of a small market town in Staffordshire, 1693–98, showed one man and five women schoolteachers as well as a visiting writing master who came twice a year for six weeks. Four of the five female teachers were wives of day-laborers and craftsmen. One of the autobiographers tells of his mother, the wife of a weaver, who herself could read but not write, but who instructed her children with the Bible and books and helped poor children to literacy by buying books for them, sending them to school and paying their teacher.[41]

In a study based on the histories of revivalists in Scottish Protestantism, most of the thirty-six women studied were servants (32 out of 36). All the male and female revivalists could read, but nearly two-thirds of the men and only one-tenth of the women could write. Two women were self-taught readers by following the chapters of the Bible in church. One servant woman learned to read at age eighteen, when she made it a part of her employment contract in service that she should get a reading lesson each day.[42]

From the point of view of a gender analysis what matters most is whether there is a consistent difference in the literacy rate of men and women. An analysis based on marriage registers in France during the 18th century shows a rise in literacy for men between 1690 and 1790 from 29 percent to 47 percent. For women during the same period the literacy rates are 14 percent to 27 percent (figures rounded off).[43]

In the 19th century there were great advances in public education and with it the spread of literacy. The records of marriage registers kept by the Church of England from 1754 on, make it possible to summarize the ability to sign of approximately 90 percent of the population who were ever married. These figures show the following:

England Illiteracy Rate
(based on sample of 274 parishes)

1750	Male 36%	Female 64%
1850	Male 35%	Female 50%

Illiteracy Rate
(based on all parishes)

1850	Male 30%		Female 45%
1911	Male 1%	1913	Female 1%[44]

It is noteworthy that while female literacy improved greatly in the 19th century it is not until 1911–13 that male and female literacy rates are the same.[45]

It may be interesting to look at an underdeveloped country which in the 20th century instituted an unprecedented campaign against illiteracy. Czarist Russia in 1897 showed a 22 percent illiteracy rate. After the Bolshevik Revolution the campaign against illiteracy was given top priority by the government. Here are the results:

Soviet Russia Illiteracy Rate[46]

1926	Males 24–25 years old	4.3%
	Females, 19 years old	11.8%

A worldwide survey made by the United Nations (UNESCO) showed that with a very few exceptions female illiteracy exceeds male illiteracy in all the countries of the world. The exceptions are mainly countries reporting a very high literacy rate, and even in these countries sex-equal literacy exists only in the young, with the literacy rates for the population over age 35 showing strong sex-based differences.[47]

NOW LET US consider the spread of literacy in the United States.[48] The best-known study of literacy in the colonial period is that of Kenneth Lockridge, based on 3000 signature marks on wills. He showed a strong rise in male literacy over a thirty-year period, with a much slower rise in female literacy. In 1660, 60 percent of the men making wills were able to sign; by 1790 almost 90 percent were signers. For women the rates of signers were much lower: 31 percent in 1660; 46 percent by 1790. For a number of methodological reasons the Lockridge study may have underestimated female signing ability.[49] In a recent study of 907 Connecticut women signers of deeds or witnesses to deeds, arranged by birth cohort, Linda Auwers found that 21 percent of the women born in the 1660s and 94 percent of those born in the 1740s were able to sign.[50] Still, female signing ability (and with it literacy) lagged behind male.[51]

Colonial New England children of both sexes learned the rudiments of spelling and reading from their mothers or from neighboring women who kept "Dame schools" in their homes, supported by small fees paid by each pupil. The strong religious and economic impulse for promoting education at work in the colonies is exemplified by the Massachusetts law of 1642, which empowered the selectmen to check up on the ability of all children "to read and understand the principles of religion and the capitall lawes of this country." Children who were not being adequately trained could be removed from their parents and apprenticed to someone else. Similar laws were passed in the other colonies. The law of Massachusetts also specified that boys were to be taught reading and writing, while girls were only to be taught to read. It was not until 1771 that legislation stipulated that children apprenticed under the Poor Laws were to be taught: "males, reading, writing, cyphering; females, reading, writing."[52]

The ability to write was considered a craft which was difficult to teach and therefore was taught by men. Because it was considered a preparation for jobs, writing was for over a hundred years taught mainly to boys in town-supported schools, staffed by schoolmasters. From 1690 on some girls won access to these schools, but schools were closed to most girls until the middle of the 18th century, when, in 1760, Dedham, Massachusetts, became the first town to provide regular summer sessions for them. In Medford, Massachusetts, in 1766, girls were admitted to school in the afternoon only, when the boys had left. New London, Connecticut, admitted girls to school in the summer, and only during the hours from 5 to 7 a.m. As these summer sessions for girls became more widely available, female teachers were hired to offer instruction in reading, writing and ciphering.[53]

In a pattern familiar from the European past, a small elite group of boys was prepared in Latin schools and academies to enter college. After the American Revolution educational opportunities improved for children of both sexes, but the goals toward which their education was directed were farther apart than ever before. Boys were to be educated for social usefulness and political leadership as citizens of a republic; girls were to be educated for their social usefulness as wives and mothers. And although the concept of their increasing significance as "mothers of the republic" served as a spur to the spread of female education, it remained limited in scope and quality and always inferior to the education offered to males.[54]

Between 1790 and the 1840s female academies proliferated in the Northeast, in the Moravian settlements in Pennsylvania, in Georgia, frontier Tennessee and Ohio. Of equal importance was the increasing number of male academies which accepted women students either part or full time. Most of the female academies offered a curriculum, which stressed "accomplishments," and which reinforced the girls' indoctrination to a strictly gender-defined role in life. Women's academies prepared girls to function more intelligently, more effectively and more graciously in "woman's sphere," but they also raised the educational aspirations of many of their graduates.[55]

The decisive break with that tradition came in 1818 when Emma Willard drafted a plan for the improvement of female education to be submitted for the consideration of the New York State legislature. With this bold move and with the subsequent founding of Troy Female Seminary she began what would be a century-long movement by women to equalize women's access to education.[56]

Emma Willard, Mary Lyon, Catharine Beecher, and the several other women pioneers who established institutions of higher learning for women with curricula equal in content to that offered men, did not plan to challenge gender-defined separate spheres for women and men. They merely wished to upgrade "woman's sphere" and extend her educational and economic opportunities by training large numbers of teachers to furnish the newly established public schools of the nation. In this endeavor they admirably succeeded and the literally thousands of schools founded and staffed by their pupils in the 1840–70s bear testimony to their achievement. An unexpected consequence of it was that the existence of so many graduates with better educational qualifications led to an ever-increasing demand by women for access to colleges and universities. The fact that the school founders had no intention of producing such results is unimportant. What is important is the pattern they reveal, whereby women's education centered in female communities becomes the energizing force for future societal transformation.[57]

The gap in male/female literacy diminished in a pattern affected by region, class and race. By 1840, when common schools offered the same hours of instruction to boys and girls, almost all white women in the Northeast could read and write.[58] This level of literacy was not attained by Southern white women until the end of the 19th century. Rural women, immigrants and African-American women were illiterate longer than native-born, white and middle-class women.[59] But no matter what particular group of person one studies and in what particular location, the literacy gap between men and women of the same group is not closed until nearly universal literacy is reached.

A similar observation can be made by studying levels of educational achievement in various groups and classes of the population. For example, until 1837 women were unable to enroll in any college or university. By 1870, they constituted 21 percent of the total undergraduate enrollment; by 1880, women constituted 32 percent of the undergraduate student body and by 1910 almost 40 percent. While the increase in the number of college-educated women is notable, it is more significant that it was not until 1920, when women were 47 percent of the college undergraduates, that women achieved equal access to college educations with men. Yet by the end of the 1930s, while the number of female college-trained undergraduates rose slightly, the number of women trained to the professional level declined dramatically. The low point in the 20th century came in 1960, when women were 35 percent of all students with a B.A. or first professional degree, and only 10 percent of all doctorates.[60]

It is only since the 1920s that equal educational access for women has been won on all levels up to graduate school, yet vestiges of former educational deprivation continue to show up in women's lower achievement on college-level tests and in the awarding of scholarships. More important, no matter what the variation for a particular group to be considered (ethnicity, age, region, religion), what remains unvaryingly true is that women's access to education remains below that of males of their group. The single exception to this rule is the case of African-American women, who between 1890 and 1970 exceed males of their race in educational attainment. This is due to the vagaries of race discrimination, which offered little incentive for higher education for men, since even with advanced degrees they were confined to menial jobs. On the other hand, educated black women had a chance to escape domestic and menial service. Thus families had an incentive to foster the education of their daughters rather than of their sons. In this respect African-American families form an exception to the almost universal American pattern whereby families educationally deprive daughters for the sake of sons.

Thus, although educational access was won much later for all African-Americans than it was for whites, in 1960 the census shows that black female physicians represented nearly 10 percent of all black physicians, while white female physicians were 6 percent of all white physicians. Black women lawyers were 9 percent of all black lawyers, while white women lawyers were only 3 percent of all white lawyers. Similar patterns appear in the census data for schoolteachers. Ironically, one of the few gains of the 20th century civil rights movement which has remained in place is that the educational advantage of black men over black women now follows similar sexist patterns as that of white men over white women.[61]

The pattern of women's struggle for equality of access to educa-

tion in America is the same as it was in Europe: each level of institutionalized learning had to be separately and consecutively con-
quered. Resistance by individual men and by male-controlled
establishments was relentless and unwavering. At every level of the
educational establishment women had to first fight for the right to
learn, then for the right to teach and finally for the right to affect
the content of learning. The last has yet to be accomplished to any
significant extent.

WHY HAVE THERE been no great women thinkers and system builders? Where are the female Newtons, Kants, Einsteins? Virginia
Woolf's brilliant metaphor of Shakespeare's sister who, had she been
as talented as her brother, would still not have been able to accomplish what he did due to the contraints of gender definitions, has
actual historic precedents. These women existed, women of extraordinary talent, of genius, with the capacity and the will to excel, create and define. Isotta Nogarola, accused of incest with her brother to
explain her literary achievements; Sor Juana de la Cruz selling her
precious library at the Archbishop's command to show her humility;
Elizabeth Elstob serving as the governess of the Duke of Portland's
children. And that otherwise unknown girl of sixteen, one Lucinda
Foote, who was denied the admission she sought to Yale University
in 1792 with the comment that she was qualified in all respects "except for her sex." Lucinda Foote may have been only moderately
talented or possible she may have been gifted with genius. We will
never know, for she was female, and that was all that mattered.

THREE

Self-authorization

FAR MORE DETRIMENTAL than the inferior training offered to women was the misogynist explanatory system that dominated Church doctrine and shaped ideas of gender in society in general. Beliefs in the God-given inferiority of women and in their subordinate position in society antedated Christianity but were greatly elaborated in the centuries after 300, when the Church began to consolidate into a strongly hierarchical institution dependent on a male clergy. Even then, the tradition of female disciples of Christ and the Apostles was still strong enough and the presence of holy women and anchorites pervasive enough to counteract misogynist ideas. Efforts by both Church and State during the Carolingian period to control polygamy, to end the concubinage of the clergy and to restrict or forbid divorce revived and reinforced misogynist ideas. The reforms not only elevated the monogamous family to the basic economic unit of society but helped to strengthen class formation among the propertied. The effect of these innovations was to make unmarried women highly vulnerable economically, to render the possibility of upward mobility through marriage less likely, and to make the lot of former concubines of the clergy precarious. It is no accident that ideological attacks on women rose sharply and that the first witchcraft accusation against a woman occurred in this period.[1]

Misogynist ideas at first were merely an instrument of state and clerical short-range interest, but soon such ideas acquired a life of their own. The concept that women are born inferior, have a weaker mind and intellect, are more subject to emotions and sexual temptations than men and that they need to be ruled by men, had a devastating effect on women's minds. Even extraordinary women, talents which occur once or twice a century, had to struggle against this notion which deprived them of authenticity and authority. Each thinking woman had to spend inordinate amounts of time and energy apologizing for the very fact of her thinking.

Recent feminist criticism has traced and recorded the cost of this handicap for individual women thinkers, especially those living later than the 17th century. The creation of the authentic self which defines its own creativity is a historical phenomenon which for women was possible only much later in history than it was for men. St. Augustine's *Confessions*, written in the 5th century A.D., is generally regarded as the first autobiography by which such an authentic self was constructed. But that self was male; its very definition excluded the female from identifying with it. It is debatable when the first female autobiography succeeded in similarly constructing an authentic self. The works of female mystics, beginning with Hildegard of Bingen, certainly deserve consideration, over and above their description of a spiritual journey, as works of autobiography, but as such they lack precisely the authority and assertiveness whereby the self becomes an exemplar of the life leading to salvation. The female mystics rather submerged the self in order to become open to ecstatic revelations. They saw themselves as insignificant instruments through which the power of God is manifested, "God's little trumpet," as Hildegard referred to herself. The search for an authentic self had to take different forms for women than it did for men, since for men authority was assumed, while for women it was utterly denied. Thus each woman asserting authority was a self-defined freak and had to deal with that fact in her writing before her audiences could be open to her language and thought.[2]

Writing women, working prior to the recognition that women might be capable of participating as autonomous thinkers in the public discourse—a recognition we can place historically in the 17th century—had to remove three obstacles before their voices could be heard at all: 1) that indeed they were the authors of their own work; 2) that they had a right to their own thought; 3) that their thought might be rooted in a different experience and a different knowledge from that of their patriarchal mentors and predecessors. Once these obstacles were removed, writing women still faced the problem of finding or creating audiences appropriate to their work. If they addressed men, they needed to defuse and deconstruct the patriarchal frame of reference which devalued and trivialized their work. They also needed to minimize the separateness and uniqueness of their female experience, and often they ended up distorting, disguising or trivializing their own experience. If their audience was made up of women, they needed to find symbols and encoded language to enable their readers to follow the process they themselves had had to undergo in order to think at all. They had to evoke and legitimate sources of knowledge and experience women usually denied in themselves in order to survive in the patriarchal world. Somehow they had to cut through gendered metaphor and touch actual feeling and knowledge, elevate the process to the order of universality abstract thought demands, and evoke in other women the courage and daring to follow their own process and go on from there. This was a task far different from that facing the male thinker, whose authority was unquestioned, whose right to his own experience was taken as a given and who could develop his thought standing in discourse with the great thinkers before him. Women were denied all of these necessary preconditions for developing abstract thought.

Each woman asserting the right to her own voice was forced to prove that her writing was her own, and was not ghost-written by a male mentor. While the authenticity of the plays of the 10th-century nun Hrosvitha of Gandersheim was not questioned by historians and critics, her talents were dismissed as being merely imitative of the Roman playwright Terence. It was not until quite recently, in the excellent and respectful evaluation of her work by Peter Dronke, that the full scope and range of her thought were presented. Hrosvitha herself expressed her self-doubt and the obstacles she expected to meet should her talent be revealed in her first "Preface" to a series of legends.

> . . . I did not dare to lay bare my impulse and intention to any of the wise by asking for advice, lest I be forbidden to write because of my clownishness. So in complete secrecy, as it were furtively, now toiling at my composition alone, now destroying work that was badly done, I tried as best I might to produce a text of even the slightest use, based on passages in writings I had gathered to store on the threshing-floor of our Gandersheim foundation.[3]

The nun Hrosvitha hiding her writing and the sources for it on the threshing floor of the abbey of Gandersheim, a celebrated center of learning and culture, evokes the painful memory of the 19th-century Harriet Beecher Stowe hiding her writing in her sewing basket, lest family and friends disapprove of her unseemly pursuits as a writer. The manuscript on which she was then working was *Uncle Tom's Cabin*. Over a period of nearly nine hundred years women's claim to the right to think and to write remained controversial and disputed.

Hrosvitha, in a later "Preface" to her plays, gives us some indication of the near-fatal effects of female self-disparagement and self-censorship when she writes: "Hitherto I hardly dared to show the clownishness of my little composition even to a few people, and if at all, then only to intimate friends. So the task of composing something further of that nature almost ceased."[4] Hrosvitha continues with newfound confidence by asserting that her gift of writing comes from God and paraphrasing the words of the apostle Paul: "By the grace of God I am what I am" (I Corinthians 15:10), saying: ". . . I feel joy deep in my heart that God, through whose grace I am what I am, is praised in me; yet I am afraid to seem greater than I am."[5] Here, quite early in the history of women's thought the basic dilemma of women's authority is sharply and painfully delineated— her talent is inspired, yet she dreads its consequences, because the societal definition of her gender role excludes the possibility of such a gift.

The nun Hildegard of Bingen (1098–1179), appearing two hundred years later and emerging as a unique and inspired thinker out of a community of women, was much more confident in her God-inspired gifts than Hrosvitha. Yet the authenticity of her medical writings was challenged by at least one historian.[6] The authenticity of several of the 12th-century Abbess Héloïse's three letters to her former lover Abelard have been questioned by some scholars.[7] Similarly, some of the writings of the remarkable group of Provençal *trobairitzes*, who flourished in the same century, were for a long time ascribed to male troubadours supposedly writing in a female voice.[8] Marie de France, one of the great lay writers of the Middle Ages, who also lived in the 12th century, met the usual attacks on her authorship. She responded to them in the Epilogue to her *Fables*:

> And it may hap that many a clerk
> Will claim as his what is my work.
> But such pronouncements I want not!
> It's folly to become forgot.[9]

The first known woman to make a living by her pen, Christine de Pizan (1365–*c*.1430), faced the usual questions of authenticity and answered them in her sprightly way. In her allegory, *Christine's Vision*, she has "Dame Opinion" say:

> Some say that clerks or priests have written your works for you for they could not come from feminine intelligence. But those who say such things are ignorant, for they are not aware of the writings of other women wiser than you, even prophets who have been mentioned in past times. . . . so I urge you to continue your work which is valid, and not be afraid of me.[10]

We will find the same defenses against the charge of plagiarism by women in every century. The Renaissance humanist Laura Cereta (1469–99) was accused by male writers of presenting her father's work as her own, because no woman could have written such learned letters. Cereta retorted that she was pleased to find herself compared with her father whom she admired, and displayed her erudition and writing skills in her reply as proof of her authorship.[11]

Many British women authors, from the 17th to the 19th century, sought to forestall such accusations by having male authorities endorse their works. Such endorsements, while testifying to the woman's authorship, could be quite demeaning and insulting. One of the worst cases is that of Sir Egerton Brydges, M.P., whose Preface to the autobiographical work of Margaret Cavendish, Duchess of Newcastle, tells us that the Duchess:

> was deficient in cultivated judgement; that her knowledge was more multifarious than exact; and that her powers of fancy and sentiment were more active than her powers of reasoning. . . . Her Grace wanted taste. . . . She pours forth everything with an undistinguishing hand, and mixes the serious, the colloquial, and even the vulgar, in a manner which cannot be defended.[12]

Apparently undaunted by this critical judgment the Duchess insists that she writes this memoir "for my own sake . . ."[13]

In the 18th century that great rarity, an Irish tradesman's wife who wrote published verse, assured her readers that she "found leisure without neglecting her husband's business to write several little pieces." She, too, suffered the indignity of an eminent male sponsor's introduction. The great Jonathan Swift, recommending her to a patron, wrote:

> She seems to have true poetical genius, better cultivated then could well be expected, either from her sex, or the scene she has acted in, as the wife of a citizen. . . . Poetry has only been her favorite amusement;

for which she has one qualification . . . that she is ready to take advice, and submit to have her verses corrected, by those who are generally allowed to be the best judges.[14]

The list of such patronizing and deeply insulting sponsors, casting their protective arms around the frail shoulders of their victims, is not as astonishing as the sturdy persistence of the women who absorbed such insults, used them to their advantage and persisted in their efforts at self-expression.

MUCH MORE SERIOUS in its impact on female thought was the internalization by women of their inferiority, which made them uncertain or defensive as to their right to think. Medieval women writers, even the most powerful, such as the female mystics, all found it necessary to announce their unworthiness to the reader. Hildegard of Bingen, one of the most learned women of her century, referred to herself as *"ignota,"* an ignorant woman. Mechthild of Magdeburg similarly assured the reader of her simplicity and ignorance of learning. Julian of Norwich, the powerful English mystic, used almost the same language, calling herself "unlettyrde," by which she probably meant that she was uneducated in Latin, the language of learned men.[15] While both male and female mystics used the argument of their own ignorance, the "humility *topos,*" as literary critics designate it, to heighten the power and effect of their miraculous inspiration, the same was not true for the almost inevitable apologies with which women writers prefaced their work. These are pathetic remnants of what must have been agonizing struggles each woman had to conduct within her own soul and mind.

A few examples of such apologies will highlight the general pattern. Hugeburc, abbess of Heidenheim, an Anglo-Saxon nun who had settled in Germany in 762, wrote the life of two brothers, the bishop of Eichstatt and the abbot of Heidenheim. In the Prologue she speaks of herself as follows:

I am unworthy. . . . I who am as it were a puny creature compared with my fellow-Christians . . . . especially corruptible through the womanly frail foolishness of my sex, not supported by any prerogative of wisdom or exalted by the energy of great strength, but will, as a little ignorant creature culling a few thoughts from the sagacity of the heart, from the many leafy, fruit-bearing trees laden with a variety of flowers, it pleases me to pluck, assemble and display a few . . . for you to hold in memory.[16]

Her statement that her words are culled from the heart becomes the prototype for a typically female justification for thought—women think with the heart, not the brain, and that, somehow, makes their thought more acceptable. She asserts that she does not properly write, but "plucks and assembles," a minor sort of mental activity akin to flower arranging or quilting and making no claim to originality. Many other thinking women, in their public apologies for the daring undertaking by which they confronted the patriarchal doctrine of their incapacity, similarly trivialized what they were doing. They claimed merely to translate ideas, to rearrange them, anything but think for themselves.

And yet women thought and women wrote and acted in the world. Even those who apologized and seemingly accepted the humility *topos* transmitted a different attitude in the rest of their writing, as though they felt freed, once the formalities of admitting their inferiority had been satisfied, to prove their strength and talent and individuality.

THE LIFE OF Hildegard of Bingen exemplifies the breakthrough of a female genius who managed to create an entirely new role for herself and other women without, ostensibly, violating the patriarchal confines within which she functioned.

This remarkable 12th-century nun followed the tradition of strong female religious leaders in institution-building and in her leadership of two religious communities. More important, she left a large and highly original body of work, writings which were influential in her lifetime and for centuries after her death. She was a pioneer in combining spirituality, moral authority and public activism to create what was to become a new public role for women. This remarkable achievement was made possible only because God spoke to Hildegard, and not only did she believe it and know it, but she made those around her believe it and know it.

Born in 1098, she was the youngest of ten children of a noble family of Bermersheim in the Rhineland. Early exhibiting a religious inclination, she was sent at age eight to live at the Benedictine nunnery of Disibodenberg. There she came under the tutelage of the Anchoress Jutta of Sponheim, who supervised her education according to the Benedictine rule. She acquired a knowledge of writing and reading, liturgy and singing, which later found expression in her musical compositions.[17] In 1136, after Jutta's death, she succeeded her as leader of the community.

Hildegard derived her authority entirely from her visions, which began when she was five years old and which she kept secret into adulthood. She revealed her visions only at the express command of the inner voice and then only after a severe illness convinced her that this command was indeed God's will.[18] Here she describes the source of her authority and the way she responded to it:

> In the year of our Lord 1141 when I was forty-two years and seven months old, the heavens opened and a fiery light throwing off great streams of sparks utterly permeated my brain and ignited my heart and breast like a flame which does not burn but gives off heat the way the sun warms an object which it touches with its rays. And suddenly the meaning of the Scriptures, the Psalter, the Evangelium and the other catholic books of the Old and New Testament was revealed to me . . . I had experienced the power and mystery of hidden and marvelous visions since childhood, that is from the age of five up to the present, but I had revealed this to no one except to a few others who shared my way of life. I concealed it and kept silent until such time as God saw fit to manifest it through his grace.[19]

Hildegard's description of the sudden revelation experience is quite similar to that of other mystics. It involved all the senses—in other visions she described at length the feeling of sweetness on the tongue and the smell of sweetness—; it possessed the visionary physically and spiritually and it was all-encompassing. There is no way of analyzing what has happened or explaining it rationally. "And suddenly I knew. . . ." It was from this knowledge Hildegard received her self-assurance, her authentication. All mystics and visionaries so grounded their experience and explained it with the same simplicity and belief. What is remarkable about Hildegard is the use to which she put her visions and the responses they evoked. Her keeping silent about her visions is, again, quite typical of the life stories of most of the great mystics. Humility, self-doubt and the fear of censure or ridicule kept the mystic from revealing her special knowledge and perceptions.[20] Hildegard apparently did reveal what she experienced to a few of her nuns ("who share my way of life"). It was only with their encouragement and at a command of her vision that she spoke to her spiritual adviser about it. She was readily believed, which is not at all typical of the stories of the mystics. The final confirmation of her inspired gifts at the Synod of Trier gave her an authority most unusual for any mystic, much less a woman.

Her protestations of her ignorance ("since I am uneducated") have been generally discounted by modern historians, for the internal evidence of her vast literary output suggests that she must have been well educated in patristic literature, biblical exegesis, philosophy, astrology, natural sciences and music. She was well acquainted with the Latin Bible and she stated that she heard the divine voice speaking in Latin. Her medical books are so closely grounded in the theories of Galen that it is inconceivable that she did not have knowledge of his work.[21] Her conventional reference to herself as an uneducated woman undoubtedly was designed to strengthen her claim to divine revelation, as does the detailed description she gives in a letter written later in her life to the monk Guibert of Gembloux, who became her secretary:

> Whatever I see or learn in this vision, I retain as a memory for a long time, so that when I see or hear it, I remember it, and at the same time I see, hear, and know and as if in an instant, I learn what I know. But what I do not see, I do not know, since I am uneducated and have been taught only to read out letters in all simplicity. That which I write in the vision I see and hear, and I do not set down any words other than those that I hear. I bring them forth in unpolished Latin words just as I hear them in the vision, for in this vision I am not taught to write as the philosophers write.[22]

Again, there is the confirmation of the overpowering existential revelation ("I see, hear, and know and as if in an instant"). Hildegard makes a fine distinction between knowing and understanding when she writes ". . . as if in an instant I learn what I know." Her visions appear to her as physical images which she describes in great detail and with strong poetic force. But the interpretation of these images is another kind of "knowing," it is the knowing which is learned, by an added grace. Hildegard always claimed that kind of knowing, asserting the interpretation of her visions with strong conviction. Most likely it was that aspect of her belief which enabled her to create her unique public role.

The book of her visions, *Scivias*, was recommended by Bernard of Clairvaux to the Synod of Trier. Hildegard was examined by a commission appointed by Pope Eugenius III, after which he acknowledged the authenticity of her visions. This made Hildegard a public figure, whose advice was sought by high and lowly and whose influence reached throughout Europe.

In 1148 she had a vision telling her to found a new convent, but she was refused permission by Abbot Kuno of Disibodenberg. As was to be the case repeatedly when she met obstacles, she fell into a severe illness, which finally convinced the Abbot to grant her request. In 1150 she moved to the new site with eighteen nuns, all noblewomen, building the convent Rupertsberg near Bingen on the Rhine. She managed to keep her convent entirely free from the control of Abbot Kuno and recognized only the Archbishop of Mainz as her superior. More than a decade later, the Holy Roman Emperor Frederick Barbarossa not only accepted her rebuke over his policies but granted her convent his special protection during a period of warfare. Hildegard later built a second convent at Eibingen and for the rest of her life supervised both institutions.

Once started on her public career, she broke all precedent by traveling widely throughout the Rhineland, preaching in big cities, visiting monasteries, counseling clergy and laymen and distributing the texts of her sermons.[23] She wrote her second book, *Liber Vitae meritorum* (Book of Life's Rewards), in five years. Her last book of visions, *Liber Divinorum Operum* (Book of Divine Works), was finished in 1173, when she was seventy-five years old. She left a very large body of work, including two major works on medicine and natural science, *Physica or Liber Simplicis Medicinae* (Book of Simple Medicine), and *Causae et Curae or Liber Compositae Medicinae* (Book of Advanced or Applied Medicine).[24] She also left a play, *Ordo vitutum*, two books on a secret language she invented, a book of exegesis of the Psalms, and two biographies, honoring St. Rupert and St. Disibode. Her collected letters reveal an amazingly far-flung correspondence with notable political and religious leaders of her day, such as Henry II of England, Eleanor of Aquitaine, Bernard of Clairvaux, Popes Eugenius III, Anastasius IV, Adrian IV and Alexander III, Emperors Konrad III and Frederick Barbarossa and the Archbishops of Mainz, of Trier and of Salzburg.[25] She also corresponded with abbots and abbesses, nuns and lay persons. She dispensed advice, answered theological and moral questions, challenged political decisions and recommended action, always speaking in the inspired voice of "God's little trumpet." Her tone in the correspondence is authoritative and firm, showing none of the deference, timidity and humility customary for a woman of her position. She addressed popes and emperors as equals and was apparently so treated by them in response. In later centuries there would be a number of outstanding mystics and saints, such as St. Catherine of Siena and St. Teresa of Avila, who similarly combined the contemplative life of mystic visionaries with political and public careers, but Hildegard was the first to fashion such a role for herself. Undoubtedly, she was a model for others.

That she was fully aware of her powers and willing to use them can be seen in the prolonged and bitter struggle she waged in order to prevent her close friend and disciple Richardis von Stade from leaving her convent. This young noblewoman, who had for years been her amanuensis, had decided to accept an appointment as abbess of another convent. Unable to dissuade her, Hildegard protested strongly to the young woman's family, the Archbishops of Mainz and Bremen and finally even to the Emperor. Her language displayed her usual boldness and forcefulness, when she went so far as to accuse her superior, the Archbishop of Mainz, of simony. "The spirit of God, full of zeal, says: pastors, lament and mourn at this time, because you do not know what you do, when you squander offices, whose source is God, for financial gain. . . ."[26] Still, in this case all her appeals were in vain—she failed to impose her will on Richardis. It is the only known incident in her life in which she was defeated. This was true despite the fact that she never avoided controversy.

The last such incident occurred when she was eighty and became embroiled in a difficult moral and political struggle. She had granted a Christian burial within the walls of her Rupertsberg cloister to a nobleman and donor who had once been excommunicated. Hildegard believed that before his death he had made his peace with the Church and therefore she refused the order issued by the Mainz diocese, in the absence of Archbishop Christian, to have his body exhumed and cast out. For this offense she and her nuns suffered the interdict and were denied the benefit of the mass and the sacrament. Since the interdict also meant that, in case of death, she would be denied the last rites of the Church, this must have been a dire threat for the eldery abbess. Still, she stood her ground. Characteristically, she based her defiance on her inner light, which she considered to have greater authority than the command given to her. "I saw in my soul that, if we followed their command and exposed the corpse, such an expulsion would threaten our home with great danger, like a vast blackness . . . So we did not dare expose him."[27] Her reasoning was that the dead man had been consecrated by burial in holy ground and thus an insult to his corpse would be an insult to the sacraments. This profound conviction of the theological correctness of her argument enabled Hildegard to defy the interdict. Finally the Archbishop decided, on technical grounds and disregarding her theological argument, to cancel the ban and thereby vindicate her, just six months before her death.

The range and depth of her work, which encompassed medicine, natural sciences, cosmology, theology, ethics, mystical revelations and poetry, have been compared to that of the great philosopher Avicenna.[28] Her writings were not only influential and widely circulated in her own lifetime, but she was known in the 13th century and her manuscripts were published in the Renaissance (1533 and 1544). Her influence has been traced into the 16th and 17th centuries.[29] She is the first woman thinker and writer to hold such an influential position during her lifetime and for several centuries after her death. As such she deserves close consideration, especially since her work and life reveal some of the major tensions, conflicts and strength that characterize the lives and works of later female thinkers.

Hildegard overcame the biggest obstacle all thinking women faced and still face—the overwhelming burden of proving their right and their ability to think at all in opposition to traditional gender-roles they were expected to fill. As we have seen, she overcame these obstacles by removing herself from the role of wife and mother, by selecting the life of a religious and then by grounding her authority in mystical revelations and a direct relationship to God. That this adjustment was neither easy nor conflict-free can be seen in her life-long history of ill health and the nearly fatal illnesses that preceded various turning points in her life. Such an illness occurred when at age forty-two she was commanded by her inner voice to write down her revelations. She resisted that command and fell ill, and it was not until she became convinced of the seriousness of her illness that she made the connection between her resistance to her inner voice and the failing of her body. She must do as her inner voice commanded or she might die—and so she did as commanded. The same pattern was repeated when it was revealed to her that she must found her own convent and move away from Disibodenberg. The only way she could overcome the strong resistance of her male superior to this command was by again falling into a severe illness. Here is how she described what happened to her:

> But my abbot, and the monks and the populace in that province . . . were determined to oppose us. What is more they said I was deluded by some vain fantasy. When I heard this, my heart was crushed, and my body and veins dried up. Then, lying in bed for many days I heard

a mighty voice forbidding me to utter or to write anything more in that place about my vision.

A noblewoman thereupon intereceded in her behalf with the Archbishop, and thus Hildegard gained permission to move with her nuns. But they faced extreme poverty and many tribulations in the new location and Hildegard was confused about the meaning of these trials.

> Then in true vision I saw these tribulations had come to me according to the exemplar of Moses, for when he led the children of Israel from Egypt through the Red Sea into the desert, they, murmuring against God, caused great affliction to Moses too. . . . So God let me be oppressed in some measure by the common people, by my relatives, and by some of the women who had remained with me, when they lacked essential things. . . .[30]

The metaphoric comparision of herself to Moses is revealing; it shows that she felt called to spiritual leadership, that she thought of herself as a prophet and that she had no hesitation about assuming such a role. And yet the tensions and conflicts generated by such assumptions took their toll. Throughout her life she complained that her visions left her in a state of physical exhaustion; she suffered constantly from migraine and always experienced her body as weak and frail. Yet she led a life of constant activity, strenuous travel and public appearances, exhausting mental work that lasted well into old age. This hidden conflict, with its untold costs, is characteristic of many women thinkers throughout the centuries.

Hildegard was privileged in her ability to free herself from traditional gender roles by living as part of a female community, enjoying what Sara Evans has listed as a precondition for feminist consciousness, "free space."[31] This was the free space provided by convent life and the absence of women's domestic and reproductive responsibilities; but it must be understood that this relatively "free space" was a space within a patriarchal institution, the Catholic Church, in which all the higher offices and positions of power were held by the male clergy. Clearly, in Hildegard's case this free space commanded more autonomy than many female religious normally enjoyed, as can be seen in her struggle to free her newly founded convent of Bingen from the restrictive control of Abbot Kuno; in her successful campaign to be governed only by one male superior, the Archbishop of Mainz; and in her securing the protection of the Emperor Frederick Barbarossa for her convent. It also shows up again in the resistance she offered, and which all her nuns supported, in the face of suffering the interdict against what she considered an arbitrary ruling and erroneous interpretation by her superior.

As other nuns before and after her, Hildegard acknowledged and credited the strong influence of a female teacher, in her case the Anchoress Jutta. She also transmitted a similar mentorship and leadership model to her disciples, as seen in her relationship with Richardis. Another indication of her assertion of independent authority can be seen in the innovations she introduced in her order, which ranged from the practical to the spiritual—the installation of indoor plumbing at Bingen; the wearing of rings, white veils and tiaras by her nuns on festive days to celebrate the Virgin Mary. She explained and defended these innovations on theological grounds, so that we may deduce they were deliberate.[32]

Hildegard's father may have taken part in the first crusade while she was still a child. She did speak to the returning men of the second crusade and later strongly endorsed the persecution of the Cathars, whom she considered, according to prevailing Church doctrine, a heretical sect. Like her mentor and supporter, Bernard of Clairvaux, who defended the Jews against the brutal persecution they suffered in the wake of the first crusades, Hildegard was friendly to Jews and had a number of conversations with them. Apparently they came to her convent for disputations.[33]

Hildegard's vision of cosmos, nature and humankind is powerful in its holistic integration of all aspects of Creation. The beautiful illustrations of the Rupertsberg Codex, which was created under her personal supervision by the nuns in her cloister, reflect the harmony and grandeur of her vision. Concentric figures hold sea, earth, sky, stars and the heavens in balance. Symbols are as frequently female as male and worshippers are evenly balanced among both sexes. Wherever the clergy is shown, it is represented by male and female religious.[34] One senses in Hildegard a soul at ease with the physical as with the metaphysical, with life as with spirit.

Hildegard's religious writings reflect, on the whole, the prevailing Christian tradition of her day. But the extent to which she deals with the subjects of reproduction and sexuality is quite extraordinary for her time, as is her concern with defining sexual relations, their consequences for reproduction and her scheme of classifying men and women of different dispositions. She seems to accept the traditional definition of gender roles as taught by the Church fathers, that is, she repeatedly asserts that women are weaker, different in their physical and psychic structure from men and therefore destined to be subordinate to man. Man was transformed from clay into flesh and is therefore stronger; woman was made directly from flesh and is thereby weaker.[35] Since she was weaker and softer than man, it was only natural that woman should first fall to temptation and that, Hildegard thinks, was a good thing. For if Adam had fallen first, his sin would have been stronger and salvation would not be possible.[36]

Hildegard's explanation for conception also builds upon the qualitative differences between the man and the woman's contribution to the process. She explains that conception occurs when a man's and a woman's foam meet in sexual intercourse. Since woman's "foam" is weaker than that of the man she mainly acts as the recipient of his foam, which she alternately warms, cools and dries in her womb. Hildegard then explains differences in offspring as due to a combination of the strength of the seed and of the attitude of the parents. The strength of the child seems, according to her explanation to depend on the strength of the man's seed, but the character of the child depends on the love of the man and woman for each other. While Hildegard's notions of conception are pre-Aristotelian and reflect some Galenic concepts, the slight twist she gives to her explanation in introducing the question of love and mutuality changes the role and importance of the sexes in conception in a rather dramatic way. Only if the man and the woman love one another and the man's seed is strong will a strong boy be born. If one or the other partner is lacking in love, the offspring will either be a girl or an embittered boy.[37] This explanation upgrades the role of woman in the process of conception from a merely passive one to one whose feelings and attitudes have a decisive influence on the outcome. Similarly, while Hildegard reflects patriarchal values in her acceptance of the superiority of the male, her retelling of the story of Creation puts an entirely new interpretation on the words of Genesis. Her words are poetic and powerful:

> When God created Adam, Adam experienced great love in the sleep which God sent over him. And God gave form to the love of man and so the woman is the love of man. For when Adam saw Eve for the first time, he was entirely filled with wisdom, for he recognized in her the mother of his children. But when Eve saw Adam, she looked upon him as though she were looking into heaven. . . . And therefore there is only a single love, and that is the way it should be in the love between man and woman and no different. . . . The love of man alights his passion like the fire of flaming mountains, which can barely be con-

tained, but the love of the woman is like the flame in a woodfire. . . . Her love for man is like the balanced warmth of the sun's glow which brings forth fruit. . . . In this manner the woman can more pleasantly carry her fruit to term.[38]

The illumination of this vision is even more startlingly radical in its departure from traditional explication than is her text. It combines elements of the Creation story with those of the story of the Fall. In a picture dominated by the four elements, the sky, the stars and the angels, Adam lies on his side, above a picture of the two trees of paradise. From his side Eve is born, in the form of a shell containing stars, which Hildegard describes as the "precious pearls of humanity." The left side of the picture is dominated by a black figure which looks like a tree and a lake of fire and which terminates in the head of a snake, breathing fiery tongues over the shell [Eve]. This black figure represents the fallen Lucifer [devil] who takes the form of a serpent to tempt Eve.[39] The absence of a human figure of Eve is unique in the iconography of the Creation story. The balance between the stars in the heaven above the scene, which according to Hildegard represent the angels, and the stars within the shell, which stand for future human beings to be born of Eve, stresses her redemptive role rather than her role as causing the Fall.

In a similar manner Hildegard, in her retelling of the story of the Fall, removes the blame for the Fall from Eve and all women. Instead, the Fall becomes almost preordained by the bodily weakness built into Eve by the Creator. We will see this version of the Fall retold by many women in later centuries.

Although Hildegard is quite traditional in her use of the masculine designation for God—Father, King, Redeemer—in her narrative of great historical events, she uses feminine symbols for God in her description of timeless cosmic events. The predominance of feminine figures, both in her visions and in the pictorial representations, is quite startling. The three main figures to appear repeatedly are Wisdom (Sophia), the figure of Scientia Dei (knowledge of God)—who embodies both kindness and terror—and Sapientia, representing divine wisdom in Church and cosmos. Sapientia stands on a platform supported by seven pillars, which is the traditional way of representing the house of wisdom iconographically. She is both terrible and kind to mankind, revealing herself fully only to God. At various times she is refered to as Queen Consort, Bride of God. The contradictory attributes of these female figures, kindness and awesomeness, and the strongly erotic language in which Hildegard speaks of them, underline the continuity of their symbolism with the ancient pre-Christian goddesses. This is particularly notable in the representation of Sophia, wearing a stylized crown similar to the iconographic representation of the hellenistic Sophia and the Ancient Near Eastern Mother-Goddess. This continuity of ancient heathen symbolism and its transformation in the Christian tradition in the form of "sapiental theology" has been frequently noted. The conflation of the Old Testament figure of Sophia (Wisdom), representing the female aspect of God, with Mary, bride of God and Mother of Christ, is characteristic of sapiental theology and will occur frequently in the writings of later mystics.[40]

The figure of Sophia occurs in three succeeding visions (*Scivias*, II, 3–5). In the first of these Hildegard interprets her as "the bride of my son [the Church] which always gives Him new children through the rebirth out of the Spirit and the water"[41] This vision abounds in female and birth imagery. The womb of the woman represents mother love, "the net" of the Church for catching sinners in order to redeem them. The breast of the virgin represents the heart of the faithful. The female figure spreads out her glory

> like a robe and says she must conceive and give birth. This means the growth of the Church in the sacrament of the Trinity . . . . The Church is the virginal Mother of all Christians. She conceives and gives birth to her children through the secret strength of the Holy Ghost and offers them to God, so that they are called children of God.[42]

Hildegard describes the woman of another of her visions in the words she heard a "voice from heaven" speak: "This is the blossom of heavenly Zion. She shall be Mother and yet the blossom of a rose and a lily of the valleys. O blossom, you will be betrothed to the most powerful King, and when you have grown in strength, when your time has come, you will be Mother of the most illustrious child."[43] In her lengthy explication of the details of this vision, Hildegard describes the state of the Church, represented by three groups which she defines as the apostles and their followers, the clergy; "the most noble branch of heavenly Jerusalem"—the virgins and the virgin martyrs; and third, lay persons, kings, nobles and the poor. It is characteristic of Hildegard's thought that virgins, i.e., the female religious, occupy a position equal to the clergy in celebrating and maintaining the strength of Mother Church.

Hildegard, in developing her theology, linked the idea of Christ's predestination pre-eminently with the feminine. Just as she linked

Mary to Sophia in her maternal qualities, so she envisioned a female Caritas who like Sapientia is a mysterious *persona* containing elements of both Christ and the Virgin Mary. "In her right hand she held the sun and moon and tenderly embraced them" and she spoke to "the form which appeared in her busom . . . I bore you from the womb before the morning star."[44] This predestination idea was common currency in Hildegard's day, it even appeared in a favorite manual for nuns. It suggested that God created the world in order to redeem it. Thus, the virginal/motherly attributes of the three Mother figures in Hildegard's vision, Caritas, Mary and the Church, all carry out God's purpose of bringing Christ into the world in order to redeem it.[45]

Hildegard's repeated envisioning of the Church as Mother and her descriptions of the creative, life-giving aspect of the Church, which she likens to "green-ness" *(viriditas)*, her holistic symbol for the vitality of earth, nature, human life and spirituality, all express her insistence on the unity of male and female principles in the universe, on earth and in heaven. Her theology breaks sharply with the dichotomized categories of the scholastics and with the patriarchal hierarchies embedded in their thought. Hildegard's visions fuse male and female elements, the physical and the spiritual, the rational-practical and the mystical aspects of existence. It is no accident that the illuminations of her visions abound in circles, curves and waves, in *mandala*-like designs, which avoid any concept of hierarchy in favor of wholeness, roundedness and integration.[46]

It is impossible here to do justice to the richness of her visions, the complexities of her thought and the originality of much of her writing. She was influenced by Benedictine teachings and by Galen's medical theories, which defined "humors" as leading principles governing nature and humans, and "phlegm" as the main cause of disease. She incorporated principles of folk medicine and popular tradition in her medical work and her cosmology, such as belief in the curative value of minerals and precious stones. Since the Latin translations of Aristotle's scientific writings were not then available in Western Europe, she was not influenced by Aristotelian explanations of natural and biological phenomena. Hildegard was therefore quite original in her medicinal writings and especially in her poetic cosmology.[47] Her careful, often quite accurate descriptions of sexual intercourse and her insistence that sexual activity was beneficial to human beings over and above its function for procreation bespeak an unusual understanding of human nature and a rather liberal interpretation of human possibilities, especially considering that Hildegard had lived since age eight in a cloistered environment. Further, her descriptions of female and male characteristics quite independent of one another and her upgrading of woman's role in various ways in her writing indicate that, despite her acceptance of traditional gender definitions, she integrated some of her life experiences into her writing. Women, despite her insistence on their frailty and inferiority, emerge as active, strong people in her writings.

Hildegard, first of a long line of female mystics and spiritualists, derived her authority and right to speak and to think directly from God. God spoke to Hildegard—of this she was convinced and she was able to convince her contemporaries. From this she derived her enormous energy, vitality and leadership.

In three of the illuminations appearing in her late work, *De Operatione Dei*, Hildegard has painted herself into the visions. The visions are abstract and interpretative in their subject matter, representing "The Cosmic Wheel," "On Human Nature" and "Cultivating the Cosmic Tree." Each of these illuminations shows a mandala with many circles, representing various aspects of the universe, with a human figure at its center. In the left-hand corner of each of these pictures there is the figure of a seated nun, writing on two tablets shaped like the Mosaic tablets. Her face is lifted up and touched by some sort of radiance. This self-conscious self-representation may very well be the first of its kind for a woman.[48] The repetition of this motif and its placement within the illuminations dealing with the most far-reaching, philosophical themes show that Hildegard had by then transcended the conventional posture of self-effacement and humility. No longer merely "God's little trumpet," she wished to be seen in the act of writing down her visions, in the act of authorship. Wishing to be remembered in her own right, she became the first female inspired by mystical revelation to claim her place in history.

FOUR

The Way of the Mystics-1

IF TRADITION, RELIGION and daily practice inculcated in women a deep sense of mental inferiority, which they were to regard as both natural and God-given, one must wonder how some of them managed to overcome this sense and give themselves authority and warrant to think and speak, even to write. We have earlier discussed some of the obstacles they faced and the sacrifices they had to make in order to function as thinking persons. Let us now examine some of the trends and movements that fostered female spiritual and mental emancipation.

The thinkers of Classical Antiquity and the fathers of the Church had elevated man's rationality, his ability to reason logically and without the subjectivity of emotions, to a divine gift which marked the road to salvation. Because of man's capacity for reason and because of his free will, his ability to choose the good through the teachings and practices of the Church would lead from sin to redemption. Biblical interpretation was based on rational, philosophical and theological arguments, on scholastic progression from one interpretation to the other and on complex symbols, the comprehension of which demanded their interpretation through a learned clerical elite. Much of the misogynist content of patristic teaching was designed to convince men and women that this rationality was a natural ability reserved to men, while women, precisely because they lacked this capacity, were preordained to educated ignorance and intellectual dependency.

There was, however, an ancient tradition, preceding Christianity and developing within it from the start, which allowed for another mode of cognition and enlightenment. Mysticism, in its various forms, asserted that transcendent knowledge came not as a product of rational thought, but as a result of a way of life, of individual inspiration and sudden revelatory insight. Mystics saw human beings, the world and the universe in a state of relatedness, open to understanding by intuitive and immediate perception. Its practitioners saw God as immanent in all of creation, accessible through unconditional love and concentrated dedication manifested in sincere prayer and religious devotion.[1] "As if in an instant I learn what I know," wrote Hildegard of Bingen. The foremost Dutch mystic of the 13th century, Hadewijch of Brabant, wrote: ". . . Love shows that it disdains reason and all that is in, above and below reason. For what belongs to reason is opposed to what benefits the true nature of Love. Reason cannot take anything away from Love nor can it give anything to Love. For the true nature of Love is always a swelling flood without thought or forgetting."[2] After describing with great physicality the longing of her soul for union with her "beloved" (God), the 13th-century mystic Mechthild of Magdeburg described her experience poetically:

> The great tongue of the godhead
> spoke to me in many a strong word,
> this I perceived with the pitiful ears of
> my nothingness,
> and the pervasive radiance of light
> revealed itself
> to the eyes of my soul.
> In it I saw the unpronounceable order
> and I recognized the unspeakable
> magnificence
> and the unfathomable mystery
> and the unique sweetness with its gift of
> distinctness,
> and the highest satiety
> and the greatest order in the recognition
> and the delight with restraint
> toward one's (limited) forces
> and the unmixed joy in merging
> and the living life of eternity,
> as it is now and will ever be.[3]

Many mystics experienced ecstatic raptures over prolonged periods, some of them for most of their lives. Others had such intense experiences only rarely. Julian of Norwich is supposed to have experienced all her revelations in one 24-hour period of intense visionary activity. Mystics drew on the biblical tradition of prophesy and revelation and especially on the imagery of the Song of Songs, which ever since Bernard of Clairvaux's allegorical interpretation had stood for the mystical union of God and the soul. Other sources of mysticism were the works of Plato and Eastern Christian spirituality of the 4th to the 6th century, especially the work of a Syrian monk known as Pseudo-Dionysius, who provided much of the language and imagery of medieval mystical thought. While mysticism had a long history, the religious revival of the 12th century gave it new vitality in Western Europe. The founding of the Cistercian order was based on a desire of many religious for a more ascetic life and a meditative practice that sought a profound spiritual union with God. The aim of Christian mystics was spiritual union with Christ, which could be reached by ascetic practices, suffering and mortification of the flesh, meditation, and openness to the revelatory experience. Mystics described their road to God variously, but it usually included several stages: 1) a purging of body and soul by exclusion of all sensory distractions achieved by ascetic practice and prayer and an emptying of the soul of all worldly concerns. 2) This "night of the spirit" or "darkness of unknowing," when all previous knowledge has been abandoned to get the soul in readiness, is followed by a transcendent experience, a sudden illumination. Mystics described the presence of God, a sudden certainty of a metaphysical reality which they perceived as immensely joyful and reassuring. 3) The final stage, which may occur simultaneously or later, is union with Christ, in which the mystic is re-experiencing Christ's suffering and crucifixion, or which may come as an overwhelming revelatory feeling of union, a merging, and sometimes orgiastic giving-over-of-the-self to the Other. All the great mystics, male or female, described such experiences, often in words that managed to express the inadequacy of words. Hadewijch's explanation is quite typical: "For the languages of heaven cannot be understood on earth. Languages enough and Dutch enough can be found for all things on earth, but I do not know any Dutch or any language for the things of heaven."[4] Similarly, Mechthild of Magdeburg, after a highly poetic passage describing one of her visions, said in homely and rather vivid prose:

"Now my German falters. Latin I do not know. If there is something good in it, it's not my fault. For there was never a dog so mean that he did not come gladly when his master offered him a white roll."[5] Her shifting into plain speech here not only expresses the paucity of language in face of the mystical revelation, but her metaphor of the dog offered a white roll vividly expresses her sense of loss in not being offered the precious gift of the holy tongue.

WHAT THE MYSTIC learns in ecstasy and rapture is transmitted to contemporaries in revelations, prophecies, visions and spiritual commentaries. Some mystics' visions amount to a coherent theological system, others are fragmentary and unsystematic. Some build upon biblical and traditional ritual imagery; others are astonishingly original in concept and symbolism. Mystics obviously used whatever materials their own lives could provide; thus, cloistered mystics were influenced by imagery they would see depicted in the churches, the Bible and the sacred manuscripts to which they may have had access. Mystics who had long lived outside of cloisters or who came late in life to their mystical experiences, such as Hadewijch, Mechthild of Magdeburg, Margery Kempe, Dorothea of Montau and the later Protestant mystics, used imagery closely reflecting their worldly experiences. Margery Kempe, describing an ecstatic experience, drew on homely metaphors deriving from her life experience as a housewife and mother in Lynn in East Anglia. She described wonderful sounds she heard: "One was a sort of sound as it if were a pair of bellows blowing in her ear. . . . it was the sound of the Holy Ghost. And then Our Lord turned that sound . . . into the voice of a little bird which is called a red-breasted, that sang full merrily oftentimes in her right ear."[6] The 17th-century Pietiest mystic Anna Vetter had visions of Christ dancing with her at a wedding feast and of some mystic presence intervening in a quarrel in a tavern.[7] The mystics' visions are generally amazingly concrete in detail. There can be no question that they described actually lived experiences, whether these were visions, dreams, hallucinations, out-of-body states. In the case of Hildegard of Bingen and Julian of Norwich, the visions came during their full consciousness in the form of "showings," visual and auditory images, later explained by "voices." The important achievement of all the mystics we know is that they not only had these extraordinary experiences, but that they could convince contemporaries not only of their actuality, but of their spiritual meaning.[8] Male mystics in the Middle Ages were all clerics who needed no other authorization than that of their religious training to assume a public role. But for women the private discipline, suffering and rewards of the mystical life could sometimes be transformed into public roles of leadership unusual for their sex, as can be seen in the case of Hildegard of Bingen and, later, St. Catherine of Siena and St. Teresa of Avila.

Hugh of St.-Victor, one of the early mystics, believed, as did most others, that scholastic learning and institutionalized ritual were not conducive to spiritual preparedness. The mystic's way of perceiving was, then, an alternate mode from the dominant religious/theological mode of perceiving and knowing. It was particularly suitable for the unlettered, the humble, those despised in the eyes of society. For had not Jesus spoken of just such men and women, those humble in spirit, that they would enter his Kingdom? Each of the female mystics dealt in some manner with this problem of her unworthiness for the role she was assuming. In a way, which occurred so frequently among women asserting their right to think that one might call it a pattern, they transformed this imputed weakness of their femaleness into a strength. It was precisely because they were weak, uneducated and simple, and because they were excluded from the great privilege of the priesthood, that God had chosen them as His instrument for salvation. This argument recurs throughout the centuries. Hadewijch dealt with it several times in her book. In a section entitled "Of this book and its writer" she asked in prayer why she was commanded to write it.

> Ah Lord! were I a learned priest
> And hadst Thou worked this wonder in him
> Then hadst Thou endless honor therefrom.
> But how can any believe
> That on this unworthy soil
> Thou couldst raise up a golden house . . .

To which the Lord replies:

> One finds many a wise writer of books
> Who in himself, to My sight, is a fool.
> And I tell thee further, it greatly honours Me
> And strengthens mightily Holy Church
> That unlearned lips should teach
> The learned tongues of My Holy Spirit.[9]

In another characteristic passage she had the Lord remind doubters that the apostles, too, at first were weak, that Moses hesitated to take up his power. "And ask yet further how it was that Daniel was able to speak (so wisely) in his youth?"[10]

The apologetic stance of Mechthild of Magdeburg, an uncloistered Beguine, toward her own prophetic gifts may have been due to her marginal social status, as the medievalist Caroline Bynum has remarked. Bynum noted that the nuns of the convent Helfta, living a generation later in a large and powerful community of women, spoke in a more confident tone of their right to teach and to counsel other Christians. Mechthild of Hackeborn and Gertrude, her sister, who was the abbess of Helfta, accepted the authority given them by their visions to be mediators, "preachers and teachers." Bynum points out that this authority came precisely because women were denied active roles in the institutionalized Church.[11]

The mystics' way of knowing and perceiving transcended national and religious boundaries. Practicing mystics can be found in all religions and in most historical periods. To demonstrate the universality of the mystical experience it is interesting to compare the accounts given above with that of a 19th-century African-American evangelist.

Julia Foote, the daughter of slaves, but herself born free, was raised in New York State and later moved with her husband to New England. She early experienced a strong religious calling, but when she had two visions in which an angel held up a scroll to her which commanded her to preach, she resisted. "No, Lord, not me . . . I thought it could not be that I was called to preach—I, so weak and ignorant. . . . I had always been opposed to the preaching of women, and had spoken against it."[12] Following a familiar pattern of earlier mystics, she fell severely ill. Her friends and relatives gathered at her bedside, expecting her to die. She then had a vision of the Trinity in a garden. She was led before God the Father, the Son and the Holy Spirit and many angels. The Father asked her to decide whether she would obey him. She agreed, then Christ led her to a water, "and stripped me of my clothing . . . . Christ then appeared to wash me, the water feeling quite warm . . . ." She then heard sweet music and an angel held out a robe to her. The Holy Ghost plucked some fruit from a tree and fed her. Then God the Father commanded her to go, but she insisted that people would not believe her. Christ then appeared to write something with a golden pen and golden ink, upon golden paper. "He rolled it up and told her to put it in her busom and said, '. . . wherever you go, show it and they will know that I have sent you to proclaim salvation to all.' "[13]

Like so many mystics before her Julia Foote met severe disapproval. She was excommunicated from her church, censured by her bishop and often denied permission to speak or preach. But she persisted and won many adherents to her doctrine of Sanctification. Thirty years later she commented on these efforts to deny her authority to preach:

> We are sometimes told that if a woman pretends to a Divine call . . .
> she will be believed when she shows credentials from heaven: that is,
> when she works a miracle. If it be necessary to prove one's right to
> preach the Gospel, I ask of my brethren to show me their credentials,
> or I cannot believe in the propriety of their ministry.

Again, following much earlier precedent, Julia Foote then cited the Bible in defense of woman's right to preach. She quoted earlier prophets and especially Paul. "When Paul said 'Help those women who labor with me in the Gospel' he certainly meant that they did more than pour out tea."[14] With this acerbic comment this self-educated African-American 19th-century evangelist joins the long line of Christian women who base their authority as teachers and preachers on their mystical experiences and on citations from the Bible.

IT IS EVIDENT from the historical record that mystical thought had a special appeal for women and that female mystics appeared to cluster in certain periods and regions. In their study of the sociology and origin of 864 saints in the Christian era, Weinstein and Bell report that the overall proportion of male to female saints was five to one. While not all mystics became saints, the Weinstein-Bell study illustrates patterns which hold for mystics as well as for saints. Weinstein and Bell found a gradual rise in the proportion of female to male saints from the 11th to the 13th century, with a sharp rise in the 14th and 15th centuries, when one of four saints was female.[15] Weinstein and Bell also show the connection between mysticism and female sainthood. Even though women represent only 17 percent of all the saints they studied, they are 40 percent of all the saints known for mystic contemplation and 45 percent of all saints known for visionary experiences. The most striking characteristic of female saints seems to be their propensity for supernatural signs and communications, in which they represent 52 percent of Weinstein and Bell's sample.[16] Mystic contemplation, visions and communication with the supernatural manifested in signs are peculiarly private forms of the miraculous. Since women were forbidden the practice of the priest-hood and of most public roles, with the exception of nursing the sick, it is not surprising that they expressed their religious experi-ence in these more private mystical forms. The need of women for authorization to speak, which we have detailed earlier, also may have led them to choose these forms of mystical expression. The divine image authorizes them, sends a scroll, speaks directly to them. It engages in a mystical marriage; washes them free of sin in a baptism scene; gives warrants, signs and messages. Without these, no one would believe the female mystic. One can conclude from these sta-tistics that women tended more toward visions and mystic contem-plation than men did, but it is also possible that these manifestations were more likely to be rewarded by the granting of sainthood to female than to male religious. The gender-specific definition of women as more emotional might lead the clergy controlling the institution-alization of sainthood to favor such manifestations in women rather than in men.

Female mystics appear in clusters. The great 12th-century mys-tics, Hildegard of Bingen and Elizabeth of Schönau, both of whom died before 1180, were followed by the Beguine mystics Marie of Oignies, Hadewijch, Mechthild of Magdeburn and the remarkable nuns of Helfta, whose mysticism flourished in the late 13th cen-tury.[17] The 14th century brought the appearance of female mysti-cism in Holland, Germany, England, France and Italy. With the spread of the witchhunts and the onset of the Reformation there was a sharp drop in the numbers of female saints, followed by a steady decline. But female preachers making prophetic claims based on their visions continued to appear among Catholic and Protestant sectarians in the 16th and 17th centuries. The Counter-Reformation inspired the mysticism of Teresa of Avila and Mme. Guyon. In later centu-ries the mystic mode of thought would find expression in various Protestant sectarian religious movements, such as the Shakers, the Spiritualists and many of the smaller evangelical churches.

The local clustering of mystics may also be explained by the fact that mystical practices could be learned. The nuns in the abbey of Helfta in Saxony and the Poor Clares convent of St. Damian in As-sissi taught each other mystical practices. Christina Ebner, herself a mystic, considered it unusual that some nuns in her convent did not have such experiences.[18] How can one explain the phenomenon of the flourishing of female mysticism from the 12th to the 14th century?[19] Many historians think that the social conditions that fostered the growth of mysticism developed in the 11th century, when the Gregorian reforms of the Church expanded the clergy's influence and control over the laity. In the early Middle Ages the source of supernatural power had been manifested for the laity in daily life predominantly through the relics of saints, while the ordinary person's contact with the clergy was limited to baptism, burial and the paying of tithes. Monastic spirituality served as an ideal, while the prayers of monks and nuns assured God's grace to individual and community. By the middle of the 12th century the reforms in the Church, the spread of clerical celibacy, the refinement of canon law and the secure monopoly of the Church over education had enhanced the position of the clergy, while it separated the spiritual and material worlds more sharply. The spiritual world was more and more seen as dominant over the secular. Theologically, the office of the priest was greatly increased in importance due to his authority to dispense the sacrament in the form of the mass and the Eucharist. This was reflected also in the sharp increase in the number of monastic orders founded. The order of Fontevrault, founded by Robert of Arbrissel in 1100, grew rapidly in membership. The Cistercians, under the leadership of Bernard of Clairvaux, expanded greatly during the 12th and 13th centuries. By 1270 their abbeys in Western Europe numbered 671. The Premonstratensian order, founded by St. Norbert in 1120, evangelized the German domain.[20]

As the role of the educated clergy was enhanced, the role of women as both uneducated and unfit for clerical office became more sharply delineated, which, in fact, meant for women a restriction in their connection to the world of the sacred. This spiritual loss was paralleled by a loss of visible authority for women. While the number of people who joined monastic orders increased dramatically in the 12th century, changes in the form of monasticism also worked to decrease the autonomy of women religious. By the end of the century double monasteries ruled over by abbesses had virtually disappeared in England and Western Europe. The three new orders, at first reluctant to admit women, later set up separate houses for them, but defined the rules for women religious more strictly than they had earlier been. By the middle of the 12th century, total enclosure for women religious and their spiritual guidance by priests had become the norm. In the same period the educational goals for nuns were redefined and the study of Latin by nuns became the exception.

Yet the same period saw the development and spread of new forms

of religious vocations. The apostolic life was now sought by a proliferation of lay groups in which men could pursue sanctity in new
forms. Some withdrew to the wilderness to live in poverty and prayer;
others formed wandering bands that attracted followers to their religious fervor. The second half of the 12th century saw the rise of
the Albigensian heresy (the Cathars in southern France were known
as Albigenses). Some lay spiritual dissenters like Peter Valdes wanted
to reform the clergy by their exemplary life of poverty and good
works. He formed the Waldensian movement, consisting of lay persons who chose to live a life approximating that of Christ and the
Apostles. His movement, at first tolerated by the Church, was soon
condemned as a heresy. On the other hand, Pope Innocent III approved of idealistic movements which sought to regenerate the Church
from within, such as that of the new orders of friars, both the Dominicans and the Franciscans. Friars resembled monks in their religious vows, but they did not live in monasteries. They lived in the
world, begging for their subsistence, and devoted themselves to good
works and preaching. The movement founded by St. Francis of Assisi inspired St. Clare to become his follower and to found, with his
approval, the order of the Poor Clares. Women flocked to the wandering preachers and their sects, many of them joining heretical
groups, as we will discuss later. Thus, the outburst of religious fervor among women persisted over male resistance.[21]

Women found temporary, often short-lived support for the notion of their innate equality with men as creatures of God in the
heretical sects. Women in great numbers were active in organizing
and proselytizing for the heretical sects and were visible among those
suffering persecution and martyrdom. In this, they followed a pattern already noted in the history of early Christianity: as long as
movements were small, loosely structured and persecuted, women
were welcomed as members, given access to organizational leadership and shared authority with men. When the movement became
successful, it became more tightly structured, more hierarchical and
more male-dominated. Women were then relegated to auxiliary roles
and to invisibility. This can be illustrated by the case of the Cathars.

The Cathar heresy flourished in the 11th century in the Languedoc and in the 12th century continued there and spread into Italy,
the Rhineland and the Low Countries. Its dualistic belief system rested
heavily on Gnostic texts and interpretations.[22] Cathar doctrine taught
that there were two distinct gods, one the creator of good, the other
of evil. The material world was created by the evil god and its re-

production was by definition evil, hence Cathars rejected marriage and what they defined as the fruits of copulation, meat and milk. Since sin originated in Satan, Cathars held Eve blameless in the Fall; they saw her merely as Satan's tool. Following Gnostic doctrine, Cathars believed that Mary Magdalen had been the wife or concubine of Christ. They denied the doctrine of physical resurrection and held that resurrection referred purely to the soul. It was the evil god that created male and female; in the heavenly kingdom all creatures would be angels without earthly sexuality. These doctrinal differences from Catholic orthodoxy enabled Cathars to see men and women as more alike than different in the divine purpose and in their religious potential. Cathars believed that it was possible for human beings to come closer to perfection through ascetic living; those who succeeded were called *perfecti*; both men and women could reach that stage. In practice most people reached that stage only shortly before their death. While marriage was tolerated for the ordinary believer, it was forbidden to *perfecti* and *perfectae*. One reached that stage through the ceremony of the *consolamentum*, a sort of baptism by the laying on of hands. This meant that ordinary believers had a great deal of freedom in sexual matters during their lifetimes, since they were assured that after confession and receiving the *consolamentum* they would be perfected and saved. It is significant for the high status of women among the Cathars that, at least in theory, men and women could administer the *consolamentum*, although in practice few women ever did.[23]

Catharism developed in the cities of the Languedoc, especially in Toulouse, the center of textile production and trade. Large numbers of women in the textile manufacturies became Cathars, as did male artisans and textile workers. Since the wages of female textile workers were much below those of male workers, even fully employed women could barely support themselves. To such women Catharism may have offered hope of salvation and practical communal support. The disproportionately large number of females among these heretics was noticed even by contemporaries.

A number of Languedoc noblewomen are known as leaders of Catharism and as *perfectae*. Phillipa, wife of the Count de Foix, led a convent of *perfectae*; one of the count's sisters was Esclarmonde de Foix, the "Princesse Cathare." After the death of her husband, she returned to the court of her brother, who built a house in which she, his former wife and other *perfectae* lived. In 1207 there was a public dispute between several bishops and representatives of Waldensians and Cathars. It is indicative both of her high status and of the limitations of her position that Esclarmonde participated in this public dispute on the side of the heretics and that the bishops reprimanded her and told her to go back to her spinning.[24]

In the second half of the 12th century many Cathar women's convents were founded for unmarried daughters and widows of the lower nobility. These communities, led by *perfectae*, were under the spiritual guidance of a heretical bishop. While these Cathar women, like Catholic nuns, were active in education, spinning and weaving, they also proselytized and performed some religious ceremonies.[25]

Constant persecution of the Cathars by the Inquisition made severe inroads in the strength of the movement. The violence of the Albigensian crusade of 1209 fell with particular brutality upon women. That year there was a massacre of heretic women and children in Beziers, and a year later, in Minerve, Cathars were given a choice of abjuring their belief or burning. One hundred forty male and female Cathars jumped into the flames. When crusaders started a reign of terror against the *perfectae*, the local population at times defended the heretics. In 1234 in several communities, armed women and other citizens prevented the arrest of female heretics. In 1243 women actively fought in defense of Montsegur castle, the last stronghold of the Cathars. During the siege almost all the noblewomen in the castle made a pact with the bishop to give them the *consolamentum* in case they were wounded and could not speak. The agreement was fulfilled when the situation in the fortress became hopeless. After the defeat, the military defenders of the fortress were allowed to retreat unharmed, but 200 male and female Cathars were burned on a great pyre, among them a number of well-known *perfectae*. After Montsegur the nobility largely withdrew from Catharism, and Cathar convents gradually disappeared.[26]

By the end of the 13th century, Inquisition records no longer mention *perfectae*, which indicates that they lost their leadership position in the sect. In its declining phase Catharism attracted more adherents of the urban middle classes. Members of the middle class were drawn to Catharism because it allowed profit and interest, which the Church opposed.[27] The Cathar women among this group appear in the record as among the faithful, but not as leaders. They supported the movement by raising funds, giving help to fugitives and doing missionary work. With the destruction of the Cathar convents the opportunity for women to exercise autonomous power and even political leadership disappeared. Many former *perfectae* joined the

Beguines; others found refuge in Catholic convents. By the middle of the 14th century, Catharism had virtually disappeared. As would happen so often later in revolutionary and heretical movements, Catharism had seemed to promise women a role of spiritual and theological equality. Under the impact of persecution and of middle-class respectability this promise had given way to male dominance and patriarchal structures. The courage of the armed women defending their villages in the Languedoc against invading crusaders was only a singular outcry, throttled, and quickly forgotten.

THE DEVELOPMENT of the Beguine movement shortly after 1200 in the Low Countries, the Rhineland, Switzerland and northern France offered a new road to sanctity for women. Beguines—lay women pledged to poverty, chastity, manual labor and communal worship—lived in all-female, self-governing communities. In addition to the spiritual reasons discussed above, there were also economic reasons for the spread of this movement in certain regions. There was in the 12th and 13th centuries a surplus of females in the population, which made many women unmarriageable. It did not require a dowry to join a beguinage, as it did to join a convent, and this fact may, according to some historians, explain the rapid spread of the Beguine movement.[28] Beguine communities not only offered sanctuary and a new lifestyle to single women, they also promoted the reading of the Bible in the vernacular, which increased the potential for unschooled women to express themselves religiously. It is of interest here that several Beguines became celebrated mystics. Although the further spread of the Beguine movement was halted in the early 14th century by accusations of heresy and witchcraft, mysticism continued to flourish.[29]

I began this discussion by defining mysticism as an alternate mode of thought to patriarchal thinking. If this is true, then the fact of its appeal to women in a period of social upheaval, when avenues of self-realization and religious expression were restricted for them, makes sense. Whatever motivation women may have had for becoming mystics, it was more difficult and hazardous for women than for men to make claims to mystical experiences and to sainthood. The faithful were much more likely to accept such claims from males, who usually were priests or monks. There is a noticeable difference in the popularity during their lifetime and in their later impact between women mystics who stayed under the mentorship or protection of a male spiritual adviser or of an institution supporting them and those who operated without such protection. It was quite impossible for a woman to reach sainthood without such male clerical protection and promotion. Hildegard of Bingen, despite her not infrequent conflict with Church authorities, early won the approval of St. Bernard of Clairvaux and of the Pope himself, which established her and enabled her to pursue a respectable public career. Christina of Markyate, a 12th-century Anglo-Saxon mystic and recluse, was supported by the hermit Roger and by Geoffrey, abbot of St. Albans. Margaretha and Christina Ebner were supported by their spiritual mentor Heinrich von Nördlingen. St. Clare had the support of St. Francis of Assisi; St. Catherine of Siena was encouraged by her spiritual adviser Raymond of Capua, later General of the Dominican Order. These mystics, who exerted great influence during and after their lifetime, managed to combine their unusual public roles as teachers and prophets with the traditional roles of the female religious within the Catholic Church.

It was more difficult for an uncloistered woman or one who came to the cloistered life late. She had to convince her family of origin, or if she was already married, her husband of her desire for and commitment to chastity. The struggle was often protracted and bitter, as can be seen in the case of several celebrated mystics.[30]

Christina of Markyate (b.1096), daughter of an Anglo-Saxon noble family, vowed herself to chastity at an early age. Nevertheless her family arranged for a betrothal, which Christina refused. She fled from her home and was sheltered by the hermit Roger, who became her spiritual adviser. She long lived as a recluse and later became prioress of a small Benedictine order at Markyate. Marie of Oignies (b.1176), whose marriage had been arranged at the age of fourteen, persuaded her husband to live a chaste marriage and even persuaded him to share her life of poverty. Birgitta of Sweden (b.1302 or 03–1373) similarly managed to convince her husband to live a life of chastity and asceticism, but only after she had borne eight children and lived a traditional life as mistress of a household at the royal court. After her husband died, she sought shelter and found support in the Cistercian abbey of Alvastra, whose prior became her spiritual adviser. It was there that she dictated her Revelations. She soon moved to Rome and began her public career as spiritual adviser, teacher and founder of the Brigittine order. Her daughter who became St. Catherine of Sweden (1331–81) was married at age twelve, but persuaded her husband not to consummate the marriage. Still a virgin at age eighteen, she left her sick husband in Sweden and joined her mother in Rome. God assured her in a vision that this is what she must do and that her husband would soon die, which he did. As a widow she perfected her vocation of mystic and saint.

Several other married mystics had a more difficult struggle for their right to their vocation. Dorothea of Montau (1347–94), although certain of her religious vocation at an early age, was married at sixteen and bore nine children, of whom eight died in her lifetime. She lived an ascetic life, practicing constant devotions and mortifications of the flesh, which interfered with her duties as a housewife. Her husband abused and beat her for these transgressions, but she considered all of her suffering, whether self-inflicted or inflicted by her husband, as a special dispensation of God which increased her raptures and trances. While she was on a pilgrimage her husband died and she put herself under the protection of John of Marienwerder, who promoted her fame as a miracle worker and wrote two *vitae* of her. Dorothea of Montau lived out the last years of her life as an anchoress, walled off in a cell in the cathedral of Marienwerder.

Clara Gambacorta (d. 1419), the offspring of a prominent family in Pisa, was betrothed at age seven and sent to live in the house of her betrothed at age twelve. When he died before the marriage could be consummated, the family wanted her to enter a second betrothal, but she refused, citing the example of Catherine of Siena, and escaped to join the Poor Clares. Her brothers came with an armed gang and threatened to burn the convent down if she were not released. The nuns sent her back to her family, where she was held prisoner in her room for many months, until her father finally became convinced of her vocation. He endowed a new Dominican community for her, of which she later became the prioress.

Women who lived without parental or male protection were always very vulnerable to accusations of heresy. The mystics who lived as Beguines were often under suspicion of heresy and under attack. The Beguine Hadewijch of Brabant, who lived in a community of women, whose spiritual guide she was, supposedly escaped persecution as a heretic only by leaving this community and living in isolation. The Beguine Mechthild of Magdeburg had to seek shelter and protection in old age at the convent at Helfta. Most of the uncloistered women mystics, down to the 19th century, report harassment, ridicule and public condemnation. During the period of the witch-craft trials, such women were particularly vulnerable to prosecution and death.

The case of Marguerite Porète is a significant example of this phenomenon and one of the few examples in which the actual words and beliefs of the accused heretic are available to us through her writings, not through the interpretations of inquisitorial proceedings or courts. Since many different contemporaries refer to her as a Beguine, we may assume that she was one and that this fact contributed to the suspicions centering upon her. Marguerite Porète was born in Hainaut and wrote her famous book, *Le Miroir des simples âmes* . . . (Mirror of the Simple Soul) sometime between 1296 and 1306. Her long work, made up of verses and commentary, is in the form of a dialogue of Amour and Raison concerning the conduct of the soul.[31] It postulates seven states of grace which lead up to the union of the soul with God. At the fourth stage the soul is at a level of contemplation in which it is free of all obedience to external authority and laws. In the seventh stage the soul arrives at a level of "glorification" in which "all the works of virtue are enclosed in the soul and obey her without contradiction."[32] Porète goes on to argue that in this stage the soul need not concern itself with masses, penance, sermons, fasts or prayer. She sings in rejoicing: "Virtues, I take leave of you for evermore:/ I'll have a freer heart for that—more joyful too./ Your service is too unremitting—indeed I know./ . . . I have quit your tyrannies; now I am at peace."[33] This belief, bordering on Antinomianism, was of itself offensive to the orthodox. In 1306 her book was condemned before an ecclesiastical court at Valenciennes as heretical and burned in her presence. She was warned not to disseminate it or her ideas any further. In 1308 she was brought before the new Bishop of Cambrai, Philip de Marigny, and the Inquisitor of Lorraine under the accusation that she was still circulating copies of her book. She was then sent to Paris to be examined by the Dominican Inquisitor, but there she refused to answer any questions and to take the vows necessary for her examination. She was then imprisoned and stayed in prison for one and a half years. When she was finally brought to trial in 1310, the Inquisitor extracted a list of articles from her book, which the judges then declared heretical. The Inquisitor particularly objected to the passage in the *Miroir* which stated "a soul annihilated in the love of the creator could, and should, grant to nature all that it desires." The examiner, citing this offensive passage against her and pointing out its similarity to the beliefs of the Free Spirit adherents, had deliberately left out the next sentence in the text, which qualifies this statement by explaining that the soul, thus transformed and glorified is so well ordered "that it does not demand anything prohibited."[34] Her defense that before her trial she had sent the book to three high Church authorities for their judgment and that they had not considered it heretical worked against her. Because she had ostensibly by her presence at the book-burning in Valenciennes abjured her heresies, the examination commission found her current offense the more deplorable and condemned her as a "relapsed heretic." She was immediately transferred to the secular courts and a few days later was burned at the stake at the Place de Grève in Paris. A contemporary witness testified to her unusual dignity and courage which made many who were present at her ordeal weep.[35]

Marguerite Porète indeed believed in "free souls," but she meant by this an invisible community of free souls united in the love of God. In the *Miroir* she pointed the way by which such a level of love and spirituality might be attained. Going this far, she was still within the realm of accepted mystical thought. Her doctrine of mystic union with God reflects ideas found in the writings of Hildegard of Bingen and Mechthild of Magdeburg, but, unlike these authors, Marguerite Porète did not respect the established Church as the only or chief vehicle toward salvation. Porète contrasted her greater Church with the "little Church" established on earth. As she saw it, the greater Church of the free spirits could override the lesser, the scholastic church establishment. It is this unorthodoxy which distinguished her from most of the other mystics. Her writing becomes sharp, almost polemical when she deals with this subject:

> Theologians and other clerks,
> You won't understand this book
> —however bright your wits—
> if you do not meet it humbly,
> and in this way Love and Faith
> make you surmount Reason:
> they are the mistresses of Reason's house.

And in her "Farewell Song," she again sounds a note of defiance:

> Beloved, what will beguines say and the pious throng
> when they hear the excellence of your divine song?
> Beguines say that I am wrong, priest and clerk and preacher,
> Austins and Carmelites and the Friars Minor,

wrong in writing of the being of this noble Love.
I am not— . . .[36]

Still, her theoretical deviations from orthodoxy were too slight to explain her fate. The historian Robert Lerner thinks that her persecution was due to the fact that she was uncloistered and happened to be tried at a time when, for political reasons having nothing to do with her, King Philip had to demonstrate his orthodox zeal. Lerner thinks Porète rather arbitrarily fell victim to this political necessity when Bishop Marigny, her accuser and King Philip's close adviser, misinterpreted certain passages in her book as an attack on the King.

Yet, despite her death as a heretic, and even though the Inquisition declared that to retain a copy of her book made one subject to excommunication, the *Miroir* was widely read and cherished in succeeding centuries. One copy of the original in French was saved, but there were five medieval translations (two Latin, two Italian and one Middle English) in which the book survived. For a time, it was even ascribed to the celebrated male mystic Ruysbroeck, whose orthodoxy was unquestioned.[37] Porète's work was always more acceptable than her person and her attitude toward authority. Other rebellious women affiliated with social movements considered heretical or revolutionary were savagely persecuted for such affiliation, but Porète represents a more solitary figure. Like Joan of Arc, and, much later, the Quaker Mary Dyer, she followed her inner voice and refused to cooperate with Church or state authority. The fact that, after a year and a half in jail, she remained silent during her trial and refused to obey all orders asking her to renounce and abandon her own writings makes her a heroic figure, braver than Galileo and many others, better known and more celebrated. Galileo, after recanting his theories under pressure from the Inquisition, is said to have stated on his deathbed, "And yet it [the earth] moves. . . ." Marguerite Porète, never recanting, anticipated her martyred death and, after listing all those who would say that she was wrong, defied the future with her proud assertion: "I am not [wrong]."

WE HAVE SEEN HOW mysticism offered some women a liberating path toward self-fulfillment and even toward the assumption of public roles. The mystical way empowered these women and enabled them to lead highly individualistic, heroic lives, defying all the prescriptions of patriarchal ideology. Yet these rare and certainly unusually gifted women paid an enormous price in insecurity, sickness and vulnerability. With a very few exceptions, their position was marginal and imperiled. The 15th-century mystic Margery Kempe has provided an unusually vivid description of the hazards she faced in her unusual vocation and life style in her autobiography, the first autobiography written by an Englishwoman. Margery was not only insecure during her lifetime, but has been equally insecure in her reputation.[38] If Hildegard of Bingen, the noble-born nun of recognized genius, represents one extreme in the spectrum of female mysticism, then Margery Kempe, the urban housewife and mother who made herself into a pilgrim and outcast, represents another.

Margery Kempe (*c.*1373–1438) was the daughter of a prominent burgher family in Lynn, East Anglia, and the wife of a merchant of Lynn. Uneducated, but resourceful, she led a fairly conventional life until her first child's delivery, which brought on a severe mental and physical crisis. She thought she would die and had a vision in which Christ appeared to her, after which she recovered. She then decided that "she was bound to God and would be his servant." Still fighting her vocation, she engaged on a career as a brewer, in which she succeeded for three years and then failed. Taking this as God's punishment for her sins, she tried again as a miller, but failed in this occupation as well. Meanwhile, her husband exercised his conjugal rights over her, which she described as so "abominable . . . that . . . she would rather have eaten or drunk the ooze and the muck in the gutter than consent to any fleshly communing, save only for obedience."[39] From this we can surmise that her fourteen pregnancies were not voluntary. In her autobiography, in which she mentions many trivial incidents with much detail, she never speaks of her fourteen children, except for one son, a great sinner whom she helped to repent and reform.

Margery Kempe's struggle for marital chastity was protracted and clearly long unsuccessful. She felt a great urge to go on pilgrimages and overcame her husband's reluctance, getting him finally to accompany her. On the first voyage, after they had been observing eight weeks of voluntary chastity, the crucial incident occurred. Margery Kempe describes it in her usual simple and down-to-earth manner, remembering such homely details as that it was "right hot weather," that they were coming from York and that she was carrying a bottle of beer for her husband. John Kempe asked her if she would rather see him beheaded than sleep with him again. She answered, "with great sorrow:—Forsooth, I would rather see you being slain, than that we should turn again to our uncleanness." And he replied; "Ye are no good wife," but he offered her a compromise. He would not "meddle with her" again, if she would pay off his debts; he demanded that they continue to lie in bed together and that she should eat and drink with him again on Fridays as she used to do.[40] Readily agreeing to the first two points, Margery sought reassurance from Christ on the decision not to fast on Fridays, was apparently reassured, and agreed to the bargain her husband had proposed. Thereafter they lived a chaste married life on its terms.

The simplicity and naiveté of Kempe's account partially account for her bad reputation among historians, who consider her a hysteric or a fraud. Her extroverted scandalous behavior is often unfavorably contrasted with the introverted, deep mysticism of cloistered women. But it is precisely the newness of the role she created, which made the way of the mystic accessible to ordinary women living in the world, that is of interest here. Kempe perceived her mission to be in the world, to be a mirror to sinners, so that by her example they might be saved. From the time of her first vision of Christ she lived ascetically, did much fasting and penance and took communion frequently. Yet her visions came easily and seemingly without the self-inflicted agonies so many of the mystics paid for their raptures. She spoke to Christ as familiarly and plainly as to her husband and to other contemporaries. She frequently went on errands at the Lord's command, delivering his messages. Once, shortly after childbirth, the Lord commanded her to go to the Vicar of St. Stephen in Norwich and "shew him thy secrets, and My counsels such as I shew thee." She explained to the Vicar "how sometimes the Father of Heaven spoke to her soul as plainly and as verily as one friend speaks to another. Sometimes the Second Person in Trinity, sometimes all Three Persons in Trinity, and one substance in Godhead spoke to her soul. . . . Sometimes Our Lady spoke to her mind; sometimes St. Peter, sometimes St. Paul, sometimes St. Katherine. . . ."[41] She acknowledged that many people slandered her and did not believe that she spoke the word of God, but she managed time and again to convince monks, friars, bishops of the truth of her claims.

Margery Kempe was concerned with money, with debts, with how to secure food and drink and lodging. Her spirituality is rooted in ordinary dailyness. Precisely that lends her account its uniqueness and makes it a convincing source of social history, quite apart from its intrinsic interest.

Kempe was unable to write or read, and her autobiography was dictated to two scribes when she was over sixty years old. It is written in the third person and she refers to herself throughout as "this creature." The book exists in a 15th-century manuscript, which remained undiscovered until 1934 in a Lancashire home. Thus, it lacks all the hagiographic conventions and formalities of the lives of most of the mystics who have come down to us in history. Kempe was largely unknown outside of a circle of neighbors and acquaintances during her lifetime and had no following to perpetuate her memory. She intended the book as a testimonial of "the high and unspeakable mercy of our Sovereign Saviour" and hoped it would encourage other "sinful wretches" to take solace and comfort in Christ's mercy. She is thus closer in tone and attitude to the left-wing sectarians of the Reformation and to the black evangelicals of the 19th-century United States than she is to the more theologically oriented mystics discussed earlier.

After she had won her freedom to go on pilgrimages as God commanded her, Margery Kempe proceeded to fashion a unique and somewhat notorious career. The Lord commanded her to wear only white clothing, which caused her much grief and attack from contemporaries. But it did serve to set her off from others as unique and strange. She lived a life of almost constant pilgrimages, apparently without the support of husband and family. She traveled to Germany, to Rome and to the Holy Land. She recounts innumerable difficulties because of her itinerant and deviant life. In her day reputable women of good family did not travel alone, so Kempe was always trying to attach herself to groups of pilgrims. But her peculiar form of devotion, loud and pitiful sobbing and weeping in churches and holy places, made her conspicuous and obnoxious to her fellow pilgrims, and time and again they cast her out. While she had earlier fallen into fits of "holy tears" and loud weeping whenever she contemplated the passion of Christ, this escalated when she was in the Holy Land on Mount Calvary. "She fell down because she could not stand or kneel, and rolled and wrested with her body, spreading her arms abroad and cried with a loud voice as though her heart would have burst asunder."[42] This kind of crying and shouting came over her at the sight of the crucifix or in other holy places or when she saw an animal or a person hurt. Contemporaries (and later readers) considered her crying extreme. At first it came over her infrequently, but later daily; one day she had seven fits. She would try to control herself, but could not. "Some said that a wicked spirit vexed her; some said it was a sickness; some said that she had drunk too much wine; some banned her . . . some wished she was on the sea in a bottomless boat."[43] It is clear that the crying and weeping were out of her control and brought her mostly grief. Yet it served to impress her contemporaries with her strangeness and power and, combined with her visions and her energy, made her mystical qualities believable.

Kempe reports that she performed a number of miracles, such as saving the Guildhall in King's Lynn from a fire by her prayers, which brought on a snowfall. She had a following among people who wanted her to weep for them, especially the dying or the sick, and she reported some successes in curing the sick with her tears and prayers. During long years of pilgrimages and voyages, she spent much time among strangers, and the precariousness of her existence led to her being accused of heresy and, once, of being a Lollard. She was imprisoned and questioned, but her answers to theological questions were so orthodox, that she was released. When she found herself in dangerous situations of this kind, she did not hesitate to invoke her respectable family ties as the daughter of an outstanding burgher of Lynn and the wife of another. She assured her accusers that she had her husband's permission to travel. At various other times, higher ranking clergy, to whom she appealed boldly when she was in trouble, sympathized with her and offered her protection against the lower ranking clergy who accused her. In these encounters she showed great fortitude, wit and resourcefulness.

Once the Archbishop of York tried to make her promise not to teach in his diocese, but she insisted that she would continue to "speak of God." The monks invoked St. Paul against her, but she had a ready answer. "I preach not, sir; I come into no pulpit. I use but communication and good words, and that I will do while I live."[44] She was repeatedly accused of sexual misconduct and often felt herself threatened by rape. It is noteworthy that her exaggerated weeping, anxiety and fear of rape and persecution were all traits common to other women of her time, which she managed to dramatize and put into the service of her vocation. She lived in a harsh world in difficult times, having removed herself from the comfort, security and protection which she had had as a burgher's wife in Lynn, and making herself conspicuous and suspect by her unusual behavior. While her outbursts reinforced the stereotype of the ultimate victim, the uncontrollably weeping female, she was active, shrewd and gifted with a talent for self-preservation. At times of crisis she showed a cocky self-assurance and a sure instinct for appealing to the most important male officeholder to whom she had access. Margery Kempe shows little introspection and seldom rises to theological speculations. Her greatest worry was whether she could trust her visions or whether she might be deceived by the devil. She consulted the Dominican anchorite Julian of Norwich and was reassured by her, "Daughter, ye suck even on Christ's breast, and ye have an earnest-penny of Heaven."[45] Several monks and bishops whom she consulted believed in her divine inspiration. Her pilgrimages strengthened her faith in herself, and she always found people who believed in her and supported her in her work. Despite all accusations of heresy, she remained a faithful daughter of the Church all her life.

Margery Kempe's conversations with Christ are unaffected, almost simple-minded. As a mystic, she has the quality of woodcutters and painters who decorate the village churches with their starkly beautiful, yet coarsely made works of art. She was self-made, original, devout and utterly human in her energy for survival and her insistence on making herself heard. In her, the affective aspect of mysticism was developed to excess, yet it was always held in check by her good common sense and her ability to deal with people. Where patriarchal society had confined women to the choice between cloistered virginity or domestic drudgery, Margery Kempe developed a new way, to be followed by housewives, mothers, secular self-made charismatics and reformers. She stood at the end of a long line of saintly women, slightly shop-worn and at times a bit comical, but sturdy and solid and pointing toward other choices for women in the future.

FIVE

The Way of the Mystics-2

WE HAVE SEEN HOW women through mystical experience found the assertiveness and authority necessary to speak, teach and influence people. Others found different ways to assert their claim to religious equality. The effort on the part of individual women, each acting in her own way, persisted over the centuries. It took a variety of forms: 1) the development of female God-language and symbolism; 2) the re-conceptualization of the Divine as both male and female; 3) women's direct intervention in redemption and salvation; and 4) a deliberate and often scholarly feminist Bible criticism, which I will deal with in a separate chapter.

The development of female God-language and symbolism has a complex and ambiguous history, because both men and women engaged in the enterprise, although possibly for quite opposite reasons. The medievalist Caroline Bynum has studied the various female symbols attributed to Christ by male and female mystics during the late Middle Ages—Christ the Redeemer as a mother nourishing and saving her young; the feeding of the soul through the Eucharist likened to a mother nursing her baby; the image of nursing the soul through feeding or drinking of the blood of Christ's wounds; and the frequently used image of the Church or the priest as a mother nourishing souls with the milk of religion. These images were used by male and female religious, but, as Bynum observes, such "female" images were more frequently used by men than women. Women seemed to prefer the images of being the child of Jesus or being his bride.[1] She observes that the metaphor of the leader as "mother" was usually applied to male authority figures—the apostles, abbots, bishops. She sees this expressing a desire of 12th-century monks to project a more loving, less authoritarian image of leadership and she cautions us not to confuse this with their high valuation of contemporary women. In fact both the cult of Mary and the use of female symbolism in God-language coincided with misogyny and the curtailment of women's power and influence in Church and secular life.[2]

The image of the women mystic as the bride or lover of Christ occurs repeatedly. I will give just one example of it. Hadewijch, in one of her visions expresses herself in characteristic erotic imagery:

> On a pentecost I had a vision at dawn. The mass was being celebrated in the church and I was there. My heart and my veins and all my limbs shook and trembled with longing . . . and I felt in so fierce and terrible a mood that I thought I could not satisfy my beloved and my beloved did not fill me entirely: it seemed I had to die raging against myself and dying had to continue to rage against myself. . . . I longed to enjoy my beloved, to recognize and feel him in order to experience my humanity in fullest measure by feeling his humanity . . .
>
> Then He came from the altar in the shape of the child; and the child was in the shape He had in the first three years of His life. He turned toward me, took his body from the Ziborium into his right hand and into his left he took the Cup. . . .
>
> Then he came in the shape and dress of the man, as he was on the day when he first gave us of his body; entirely human and male, wonderful and beautiful with a glorified face he approached me in an attitude of humility, as someone who entirely belongs to another. He gave himself to me in the form of the sacrament, in the form in which one usually partakes of it; and afterwards he himself offered me the Cup to drink with its taste and form as usual. But then he came to me himself, took me into his arms and pressed me to him; and all my limbs felt his in the fullness of my heart's desire and my humanity. . . . But after a short time I lost the beautiful man in his external form. I saw him disappear and melt into Oneness so I could no longer separate him as outside of myself and I could no longer perceive him. It seemed to me that we had become One without distinction. . . . And so I rested in my beloved in dread and awe, so that I fully melted into him and there remained nothing of myself to myself; I was transformed and accepted into the spirit; and this vision lasted for hours.[3]

Not many mystics take the erotic imagery so literally, but most of the women mystics use gender-specific bodily metaphors to express their unfathomable and mysterious transcendent experiences. They describe themselves as nourishing, sometimes as breast-feeding the Christ child; they cradle and fondle the child; they experience the sensation of feeding on the blood of Christ as they receive the Eucharist. Caroline Bynum has shown that Eucharistic devotion is a largely female contribution to Church ritual.[4]

The re-conceptualization of the Divine as both male and female appears already in the work of Hildegard of Bingen (discussed in Chapter Three). The archetypal maternal figures in her visions— Caritas, Mary and Ecclesia—mediate between God and humanity in her "richly nuanced theology of the feminine."[5] Yet, ultimately her addition of a female element to the divinity, while powerful and persuasive, is incremental in a theology in which the Trinity remains male-described and male-personified.

The most far-reaching re-conceptualization of the Divine occurs in the work of Julian of Norwich, an English 14th-century mystic and recluse. In sixteen visions which she recounts in her book *Revelations*, Julian presents us with an androgynous God, a God essentially expressed in male and female symbols.

> And thus in our Creation God almighty is our kindly Father, and God Who is all wisdom is our kindly Mother, with the love and the goodness of the Holy Ghost—all of Whom are one God and one Lord. . . . Thus in our Father God we have our being, and in our Mother of mercy we have our reforming and our restoration, in Whom our parts are united and all made into perfect men, and by the yielding and giving grace of the Holy Ghost we are fulfilled . . . for our nature is whole in each person of the Trinity which is one God.[6]

Julian elsewhere elaborates on the metaphors of motherhood. As the mother gives suck to her child, so Jesus, our Mother, feeds us with Himself. As the mother lays the child to her breast, so Jesus, our Mother, leads us to his breast. She continues:

> To the property of motherhood belong nature, love, wisdom, and understanding, and it is God. Although our bodily birth may be insignificant, meek and humble compared to our spiritual birth, yet it is He Who enables creatures to give birth. . . . He is our Mother in nature by the operation of grace in the humble part for love of the higher part.[7]

While other theologians before her had used the metaphor of God as both father and mother, Julian's re-visioning makes this concept central to her entire theology. The idea of an androgynous God or a female part of the Trinity appears again in the work of the mystic Jacob Böhme and later in some of the left-wing sects of the Protestant Reformation, which we will discuss below. Interestingly, women do not take up the concept again until the 18th century, when Ann Lee develops a theology based on the full equality of the male and female aspect of the Divine.

The major emphasis in the feminine re-thinking of Christian theology next to Julian of Norwich is on re-visioning the female role in salvation. A radical expression of this tendency appears in the 13th century among a small group of heretics named Guglielmites. We know of them only through the records of the inquisitorial process against the followers of one Guglielma of Milan (1210–81), who was worshipped as the incarnation of the Holy Spirit. She was a somewhat mysterious figure, most likely a daughter of the King of Bohemia who, together with her young son, fled from her family to live the life of a Cistercian Tertiary in Milan. She was connected with the abbey of St. Maria di Chiaravalle, but did not enter the order. She preached, advised people and reported on her visions, soon acquiring a steady following of men and women who considered her a saint. Her adherents spread the word that she was the bodily equal of Christ, that she would die in order to save the unconverted, and that Redemption was only possible through the Incarnation of the Divine in both male and female. She selected a woman to represent her as a true Pope, as St. Peter represented Christ. Her candidate for the female papacy was Manfreda da Pirovana, a cousin of Milan's ruler Matteo Visconti. After Guglielma's death in 1281, her followers expected that she would bodily ascend to heaven. According to her wish, she was buried in Chiaravalle, which became the center for her veneration as a saint, with pilgrims, miracles, relics and several holidays devoted to her.

A month after her burial her corpse was exhumed and subjected to a ceremonious washing. The corpse was then dressed in the habit of the Tertiaries and reburied. The water in which her corpse had been washed was kept by Manfreda and used as a miracle-working fluid. Guglielmites held preaching and prayer meetings and celebratory memorial meals. Manfreda asserted Guglielma's divinity and preached her doctrine and went so far as to twice celebrate the Mass and give her followers the Eucharist, functions reserved to the male priesthood. Nineteen years after Guglielma's death the Inquisition examined Manfreda and several of her sect twice before concluding that not only Manfreda and her followers but, above all, the dead

Gulgielma were guilty of heresy. Manfreda and two of her male followers were burned in Milan in 1300, together with the exhumed body of Guglielma, a measure which seems to indicate that Church authorities feared her appeal and wanted to forestall any cult attached to her remains.[8]

A similar claim to female agency in the bringing of salvation appears shortly after this trial. One Prous Boneta was arrested in Montpellier and brought before the Inquisition in Carcassonne. There, on August 6, 1325, she made a public confession and was burned at the stake. Boneta, an unlettered simple woman, was apparently the center of a small group of radical sectarians, a fact which was confirmed by the confessions of her sister and another woman accused with her. Boneta claimed that the then current Pope, John XXII, was a veritable Antichrist and that under his reign no more souls could be saved. She regarded her own condemnation as the redemption of the Holy Ghost, necessary to achieve the salvation of humankind. For she, Prous Boneta, had been selected as the representative of the Trinity and as the giver of the Holy Ghost to sinful humanity. She does not seem to have had a large following, but her confession is another instance of a woman trying to formulate a fully elaborated theological doctrine that puts women into the center of the divine design for salvation.[9]

We do not know how many of the women accused of witchcraft and burned at the stake in the next two centuries held similar views. But we do need to notice that there was no transmission of such ideas from one generation to another or from one locality to another. Each visionary, "crazy" woman, wrestling with the deep questions of the theological definition of humanness that eliminated her from God's design, played out her local limited role and vanished. There are only traces left of women asserting their full equality as human beings and searching to find the proper form of expression for such notions, longings and intuitions.

I find particularly interesting the visions of women mystics in which they are involved in the birth of Christ. Such visions are scattered through the centuries, deriving out of rather varied circumstances. In such visions the visionary is not identified with Mary, mother of Christ. Quite the contrary, the visionary is placed in an exceptional, active and generative role without which the miracle of Christ's birth could not happen. As we will see, in some cases this particular female agency is interpreted as being essential to the second coming of Christ.

One of the simplest and most compelling of these visions is the one reported by Christina Ebner (1277–1356), a German nun at the Dominican convent in Engelthal, who practiced a regime of severe self-deprivation and self-flagellation and who, after a serious illness, began to have visions at the age of sixteen. She recorded these with the help and encouragement of her spiritual guide, Konrad von Füssen. By the age of twenty she was famous outside of her convent, and in 1350 the Emperor Charles IV sought her blessing. Heinrich von Nördlingen, who also befriended other women mystics, visited her for three weeks and corresponded with her. She authored a book of her visions, which appeared in several versions, and also wrote *Engelthaler Schwesternbuch*, a collective biography of her convent.

> At a time when she was well and 24 years old she dreamed that she was pregnant with our Lord. She was so filled with grace that every part of her body felt this grace. And she experienced such tenderness toward the child that she had to guard herself for his sake. . . . And after a while she dreamed that she gave birth to him without any pain and she experienced such extraordinary joy that after she had carried it within her for a while she felt she could no longer deny it and so she took the child in her arms and brought it before all those assembled in the refectory and said, "Rejoice with me. . . . I conceived Jesu and now have given birth to him" and she showed them the child and when she was full of joy as she walked around with him, she awoke.[10]

Christina Ebner put no theological interpretation on this delightful and joyous experience. Rather, she described it as part of her road toward *imitatio Christi*, her empathetic re-living of the life of the Saviour.

The next visionary who uses this metaphor comes out of one of the radical sects of the Protestant Reformation. Before discussing her, we need to pause to consider the important changes in form and meaning of the religious discourse in Protestantism and especially its impact on women.

THE QUESTION of the effect of the Protestant Reformation on women has been the subject of considerable controversy, especially among feminist scholars. The debate concerns contradictory interpretations in Luther and Calvin of the nature of the female and of her societal role. Those who hold that women's lot was improved by the Reformation usually point to the spread of education and to the enhanced role of women as mothers and guides of the young. Those who see the Reformation as disadvantaging women point to the increasing patriarchal orthodoxy within the Reformation churches, to the continuing restrictions on women's civil rights and public roles and to the weakening of nunneries, which can be seen as having provided privileged space for women. The controversy cannot be readily resolved, since, like so many reforms in patriarchally structured societies, the results of the reform tend to be ambiguous in effect. I believe that viewed from the vantage point of intellectual and religious history, the Reformation was a decisive turning point for women and very positively affected their ability to come to feminist consciousness. The breakthrough in theological and religious thought was Luther's insight that every soul has equal access to God, and his revolutionizing statement that there is no need for mediation between God and human beings. All at once, as though the ancient veil had been ripped off, women were told that they could directly speak to God and that God could and would speak to them. It is true that orthodox Catholic women had managed to demonstrate that very fact through mystical practice, but clearly only the few, the rarest human beings, could become mystics. Mystical insight was a grace, a gift, won by hard sacrifice and ascetic practice. Now, Luther proclaimed, this gift was open to all, to everyone, female and male.

Practically speaking, due to the increasing orthodoxy of the Protestant church establishment, these revolutionizing ideas were worked out more fully in the left-wing groups of the Reformation. Women actively participated in a number of these left-wing sects, the Anabaptists, Quakers, and the strongly mystical movement of Pietism. We are fortunate to have available a number of primary sources, testimonials, autobiographies and visionary accounts of German Pietists in which these women speak for themselves. While some of these women visionaries can be compared to the medieval Catholic mystics, they were of distinctly lower-class origins. They were urban women, wives and daughters of artisans, and saw themselves as teachers, preachers and popular speakers. German and Dutch Pietists shared with other Protestants the belief that women should not speak in public on religious matters, but they developed in the *huiskerk*, a prayer meeting in a home, a forum where women could teach and preach.[11]

A German Pietist, Anna Vetter, "a simple-minded, lowly woman," as a contemporary characterized her, left a particularly vivid account of her life and visions, which is of interest here because she picks up the theme we have earlier encountered of women's enhanced role in bringing about the second coming. Anna Vetter was born in Franconia, the daughter of a smith.[12] When she was four years old, soldiers invading the small town of her birth robbed the family and beat her father so severely that he died as a result. Her mother and the four children lived in poverty and exile, with Anna contributing to their survival by becoming a seamstress. She married a mason, who she says had no interest in spiritual matters. Within ten years she had given birth to seven children, of whom four survived. At age thirty she almost died of a severe illness, during which her husband raped her. The pregnancy resulting from this rape prolonged her illness; the child died soon after its birth. Anna Vetter interpreted these events theologically. "It was because I was supposed to become an entirely different person, physically and spiritually renewed."[13]

It was after these events that she began to have visions, which she recorded. The fact of this record was in itself miraculous: Anna Vetter, who had been illiterate until the moment of her visions, was commanded by God to write these down neatly so that they could be shared with her people. So she learned to write in one night and wrote her autobiography. Her local priest testified to these facts and argued from them that such an event was a sign of true inspiration. When others protested to Vetter that she should follow the advice of St. Paul, she answered that Paul had to be responsible for his community, and she had to be responsible for hers. His rules did not concern her, but she believed that her preaching was in the same spirit as that of St. Paul. She saw herself as a prophet, like Hosea and Jeremiah, and felt it her duty to save the sinful German cities, specifically Nürnberg and Weissenbach, where she lived. Following God's command she devoted herself to speaking and preaching in the marketplace, neglecting her household duties. She also lived as though she were a widow, although her husband was still alive.[14] She says in her life story that she was inspired by God to be his spokesperson until St. Bartholomew's Day in 1663; after that she "calmed down and had no more visions."

Anna Vetter wrote in the plain vernacular of the uneducated person and in her account mixed dream, vision and daily events without transition or explanation. This makes her account particularly compelling, for it obviously does not bear the marks of literary editing and "improvement." The city to which she refers in the following vision is Nürnberg.

At last I saw the city as a pregnant woman in labor and all her midwives sat around her and they could not make the child come to birth. And mother and child were doomed to die and to eternal damnation. Then I thought I must not let this woman and her child perish and I went to the woman and with her I gave birth to a little boy whom I brought to God; I had such terrible pain just like the woman giving birth with her screaming; God be praised who helped me to overcome, but it cost me blood . . . I saw that all the souls of the people in the city were represented in the form of this boy child, who had to be born out of the heart above and not like a physical child that breaks out of the mother below. This one had to come out of the heart and that bitter labor pressed my blood out of my right side. . . . My own daughter . . . and this boy were as one; I lay in chains and fetters for them for 27 weeks until I brought them both to God and since I prayed more for the little boy in whose shape all the people were represented my own child was not written in the book of life until I had overcome and reconciled; then there came two angels from heaven and they wrote on the cradle of my child . . . thus my daughter and the little boy were written into the book of life again. . . . Then I took a knife and cut the iron chains and fled toward Wedelsheim five miles from Anspach; if I had not born the child out of that woman no one would have been saved.[15]

This remarkable vision unself-consciously combines the pedestrian details—she fled and gives us the names of the villages and the exact distance between them—with elaborate religious metaphors, such as her responsibility for the sinful city as a sister, her attendance by angels, her miraculous cutting of iron chains, her redemption of others through pain and sacrifice. Like Abraham, she gives up her own child in obedience and thereby becomes an instrument of sanctification. Like Christ's blood, her blood flows from her right side to testify to her labors of redemption. The birth of the boy child echoes the birth of the Saviour and her phrase "the little boy in whose shape all the people were represented" alludes to the Second Coming. According to Vetter's imagination Redemption is impossible until the second boy child is born and offered up to God. But what is new and different in Anna Vetter's vision is her active role in the process of Redemption. She starts out claiming to be a prophet and warning the sinful city, but in fact she does more than that— she gives birth to the miraculous boy child through whom the city and all its inhabitants are actually saved. "If I had not born the child out of the woman, no one would have been saved." The phrase is telling if ungrammatical—she does not claim to have assisted the woman, which would have placed her in the familiar role mystic women envisioned, that of a sympathetic helper to the Virgin Mary.

But through her labor—after the failure of the physical mother and all the assembled midwives—Anna Vetter herself claims to have given birth to the child, who is clearly not the Christ child, but the Saviour of the Second Coming who redeems the sinful world. This is a leap forward in the female imagination, making claims for its essential agency in the divine plan. There is no way Anna Vetter could have known of the ideas of the burned heretics Guglielma of Milan and Prous Boneta, four hundred years earlier. But hers was a similar insight: Redemption is impossible without that ultimate female function, the holy woman giving birth.

This vision, had it been that of a cloistered religious and the result of hard ascetic practice, would be significant and unusual. But Anna Vetter was an artisan's daughter and an artisan's wife, the mother of seven children. The daughter of her vision was the child born after the marital rape, the event that produced the prophetic visions in the first place. One might have thought that a woman subjected to the pain and indignity her husband had inflicted upon her would blame him for causing the child's death or would accept that death as the will of God. But Anna Vetter transformed the event into a powerful prophetic vision in which she transcended her earthly role and fate and boldly asserted the most powerful claim any woman could make: she and by implication all women with her, were essential agents in God's plan for the redemption of humankind.

Anna Vetter's vision was informed by the ideas of male and female Pietists whose theology challenged orthodox Christian beliefs about the role of women in state and church. From its inception, Pietism treated the prophesies and visions of women with great respect. Adelheid Sybilla Schwarz and Rosamund von Asseburg were admired by male co-religionists for their wisdom, their insight, their piety and were considered to be saints. Pietists saw women's emotionalism as a strength that led to deeper religious insights. At the time Anna Vetter preached and prophesied in and around Nürnberg, a Pietiest named Antoinette Bourignon (1606–80) lectured and wrote tracts in Holland. She was hounded by the Jesuits, who forced her to burn one of her tracts; she fled from Brabant to Holland and from there to Hamburg and back again to Holland trying to escape persecution. She was a prolific and apparently popular writer. The venom and hatred she aroused in her enemies are a measure of her impact. One polemicist, writing a pamphlet against her, reversed the birth metaphor to ridicule and caricature this woman who was literally hounded to death by her persecutors (she died in flight from Hamburg to Holland). He wrote:

> Now in the rear there comes an old woman riding on some animal and bawling that her time of birthing has come/ she chooses the Northcoast/ to hold her childbed/ and to spew forth her old dragon seed. . . . I should have let her hide out there except that certain people surfaced who inclined to taste the milk of the old sow therefore I wanted to take pen in hand. . . . many . . . perceive the horror of the devil in this woman and begin to hate her. . . . The woman is foolish, crazy and godless.[16]

Again, as so often, her writings are lost to history, but we can get a sense of her impact on contemporaries by the extremity of the attacks upon her. We also know from the writings of male Pietists, that Bourignon was considered a heroine and model of piety. Gottfried Arnold, who recorded many of the *vitae* of Pietists and who was himself one of the leaders of the sect, recommended Bourignon's writings to all Pietists.[17]

Another of this group of German Pietists, Beate Sturm, was reputed to have committed the entire Bible to memory. She was able to recite all the portions of the Bible and to comment on the sermons she had heard at Saturday meetings of her group. In this manner, she developed a purely feminine form of religious teaching. One is reminded of a similar practice by Anne Hutchinson in colonial Massachusetts, which led to her excommunication and expulsion from the colony. Beate Sturm felt a call to public preaching; her sermons addressed religious and political topics, sometimes they lasted as long as four hours and were heard by hundreds of people.[18]

Another female Pietist leader, Johanna Eleonora Petersen (1644–1724), left a long autobiography, with accounts of her visions, which was written between 1688 and 1719. Of particular interest is her last vision in which she was a prisoner in a house which contained twenty-four pictures. Following these pictures as though they were guides, she freed herself, but then she was confronted by a closed door behind which lies the secret, "a father, a mother and a son." She could not remember what to do to open the door, but then she recalled that in an earlier picture she had seen a nightingale and interpreted this to say that she must be a nightingale and "when I commenced to sing and my voice grew stronger and stronger, the door opened, and I felt wonderfully well and awoke from my sleep." She interpreted this last image as that of the holy Trinity—Father, Son and "the fruitful mother and breeding dove [the Holy Ghost]."[19]

Women such as these influenced the thinking and theories of Count Nikolaus von Zinzendorf, who in 1730 founded together with his wife Erdmuth the most important Pietist community of the Moravian brethren at Herrnhut.[20] Largely influenced by his personal religious development, which he credited to the influence of his grandmother, Zinzendorf set out deliberately to upgrade the role of women in the community and showed by biblical argument that Jesus regarded women as evangelists. Zinzendorf wanted women to be preachers because he believed that they carried greater emotional conviction than men. His theological argument was that Adam was androgynous before the Fall and that men must become more female in their nature before Redemption could take place. These revolutionary ideas about gender led to conflict with more traditionally minded men in the Pietist communities. After Zinzendorf's death the more patriarchal men prevailed, and in 1764 the Synod excluded women from leadership positions in the community.[21] Thus, for several decades Pietism, both in Europe and in the Philadelphian utopian communities in the United States, provided some space and scope for women's religious leadership and a theology to support such undertakings. Then, as we have seen it happen in so many other revolutionary movements, orthodoxy triumphed and women returned to their more traditional subordinate roles.

The medieval mystics had created and perpetuated a role for women religious which, under male sponsorship and tutelage and within the protection of the cloistered life, allowed them to influence Church and secular policy and assume an honored and respected public role. Within the heretical sects of the 12th to the 15th centuries women assumed public roles as teachers, preachers, proselytizers and martyrs, but we have no record of their actual words. The contributions of Anna Vetter, Beate Sturm and Johanna Petersen to women's theological re-thinking appealed to their contemporaries, but they could not be transmitted to others and reproduced by them because the female network out of which they had arisen no longer existed. But the transmission of such ideas and practices continued among another Protestant sect, the Quakers, and it is among them that we next find women making significant intellectual advances.

From the first establishment of Quakerism, women, in their Women's Meetings and through a Board of Women Elders, gave religious and moral guidance to female Friends. Quaker women were generally better educated than their female contemporaries and had a tradition of public speaking and religious leadership. They took active roles in establishing Quaker churches (Meetings); they were ministers, preachers, missionaries on several continents. Many of them suffered imprisonment and even death for their religious convictions, such as Mary Dyer in Boston in 1660.[22] After the Restoration of the monarchy in England, many radical women petitioned and pamphleteered for the abolition of tithes. Some went even further and prophesied the destruction of sinful cities.[23]

Some English Quaker women had offered a radical critique of St. Paul's teaching and of misogyny since the early 1650s. Possibly in response to such views, George Fox, the founder of Quakerism, in his pamphlet *The Woman Learning in Silence* (London, 1656) articulated the principle basic to Quaker beliefs: God made all human beings equal by implanting the Indwelling Spirit in everyone. He interpreted that to mean that therefore Christ's spirit might speak in the female as well as in the male. Drawing on these antecedents, Margaret Fell expanded his doctrine to include the right of women to preach.

Margaret Fell (1614–1702), a close coworker and after 1669 the wife of George Fox, had an active public career as missionary, preacher, teacher and writer. Her books were translated into Hebrew, Latin, and Dutch. She annually made long journeys through England, visiting Quaker Meetings and defending Friends who had been imprisoned and had suffered physical attacks. She and George Fox were tried in 1664 for refusing to take the Oath of Allegiance and for holding Quaker meetings. Her sentence deprived her of all her property and ordered her imprisoned for life. After four years she was released from jail on orders of the King, but she was twice more imprisoned in later life. While she served her first prison sentence, she wrote and published *Women's Speaking Justified*, a fully developed scriptural argument justifying women's active role in biblical history and their right to participate in public religious life.[24] She wrote a coherent theological brief; her tone is self-confident and assertive without any of the apologies present in women's writings for centuries.

> Those that speak against the Power of the Lord, and the Spirit of the Lord speaking in a woman, simply, by reason of her Sex, or because she is a Woman, not regarding the Seed, and Spirit, and Power that speaks

in her; such speak against Christ, and his Church, and are the Seed of the Serpent. . . .

The Lord God in the Creation, when he made man in his own image, he made them *male* and *female*; and . . . Christ Jesus was made of a Woman, and the power of the Highest overshadowed her and the Holy Ghost came upon her . . . .[25]

She cited chapter and verse in the Old and the New Testament, naming every woman who had prophesied, spoken or argued, and providing powerful ammunition for any woman who would reason against orthodox misogyny from the scriptural text.

Margaret Fell's pamphlet, her life and her career illustrate the qualitative leap forward women were enabled to make intellectually as a result of the Protestant Reformation. The fact that Protestant women after her still had to argue, reason and persuade to win equality within church and state speaks to the negative side of the Reformation, its institutionalization of patriarchal orthodoxy and its resistance to fundamental change.

Thus, Margaret Fell's bold re-thinking found no echo until the 18th century, when Ann Lee founded the sect of the Shakers and asserted the role of women as the essential agent in the Second Coming.

Ann Lee (1736–84) was born in England into the family of a poor blacksmith. In her twenties she joined a sect which had split off from the Quakers and became known as Shakers, due to their singing, dancing and shouting worship. She married a few years later and had four children in quick succession, all of whom died in infancy. Like so many other women mystics, the near fatal illness following upon her last childbirth brought her to a deep crisis of feeling. She became persuaded that the death of her children had been a punishment for her sin of concupiscence. Afraid to sleep with her husband, lest she "awake in hell," she spent the nights walking around, praying and groaning. She then refused all food in order to mortify her body so that her soul might "hunger for nothing but God." In this state she had a profound psychic experience. She believed she was reborn into the spiritual kingdom. Lee then entered upon a period of preaching and teaching, and a few years later became the leader of the small sect of Manchester Shakers. Although she converted her father and one of her younger brothers, another brother once tried to break her resolve by savagely beating her about the face and head with a stick. But Ann Lee cried for help to God. "While he

[her brother] continued striking, I felt my breath, like a healing bal-
sam streaming from my mouth and nose . . . so that I felt no harm
from his stroke."[26] This was only the first of many occasions on
which she suffered beatings, imprisonment and harassment with the
stoicism of a martyr. In 1772, and again a year later, she spent time
in jail for breach of the Sabbath, because of her group's dancing
worship. While in prison she had her grand vision of the scene of
the Fall which led her to understand that "lustful gratification of the
flesh [was] the source and foundation of human corruption." She
now knew that she had a special commission to fulfill Christ's work.
"It is not I that speak, it is Christ who dwells in me."[27] Thereafter
she lived a celibate life and enjoined celibacy on her followers. They
regarded her as embodying Christ of the Redemption, and called her
Mother Ann Lee of the New Creation.

To escape persecution Ann Lee and eight followers traveled to
New England and soon settled near Albany, New York, where she
founded a utopian colony and continued her preaching and proselytizing missionary work. Here, too, she suffered much persecution at
the hands of angry mobs who believed her to be a heretic and even
a British spy. Still, she and her group persisted.[28]

Ann Lee's doctrine revitalized the concept of an androgynous
God—Sophia, Holy Wisdom of the Bible, was the female element in
God; in Christ the masculine side had been made manifest and in
Mother Ann Lee the feminine had been reincarnated. Ann Lee's rev-
elations indicated that the millennium was at hand and that the
Shakers, with their celibate, pious life would hasten its coming. Mother
Lee continued her mission until her death, and the work of the sect
was continued and expanded by her successors.

In line with Mother Lee's theology, Shakers believed in the equality
of the sexes. In their communities leadership was shared between
men and women and they practiced their belief that women, as well
as men, could be teachers and preachers.[29]

American-born Jemima Wilkinson (1752–1819) continued the
tradition of women prophetesses. Wilkinson was raised as a Quaker,
but was dismissed from the Society because she attended the meeting of a New Light Baptist group. When she was twenty-three years
old she almost died of a fever and during her illness had a vision
that she had actually died and had returned from heaven. From the
time of her recovery on she changed her name to that of Publick
Universal Friend and for more than forty years preached and prophesied her millenarian doctrine. She felt called upon to build a uto-

pian community, New Jerusalem, near Seneca Lake, where more than two hundred settlers followed her. Despite legal harassment, Wilkinson's charismatic style attracted many believers and her community held together until her death.[30]

Joanna Southcott (1750–1814), an English contemporary of Ann Lee and Jemima Wilkinson, was a servant girl and an upholsterer's apprentice, who at age forty-two began to have visions. She recorded these later in no less than 65 books and pamphlets, which were published between 1801 and the time of her death and received wide circulation. Southcott claimed to be the woman of Revelation, "a woman clothed with the sun . . . and she being with child cried, travailing in birth, and pained to be delivered." She developed a feminist theology, arguing that since woman first plucked from the sinful fruit, so she must bring knowledge of the good fruit. She believed in the imminence of the Second Coming and that she had been chosen to bring it about. Quite in the spirit of earlier mystics, she did not seek out this distinction and at first resisted it:

> This is a New thing Amongst mankind, for a woman to be the Greatest Prophet that ever came into the World, to bring man out of darkness, into My marvellous light. . . . And what a profound, conceited fool must I be, to say of myself, I have more knowledge than the learned, and can tell them better than they know from my own wisdom. Shall I say I know it from philosophy, and do not understand one planet? Shall I say I know it from divinity, and never studied the Bible in my life, no further than I thought necessary for my own salvation . . . I always deemed myself [the simplest of my father's house]; but the Lord hath chosen the weak foolish things of this world, to confound the great and mighty.[31]

Southcott got her revelations from The Spirit, a voice that regularly communicated with her. When she wrote these down, no one could read them because her handwriting was so poor. Later she acquired an amanuensis from among her followers. Beginning in 1801 she lived in London, gathering adherents and writing profusely. Part of each year she spent traveling, lodging in the homes of her followers, speaking all over England. In 1804 the wealthy Jane Townley became her devoted disciple and invited her to join her household, after which Southcott lived with her and was fully supported by her. Southcott at first sought the approval of the Methodist Church and managed to convince a few prominent churchmen of her cause, but she never was accepted by the Church. Instead, she bound her followers to her by giving them "a seal," a document with the believer's name on it and Southcott's signature at the bottom. This seal was supposed to confer protection upon the believer, even should Napoleonic troops invade England. The success of her mission is reflected in the staggering growth of her supporters: beginning with 58 in 1803 her ranks swelled to 20,500 by 1815, a year after her death. Her enemies claimed that she had upwards of 30,000 loyal followers.[32] Her feminist God-language and argument must have appealed to women, since 63 percent of her followers were women. Perhaps her appeal was based on writings such as this, when Southcott spoke in the voice of Christ:

> They [women] followed me to my Cross, and stood weeping to see me crucified; they were the first at My Sepulchre to see My resurrection; now I will not refuse women that assist thee . . . . It was by a woman I came into the world in the form of a man; and now by a woman I will reveal Myself unto men. . . . and now from the woman shall my second coming be revealed that no man may boast nor be worshipped in My stead. . . . But no Saviour can arise in a woman for her to be Christ. For here I am . . . come to heal the fall of women, which *must* first be healed before man's redemption can come . . . .[33]

Had Joanna Southcott had knowledge of Anna Vetter's visions, one might conclude that she was elaborating on them and carrying them forward. But no such knowledge of the past thought of women was ever possible for women in the 18th century, and so we see here, once again, an example of a woman reinventing a revision of patriarchal doctrine that had already been made earlier by another woman. Southcott was quite explicit about woman's role in the Redemption—without the prior elevation of woman there would be no Redemption. Yet she ended her life with an elaboration of her metaphoric conceit which became pathological and, surely, was pathetic.

In 1813 the Spirit announced to her: "This year, in the sixty-fifth year of thy age, thou shalt have a SON by the power of the most HIGH." The child's name was to be Shiloh, and he was to be Christ's pro-consul on earth, to prepare the way for the Second Coming.[34] Southcott, during a period when her following was beginning to fall off, testified that she felt "a powerful visitation working upon my body." Believing she was pregnant by a miracle similar to that visited upon the aging Sarah in the Old Testament, she invited a committee of physicians to examine her and observe her. Twenty-one physicians accepted that invitation and seventeen of them confirmed her pregnancy, although owing to modesty she refused to let them give her a pelvic examination. Believers flocked to her home in London, sent her expensive gifts, circulated fake reports and false "seals" and turned her sickbed into a public circus. Southcott arranged that should she die in childbirth, no delivery of the child should be made until four days after she was dead. She was, in fact, dying during the long weeks past her ninth month of "pregnancy." After her death, an autopsy revealed no pregnancy but showed an enlarged liver, and the expert physicians testified that no physical cause for her death could be found.

Joanna Southcott took her passionate revision of patriarchal theology further than most and was defeated, but the enterprise, no matter how often thwarted, would not die.

WE WILL NOW CONSIDER two groups coming out of different racial and ethnic cultures—African-American and Jewish women—and compare their efforts at theological re-vision with those of the women earlier discussed. African-American women in the 19th-century United States, while they shared the theological tradition and sources of the dominant white Protestant religions, came out of African-American churches which had their own language, symbolism, structures and traditions. We cannot here attempt to do justice to the complex history of differentiation, self-definition and spiritual re-vision of the African-American churches but, for purposes of comparison, will consider a small sectarian group whose practices and visionary inspiration can well be compared to the left-wing Protestant sects of the Reformation which we have discussed above.

In the 1830s to the 1870s a remarkable group of black women spiritualists and prophets appeared on the Eastern seaboard, where they had active public careers. The best-known of these during her lifetime and after, was Isabella Baumfree, who after a revelation experience renamed herself Sojourner Truth (c.1797–1883). Born a slave in New York State, she saw her siblings sold off and was herself sold as a child. Her master raped her and later forced her into marriage with an older slave by whom she had five children. Freed by New York State law in 1827, she rescued one of her children from slavery. While still a slave she had frequent, often daily conversations with God and from them drew strength to endure her lot. At various points in her life she was aware of Jesus' interference in her life and his protection. Her rich inner religious life culminated in a vision, during the time she was living in New York City and supporting herself by doing domestic work. That vision commanded her to leave the city and "declare the truth to the people." From that time forward she traveled as an itinerant preacher in the North, advocating abolition, women's rights, the protection of the poor and her own brand of pragmatic Christianity.[35]

Like the mystics and prophets before her, Sojourner Truth derived her authority from her direct communication with God. She was a charismatic speaker who had a strong effect on audiences, and she often tamed hostile crowds by her fearless attitude and pithy comments. The speech which most succinctly embodied her race-based feminism was given at the Akron, Ohio, Woman's Rights convention in 1851. Rising from the back of the audience and insisting on being heard, she said:

> That little man in black there, he says women can't have as much rights as men 'cause Christ wasn't a woman. Where did your Christ come from? Where did your Christ come from? . . . From God and a woman! Man had nothing to do with Him. . . . If the first woman God ever made was strong enough to turn the world upside down all alone, these women together ought to be able to turn it back, and get it right side up again![36]

Sojourner Truth stands virtually alone among black women in the 19th century in staunchly combining the defense of her race with a defense of her sex.[37] Even in very old age she insisted on stressing the duality of black women's oppression, as members of the race and as women. She said, as late as 1867:

> I want women to have their rights. In the courts women have no right, no voice; nobody speaks for them. I wish woman to have her own voice there among the pettifogers. . . . We do as much [as men], we eat as much, we want as much. I suppose I am about the only colored woman that goes about to speak for the rights of the colored women.[38]

She was a unique figure in her day, both in the *persona* she created for herself and in her self-supporting itinerant ministry and reform activities, which she pursued into old age. She was quite different from the other African-American women mystics of her time in operating in the general reform community and not out of a specific church, even though she had contact with a number of evangelical churches at the beginning of her career.[39]

Nancy Prince, Jarena Lee, Amanda Berry Smith, Julia Foote and Rebecca Jackson all developed their religious lives in the African

Methodist Episcopal Church. In this church the institution of the "praying bands," women's meetings in which women preached and talked about Scripture and out of which some of them moved into public preaching, provided that rare "free space" for women which allowed leadership talent to flourish. The women offered each other support and encouragement and pairs or groups of them braved the censure and difficulties of women's preaching in public.

We have earlier discussed Julia Foote's mystical experiences. The visionary autobiography of Rebecca Jackson is particularly interesting in the context of the mystics and prophets we have discussed in this chapter, because of its striking similarities to those of some of the other women mystics and because it expresses the struggle for women's religious agency in the context of race consciousness.

Rebecca Jackson (1795–1871) was raised in Philadelphia, where her mother took the children after her father's death. Her mother remarried and had more children, for whom young Rebecca cared while her mother worked. For this reason she received no schooling. Her mother died when Rebecca was thirteen and there is nothing known of her life until the beginning of her spiritual autobiography in 1830, when she was twenty-two.

At that time she was married to Samuel Jackson, and they both lived with her older brother Joseph, Rebecca taking care of his four children and working as a seamstress. Although her brother was a minister in the AME Church, Jackson never formally joined the church. She had a spiritual awakening and felt herself sanctified, although at first she doubted the authenticity of her visions. But after a few miraculous occurrences, Jackson more and more trusted her inner voice and convinced her family of its authenticity. She received a "gift of healing" and was freed from "lust of the flesh." She made a binding covenant with God, promising to obey the commands of her inner voice completely. Like the medieval mystics, she then began a systematic routine of fasting the first three days of each week, while doing all her usual work. She combined this with systematic sleep deprivation and rejoiced in the increasing intensity of her visions.[40] As with other married women mystics, Jackson needed to find a way of freeing herself from her marital obligation. She wrote:

> Of all things it [the lust of the flesh] seemed the most filthy in the sight of God—both in the married and in the unmarried, it all seemed alike

in the sight of a holy God to me, although I had never heard anybody say it was wrong.[41]

But she did not as yet speak of this to anyone. Jackson began holding prayer meetings in her home and soon acquired a sizable following among black Methodists. In this period she had three dreams which encouraged her to the ministry. Like the dreams of Anna Vetter, her dreams use homely, typically female symbols. In one dream she made cakes at the hearth, which many people ate and enjoyed. In another dream she washed three quilts and with them was transported to a strange place and a white cottage in which she was to live. In another dream she exchanged an old broom for a new and received a casket with a golden treasure from her grandmother and a mysterious old woman.[42]

Like several of the mystics we have discussed, Jackson miraculously received the gift of reading. She had asked her brother to teach her to read, but he stopped after two lessons. When she asked him to write her letters for her, she found he had corrected what she was telling him to write. She objected:

> Thee has put in more than I told thee. "This he done several times." I then said, "I don't want thee to *word* my letter. I only want thee to *write* it." Then he said, "Sister, thee is the hardest one I ever wrote for!" These words, together with the manner that he had wrote my letter, pierced my soul like a sword. I could not keep from crying.

She prayed for God to teach her to read.

> And when I looked on the word, I began to read. And when I found I was reading, I was frightened—then I could not read one word. I closed my eyes again in prayer and then opened my eyes, began to read. So I done until I read the chapter. I came down. "Samuel, I can read the Bible." "Woman, you're agoing crazy!" "Praise the God of Heaven and of earth, I can read His holy word!" Down I sat and read it through. And it was in James. So Samuel praised the Lord with me.[43]

Jackson spiritually liberated herself through this act of conquering her illiteracy. She then took the next step by convincing her husband that he had no power to touch her, since the divine spirit inhabited her. Still, they lived together, presumably in celibacy. During a severe illness, possibly a series of heart attacks, Rebecca Jackson had the sensation of repeatedly leaving her body and of communing with the angels. These increasingly strong divine messages convinced her to begin a career of traveling and preaching in

1833. When she returned, her husband was enraged with her and threatened her with violence. "If I had not had the gift of foresight given to me at the beginning, I must have fell in death by his hands. . . . I always was able to know what he was agoing to do before he did himself." Seeing that he could not intimidate her, Samuel repented and said, "Now Rebecca, you may sleep at your own house, I will trouble you no more. Go forth and do the will of God . . . I never will trouble you."[44]

Like Dorothea of Montau and Margery Kempe, guided by her visions and dreams, Rebecca Jackson, freed herself from her sexual obligations in order to focus on her religious mission. But in her case this feminist self-authorization took place in the context of her life as a black woman. The long tradition of black women's religious leadership and the existence of the "praying bands" helped to foster her ministerial role. During her many years of itinerant preaching, she never lacked for an audience, although she also met much opposition. Her advocacy of celibacy was considered very threatening by the male ministry. In 1837, when she was accused of heresy, Jackson asked for a trial at her own house before representatives of black Methodist and Presbyterian churches. She also asked that "mothers of the church" be present, but she was refused a trial and broke with the AME Church thereafter. It was during this period she met Rebecca Perot, a black woman who became her constant companion in life and missionary work to the end of her life.[45] Jackson and Perot lived with a group of white Perfectionists in Albany, New York, for a while and in 1843, after two visits to the Shaker community at nearby Watervliet, they and others of that group joined the Shakers.

Jackson saw many parallels to her own theology in Shaker doctrine and quickly assumed a leadership role in the mostly white community by preaching to Shaker meetings and "in the world." After she joined the Shakers, Jackson's visions include female divine figures and, where formerly in her dreams she had been guided by a white male figure, she now pictured a beautiful black-haired woman as her instructor in a dream.[46] She also had a vision of Holy Mother Wisdom and expressed her feminist re-visioning as follows:

Oh, how I love thee, my Mother! I did not know that I had a Mother. She was with me, though I knew it not, but now I know Her and She said I should do a work in this city, which is to make known the Mother of the New Creation of God. . . . And none can come to God in the new birth but through Christ the Father, and through Christ the Mother . . . . And then I could also see how often I had been led, comforted, and counseled in time of trial by a tender Mother and knowed it not.[47]

Despite Jackson's theological agreement with the Shaker community, she was deeply disappointed in their insufficient efforts to recruit more Blacks. Jackson primarily saw herself as a missionary to the African-American community, and after some conflict with the Shaker Eldress who at first refused them permission to leave, she and Perot did missionary work in Philadelphia and set up a mostly black, largely female Shaker society, in which both women were Eldresses. The "sisters" lived together in a well-furnished big house, supported themselves by daywork, seamstressing and doing laundry. The society survived forty years after Jackson's death.[48]

The group of 17th-century German Pietist women mystics and the 19th-century African-American Spiritualists seem to have had little in common but their womanhood and their religious quest. Yet both groups were marginal to society as lower-class, self-supporting women and both were centered in small religious movements that offered them some free space and a network of support. The commonality of their experiences, their language, their visions and their self-defined lives, despite the enormous cultural differences among them, speaks strongly for the existence of a female culture modified by factors of race and ethnicity.

FINALLY, LET US consider how Jewish women expressed their religious quest and participation out of a quite different historical context from that of the women we have earlier discussed. The most important religious duty, the study of Torah, the holy books and Jewish law, was generally reserved for men. While in the earliest centuries there are recorded examples of Jewish women who were taught to read the Torah and even interpret it, they were exceptions. In the period of the Jewish diaspora there are again a few examples of learned women, which we have cited above, but by and large among European Jewry women rarely mastered Hebrew, the language of the religious texts. Up until the 19th century, those among European Jewish women who were literate, wrote in the vernacular, Yiddish. Women were excluded from houses of study and from the rabbinical courts. The basic unit of the community of worship, *the minyan*, was defined as a community of ten men. In the synagogue women were seated in the balcony or even in a separate room, participating in public worship only at a remove. Still, Jewish women lived intensely religious lives that held great spiritual meaning for them.[49]

The religious historian and folklorist Chava Weissler, who has studied the extensive Yiddish devotional literature written for and by women, has uncovered evidence of the hidden voices of women in a variety of expressions. In particular, she found in 17th- and 18th-century collections of *tkhines*—prayers usually recited by women in the home—evidence of efforts at upgrading women's religious significance. In a commandment for women's observance, "taking *hallah*," separating portions of the bread dough, the prayer compares the acting out of this ritual to the service performed by the high priest which caused sins to be forgiven. The woman prays: ". . . so also may my sins be forgiven with this. May this *mizvah* [good deed] of the *hallah* [making of the holiday bread] be accounted as if I had given the tithe."[50] Thus she associates herself with the ancient biblical tradition of tithes and with the high priest. In the *tkhine* for candle lighting in the same collection the woman prays that her " 'mizvah' of the candle lights be accepted like the *mizvah* of the high priests who kindled the lights in the dear Temple."[51]

In their domestic prayers which flowed from the mundane activities of wives and mothers, Jewish women expressed their connectedness with the sacred and ancient traditions, which many of them came to know only by oral transmission. In a number of the prayers to be recited during the domestic ritual of preparing the candles for Yom Kippur, the women appealed not only to the patriarchs, but also to the matriarchs, Sarah, Rebecca and Rachel. They did so with an important difference: the patriarchs were mentioned formulaically, as passive recipients of God's aid, while the matriarchs were described as acting to save their children and therefore were appealed to as advocates. The prayers affirmed and celebrated the women's power as mothers to save the people of Israel.[52]

Another Eastern European *tkhine*, important because the identity of its author is known, "The *Tkhine* of the Matriarchs for the New Moon of Elul," states that it was written by one Serel, a rabbi's wife of Dubno. It is a woman's prayer to be recited during the blowing of the ram's horn on the New Year's Holy Day; it asks the matriarchs to intercede with God for the praying woman. Each of the matriarchs is reminded of her own suffering for her children, so that she may be moved to prevent similar suffering by other mothers.

"We ask all our mothers to plead for us that we may be inscribed for life and for peace and for livelihood."[53]

The most interesting of these *tkhines* was written by a woman celebrated during her lifetime for her Talmudic knowledge. Sarah Rebecca Rachel Leah Horowitz (known as Leah Horowitz) was born around 1720 in Poland and died in 1800. She was the daughter of a rabbi and the wife of Rabbi Shabbetai. From anecdotes told about her it appears that she surpassed her father's students in learning and in the ability to explicate Talmudic texts. The prayer she wrote is in three parts: a Hebrew introduction, a prayer in Aramaic and a Yiddish translation of this prayer. Obviously, Horowitz wanted to be read not only by women but also by Hebrew scholars. In the Introduction she discusses women's duties toward their husbands and takes the traditional view that they must do their husbands' bidding. The prayer itself includes an appeal to the matriarchs for intercession and asserts that women's prayer and tears, which are described as having great redemptive power, should be offered for the sake of the Shekinah, the female spirit of wisdom. The repeated referencees to the Shekinah are drawn from kabbalistic literature and show Horowitz's familiarity with Jewish mysticism. Essentially, her message to women is that they must fully use the powers given to them in their traditional roles, and that their spiritual powers are greater than they realize.[54]

Jewish mysticism, which like Christian mysticism, was influenced by Gnostic thought in the 1st and 2nd centuries, flourished in the Middle Ages in Germany, France and Spain. At the height of Spanish Kabbalah (Kabbalah is the Hebrew word for mysticism, literally "tradition"), the *Zohar* (Book of Splendor), its classic text, was written in the 13th century. All later Jewish mystic systems were based on this book. A renaissance of Jewish mysticism occurred in the 16th century around the figure of Isaac Luria. A century later European Jews, especially in Poland, incorporated Lurianic Kabbalah in the Chassidic movement.

Kabbalah stressed the mysteries contained in the words and letters of the Old Testament. Like other mysticisms, it emphasized intuitive knowledge of the Divine. It posited the existence of a primordial hidden Godhead, *En Soph*, from which ten divine potencies or *Sephirot* emanated, one of which was the Shekinah, the female form of the Divine. Human sin, particularly the sin of Adam and Eve, caused a separation of the male and female aspects of the divine emanations. This could only be repaired by reuniting these divided aspects through mystical prayer and practice. Thus, one of the theoretical foundations of Kabbalah seemed to offer an opening for a more female-oriented theology, which would upgrade women's role and participation.[55]

Eighteenth-century Chassidism was inspired by Israel Baal Shem Tov, a saintly man who had no talmudic training. He appealed to women, to the poor and the unlearned, and encouraged their religious expression, especially in the early stages of the movement; yet the structure of the movement was patriarchal. His followers created exclusively male communities around a *Zaddik* (a holy man) in which they celebrated and worshipped with song and dance after communal meals.

The extent of the participation of women in these movements is a matter of dispute among experts. Gershom Sholem, a religious historian of the movement, says: "The long history of Jewish mysticism shows no trace of feminine influence. There have been no women Kabbalists." He explains this "exclusive masculinity" of Kabbalism by the stress it places "on the demonic nature of woman and the feminine element of the cosmos." The demonic, according to the Kabbalists, is connected to the feminine sphere, thus women's contributions to both the theory and practice of the movement were rejected.[56]

On the other hand, there is some evidence that certain women, usually daughters or wives of Chassidic rabbis, were recognized scholars in their own right and had a following of male students. An earlier example of a woman taking a leading role in a sect was Eva Frank, daughter of Jacob Frank, the founder of a messianic movement in Poland. She became co-leader of the sect with her father in 1771, and after his death led the sect until her death, when it dispersed.[57]

There were a number of Chassidic women celebrated for their learning. One of these was Hannah Havah Twersky, daughter of a rabbi, who considered her to have been "endowed with the Holy Spirit from the womb and from birth." Her aphorisms and fables became famous throughout Poland. She gave religious guidance to women and urged them to pursue their education.[58] One historian cites at least ten Chassidic women of learning, all related to famous rabbis, who taught and commented of the holy texts and may have had a following in their own right.[59]

The most famous of these women of learning is Hannah Rachel Werbemacher, (c.1815–92), known as "The Maid of Ludomir." She was taught in the home of her wealthy father and received a thorough religious education. She was betrothed at an early age to a young man she loved; her mother died before the marriage took place, after which event the young woman became very withdrawn. She experienced visions at the grave of her mother and fell seriously ill. After her recovery, in a pattern reminiscent of that of many Christian mystics, she declared that she had been given a new soul in heaven. She then wore *Tzitzit* and *Tallit* and laid *Tephillin* (all attributes of religious practice reserved to men) and spent her time studying Torah and praying. Her bethrothal was annulled. After her father's death Hannah Rachel built a house of study near her home, where every Sabbath she lectured and discoursed with the scholars who came to eat at her house. She did so through the open door of an adjoining room, so that she might be unseen, as custom required. She acquired a large following and a special group of Chassidim formed around her, treating her as their leader. At age forty, she married a talmudic scholar, but the marriage was short-lived and ended in divorce. After her marriage her influence waned, and she emigrated to Palestine, where she again acquired a following as a spiritual leader.[60] How great the influence and reputation of "The Maid of Ludomir" actually was, is difficult to ascertain from the available sources. But the similarity of her life story to that of some of the female Christian mystics is unmistakable and worth noting.

WOMEN'S SEARCH for the Divine and through it women's search for full humanity, transcending differences of class, race and religion, continued and found expression in the most unlikely, the most humble places.

On January 5, 1839, a thirty-six-year-old spinster, living on what was then the Ohio frontier, wrote her religious musings into her diary. She lived alone on an isolated farm with her aging mother; wolves howled outside of their cabin; the handyman who occasionally came to help out the women, frightened her with his sexual advances. Marian Louise Moore was unacquainted with literature except for the sentimental tales of Lydia Sigourney and the religious orthodoxies of Hannah More. But she fashioned her own feminist statement, groping for words and examples, as had so many women throughout the centuries before her. "Methinks, were I to address myself to mothers . . . I would still proclaim, thou art responsible . . . oh mothers." She then cited the usual group of biblical heroines and reasoned that it was women's role "like an angel here to guide, aid, and accompany man to a nobler paradise . . ." This fairly traditional view of women's role is sharply re-defined in her diary entry three years later, when she wrote:

> Now my Saviour I ask that woman may be found worthy before God to stand upon a platform of equal rights as the first major stroke in these United States of America . . . Lord, increase my faith. I wish her to be exalted, not to do evil, but to do good. . . . I pray to God to this effect. If there is not another woman in America pleading to that effect, I am pleading . . . Oh, my saviour, if I may experience the heaven of my late-mentioned desires, my soul shall praise thee.[61]

Marian Moore did not know that there was another woman in America asking for women's rights in 1842, but she wrestled with God about it, seeing herself as part of an as yet unconstituted collectivity of women who needed "a platform of equal rights."

The concept of the divine female, Great Goddess, procreatrix, goddess of life and death continued to inspire women two thousand years after her passing. Despite all the gender indoctrination and the intense pressure toward submissiveness, women, obsessed or rational, wrote themselves into the story of redemption. They would speak to God, represent the Divine, give birth to the redeemer, assert the feminine element in the divinity and usurp, by ecstatic vision, mad inspiration, simple faith or any means they could muster, the right to define the Divine and with it the right to define their own humanity.

SIX

Authorization Through Motherhood

ALONGSIDE THE WOMEN mystics and those motivated by religious impulse there were always others, writers who sought a different source of female authority. They found it in the most basic and common experience of women—motherhood. As mothers, their duty to instruct the young provided them with the authority to express their ideas on a broad range of subjects. Armed with such authority, they could give advice, instruction in morals and even offer theological interpretations. In the modern period, women would reason their way to claims of equality based on motherhood and later even to group consciousness.

The concept of "motherhood" contains a broad range of meanings. The subject is vast and complex and has become a central focus for feminist scholarship. There is the physical aspect of motherhood, both as the ability to give birth and as the practice of nurturance. The two are historically not always connected, such as in the case of medieval women who left their children in order to devote themselves to religious duties or, in the 17th century, in the case of women who gave their children to the care of wet nurses.[1] Then there is "motherhood as an institution" or "the social construction of motherhood." This encompasses the legal, economic and institutional means by which society defines the roles, rights and duties of mothers. The "institution of motherhood" changes over time and is different in different places or when applied to women of different ethnic or racial groups.[2] Finally, there is the ideology of motherhood, its symbolic meaning as defined in particular periods and under different circumstances. I am, in this chapter, mostly concerned with the last definition of "motherhood"—its symbolic and ideological meaning *as seen by women.* I find it remarkable that over many centuries some women find their identity primarily in motherhood and that they think of their group identity first as mothers, long before they begin to conceive of the possibility of "sisterhood."

The two earliest known female writers in Europe, Dhuoda and Frau Ava, grounded their quest for self-expression in their status as mothers. Dhuoda, born in 803 into a noble family in the Frankish kingdom, married Bernard of Septimania, a relative of the Carolingian kings. She was deprived of both her sons by her husband, who sent the elder as a hostage to a distant court—a not uncommon practice at the time—and wished the other to be educated under his control and away from his mother. This absence from his wife may have been owing to his affair with another woman.[3] It is striking that Dhuoda did not complain of it or consider it a breach of his marital obligations. In forced separation from her children and exiled by her husband, Dhuoda wrote a manual of conduct for her elder son. Her justification for writing at all was that she was a mother, deprived of her children.

> Knowing that most women in the world have the joy of living with their children and seeing that I, Dhuoda, am withheld from you, my son William, and am far away—as one anxious because of this, and full of longing to be useful, I am sending you this little work of mine. . . . I'd be happy if, since I am not physically present, the presence of this little book call to your mind, as you read it, what you should do for my sake. . . . I, Dhuoda, though frail in sex, living unworthily among worthy women, am nonetheless your mother, my son William.[4]

And once again, addressing herself to God, she stressed the uniqueness of her relationship to her son: "He will never have one like me to tell him this, /I, though unworthy, am also his mother."[5] She then proceeded to lay out a plan for her son's education, urging him to become learned, pious, develop chivalric skills and honor, and live with humility. She urged him to honor and obey his father and expressed the hope that there would never be discord between father and son. Finally, she stated that in order to "help my lord and master, Bernard," she had saddled herself with great debts and asked her son should any remain unpaid after her death, to pay back from her estate and his whatever was due.

Her moving conversation with her son is pathetic in its unquestioning acceptance of the bitter fate imposed upon her by her husband, yet her agony and personal loss impelled her to an act of self-assertion which will not appear again in female writing until the 12th century—to write because of her authority as a mother and a woman.

The first known female poet writing in German was a certain Frau Ava, who has been identified with a nun named Ava in the abbey of Melk. She died in 1127 and is known to have lived a secular life before taking religious orders. She was the author of four long religious poems, written in Old High-German, one of which dealt with the Last Judgment. At the end of this poem there occurs the only autobiographical reference in her work, in which she identifies herself as Frau Ava, the mother of two sons. She said:

This book was written by the mother of two children . . .
The mother loved these children, one of whom left this world.
Now I ask you all, great and small,
whoever reads this book, command his soul to grace.
and the one who is still alive and who for his work does strive,
wish him grace as well as his mother, who is AVA.[6]

The biographical information she offers is slight, but her primary characterization as the mother of two children who wrote this book of poems is significant. She offers two personal notes: one of the sons died young; the other strives to do good work; she urges the reader to pray for the salvation of the departed son and for the success of the living son and of herself, identified only as his mother. The last lines give the impression that the whole work was undertaken in order to secure greater blessings to her sons and, with it, to herself. Since at the time of the writing she was presumably living a cloistered life, this speaks strongly to her authorization through motherhood.

The next writer who, at least partially, motivated herself through motherhood lived nearly 300 years later. The French author, Christine de Pizan was driven to writing not only because of her love of learning but because of dire necessity. Although she offered a much more complex argument for women's emancipation than anyone had before her, she also authorized her writing by the fact of her motherhood and of her understanding of woman's lot.[7] She, like Dhuoda, left an advice book for her son. But unlike Dhuoda, who instructed her son above all to honor his father, Christine exhorted her son, "Thou shall not deceive nor slander women but respect them."[8]

It is only in the 15th century that we first find a sizable number of secular women authors, learned women and poets. As these educated women created a body of work which their contemporaries read and appreciated, they also began to argue for their sex. Most of them limited themselves to an argument for women's education on the grounds that women were capable of benefiting from education and that to offer them that chance would improve society. They also began the long tradition of feminist Bible criticism by reinterpreting the core stories which were used to legitimate women's subordination. All of them accepted the gender differences which they thought "natural," namely, that woman's main and proper role is that of wife and mother.

It is my assumption that all human beings develop ideas based, at least in part, on their own experience. Women, because of educational deprivation and the absence of a usable past, tended to rely more heavily on their own experience in developing their ideas than did men. Wifehood and motherhood were the experiences most females had in common with other females. But wifehood, under patriarchy, involved women in competition with other women, both to secure and find a man who would offer them support and protection and, once they had married him, to hold him. Up to the middle of the 19th century, women were structured into society as dependents, first of fathers, then of husbands.

Even though inheritance rights varied widely over the centuries, women property owners depended on their dowries or inheritances, which were under their fathers' control, to secure marriages or even to take up the life of a religious. Once married, women of the nobility depended on their ability to produce male heirs to keep their often considerable power and wealth. Failure to produce sons would make such wives liable to the loss of all their privileges to another woman. Some of the fierce power struggles among women of the nobility under feudalism were struggles over inheritance and the succession of bastard versus legitimate sons. When we consider that as late as the 11th century men of the European nobility still engaged in concubinage, the competition was real and tended to divide noble women one against the other. Not only concubinage but also male adultery with lower-class women posed a threat to the economic security of wives.

Peasant women's access to economic resources and, above all, land came through a man—father, husband, son or lord. Even so, peasant women were valued as helpmates of their husbands and made essential contributions to the household and the economy. In the early Middle Ages women were valued more than men in rural communities for their labor, which can be seen in the fact that in some communities daughters remained in their fathers' house for some time after marriage.[9] Peasant families had to work as a team, with each member of the household providing labor for necessities and the service of the lord. The institution of serfdom rested upon a set of mutual obligations between the serf and his family on the one hand and the lord of the manor on the other.[10] Male and female serfs owed part of their weekly labor to the lord. The protection given to serf families, in addition to economic obligations, also always involved the military services the serf owed the lord. The lord had the authority to approve of or forbid the marriage of serfs. Landowners generally did not interfere with their serfs' or peasants' marriage choices, as long as the peasant did not leave the land. In many places and for many centuries the lord had the right of the first night with the bride of his serf.[11] With that important exception in mind, one can see that peasant women had relatively more freedom in making marriage choices than women of the nobility.[12]

Demographers tell us that there has always been a group in each population, estimated as reaching as high as one-third of all women, who were single, that is, not-yet-married, never-married or widowed. Yet, until the 19th century the choice of remaining single was only a choice of one kind of dependency over another. Single women might choose celibacy and the religious life, in which case they depended on their superiors and the male clergy; they might choose celibacy and dependency on male members of their family of origin; they might barely make a living as servant or governess in the household of strangers, in which case their dependency was thorough and humiliating. A single woman might choose the life of prostitution, in which case she could hardly be considered independent, since her very existence depended on the "protection" and sanction of various authorities. A small percentage of all women led economically self-dependent lives on the margins of society (in the Middle Ages literally on the outskirts of towns) as peddlers, vagrants, beggars, thieves. Additionally, there were throughout the period under consideration always a small percentage of single women working as spinsters, brewers, innkeepers and farm workers. There also were propertied widows who could live independent lives, but their properties originated in a prior dependency on a man. For the vast majority of women, marriage and motherhood were their lot and their main means of securing access to resources and economic protection. This was the reason women could not readily conceptualize bonds of sisterhood or develop a consciousness of common interest through their status as wives.

But motherhood was different, both as an actuality and as a unifying concept. Women shared the life experience of motherhood—frequent pregnancies, miscarriages, births, deaths of children and birth-induced disabilities. Even those who could not conceive did not escape that cycle of female tribulations, since they too were subject to menses, attempted pregnancies, and the ever-present threat of rape.[13] For peasant women who were serfs or domestic servants in the manors of their lords, sexual attack by their masters was a constant and unavoidable threat.

The meaning of motherhood differed for women by class. Until the middle of the 18th century in Europe and the United States, 90 percent of women lived in the countryside, so we should consider peasant women first. The lives of peasant women followed remarkably constant patterns throughout the Christian era despite the vast political and technological changes occurring in the states and nations in which they lived. Peasant women, generation after generation, accepted the double burden of work and reproduction, taking responsibility for the survival of their families and doing whatever work it was necessary to do.[14] Demographers estimate that women's life expectancy was less than that of men in the early Middle Ages, but that it changed dramatically in the 11th century owing to changes in agriculture that brought better nutrition. Still a survey made in the commune of Florence in 1427 shows the average age for men to be 28 years and the average age for women 28.51.[15]

Demographers generally hold that women might have five to seven successful pregnancies during twenty years of their childbearing age; given the life expectancies just cited, four to six successful pregnancies would seem more likely. With the high rate of miscarriages and stillbirths before the 20th century, this meant that a woman would be pregnant or nursing a child for most of her adult lifespan, while working without letup in home and field. Infant mortality rates were high; peasant women could expect half of their children to die before age twenty. Twenty-five percent of children born in England up until the 18th century died in their first year.[16]

Had the average peasant couple produced three adult children out of an average six births, the peasant population of Europe should have grown, but in fact it did not. Only in the aftermath of mass disasters, such as the bubonic plague of the 14th century and the Thirty Years War of the 17th century, did peasant populations increase. This indicates that peasants, living under conditions of bare survival, controlled their birthrates. They did so by delaying the age of marriage, practicing various forms of birth control and, when times were bad, resorting to infanticide, usually the killing of female children.[17] Even though it is impossible to know whether these demographic decisions were made by women or by men and women jointly, one can interpret the overall patterns to mean that motherhood for peasant women was part of their fate—not to become a mother was considered a failure—but also that they exerted some measure of control over the frequency of their pregnancies.[18]

For women of the nobility, motherhood was often imposed upon them by the men on whom they depended or by the structural obligation to produce sons and heirs or lose their place as wives to other women. For women of all classes the raising of sons into adulthood was a means of securing their own support in old age.

Motherhood, as fate and experience, was something women could share with other women. The rituals of motherhood involved women with one another and were dominated by female support networks, whether made up of female kin or neighbors. Births, infant deaths, sickness and succor from marital abuse were all experienced by women among women. Motherhood was then the only basis on which sisterhood could even be conceptualized. It is therefore not surprising that for nearly 350 years the main argument women advanced in favor of their claim for equality was based on motherhood.

But there was another, more powerful aspect to the unifying potential of motherhood. Women created new life out of their bodies and sustained it by nursing and their maternal care, connected to other women, sustained by female prayer and ritual. This experience, which many women felt as empowering, connected them with other women and with the metaphysics of the ancient Mother-Goddess religions, in which the ability to give life, to create and procreate, was experientially and metaphorically fused. Even though the Christian religion recognized and honored the procreative but not the creative power of women, we find evidence of the continued survival of images of the Mother-Goddess in folklore, myths, folk belief all through the early centuries of Christianity, which speaks to the strength of the concept of motherhood.

In the earliest centuries of Christianity the worship of the harvest goddesses Ceres and Demeter was widespread in the Mediterranean area. In Europe, heathen practices like the celebration of festivals outdoors near certain stones and springs previously identified with goddesses, continued for centuries after the acceptance of Christianity. True to the syncretism of Christianity, many of these rituals were incorporated into officially sanctioned Church feasts and celebrations. Several shrines and churches dedicated to Mary were situated in locations where earlier the worship of goddesses had taken place. Herbs previously dedicated to the German goddess Freia were in the early Middle Ages called "Maria's herbs" and used for the festival of Mary's Assumption.[19] The mysterious life-giving forces of the Mother-Goddess continued to be celebrated in folklore and folk memory, such as the custom of drawing the goddess in a wagon around the fields to ensure the success of the crops. This "wretched custom" was described by Gregory of Tours as being practiced in Autun in France in the 6th century. The custom lived on in legends concerning certain Christian female saints and finally, the Virgin Mary, whose "grain miracle" during the flight into Egypt recounts her miraculous ability to make the grain grow immediately after sowing. The story recurred in 12- and 13th-century texts and art works, when its connection with the Mother-Goddess had been long forgotten.[20]

It is an open question whether the development of the cult of the Virgin Mary was a response of the Church to actual popular beliefs and practices deriving from Mother-Goddess worship or whether popular practice developed certain aspects of the role of Mary to fit into the more ancient tradition. The fact is that the figure of Mary, Mother of Christ, gradually—over a few centuries—became transformed from a minor figure in the drama of Christ's martyrdom to a major figure close to the Trinity and seated, quite figuratively, to the right of God or next to the Christ, as mediator between God and humans.

The cult of the Virgin Mary had dual roots, in folk religion and in the Church. In nearly all its manifestations it carried multiple, often contradictory meanings about the nature of woman and about motherhood. Popular devotion to the Virgin started in Byzantium before the 5th century A.D. In Western Europe the cult of Mary began in the 9th century in local "Mary festivals" in German villages and towns. In popular belief, the Virgin Mary acquired and retained some of the characteristics of the old goddesses. Many legends centering on Mary already had wide circulation among the people when the nun and playwright Hrosvitha of Gandersheim wrote a hymn to Mary recounting most of these legends. In her hymn she referred to Mary by a series of epithets, which hark back to language in which a millennium earlier people had addressed the various Mother-Goddesses: "Mistress of Heaven; holy Mother of the King; Shining star of the sea." Hrosvitha restated the main theological argument by which Mary's role was elevated and which entitled her to be the object of religious worship: "Through your son, kindly virgin, you returned to the world that life which the first virgin [Eve] destroyed."[21]

The theological argument on which Hrosvitha's poem rests had already been made in the second century by the apostle Paul, who called Mary the second Eve. Iraneus (d. 202 A.D.) pursued the theme: "As the human race was sentenced to death by means of a virgin, so it is now set aright by means of a virgin. . . . A virgin's disobedience is saved by a virgin's obedience."[22] Jerome wrote in the 4th century: "But after a virgin conceived in the womb and bore for us a child . . . the curse has been abrogated. Death came through Eve, life through Mary."[23] This interpretation won wide acceptance and formed one of the doctrinal foundations for the devotion to Mary.

Popular devotion to Mary was greatly increased when merchants and pilgrims brought to the West information about the relic worship and cult of the Virgin practiced by the Eastern Church. Romanesque sculpture showed the Madonna and Child in majestic enthronement, which emphasized her role as *Theotokos*, bearer of God.

The religious developments of the 11th century, especially the reforms within the Church and the greater emphasis on celibacy of the clergy, affected the theology of and devotion to Mary. To many of the male clergy she became a spiritual mother, the object of affective piety and worship which tried empathetically to enter into the sufferings of the mother of the crucified Jesus. The devotion to Mary of two mystics had a particular impact on the development of her cult in Western Europe. Elizabeth of Schönau (d. 1164), recording and reporting her visions of Mary's bodily assumption into heaven, helped to advance the celebration of that event and give it iconographic concreteness. Devotion to the Virgin was further promoted by the mystic Bernard of Clairvaux, who made it a central aspect of the ritual practice of the Cistercians. The order dedicated all its monasteries to the "Queen of Heaven and Earth"; its members wore white robes in honor of her purity and built special lady chapels in their churches. We have discussed earlier how Hildegard of Bingen revived the iconography of the Mother-Goddess in her images of the Virgin Mary, Sophia and the Church personified as a female figure. Hildegard's fusion of Mary and Wisdom and/or the Church resulted in a powerful representation of the female aspect of the Divine.[24]

The cult of the Virgin Mary was made official when in 1095 Pope Urban II at the Council of Clermont launched the first crusade under Mary's protection. It fully developed in the 12th and 13th centuries into the glorification of Mary, with prayers, hymns, liturgical drama, legends and artistic representations devoted to her. In Gothic architecture and portraiture Mary appears seated next to the adult Christ in heaven, vested with power in her own right, the Virgin Triumphant. In still other representations she appears as the "Queen of Heaven" in full glory, surrounded by angels and the saints.[25] Mary wonder tales flourished from the 12th to the 15th century and appeared in Latin, Greek and Coptic texts.[26]

In the 12th century many cathedrals and churches were built in honor of the Virgin, among them the cathedral of Notre Dame in Paris, rebuilt on the site where Mary's veil, a relic given to the church in the 9th century, was miraculously left intact when in 1194 a fire entirely destroyed the old church.[27] The founding of shrines to the Virgin Mary, based on miracles and visionary appearances, continued from the 16th into the 19th and 20th centuries, the most prominent of these—the shrines of Loreto (1503), Lourdes (1858) and Fatima (1917)—continuing in popularity as the objects of pilgrimages and worship.

Mary's holiness due to her virginity and her own immaculate conception reflected qualities worshipped for millennia in ancient goddesses. Mary's divine motherhood echoed the power of ancient mother-goddesses as givers of life and as the protectresses of women in childbirth. Popular belief and custom persistently stressed these aspects of Mary's sacredness. A merchant in Milan had a vision of Mary as a goddess in a robe strewn with ears of corn. He commissioned a painting of his vision and donated it to the Milan Duomo, where the faithful worshipped the "corn maiden" with garlands of flowers to secure their own fertility. This image was also popular in the 15th century in Tyrol and Germany.[28] In many Renaissance images of Mary with her child, she or the child is shown holding a pomegranate, an ancient symbol of fertility.

The popular belief in Mary as protectress of pregnant women persisted. In medieval villages, pregnant women wore amulets of female figures which resembled the pregnancy amulets of the first millennium B.C. Childless women begged her intercession as did women in labor. Queen Anne of Austria, wife of Louis XIII, barren after twenty-two years of marriage, prayed at the shrine of Mary at LePuy, and had the relic of the girdle of the Virgin, which was kept there, brought in its casket from the cathedral to her bedroom. Her prayers were answered and she gave birth in 1638 to the future Louis XIV.[29] In numerous churches, believers dedicated their wedding dresses or china dolls representing babies to the Virgin in gratitude for prayers answered.[30]

In her role as "Queen of Heaven," Mary was often identified in metaphors and iconography with the moon, the stars and the sea, again reflecting and echoing ancient pagan beliefs. The Virgin's association with the moon's fertility, her celebration as mistress of the waters and as shining star, all hark back to qualities held by the ancient moon goddesses.[31]

Interestingly, Mary shared another set of characteristics with the ancient mother-goddesses—her patronage of war and violence. During the siege of Constantinople by Avars in 626, the patriarch had an image of the Virgin and Child painted on the city gates; the same image carried around city walls protected it against Arab attackers in 717. In the 9th century defenders of Chartres against the Norsemen flew the Virgin's tunic from their Bishop's staff.[32] Mary, as Queen and protectress of a particular king, was used to bolster his claim for supremacy with her divine blessing. The crusaders were told that Mary blessed their mission and many of them visited shrines to the Virgin on the way to the Holy Land. The power of Mary's image to inspire men to battle was manifest four hundred years later, when in 1620 near Prague, the Catholic troops of the Holy Roman Emperor Ferdinand of Austria advanced, crying "Saint Mary," and defeated the Calvinist enemy.

The image of the Virgin was also used to justify the persecution of the Jews. In the 12th century, when the persecution of European Jews was at its height, many of the miracle tales of Mary were also anti-Semitic and depicted Jews as villains who threatened the lives of Christian children.[33] A century later, similar mythical tales, when told in response to an actual event like the disappearance or the death of a Christian child, provided the excuse for attacks on Jewish communities.[34] Late in the 15th century the appearance of an image called "beautiful Mary" together with an image of the bleeding Christ inspired pogroms against Jews in Bavaria.[35] One historian of the cult of Mary concludes: "As guardian of cities and nations and peoples, as the bringer of peace or victory . . . the Virgin resembles Athene."[36]

The complex theological arguments underlying the cult of Mary lie beyond the scope of this book. But we can note that devotion to Mary is fundamental to essential points of Catholic doctrine; that it forces the issue of a feminine element in the Divine into consciousness and ritual and that it is both responsive to and reflective of popular belief and practices as it tries to shape them. The basic doctrinal concepts underlying the devotion to Mary are: her divine motherhood; her virginity; her conception without original sin and her bodily assumption into heaven. All of these concepts are enigmatic and contradictory and presuppose acceptance of the miraculous. Her divine motherhood is the most easily accepted aspect of this doctrine, and is in fact accepted by Christian churches of all denominations, since it is grounded in the Gospel texts. In the Annunciation the Virgin, still fully human, is touched by the Divine. The miracles of her post-partum virginity and of her own miraculous Immaculate Conception by the aged Anna are essential points of Catholic doctrine which make Mary more than human, but not divine. The crucial doctrinal point of the Immaculate Conception, debated by churchmen since the 5th century and adopted by the Church as official doctrine in 1854, is that by this miracle Christ was born free of the original sin embodied in the sexual act necessary for the procreation of mortals. The concept that Mary herself was immaculately, and thus miraculously, conceived elevates her to same position as Christ in being free of original sin.[37] Finally, the miracle of Mary's full bodily assumption to heaven, an event popularly celebrated since the 7th century and the subject of fierce doctrinal disputes among theologians, became official Catholic dogma only in 1950. The doctrinal argument was that Mary, in being free of original sin like Christ, was not subject to the bodily corruption of death. The elevation of Mary, body and soul, into heaven transformed her from a miraculously sanctified mortal into a semi-divine figure, appropriately placed in iconography next to Christ as his Mother and as Queen of Heaven.

Her multiple and contradictory functions were interpreted by theologians and Church officials in the most conservative and patriarchal way: Mary's virginity elevated that condition as a sanctifying choice for ordinary women; her submissiveness to the divine will in the Annunciation was to be the model for female behavior toward fathers and husbands; her tragic motherhood was the model for ordinary mothers' silent submission to their female destiny of suffering and loss, and even Mary's Assumption was read and preached as symbolizing her acceptance of the appropriate role of handmaiden and intercessor. Mary, enthroned in Heaven, was not to be seen as a goddess, but as the interceder, through her maternal influence on her son, for mortal sinners.[38]

Mariology was not developed by women, nor was the theology surrounding Mary developed by female saints and prophets. Yet several of the great female mystics, Hildegard of Bingen, Mechthild of Magdeburg, Gertrude of Helfta and Elizabeth of Schönau, worshipped Mary with special devotion. Among the people, the worship of Mary was largely female worship and may have been based on the appeal Mary as a sacred figure had for women. Most simply, women could feel and share Mary's experience. Mary was worshipped because she was a mother, a very special mother of a very special son, but a mother nevertheless, who had humbly submitted to God's command and will the way other women submitted to the command and will of their husbands. And Mary had raised a son whom she must lose soon, an experience, surely, with which all mothers could identify. The iconography of Mary with the child, as it appeared in countless churches, an earthly mother, nurturing a special, but earthly baby, reinforced this identification.

The theological significance of the transformation of Mary, the Mother, to Mary, the intercessor between humans and Christ, Merciful Mother—a divine or semi-divine figure, is difficult to describe without ambiguity. Modern observers have noted that Mary in that new role was a figure to which no female could aspire, since her sanctity was based on two miracles, that of her birth without original sin and that of her virginal pregnancy, a feat clearly impossible to mortal females. Was the Assumption of Mary and her triumph in heaven a theological concession to the female principle in the Divine? Or was her subordinate role in heaven, her agency solely as pleader for human sinners and intercessor for human interests another form of defining women as "helpmeet" and subordinate? Both interpretations are based on evidence extending over many centuries; both represent different aspects of the complex belief systems clustering around the figure of Mary. But we should note that either interpretation speaks to the glorification of motherhood.

THE THEME OF FEMALE bonding and the honoring of motherhood is unexpectedly conveyed in a pamphlet in defense of women written by an Englishwoman under the pseudonym Constantia Munda in 1615. This learned, witty, invective-laden pamphlet is prefaced by serious Dedication written in quite a different tone. It reads:

> To the Right Worshipful Lady her most dear Mother, the Lady Prudentia Munda, the true pattern of Piety and Virtue, Constantia Munda wisheth increase of happiness.

> As first your pains in bearing me was such
> A benefit beyound requital, that twere much
> To thine what pangs of sorrow you sustain'd
> in child-birth, when mine infancy obtain'd
> The vital drawing in of air, so your love
> Mingled with care hath shown itselfe above
> the ordinary course of Nature. Seeing you still
> Are in perpetual Labor with me, even until
> The second birth of education perfect me: . . . Thus
> I pay my debt by taking up at interest, and lay
> To pawn that which I borrow of you; so
> The more I give, I take; I pay, I owe.
> Yet lest you think I forfeit shall my bond,
> I here present you with my writing hand. . . .
> Your loving Daughter
Constantia Munda[39]

The theme of mother-daughter bonding, which will appear so frequently sentimentalized in the poetry and fiction of later centuries, is here struck coolly and metaphorically. The labor of childbearing and nurturing is compared to the "second birth of education" in an elegant equation of effort and investment, by which the learned daughter repays her debt to her mother by writing and publishing in defense of women. This is an early example of a work expressing feminist consciousness in terms of female culture.

THE PROTESTANT REFORMATION was the major intellectual watershed for women in a variety of ways. We will here discuss only its impact on female education and its upgrading of the role of mothers.

The establishment of Protestantism fostered the development of public education in Protestant cities and, generally, such rudimentary education was made available equally to boys and girls. Protestant doctrine demanded that each father and head of household be held accountable for the religious instruction of all family members. Practically, this meant an upgrading of the role of the mother. Protestant mothers were expected not only to be able to read the word of God directly from the Bible but to instruct their children in the elements of reading and writing and in religious knowledge. This shift in doctrine authorized women to be educated and authorized individual women to speak and to teach. Protestantism set strict limits to this authorization of women as educators: Protestant churches restricted women as much from equal participation in service and government as did the state, and the issues of women's right to learn and to teach on a basis of equality with men had to be fought out bitterly over three centuries. Nevertheless, the doctrinal basis for accepting mothers as educators had been laid.

A striking example of a woman authorizing both her poetry and her theologizing by her motherhood is Anna Ovena Hoyers (1584–1655), daughter of a well-to-do astronomer, Hanns Ovenn, in Holstein. She married Hermann Hoyers, a wealthy official, at age fifteen, and had nine children. After her husband's death she managed her property and supported six surviving children. After her conversion to Anabaptism she began to write religious and political pamphlets and didactic, satirical and religious poetry. Persecuted for her sectarianism and in financial distress, she was forced to sell her estate and was abandoned by her friends. In 1632 she fled to Sweden, where she was protected and supported by the king's widow, Marie Eleonore. A selection of her poems, printed in 1650, was burned in a number of places because of her heretical views.

She defied her critics by asserting, "I can and will not be silenced" and "I am driven/ have to speak out/ Have written it down / will dare more/ even if it costs me my head."[40]

Her poems are well crafted and abound in acrostics and other poetic devices which incorporate her name in various ways in the poems. This is particularly evident in a joyous and confident hymn called "Up, Up, Zion" in which she sings to the glory of Zion, and uses a rhyme scheme in which each stanza ends with "Sing, Hoseanna, and thus sings with you Hanns Ovenn's daughter Anna." In stanza 12 she begins to change her refrain, referring not to her daughterhood, but to her motherhood. "You, my three sons sing loud and bright./ Sing it Hoseanna, you two daughters be joyous with your mother Anna." This pattern is repeated for two more stanzas, then the last stanza ends with her signature as Hans Ovenn's daughter Anna. This gay and self-confident song is unique in my reading of women's literature in its constant reiteration of her name and her claim to fame as daughter and mother.[41]

One of her lengthy poems, "A Spiritual Discussion Between

Mother and Child About True Christianity," represents her own theological interpretation of basic doctrine and thus is a literary form of preaching. Her only justification for such an undertaking is the fact she is a mother instructing her child.[42] The child asks her questions unlikely to be asked by any child: "How can I get closer to Christ?" "Oh, Mother, I'm too weak to renounce the world and to follow my Lord Jesus. What do I do?" Her replies to the child's theological questions take forty-one pages. Although the child functions mainly as a literary device, she keeps her answers simple, on the level of a child. After her instruction the child says: "Yes, Mother, I thank you for this. You have shown me the way, and through your motherliness you have taught me and have given me access to beautiful books in which God reveals his glory to me morning and night. All that will stick to my heart, will bear fruit in my life."[43] Thus, the fictionalized child authorizes the mother's daring venture into theological interpretation.

A 17TH-CENTURY JEWISH-GERMAN housewife and mother has left a fascinating account of her life, her theological ideas and her activities as a mother. Shortly after the death of her husband, Glückel of Hameln (1646–1724) wrote her memoirs in the form of a diary addressed to her children.[44] She began with a summary of her theological and moral beliefs, which she exhorted her children to carry into practice. The story of her life encompassed many public events, which affected her security and threatened her survival as a Jew in the German lands torn by the religious conflicts of the Thirty Years War and its aftermath. Married at age fourteen, Glückel bore fourteen children, of whom two died in infancy. In a tone somewhat reminiscent of the practical, pragmatic style of Margery Kempe, she tells of her marriage, her activities as a businesswoman, her efforts at securing favorable marriages for her children. She lived through war, anti-Semitic persecutions and pogroms, the arrival of the false Messiah Sabbtai Zevi, pestilence, sickness and the death of her husband. Widowed, with eight children still at home, she salvaged the family fortune by her shrewd trading activities, which necessitated far-flung travels to most of the cities of Europe. She married a second time, much later, hoping to find some security in her old age, but her husband's business failed and he barely escaped imprisonment. He died impoverished and she had to accept the offer of one of her sons-in-law to move into his house, where she remained the rest of her life.

Glückel's memoirs are the only first-person account of a Jewish woman's life in the 17th century available to us. They give a vivid picture of the social scene and of Jewish life, its hardships and of the strong support network of the Jewish communities. There is one particular scene in her book which exemplifies woman's culture. She and her young husband were living in her father's house in Hamburg at the time of her first pregnancy. Her mother was at that time also expecting a child:

> My dear mother had reckoned our time for the same day. However, she had great joy in my being brought to bed first, so she could help me a little, young girl that I was. Eight days later my mother likewise brought forth a young daughter in childbirth. So there was neither envy nor reproach between us, and we lay next to each other in the selfsame room. But Lord, we had no peace, for the people that came running in to see the marvel, a mother and daughter together in childbed.[45]

Glückel continues the story of how she and her mother nearly exchanged babies by mistake "in laughter . . . the word went round, 'A little more, and we'd had to summon the blessed King Solomon himself.'"[46]

The theme of motherhood appears in an experiential way in the work of several other 17th-century writers. These women not only felt authorized to write and teach because they were mothers but they considered their experience as mothers a fit subject for their literary work. This represents a new level in the development of women's consciousness.

A poem in a humorous vein continues in the tradition of mothers' instructing their sons. It appears in a collection of poems by one Mrs. Barber, wife of a tradesman in Dublin, who, as the male writer of the Preface informs us, "found leisure without neglecting her husband's business, to write several little pieces." She complied with convention in explaining that she writes solely for the edification of her children. That she was able to publish at all, despite her humble social station, was due to the patronage of some women and men of learning, including Lady Carteret and Jonathan Swift, whose patronizing comments we cited earlier.[47] Mrs. Barber held her own against those patronizing her and wittily answered in kind:

> Conclusion of a Letter to the Rev. Mr.C.
> 'Tis time to conclude; for I make it a rule
> To leave off all writing, when Con. comes from school.
> He dislikes what I've written, and says I had better
> To send what he calls a poetical letter.

To this I reply'd, you are out of your wits;
A letter in verse would put him in fits;
He thinks it a crime in a woman to read—
Then what would he say should your counsel succeed?

I pity poor Barber, his wife's so romantic:
A letter in rhyme!—Why, the woman is frantic!
This reading the poets has quite turn'd her head!
On my life, she should have a dark room and straw bed.

    · · · ·

    Her husband has surely a terrible life!
There's nothing I dread like a verse-writing wife. . . .

If ever I marry, I'll chuse me a spouse,
That shall *serve* and *obey*, as she's bound by her vows
That shall, when I'm dressing, attend like a valet;
Then go to the kitchen, and study my palate.
She has wisdom enough, that keeps out of the dirt,
And can make a good pudding, and cut out a shirt.
What good's in a dame that will pore on a book?
No!—Give me the wife that shall save me a cook.
Thus far I had written—Then turn'd to my son
To give him advice, ere my letter was done.
My son, should you marry, look out for a wife,
That's fitted to lighten the labours of life.
Be sure, wed a woman you thoroughly know,
And shun, above all things, *a housewifely shrew*. . . .

Chuse a woman of wisdom, as well as good breeding,
With a turn, at least no aversion, to reading.
In the care of her person, exact and refin'd;
Yet still, let her principal care be her mind.
Who can, when her family cares give her leisure,
Without the dear cards, pass an evening with pleasure
In forming her children to virtue and knowledge,
Not trust, for that care, to a school, or a college. . . .

A husband first praise is a Friend and Protector.
Then change not the titles, for Tyrant and Hector.
. . . Chuse books, for her study, to fashion her mind,
To emulate those who excell'd of her kind.
. . . So you, in your marriage, shall gain its true end
And find, in your wife, a Companion and Friend.[48]

    Mrs. Barber not only cleverly subverted domestic ideology and
gender roles by instructing her son to choose what her contempo-

raries regard as an aberration, namely an educated wife, but she also elevated the dailyness of her housewife's existence to the subject matter of poetry. In this, she anticipated a development of female literary expression which would not come to full flowering until the 18th century in Europe.

A DIFFERENT APPROACH to the subject is found in the work of a German poet. Margaretha Susanna von Kuntsch (1651–1716) was the daughter of a municipal court clerk in Eisleben, and received some education in Latin and French. She got married in 1669 and had fourteen children, of whom only one daughter survived her. She wrote many poems occasioned by the death of her children. After her death her grandchild edited a volume of her poetry. In one of her poems she deals with her pathetic life experience in a rather remarkable way, infusing her tragedy with larger meaning. The poem is entitled "Occasioned by the Death of My Fifth Born Little Son, the Little Chrysander, or CK on the 22nd of November, 1686" and consists of seven rhymed stanzas. The first two stanzas tell how an artist who attempted to paint the grief of Agamemnon at the sacrifice of his daughter Iphigenia was unable to show the hero's face because the blow of fate was too strong and shocking. The third stanza continues:

> What is one-time grief?
> One should compare me with Agamemnon.
> Me, who all my hopes and joys
> had to bury in the tomb
> with my ninth child
> sacrificed to death's knife.
>
> He was a courageous hero,
> a king used to command and reign,
> a warrior leading his men
> into battle against the foe,
> and yet his usually brave heart
> faltered overwhelmed by his grief. . . .
> Who gives me the courage,
> who will sharpen my pen with craft
> when my blood is stirred
> to try in words to describe my feelings,
> I who am merely a woman?
> Alas, my senses falter.
>
> My hand trembles,
> the pen refuses me service.

> The paper is shaking
> and cannot bear the words of grief.
> Let my silent suffering
> Bear witness to my desolation.[49]

Here, for once, a woman elevates her experience of motherhood to equal status with that of the warrior-hero, subtly challenging the patriarchal value system that renders her heart-wrenching experience insignificant.

BEGINNING IN THE 17th century, debates about the responsibilities of mothers to breastfeed their children began to take on ideological freight. A new emphasis on childhood and on the benefits and joys of domesticity developed by the 18th century into a full-fledged "cult of motherhood and domesticity." Advice literature, sermons and novels glorified motherhood and romanticized women as primarily maternal beings. Advice literature urged wealthy women to breastfeed their children; a new literature on childrearing became popular; iconographic representations of sentimental motherhood became pervasive.[50]

Women seemingly embraced the concept and adapted it to their own uses, chiefly as a literary genre. It appeared first in collections of verse by women addressed to a female readership, then, increasingly, in the journals and magazines for women, which proliferated in the late 18th and early 19th century. At the same time many newspapers and reform journals adopted the custom of publishing a "woman's page" on which poems by and for mothers regularly made their appearance. The genre is sentimental and generally of low literary quality, with religious sentiments, consoling thoughts or moralistic generalizations the prevailing message. It is difficult to see any feminist consciousness in these productions, yet we should note that the emphasis on the maternal experience of the deaths of children constitutes a rudimentary recognition of motherhood as a collective cultural concept.

The concept of motherhood was also redefined in a political and feminist way in the wake of the great revolutionary movements of the late 18th century. For example, the 17th-century English author Bathsua Pell Makin argued that women in their role as educated mothers would benefit the nation. This argument for "Republican Motherhood" would be a theme frequently sounded by later feminists as well and will be more fully explored in Chapter Nine.

It is striking to see how frequently the argument made by early feminist thinkers for equality as citizens was based on an elaboration of woman's role as mother. Even the first major feminist theoretician, Mary Wollstonecraft, appealed to women as a group mainly in terms of their motherhood. Her chief argument to both men and women was that better educated women would make better wives and mothers. Yet Wollstonecraft challenged her own argument in referring to women's domestic and motherly work as their "simple duties . . . but the end, the grand end of their exertions should be to unfold their own faculties and acquire the dignity of conscious virtue."[51] Where earlier advocates of women's education had argued that women as moral creatures under God were entitled to equality, she secularized this argument, grounded it in natural rights, yet again and again conflated women's citizenship with motherhood:

> The being who discharges the duties of its station is independent; and, speaking of women at large, their first duty is to themselves as rational creatures, and the next, in point of importance, as citizens, is that, which includes so many, of a mother.[52]

She goes much further in a feminist direction in her two works of fiction, *Mary* and *Maria*. There she offers concrete evidence of cross-class solidarity among women and attacks marriage as an institution. The heroine of *Mary* dies with the joyous thought that "she was hastening to that world where there is neither marrying, nor giving in marriage."[53] *Maria* ends tragically for the heroine, who is an abused wife. Yet in both works the solidarity of women is made possible only by the commonality of their experiences of wife- and motherhood.

The theme of motherhood was countered by a very different theme, that of independent womanhood, by the pioneers of feminist thought in 17th-century England and France. Women like Sarah Fyge, Bathsua Pell Makin, Mary Astell, Lady Mary Chudleigh in England and Marie de Gournay in France, despite differences in their backgrounds and political beliefs, had in common their commitment to women's independence, to their development of social roles outside of marriage and to their intellectual advancement. These early feminists began to define women as a coherent social group whose subordination was neither natural nor divinely ordered; they mounted a strong challenge to the claim of women's intellectual inferiority, demanded institutionalized education for girls equal to that for boys— and assumed implicitly that women of their class would have a common interest in advancing these claims. We will discuss them more fully below, but we should note here that they were the first to think in terms of sisterhood as a collectivity.

The early English feminists, like their European counterparts, were savagely attacked, ridiculed and slandered. Designated as "bluestockings, old maids and strong-minded women," they were considered "de-sexed" and unfeminine, compared with the idealized wife and mother of prescriptive literature.

At this early stage in feminist thought the recognition of group interest beyond that of motherhood had to be merely a utopian projection, a tentative hope without practical or political consequences. Yet it was the ideas of the early feminists that foreshadowed the development of feminist consciousness a century later. It was only in the 19th century, when in both the United States and Great Britain educated middle-class women organized for religious and community welfare and when working women began to organize *as women* to improve their economic conditions, that the idea of sisterhood could become a central issue of feminist thought. And even then and well into the first decade of the twentieth century, women would argue for their feminist agenda on the grounds of their common experience as mothers. In Western Europe and in the United States, the claim of women's moral superiority over men because of their concern with the welfare of children and therefore with the welfare of the community was long used to justify women's claim to the ballot. Because they were mothers, some women argued, women voters would improve politics.

Until marriage was no longer the chief means of support for most women and until large groups of women no longer needed to spend most of their lives as child-bearers and child-rearers, the main concept through which women could conceptualize their group identity was their common experience of motherhood. This experience allowed them to make claims to equality long before the concept of sisterhood could develop.

SEVEN

One Thousand Years of Feminist Bible Criticism

WHATEVER ROUTE WOMEN took to self-authorization and whether they were religiously inspired or not, they were confronted by the core texts of the Bible, which were used for centuries by patriarchal authorities to define the proper roles for women in society and to justify the subordination of women: Genesis, the Fall and St. Paul. Since male objections to women thinking, teaching and speaking in public were for centuries based on biblical authority, the development of feminist Bible criticism can be seen as an appropriate and perhaps not unexpected response to the constraints and limitations imposed upon women's intellectual development by religiously sanctioned gender definitions. These biblical core texts sat like huge boulders across the paths women had to travel in order to define themselves as equals of men. No wonder they engaged in theological reinterpretation before they could move on to other, more original and creative ideas.

It may also have been the case that women took up Bible criticism mostly because the Bible was the one text available to them. If so, their act of critique and reinterpretation would be a prime example of their subversion and transformation of patriarchal doctrine, in itself a feminist act. Such an act implies that the person engaging in reinterpretation considers herself fully authorized and capable of challenging expert theological authority. It is amazing to see how woman after woman engaged in such criticism without reference to theological authorities and without apology. The same women who endlessly apologized for their audacity in writing or teaching, confidently corrected Church fathers, popes, priests and preachers. Usually they offered their own version of God's intent, not, as the mystics did, on the basis of special revelation but simply because they reasoned as they did and believed they had every right thus to reason. There is no stronger evidence available to show that there always were women who never accepted the patriarchal gender definitions which defined them as inherently inferior and incapable of reasoning. Long before organized groups of women challenged male authority, the feminist Bible critics did just that. Without making any special claims for their right to preach or teach, women simply did both, appropriating the Bible and using it for their own purposes. The long trail of evidence of this process, to be found in the work of most European women writers over many centuries, is only the tip of the iceberg. For every woman who wrote in this manner, there must have been many, anonymous and unknown, who thought that way and taught their children that way.

This chapter deals with examples of women's Bible criticism from many places and made in different periods, although the selections in the modern period are made mostly from British and American sources. This is a pragmatic choice; the sources on this subject are very rich and one could prove the same points from sources in many different Western European cultures. The point is to illustrate the lack of continuity and the absence of collective memory on the part of women thinkers. It is interesting to note that individual women thinkers in different countries and at different times proceeded along similar intellectual routes in developing their arguments for the equality and emancipation of women. Yet they hardly ever based their work on that of another woman, and they were seemingly ignorant of a feminist tradition of Bible criticism. I have selected the most telling examples from many times and places to illustrate this discontinuity.

There is, on the other hand, a continuing tradition of women's religious writing. Women's creative energies were for centuries channelled into religious writing, with other forms of expression discouraged or foreclosed. Thus there is a large corpus of women's religious texts which simply repeat traditional interpretations. Especially, during the 18th and 19th centuries, traditionalist female religious writers found outlets and readers and sometimes acclaim. I have not considered these writings here, since they do little or nothing to challenge the patriarchal tradition.

POSSIBLY THE EARLIEST known example of a woman's Bible commentary concerns one Helie, in the second century A.D., who wanted to remain a "consecrated virgin" and who argued with her mother and a judge to whom her parents had brought her. When the judge cited St. Paul, "It is better to marry than burn" against her, Helie replied: "It is true that Scripture says it is better to marry than burn; but not for everyone, that is, not for holy virgins." She pointed out that "men are not bound by laws promulgated for women." and with that argument won the right to stay a virgin and to take Christ as her husband.[1]

The teachings of the medieval Church in regard to women were based on several biblical core texts in the Old Testament: Genesis 1:27 (God created mankind in his own image; in the image of God created he him; male and female created he them) and the old Yahwist account, Genesis 2:20–23, the story of Eve's creation from Adam's rib. These were frequently linked in Christian exegesis with the story of the Fall, Genesis 3:1–24. The New Testament texts most frequently cited all derive from St. Paul and seem to dictate women's submissiveness and public silence: I Timothy 2:8–15; I Corinthians 14:33–35; Ephesians 5:22–23. St. Paul himself took a teleological view by connecting earlier and later Old Testament texts, reading backward from the Fall to interpret Genesis, as in I Corinthians 11:7–9 ("For a man indeed ought not to cover his head, forasmuch as he is the image and glory of God: but the woman is the glory of man. For the man is not of the woman; but the woman of the man. Neither was the man created for the woman; but the woman for the man"). Modern biblical scholarship has reached near-consensus in the judgment that most of the comments pertaining to women attributed to Paul were not in fact written or spoken by Paul but were the product of post-apostolic writers who ascribed the texts to him for greater authority. This includes the admonition most often cited: that women "must learn in silence and with all submissiveness. I permit no woman to teach or to have authority over men; she is to keep silent" (I Timothy 2:11). Knowledge of this erroneous ascription was, of course, not available to women until the present day, so that for nearly 2000 years the misogynist Paulinist tradition, which has dominated biblical interpretation, was regarded as apostolic.[2]

The second-century Church father Tertullian (A.D. 160–225) expressed these misogynist ideas forcefully in speaking to Eve:

> You are the Devil's gateway. You are the unsealer of that forbidden tree. You are the first deserter of the divine Law. . . . On account of your desert, that is death, even the son of God had to die.[3]

Two hundred years later, Ambrose, the bishop of Milan, commented that Eve was more to blame for the Fall than Adam, because, right after she ate the apple, she realized her sin, but still continued to tempt him. "She ought not . . . to have made her husband a partaker of the evil of which she was conscious. . . . She sinned therefore with forethought."[4]

In the 5th century, St. Augustine of Hippo argued that woman was not created in God's image but only in his "likeness," which supported the idea of her "weakness" and greater propensity for sin. He argued that "even before her sin, woman had been made to be ruled by her husband and to be submissive and subject to him," but that condition was without resentment, while after the Fall "there is a condition similar to slavery."[5] In another, often quoted statement, Augustine said:

> I have said, when I was treating of the nature of the human mind, that the woman together with her husband is in the image of God...but when she is referred to separately to her quality of "help-meet," which regards the woman herself alone, then she is not the image of God, but as regards the man alone, he is the image of God as fully and completely as when the woman too is joined with him in one.[6]

This passage has been controversial not only among theologians, but also among modern feminist critics. It has been interpreted both literally, as showing the innate inferiority of woman, and allegorically, as referring to two aspects of the human mind, the higher intellect (male) and the lower reason (female), being inextricably linked one to the other.[7] Whichever interpretation one is inclined to accept, it is obvious that the text offers support to those arguing for female intellectual inferiority. Some theologians and later some feminist thinkers used St. Augustine to argue for women's equality, but the overwhelming thrust of interpretation, as it came down to the common people, was in the misogynist direction.

Nearly a thousand years later the Dominican Thomas Aquinas, influenced by Aristotelian thinking which defined women as incomplete and inferior to men, showed that the male was created with superior capacity for knowledge and with a rational soul, whereas the woman was created chiefly as an aid in reproduction. Although

Aquinas qualified this harsh judgment on women by saying, "despise not yourselves, women, the son of God was born of woman," he thereby merely elevated motherhood as woman's only route toward the Divine, while he firmly held woman to innate inferiority by divine design.[8] This woman-blaming doctrine was accepted as truth by all medieval theologians. It was an argument frequently subverted by feminist re-interpreters who reasoned that Eve could not help her inborn weakness and that therefore her sin was less than Adam's.

Although the biblical and apostolic texts were by no means unequivocal in their position on women, during the Middle Ages two assumptions regarding woman's nature were accepted as basic truths: that women were created inferior and for a different, lesser, purpose than men and that by their nature and weakness they had a greater propensity toward sin and sexual temptation than did men. A third widespread assumption about the nature of women derived from early patristic interpretation of the core texts, chiefly by Origen and St. Augustine, namely, that Adam and Eve's sin is transmitted from parent to child through concupiscence, which invariably is part of the act of generation. Since that sin had already been blamed on Eve, all women were charged with a heavy load of guilt for the Fall and original sin.[9]

A POPULAR VERSION of these woman-blaming beliefs is expressed by a medieval Irish poet, when he had Eve speak as follows:

> I am Eve, the wife of noble Adam; it was I who violated Jesus in the past; it was I who robbed my children of heaven; it is I by right who should have been crucified. . . . It was I who plucked the apple; . . . there would be no hell, there would be no grief, there would be no terror but for me.[10]

It is against the background of this thousand-year-old tradition of patristic interpretation that one must view the daring and persistent efforts at feminist Bible criticism.

The first and highly original reinterpretation of the story of Creation from a woman-focused point of view is to be found in the work of Hildegard of Bingen. She returned to the theme repeatedly and throughout her lifetime. I have earlier discussed Hildegard's theology in which the Eve—Mary—and the Woman-clothed-with-the-sun images merge and symbolize the feminine aspect of the Divine. She regarded Eve as prefiguring Mary, the symbol of divine humanity "in which the whole human race lay hidden until it should come forth in God's mighty power, just as he had brought forth the first man. Male and female were joined together, therefore, in such a way that each one works through the other."[11] Hildegard sees man and woman as complementary and interdependent, yet she thinks the woman is weaker than the man, because he was formed from earth and she was formed from flesh. Still, in her beautiful version of the Creation, which I have cited earlier, she movingly describes Adam's prophetic wisdom, "for he saw the mother through whom he would beget children," and Eve's longing for fulfillment "for she set her hope in the man."[12] Hildegard envisioned Adam and Eve before the Fall in a state of perfection, a wholeness of mind and body in which sex was free of lust and in which state Eve would have given birth to a child painlessly from her side, the way she was created out of Adam. In a departure from traditional patristic interpretation regarding innocence before the Fall, Hildegard speaks of the "love" Adam felt for Eve. "And God gave a form to the love of the man, and so woman is the man's love."[13] This harmonious vision, so different from the Augustinian condemnation of sexuality, also echoes in the tolerant and egalitarian way in which Hildegard, in her medical writings, describes human intercourse as a joining of two equally important forces, both of which determine the nature of the child.[14]

The next Bible commentary by a woman comes from the pen of the 14th-century author, Christine de Pizan (1365–c.1430), and derives from a quite different context than that of the visionary Saint Hildegard. Christine was born in Venice and a few years later was taken to Paris, when her father was called to assume the post of court astrologer for King Charles V. She obtained an excellent education despite her mother's opposition and at age fifteen married Estienne de Castel, a notary. Her husband encouraged her literary activity and the marriage was very happy. Her husband died in 1389, not long after her father had died impoverished. At age twenty-five Christine was widowed, without income and faced with her husband's debts. She supported herself, her mother and her three young children by copying and producing books, doing illustrations and possibly by doing the work of a notary, all the while making her reputation as a writer. She lived her life in the world, engaged in court and politics, ambitious for fame and reputation. Soon she was recognized as a poet and received a commission to do the biography of Charles V. She made her reputation as a defender of women when she attacked Jean de Meung's popular *Roman de la rose* for its mockery of women. This led to an exchange of letters with some of the leading male humanists of her day, in which her reputation was attacked and which started a three-century-long debate on the status of women, known as the *Querelle des femmes*. Christine continued her argument in her major work, *The Book of the City of the Ladies* (1405), a spirited defense of women and a deliberate effort to constitute a history of women, which I will discuss more fully in Chapter Eleven.[15]

Not surprisingly, Christine de Pizan's Bible commentary is phrased with her usual assertive confidence:

> There Adam slept, and God formed the body of woman from one of his ribs, signifying that she should stand at his side as a companion and never lie at his feet like a slave, and also that he should love her as his own flesh. . . . I don't know if you have already noted this: she was created in the image of God. How can any mouth dare to slander the vessel which bears such a noble imprint? . . . God created the soul and placed wholly similar souls, equally good and noble, in the feminine and masculine bodies. . . . [W]oman was made by the Supreme Craftsman. In what place was she created? In the Terrestrial Paradise. From what substance? Was it vile matter? No, it was the noblest substance which had ever been created: it was from the body of man from which God made woman.[16]

Christine, who although self-taught, was very well read and was familiar with classical and patristic literature. She may have been familiar with Hugh of St.-Victor's statement that woman was not created from man's head, and is therefore not meant to be his mistress, and that she was not created from his feet, and so is not meant to be his slave.[17] She interpreted Augustine's remark that woman was not created in God's image but in his "likeness" allegorically and utilized his statement that God created not the body, but the soul, which allowed her to stress the equality of the sexes regardless of their bodily differences. Her assertion that the substance from which Eve was created was "the noblest substance," namely, the body of man, represents a neat, common-sensical inversion of the male claim to superiority by precedence. She here used a device women often have used to discredit patriarchal ideas—she seemingly accepted them, but cleverly subverted them by drawing different conclusions from them than do the patriarchal thinkers. If man was noble by his earlier creation, Eve surpasses him by being created of nobler substance than he was. This is a logical advance over Hildegard's acceptance of female weakness because she was born from flesh, not from earth.[18]

Christine is equally assertive in her handling of the Fall.

> And if anyone would say that man was banished because of Lady Eve, I tell you that he gained more through Mary than he lost through Eve when humanity was conjoined to the Godhead, which would never have taken place if Eve's misdeed had not occurred. Thus man and woman should be glad for this sin, through which such an honor has come about. For as low as human nature fell through this creature woman, was human nature lifted higher by this same creature.[19]

Here we see Christine push the patristic argument that Mary's grace redeemed the sin of Eve a step further by her assertion that Mary's role in lifting human nature higher surpassed the harm created by Eve.

The construction of Christine's major feminist work, *The Book of the City of the Ladies*, enabled her, one by one, to respond to and to demolish all the major and minor charges leveled against women. She did this by raising all the misogynist charges against women in a dialogue with Lady Reason, an allegorical figure of great serenity, who answered each charge with arguments, examples from history, myth or fable and with appropriate excerpts from the Bible. What is most unusual about Lady Reason's defense of women is that it confidently reversed the existing order of gender—she unabashedly depicted women in a better light than men and praised their virtues without apology.

For example, Christine said that men have burdened her with "a heavy charge" by using a Latin proverb, "God made women to speak, weep, and sew," to attack women. Lady Reason answered that the proverb is true and showed how these very qualities have saved women. "What special favors has God bestowed on women because of their tears! He did not despise the tears of Mary Magdalen, but accepted them and forgave her sins and through the merits of those tears she is in glory in Heaven."[20] She then proceeded to cite similar examples from among the saints. As for women's speaking, Jesus Christ wished that his resurrection be first reported by a woman; he had mercy on the woman of Canaan who would not stop shouting her plight in the street, and he discussed her salvation with the Samaritan woman at the well. "God, how often would our contemporary pontiffs deign to discuss anything with some simple little woman, let alone her own salvation?'' [21]

Christine's culling the Bible for worthy heroines and examples set a precedent which would be followed for centuries, yet none of the women writing in the same vein ever cited her. Nor is there any evidence that they knew of her or her work. Yet it was Christine de Pisan who launched women's participation in the debate over women's status in society represented by the *querelle des femmes* which would go on for three centuries in various parts of Europe and in England. It developed as a playful and at times bitter exchange between feminists and antifeminists of both sexes and represented the first serious discussion of gender as a social construct in Western European history.[22] During the Renaissance the main ground of the debate was biblical reinterpretation and an effort to describe the character and nature of Christian woman as different from the woman, actual and mythical, of Antiquity. Female and male defenders of women ascribed heroic qualities to the "virile woman" who transcended her sex by her virtue, nobility and courage. The ideal type of the defenders of women emerged as an androgyn, a person with both "feminine" and "masculine" virtues. The debate was, for over two centuries, highly abstract, intellectual and rhetorical. It was not intended to nor did it produce proposals for societal change; what it did offer was a counter-weight to the overwhelmingly misogynist tradition of the Church. The long lists of heroic women *exempla* presented by feminists were contrasted with the degraded presentations of womanhood in sermons, prescriptive literature and in popular belief. Women taking part in that debate almost invariably made biblical reinterpretation a part of their argument.

One of the learned women of the Renaissance, Isotta Nogarola (1418–66), engaged in such an argument over biblical interpretation. It took the form of a dialogue in letters with a distinguished male humanist, the Venetian Ludovico Foscarini, over Adam's or Eve's responsibility for the Fall. Ludovico argued that Eve was more guilty than Adam because she received the harsher punishment, caused Adam's sin and acted out of pride.[23] Isotta, like Hildegard before her, accepted Eve's greater weakness as a fact:

Where there is less intellect and less constancy, there is less sin; and Eve [lacked sense and constancy] and therefore sinned less. Knowing [her weakness] that crafty serpent began by tempting the woman, thinking the man perhaps invulnerable because of his constancy. . . . [Adam must also be judged more guilty than Eve, secondly] because of his greater contempt for the command. For in Genesis 2 it appears that the Lord commanded Adam not Eve. . . . Moreover, the woman did not [eat from the forbidden tree] because she believed that she was made more like God, but rather because she was weak and [inclined to indulge in] pleasure. . . . and it does not say [that she did so] in order to be like God. And if Adam had not eaten, her sin would have no consequences. For it does not say: "If Eve had not sinned Christ would not have been made incarnate," but "If Adam had not sinned" . . . Notice that Adam's punishment appears harsher than Eve's; for God said to Adam: "to dust you shall return," and not to Eve, and death is the most terrible punishment that could be assigned. Therefore it is established that Adam's punishment was greater than Eve's.[24]

Ludovico responded that at any rate Eve was responsible for her sin and she sinned worse than Adam because she induced him to sin. Further, her sin was not weakness but pride. Isotta disagreed:

It is clearly less a sin to desire the knowledge of good and evil than to transgress against a divine commandment, since the desire for knowledge is a natural thing, and all men by nature desire to know. . . . Eve, weak and ignorant by nature, sinned much less by assenting to that astute serpent, who was called "wise," than Adam—created by God with perfect knowledge and understanding—in listening to the persuasive words and voice of the imperfect woman.[25]

Isotta's argument is ingenious and learned. She freely cited from and commented on the fathers of the Church and various patristic texts. It is noteworthy that when she defended Eve against the charge of pride she said that the desire for knowledge is natural and common to "all men." Obviously, she meant by that all men and women, thereby anticipating the natural rights argument of a later time. Yet, she insisted on Eve's weakness. The fact that she bolstered her other arguments with patristic sources, but did not bolster this argument by citing Hildegard of Bingen, who earlier made it, shows that she must have been ignorant of Hildegard's work.

On the other hand, Laura Cereta (1469–99) a generation later and representing the third generation of Italian women humanists, was familiar with Nogarola's work.[26] Born in Brescia, she was very well educated and had an unusual interest and training in mathematics through her father, who supervised military construction. Married at fifteen and early widowed, she not only continued her literary correspondence and studies during her marriage, but recovered from her great grief after her husband's death by continuing her writing. She suffered much disparagement from male humanists, who charged that her father must have written her letters because no woman could have done so. Cereta answered her detractors with spirited invective. In one letter she attacked a male humanist who paid too much attention to women's appearance:

> Therefore, Augustine, ... I wish you would pay no attention to my age or at least my sex. For [woman's] nature is not immune to sin; nature produced our mother [Eve], not from earth or rock, but from Adam's humanity. . . . We are quite an imperfect animal, and our puny strength is not sufficient for mighty battles. [But] you great men, wielding such authority, commanding such success . . . be careful . . . .For where there is greater wisdom, there lies greater guilt.[27]

Here, she clearly relied on Nogarola's line of reasoning in defense of Eve.

Marguerite d'Angoulême, Queen of Navarre and sister of King Francis I (1492–1549), in her *Mirror of the Sinful Soul*, published 1531, offered a feminine and at times feminist theology. She was a humanist and greatly influenced by Calvin's theology, although she never left the Catholic Church. At her court, she became a protector of humanists and Protestant reformers. In her writings she accepted the Lutheran concept of *sola fides* (by faith alone) when she stated in her Preface that only "the gift of faith . . . gives one knowledge of Goodness, Wisdom and Power."[28] Marguerite, through her mentor Lefevre d'Etaples, was most likely familiar with the writings of the mystics Hildegard of Bingen and Mechthild of Hackeborn, which may have strengthened her conviction in her religious mission and her right to offer her own spiritual insights. She chose a female narrator and interpreter for her book and focused in her citations on biblical passages relating to women. Echoing the mystical ecstasy of her female predecessors she stressed God's special blessing bestowed on her as a woman:

> You call me friend, bride, and beautiful:
> If I am, you have made me so. . . .
> As I listen to you I hear myself called Mother
> Sister, Daughter, Bride. Ah, the soul that can
> Feel this sweetness is all but consumed,
> Melted, burned, reduced to nothing.[29]

In a passage describing the torment of the sinful soul, whom she identifies as herself, she interpreted a biblical passage quite literally in such a way as to give heightened significance to the female in relation to the Divine:

> Will my spirit dare speak out
> and name you Father? Yes, and ours:
> This you have permitted in the Our Father. . . .
> But Lord, if you are my Father
> May I think that I am your Mother?
> To engender you by whom I am created:
> This is a mystery I cannot comprehend:
> But you ended my doubt
> When, in preaching, stretching forth your arms
> You said: "Those who do the will of my Father
> Are my brothers, and my sisters, and my mother."[30]

Marguerite's bold suggestion of the "mystery" that she might "engender you by whom I am created" assumes at the very least woman's total equality with man in relation to the Divine and hints at the mystery of Mary's role in the Redemption. It is typical of the "slant" way in which women reinterpret scripture that it is hidden in the respectful question of a sinful soul to God, yet it is bolstered by a carefully chosen biblical text which Marguerite does not hesitate to interpret freely and with assurance.

Such assurance undoubtedly derived from the queen's powerful and privileged position in society. On the other hand, as we have seen earlier in the case of Marguerite Porète, unorthodox interpretations of the biblical texts on the part of unprotected women were highly dangerous and could lead to accusations of heresy and witchcraft. An English contemporary of Marguerite de Navarre, Anne Askew, daughter of a courtier of Henry VIII and well educated, found herself gravely at risk when her uneducated Catholic husband cast her and her two children out, accusing her of heresy because of her membership in the Reformed church. Anne Askew demanded a divorce, which was not granted, and then lived alone and unprotected in London, moving in court circles. Officially accused of heresy, she wrote down the record of her own examinations before a religious court. It is a most unusual record, revealing Askew's courage and sharp wit and her insistence on her right and ability to interpret scripture. When the Bishop cited St. Paul against her,

> I answered hym that I newe Paules meanynge so as he, which is, i Corinthiorium, xiiii, that a woman ought not to speake in the congregacyon by way of teachynge. And then I asked hym, how many women

he had seane, go into the pulpett and preache. He sayde, he never sawe non. Then I sayd, he ought to fynde no faute in poore women, except they had offended the lawe.[31]

Askew confidently assumes her right to interpret St. Paul and to argue fine points of meaning with a bishop. When Margery Kempe, similarly accused, had used a similar defense—namely, that she was not preaching in a pulpit, but merely teaching—she had been vindicated by her accusers. Anne Askew was not that lucky. When the Bishop pressed her to "make hym an answere to hys mynde," she refused, saying, "God hath given me the gyfte of knowledge, but not of utteraunce." Kept in prison, she was further questioned by a priest who tried to gain her confidence and again she refused to answer. "I will not do it, bycause I perceyve ye come to tempt me. And he sayd it was agaynst the ordre of scoles, that he whych asked the questyen, shuld answer it. I told hym, I was but a woman & knewe not the course of scoles."[32] Here again, Askew's ability to define the discourse, even under the most adverse circumstances, is remarkable. Men who keep women out of schools, nevertheless want them to abide by the rules of schools—this she refuses. The result of her refusals is catastrophic. She was put on the rack with the object of getting her to reveal the names of like-minded members of the nobility. She remained silent under severe torture and did not crye out "tyll I was nigh dead." She was then freed from the rack and fainted. When she was brought to, "I sate 11 longe houres reasonynge with my lorde Chauncellour upon the bare floore." The description is graphic and compelling—after having been tortured by the Chancellor's orders, she sat for hours upon the bare floor reasoning with him. Such insistence on the right to reason with authority could end only one way: Anne Askew was burnt at the stake as a heretic in 1546.

Nearly forty years later a prolonged pamphlet debate concerning women and following the earlier tradition of the *querelle des femmes* in France took place in England. In both countries the debate was started by the publication of an anti-feminist pamphlet, which summarized all the arguments against women in medieval and patristic literature, which in turn led to a spirited defense of women on the part of male and female pamphleteers. In both countries the anti-feminist pamphlets enjoyed greater popularity and were much more frequently reprinted than the feminist answers.[33]

In England the earliest of the female pamphleteers, one Jane Anger, responded to a misogynist pamphlet in a woman-centered defense she called *Her protection for women . . .*[34] Anger reiterated the older interpretation of the Creation story but gave it a particular gloss:

> The creation of man and woman at the first, he being formed *In principio* of dross and filthy clay, did so remain until God saw that in him his workmanship was good, and therefore by the transformation of the dust which was loathsome unto flesh it became purified. Then lacking a help for him, God, making woman of man's flesh that she might be purer than he, doth evidently show how far we women are more excellent than men. Our bodies are fruitful, whereby the world increaseth, and our care wonderful, by which man is preserved. From woman sprang man's salvation. A woman was the first that believed, and a woman likewise the first that repented of sin.[35]

Anger's extension of the argument for Eve's superiority through the act of creation to the results of the Fall—namely, that it is Eve to whom the blessings of procreation are given after the Fall—will be much used by other female Bible commentators in later periods without their being aware of Anger's earlier argument. It appears to be original with her in this pamphlet. Anger continued that argument in a homely, common-sense manner, when she listed all the services women render to men in rather graphic detail. "They are comforted by our means," she asserted. Women nourish men and keep them clean and healthy. "Without our care they lie in their beds as dogs in litter and go like lousy mackerel swimming in the heat of summer."[36] As others before and after her, Anger listed virtuous women from Antiquity and from the Bible in support of her assertions.

In 1615 one Joseph Swetnam (pseud.) wrote an attack on women which became an instant bestseller and was constantly in print for the next one hundred years.[37] He provoked a number of answers in pamphlet form, several of them written by men, but the first of these was written by Rachel Speght, the well-educated daughter of a clergyman who at the time, by her own account, was under twenty years old. Speght's satirical answer to Swetnam is not only a brilliant deconstruction of his illogical and flawed argument, his stylistic quirks and his pompous platitudes, but an elaborate Bible argument, more fully developed than that of any woman writer up to that time, with the exception of Christine de Pisan. Not surprisingly, Speght's authorship was doubted and she was accused of claiming her father's writings as her own. This accusation deeply angered her and she referred to it in openly claiming authorship of her earlier pamphlet and of her later theological work, *Mortality's Memorandum.*[38]

In her attack on Swetnam, Speght took up the old theme that woman (Eve) was made of refined matter, while man was created from dust. She elaborated:

> She was not produced from Adam's foote, to be his too low inferior, nor from his head to be his superior, but from his side, near his heart to be his equall. . . .[39]

She interpreted the question of Eve's guilt in the Fall much as Christine de Pisan had but was sharper in her attack on Adam: "For by the free will, which before his fall he enjoyed, he might have avoided and been free from being burnt or singed with that fire which was kindled by Satan, and blown by Eve."[40] Speght was well read in St. Augustine and the Church fathers, yet she set aside their interpretation of the Fall and contradicted it with her own. She continued her argument by citing Eve's life-giving quality, arguing that although woman had occasioned sin, by "Hevvah's blessed seed" Christ had been born and in Christ male and female are one.[41] More interestingly, she offered a textual critique of St. Paul's statement "It were good for a man not to touch a woman." Speght argued historically, that this was said while the Corinthians were subject to persecution and was advice designed to protect them and their wives from imprisonment or death. She also pointed out that Paul himself later married. This kind of historical critical analysis had not been earlier offered by women.[42]

In a complex argument based on Aristotelian concepts of causation, Speght argued that the true merit of woman must derive from the final cause or end to which she was created by God. Woman like man was made to glorify God, to be a "collateral companion for man to glorify God, in using her body and all the parts, powers and faculties thereof as instruments for his honour."[43] This bold assertion of the sacredness and blessedness of the female body and all its parts was not only a fitting reply to the vile description of the female body by Swetnam but advanced the feminist interpretation of biblical texts. Speght argued also that woman's role as helper put her on an equal footing with man. She then proceeded to cull from the entire biblical texts whatever passages she thought relevant to her points. Her argument is sprightly, well documented and carefully constructed.

Two years after the appearance of Speght's pamphlet the same printer came out with another response to Swetnam's pamphlet by Ester Sowernam. The author was acquainted with Speght's pamphlet, which she considered inadequate because Speght at times condemned women. Sowerman is more aggressive in her tone than Speght and shows more self-assurance, probably based on her rather wide reading in classical literature. She stressed the positive blessings God bestowed on women. After the Fall, God punished both Adam and Eve with death, but

> Justice he administered to Adam; albeit the woman doth taste of justice, yet mercy is reserved for her. And of all the works of mercy which mankind may hope for, the greatest, the most blessed, and the most joyful is promised to woman. Woman supplanted by tasting of fruit, she is punished in bringing forth her own fruit. Yet what by fruit she lost, by fruit she shall recover.[44]

Sowerman reiterated the by now familiar argument derived from Eve's name, "the mother of the living," which expresses the role "for which in her creation she and all women are designed: to be helpers, comforters, joys, and delights."[45] Sowernam then offered an extensive list of biblical heroines from the Old and the New Testament and ended with a witty and devastating attack upon the character, mind and credentials of Joseph Swetnam.

The pamphlet war on the subject of women continued well into the late 17th century in England, when the then fourteen-year-old Sarah Fyge (Field Egerton) (1669/72–1722/23) answered a misogynist attack by one Robert Gould with a long poem, *The Female Advocate*, published in 1686. Its publication so outraged her father that he banished her from his house. Fyge used the familiar argument of Eve's superiority by her creation from refined matter and added her own gloss:

> Thus have I prov'd Woman's Creation good,
> And not inferiour, when right understood,
> To that of Man's; for both one Maker had,
> Which made all good; then how could Eve be bad?[46]

Feminist Bible criticism and reinterpretation are evident also in the work of the 17th-century English poet Aemilia Lanyer. Her volume of religious poems was published in 1611 and carried no fewer than nine dedicatory poems to royal and noble ladies. This literary device was quite common in that period and helped the author win support and favor. The fact that all these dedications are addressed to women speaks to the fact that by then there existed an influential female audience. A major part of the work is a treatment of Christ's passion in which Lanyer went to great lengths to show the active and positive role women played in aid of Christ:

> It pleased our Lord and Saviour Jesus Christ, without the assistance of man . . . to be begotten of a woman, borne of a woman, nourished of a woman, obedient to a woman; and that he healed women, pardoned women, comforted women: yea, even when he was in his greatest agonie and bloodie sweat, going to be crucified, and also in his last houre of his death, tooke care to dispose of a woman: after his resurrection, appeared first to a woman, sent a woman to declare his most glorious resurrection to the rest of his Disciples.[47]

Lanyer described how men betrayed Christ; all the judges, scribes and pharisees were men. She contrasted this with Eve's sin, which seemed small in comparison.

> Our Mother Eve, who tasted of the Tree,
> Giving to Adam what she held most dear,
> Was simply good, and had no power to see,
> The after-coming harm did not appear:
> The subtle Serpent that our Sex betrayed,
> Before our fall so sure a plot had laid . . .
>
> But surely Adam can not be excused,
> Her fault though great, yet he was most to blame;
> What Weakness offered, Strength might have refused,
> Being Lord of all, the greater was his shame:
> Although the Serpent's craft had her abused,
> God's holy word ought all his actions frame,
> For he was Lord and King of all the earth,
> Before poor Eve had either life or breath.

She continued to describe the greater responsibility of Adam for the Fall and moved from it to a strong argument for women's equality:

> You came not in the world without our paine,
> Make that a barre against your crueltie;
> Your fault being greater, why should you disdaine
> Our being equals, free from tyranny?
> If one weake woman simply did offend,
> That sinne of yours, hath no excuse, nor end.[48]

In a forceful and original passage she offered a gendered reading of Christ's passion:

> First went the Crier with open mouth proclayming
> The heavy sentence of Iniquitie,
> the Hangman next, by his base office clayming
> His right in Hell, where sinners never die,
> Carrying the nayles, the people still blaspheming
> their maker, using all impiety:
> The Thieves attending him on either side,
> The Serjeants watching, while the women cri'd.[49]

Lanyer's volume also contains a pastoral elegy in which she described a country estate inhabited only by women, Margaret Clifford, Countess of Cumberland, her young daughter Anne and Aemilia herself, who in the end are forced to separate. The idyllic description, following upon the strongly feminist re-writing of the story of the Fall and Christ's passion, represents a feminist re-visioning of the story of Eden and of the other major core texts of Christianity.

The next major theological discussion of the position of women comes from the pen of the Dutch scholar Anna Maria von Schurman (1607–78). She was perhaps the most celebrated learned woman of the 17th century and was in correspondence with a number of other women intellectuals in different countries. Born in Cologne to Reformed parents, Schurman lived most of her life in Utrecht. Her early artistic talents were matched by her precocious achievements. Her proficiency in arithmetic, geography, astronomy and music was matched by her writing and speaking knowledge of all the major European languages as well as of Latin, Greek, Hebrew, Syrian, Chaldean and Arabic. Her father encouraged her education and urged her not to marry so as not to waste her talent. Her major work, which was widely distributed and acclaimed, was an essay written in Latin, "Whether the Study of Letters is fitting to a Christian Woman," published in 1638. Schurman answered in the affirmative but wanted to restrict such study to single, well-to-do women so that it would not interfere with their domestic responsibilities. Yet the underpinning of her mildly feminist argument for female education was a strong religious argument for the equality of all souls before God. "Whatever leads to true greatness of soul is fitting to a Christian woman. . . . Whatever perfects and adorns human understanding is fitting to Christian woman. . . . Whatever fills the human mind with uncommon and honest delight is fitting to a Christian woman."[50] Schurman's theology did not allow for distinctions of sex in regard to the human mind or soul. She wanted women educated for the glory of God and the salvation of their souls, just like men.

When owing to her mother's death Schurman had to give up her contemplative life and take on the usual domestic duties of women, she sought for other modes of expression and found them in the teachings of Jean de Labadie. She joined a Pietist community and, seemingly, disavowed her earlier preoccupation with study and learning because she no longer believed they led to "true knowledge" and perfection. Rather, she became an active sectarian and recognized leader of her community. She is credited with having developed the form and structure of the Pietist "house church" which gave women unusual opportunities for religious leadership. According to at least one historian, she moved from isolated scholarship to a communal life which combined practical knowledge and spiritual growth.[51]

The Pietist movement produced a remarkable group of women lay preachers and prophets whose sermons in the marketplaces of small German and Dutch towns drew large crowds and whose spiritual autobiographies testified to women's religious leadership. As we have earlier discussed, Anna Vetter preached her vision of women's essential role in the second coming of Christ; Johanna Eleonora Petersen was a recognized leader of the sect and a correspondent with Anna von Schurman and William Penn. Her spiritual autobiography, published in 1688, helped to promote the ideas of her sect and to provide a model of religious leadership for women.[52] Another Pietist preacher and religious writer was Antoinette Bourignon (1606–80), whose tracts were widely read and who lectured and preached in Holland and North Germany. She derived her authority for this public role from "the light of God." Her interpretation of the Creation story reflects the mystical theology of Jacob Böhme, who taught that Adam was an androgyne before the Fall and that the punishment for the Fall was the division of humankind into two sexes. Antoinette Bourignon commented as follows:

> After Adam turned away from God he lost his glorious body, then God fashioned woman out of him. . . . Before the fall there was neither male or female divided but both natures were one in Adam. He created both natures in His image, namely, man and woman together.[53]

We have earlier discussed the important role played by women in the Quaker sects and the major theological work by Margaret Fell, *Women's Speaking Justified, Proved and Allowed by the Scriptures . . .* , published in 1666. Here we need only note the significance of Fell's systematic survey of all biblical texts applicable to women and of her feminist reading of them. While her work is far more extensive than that of her predecessors, she does not, on the whole, offer any novel interpretation in advance of that offered by Rachel Speght, who comes closest to her in attempting a thorough textual review of the biblical references to women. But Fell goes farther than had her predecessors, including George Fox, in her critique of the Pauline texts. Like Luther, Calvin and Milton before her, she charged these texts had been misinterpreted. Like Rachel Speght before her, she chose to read Paul's injunction that women keep silent in the churches in its historical context, saying that it was Paul's intent that both men and women who were out of order should remain silent. She argued that Pauline doctrine had been misinterpreted, and she explicated Paul's dictum "for it is a shame for women to speak in the church" by seeing it in its historical context. The Apostle intended only to eliminate confusion in the meetings by keeping confused members of the congregation from speaking. Fell asserted that all who had received the Spirit of God were released from silence and must speak out to bring about the true redemption of sinners.

Further, Paul's prohibition was to be seen as local, not universal. The argument was not new and it was to be recurrently made by women for the next three centuries. Her argument that Pauline doctrine has no validity for the large numbers of widows and unmarried women, even if one were to take it literally, as she does not, is original and bespeaks the social needs of ever-increasing numbers of self-supporting urban women of her day. Margaret Fell, like earlier mystics, counterposed revelation and the inner light to the rules and dictates of scholars and priests. "God made no difference, but gave his good spirit, as it pleased him both to Man and Woman, as *Deborah, Huldah and Sarah*."[54] Her work was influential among Quaker women both in England and the United States.

In the work of Mary Astell (1666–1731), the theme of women's authorization to prophesy received a much more logical and rational explanation than it had been given by Fell.[55]

Where shall we find a nobler Piece of Poetry than *Deborah's* Song? Or a better and greater Ruler than that renowned Woman, whose Government so much excelled that of the former Judges? And though she had a Husband, she herself judged *Israel*, and consequently was his Sovereign, of whom we know no more than the Name. Which Instance, as I humbly suppose, overthrows the Pretence of *Natural Inferiority*. For it is not the bare Relation of a Fact, by which none ought to be concluded, unless it is conformable to a Rule, and to the Reason of Things: But *Deborah's* Government was conferr'd on her by GOD Himself. Consequently the Sovereignty of a Woman is not contrary to the Law of Nature; for the Law of Nature is the Law of GOD, who cannot contradict himself; and yet it was GOD who inspir'd and approv'd that great Woman, raising her up to Judge and to Deliver His People *Israel*.[56]

Astell went further than her predecessors in questioning the authority of the patriarchal interpreters of Scripture:

Scripture is not always on their Side who make Parade of it, and through their Skill in Languages, and the Tricks of the Schools, wrest it from its genuine Sense to their own Inventions. . . . Because Women, without their own Fault, are kept in Ignorance of the Original, wanting Languages and other Helps to Criticise on the Sacred Text, of which, they know no more, than Men are pleas'd to impart in their Translations.[57]

The argument that women, because of educational deprivation, have been denied their right to interpret is here, to my knowledge, raised for the first time by a woman. It is an argument which would frequently be raised by latter-day feminists. For example, at the end of the 18th century, the American writer Judith Sargent Murray in her essay "On the Equality of the Sexes" (1790) based her defense of Eve in the story of the Fall on an alternate translation of the word "serpent":

It is true some ignoramuses have, absurdly enough informed us, that the beauteous fair of paradise, was seduced from her obedience, by a malignant demon, *in the guise of a baleful serpent*; but we, who are better informed, know that the fallen spirit presented himself to her view, *a shining angel still*; for thus, saith the criticks in the Hebrew tongue, ought the word to be rendered. Let us examine her motive. . . . It doth not appear that she was governed by any one sensual appetite; but merely by a desire of adorning her mind; a laudable ambition fired her soul, and a thirst for knowledge impelled the predilection so fatal in its consequences. Adam could not plead the same deception; assuredly he was not deceived; nor ought we to admire his superior strength, or wonder at his sagacity, when we so often confess that example is much more influential than precept. . . .[58]

In the 19th century the "faulty translation" argument reappeared in the writings of Sarah Grimké. It is also reflected in the unrewarded effort of Julia Smith (1792–1878), a New England abolitionist and woman's rights advocate, who repeated the work of Erasmus in translating the Bible five times "twice from the Greek, twice from the Hebrew and once from the Latin—the Vulgate" in order to arrive at a more authentic text. She accomplished this feat in seven years with the help of her four sisters and published her translation at the age of eighty-four. That her purpose was revisionist is clear from her introduction: "[We] were desirous to learn the exact meaning of every Greek and Hebrew word, from which King James' forty-seven translators had taken their version of the Bible. . . . It was the literal meaning we were seeking."[59] None of these latter-day authors would refer to Astell's earlier argument or indicate any knowledge of it.

Historically, we find individual women reinterpreting the biblical core texts for themselves, each woman reasoning out, as best as she could, alternative interpretations to the patriarchal interpretations she had been taught. Their criticism followed predictable patterns: they juxtaposed contradictory statements from the biblical texts (such as the two versions of Genesis); they used texts from other parts of the Bible to interpret the core texts differently (such as the Song of Deborah to contradict St. Paul); they cited different patristic authorities over the dominant ones. Some women freely reinterpreted, using only their own insight as authority; others selected from various male authorities whatever they could use to construct their arguments. Beginning in the 17th century, these internal criticisms were complemented by external criticism—doubts as to the accuracy of the translations of certain words and phrases; doubts as to the intent of the translators and doubts as to the authenticity of certain sources, such as some of the letters of St. Paul. As arguments from revelation, mystical experience and personal insights were replaced by arguments based on logic and reason, feminist Bible criticism became more systematic. Beginning with Rachel Speght in the 17th century, more critics insisted that interpretation of the core scenes must take the whole biblical text into account. Thus we find passages in which women are praised, given prominence or authority, cited to illuminate passages which seemingly reinforce patriarchal interpretations.

Historical criticism began to appear in the late 17th century, namely, that certain statements must be seen as being applicable only to the time and place in which they were made, but should no longer be considered applicable to the present. Not surprisingly, these arguments were mostly used against the dicta of St. Paul.

In the early 19th century, feminist Bible criticism became more widespread and more thorough than ever before. Much of it went over old ground and repeated arguments made earlier by other women. I will pass over these and discuss only what I regard as new trends in the United States which are significant not so much for their novelty as for their impact on the minds of the generation of women who would organize the first woman's rights movement in 1848. Many of these women came from radical Quaker sects and had for decades before the start of the new movement been engaged in a redefinition of their religious mission and in discussion of woman's place in church and state. [60]

The first American woman who attempted to write a reinterpretation of the biblical text on the scale of Margaret Fell's work was a converted Quaker, Sarah Moore Grimké. Her *Letters on the Equality of the Sexes (1838)*, written ten years before the Seneca Falls convention of 1848 and seven years before Margaret Fuller's more celebrated and widely read book, was the most radical feminist work of her time. The first major feminist book by an American, it was little known in her own day and entirely neglected for over a hundred years.[61]

Sarah Grimké (1792–1873) was the daughter of a leading planter and slaveholder in South Carolina. She had early rebelled against slavery and the subordinate position of women. She left the South permanently after the death of her father and influenced her younger sister Angelina (1805–79) to join her in Philadelphia. Strongly religious, Sarah Grimké moved from one denomination to another in search of a religion which allowed her feminism and anti-racism adequate expression. Reared as an Episcopalian, she became a Methodist, then a Quaker, but affiliated, more by accident than by choice, with the most conservative branch of Quakers in Philadelphia. Disenchanted with them and rejected by them, she was influenced by the Unitarianism of William Ellery Channing and finally, late in her life, embraced Spiritualism. Disappointed with Quaker orthodoxy, Sarah Grimké agreed to accompany her sister Angelina on a lecture tour of New England in behalf of the American Antislavery Society. During this tour, the sisters were severely attacked both in words and with physical threats for daring to speak in public on the highly controversial subject of abolition. It was something respectable women were not supposed to do. *Letters on the Equality of the Sexes* was written in response to these attacks and immediately published in serial fashion in the abolitionist paper *The Liberator.* Thus, this first full-fledged feminist argument came out of direct practical experience and action in the female antislavery movement, which explains its radical feminist tone.[62]

Still, Sarah Grimké, as did all the earlier critics we have discussed, wrote from within an orthodox Christian framework. She considered the biblical text sacred, but tainted by human frailty and error. Her stance was that of a sectarian of the radical left-wing of the Reformation in her insistence on her right to judge the meanings of the biblical text for herself. She wrote:

> My mind is entirely delivered from the superstitious reverence which is attached to the English version of the Bible. King James' translators certainly were not inspired. I therefore claim the original as my standard, *believing that to have been inspired,* and I also claim to judge for myself what is the meaning of the inspired writers.[63]

She reinforced this stance by ending the first letter, in which she discussed the story of Creation and of the Fall, with the phrase "Here I plant myself. God created us equal." This phrase, echoing Luther's statement before the Diet of Worms in 1521, asserts more forcefully than her stated arguments her claim to equality with the founder of Protestantism, with the critic of established church doctrine.[64]

Sarah Grimké, like prior commentators, stressed the early version of Genesis as decisive. She argued that Creation was filled with animals who could have been companions to Adam but that God wanted "to give him a companion, *in all respects his equal;* one who was like himself *a free agent,* gifted with intellect and endowed with immortality."[65] She interpreted the Fall as showing Adam and Eve equally guilty, an interpretation we have previously encountered on the part of a number of writers. But Sarah Grimké's interpretation of God's curse on Eve—"Thou wilt be subject unto thy husband, and he will rule over thee"—was innovative. She argued that the curse is

> simple prophecy. The Hebrew, like the French language, uses the same word to express shall and will. Our translators having been accustomed to exercise lordship over their wives and seeing only through the medium of a perverted judgement . . . translated it *shall* instead of *will,*

and thus converted a prediction to Eve into a command to Adam; for observe it, it is addressed to the woman and not to the man.[66]

The "prophecy" interpretation of this section had been earlier made by Mary Astell, but there is no evidence Grimké knew of it. Her effort to base her interpretation on linguistic grounds is original with her. More important is her insistence on the bad faith of the translators and her feminist effort to historicize their gendered view of the text. Sarah Grimké pursued that theme vigorously in succeeding letters. She charged that man had exercised "dominion" over women "for nearly six thousand years" and continued:

> I ask no favors for my sex. All I ask our brethren is, that they will take their feet from off our necks and permit us to stand upright on that ground which God designed us to occupy. . . . All history attests that man has subjected woman to his will, used her as a means to promote his selfish gratification, to minister to his sensual pleasures, to be in-strumental in promoting his comfort; but never has he desired to ele-vate her to that rank she was created to fill. He has done all he could to debase and enslave her mind; and now he looks triumphantly on the ruin he has wrought, and says, the being thus deeply injured is his inferior.[67]

Here Grimké moved far ahead of her predecessors and her contemporaries. Men have not only degraded women, but have made them mere instruments for their own comfort. They have enslaved women's minds, deprived them of education and finally robbed them of the knowledge of their equal humanity. These charges will not appear anywhere else until the 1850 Woman's Rights Convention held in Ohio and even there they appear in isolation, not as part of a feminist world view which dares to challenge patriarchal thought.[68]

Sarah Grimké proceeded to build her challenge to patriarchy by critically surveying various aspects of women's conditions at different times and in different places. She gave a cursory overview of women's status in Asia and Africa and in various historical periods ranging from Ancient Mesopotamia to Antiquity, through European history to the American present. She attacked discrimination against women in education, law, economic opportunities and within the family. Her exposure of the sexual exploitation of women in marriage was particularly advanced for her time. She argued for women's equal access to the ministry and outlined in detail all the biblical passages authorizing women as teachers and prophets. Her analysis of St. Paul was historical and critical, and she pointed out every contradiction in the biblical account. She asked, if women are not allowed to preach or teach, why then are many young women now employed as Sunday school teachers, ostensibly breaking the Pauline injunction and yet "warned not to overstep the bounds set for us by our brethren in another? Simply . . . because in the one case we subserve *their* views and *their interests*, and act in subordination to them; whilst in the other, we come in contact with their interests, and claim to be on an equality with them in . . . the ministry of the word."[69] In an earlier passage she had summarized the most advanced part of her analysis, which would be "reinvented" many times over by future generations of feminists:

> I mention [this] . . . only to prove that intellect is not sexed; that strength of mind is not sexed; and that our views about the duties of men and the duties of women, the sphere of man and the sphere of woman, are mere arbitrary opinions, differing in different ages and countries, and dependant solely on the will and judgement of erring mortals.[70]

Here, Sarah Grimké, reasoning by way of a close reading of the scriptural text and relying only on her own judgment and interpretations, defined the difference between sex and gender and stated, in terms which would not be as clearly stated again until late in the 20th century: gender is a culturally variable, arbitrary definition of behavior appropriate to each of the sexes. Feminist Bible criticism had reached the point where it led directly to a feminist world-view.

It remained for feminist criticism to step entirely outside of the bounds of the Christian world-view and to become skeptical, rational, even agnostic. This occurred in the work of Matilda Joslyn Gage and Elizabeth Cady Stanton. Both women, late in their lives, came to a position of skepticism toward all religions and a vague Deism, which found expression in their radical feminist analysis. In a sharp break with all the women we have discussed in this chapter, they no longer accepted the sacred origin of the Bible or the authority of the churches. They saw religion itself as the oppressor of women and rejected the biblical text as having no authority whatsoever over women's lives and morality.

Matilda Gage, speaking during a Free Thought convention held at Watkins, New York, in 1878, stated that "the Bible and the orthodox church were the two greatest obstacles in the way of women's advancement."[71] Her sentiments were echoed and approved by Elizabeth Cady Stanton, who recognized that this viewpoint would alienate her from the Woman's Rights movement to which she had devoted most of her life. Stanton wrote:

> The suffrage movement languishes today because the new-comers and many of the old ones are afraid to take an advanced step. We are just in the position of the churches, dead. . . . I am sick of all organizations and will not pledge myself to do one thing, except to join [the newly formed free thought organization, Women's National Liberal Union] and speak. . . . Once out of my present post in the suffrage movement I am a free lance to do and say what I choose and shock people as much as I please.[72]

The Women's National Liberal Union summarized its position in the following resolution:

> That the Christian church of whatever name, is based on the theory that woman was created secondary and inferior to man and brought sin into the world, thus necessitating the sacrifice of the Saviour. That Christianity is false and its foundation a myth which every discovery in science shows to be as baseless as its former belief that the earth was flat.[73]

Matilda Gage and Elizabeth Cady Stanton, in 1895, published their major effort at Bible criticism from a radical feminist point of view, *The Woman's Bible*.[74] As Stanton had expected, the Woman's Rights movement disavowed their book. The fact that Stanton continued for another few years in her leadership role in the National American Woman's Suffrage Association (NAWSA) was due only to Susan B. Anthony's staunch defense of her and to the respect due her as a pioneer of the movement. In fact, her anti-Church and anti-Bible position made her unacceptable to the movement. Interestingly, Anna Howard Shaw, a much more conservative woman's rights leader than Stanton and a Protestant minister, echoed her attack on interpreting the Bible as literal truth.

The Woman's Bible is a work written by committee, making no claim to serious scholarship, yet attempting to summarize then-known Bible criticism. It is arranged as a glossary on various biblical selections pertaining to women, written in an irreverent tone and encouraging the reader to think in a common-sense way about the passages she has been told are sacred. Its very irreverence is what distinguishes it from previous efforts of this kind. Thus, in discussing the story of the Fall, the authors comment that it is doubtful that the snake could stand upright or talk, that it is unlikely that an apple could grow in "the latitude" of paradise and that, at any rate, the Darwinian findings on evolution cast doubt on the biblical story. Yet, with admirable inconsistency, they accept those sections of the text which testify to the dignity of women as gospel truth. They regard Genesis 1:26 as the "first" and true account of Creation and comment that "it dignifies woman as an important factor in the creation, equal in power and glory with man. The second [account] makes her a mere afterthought." Why then two accounts? To the authors "it is evident that some wily writer . . . felt it important for the dignity and dominion of man to effect woman's subordination in some way. . . . The second version [of Genesis]," they conclude, "is a mere allegory."

In view of their intention to summarize feminist Bible criticism, the absence of any references to the prior work of women is particularly telling. Stanton as a young bride had visited the then middle-aged Grimké sisters on their farm in New Jersey. She and both sisters had attended woman's rights meetings together and Stanton was well acquainted with Angelina Grimké's writings. Although there is no direct proof available, it is hard to imagine that she had not at some time read Sarah Grimké's *Letters on the Equality of the Sexes*. And yet, this important earlier work left no seeming imprint on Stanton's work of Bible criticism. On the contrary, she and her collaborators stressed repeatedly the uniqueness of their enterprise. Possibly this was due to their very real alienation from religious thought and their rejection of all feminist Bible criticism which came from within the Christian frame of reference. More likely, it reflects the pattern of the invisibility of prior women's work to the women successors.

Sarah Grimké, in the opening paragraph of her pioneering work wrote: "In attempting to . . . give my views on the Province of Woman, I feel that I am venturing on nearly untrodden ground."[75] Nearly untrodden ground, after more than a thousand years of women's Bible criticism. . . . As one looks back at this unknown, monumental effort one is struck above all by the repetitiveness of the process. Over and over again, individual women criticized and re-interpreted the core biblical texts not knowing that other women before them had already done so. In fact, present-day feminist Bible criticism is going over the same territory and using the very same arguments used for centuries by other women engaged in the same endeavor. Just as Elizabeth Cady Stanton and Matilda Joslyn Gage undertook the monumental task of writing *The Woman's Bible* in total ignorance of the similar work done by generations of predecessors, so do some current feminist critics consider them their earliest antecedents, when in fact the tradition of feminist Bible criticism goes back to the 3rd century A.D.

This is no trivial point. I believe it marks the very essence of the different relationship men and women have to historical process. Isaac Newton, in his famous aphorism—which actually originated with Bernard of Chartres—"If I have seen further, it is by standing on the shoulders of giants," expressed the mode by which the thought of men was shaped into the major concepts of Western civilization. Men created written history and benefited from the transmittal of knowledge from one generation to the other, so that each great thinker could stand "on the shoulders of giants," thereby advancing thought over that of previous generations with maximum efficiency.[76] Women were denied knowledge of their history, and thus each woman had to argue as though no woman before her had ever thought or written. Women had to use their energy to reinvent the wheel, over and over again, generation after generation. Men argued with the giants that preceded them; women argued against the oppressive weight of millennia of patriarchal thought, which denied them authority, even humanity, and when they had to argue they argued with the "great men" of the past, deprived of the empowerment, strength and knowledge women of the past could have offered them. Since they could not ground their argument in the work of women before them, thinking women of each generation had to waste their time, energy and talent on constructing their argument anew. Yet, they never abandoned the effort. Generation after generation, in the face of recurrent discontinuities, women thought their way around and out from under patriarchal thought.

EIGHT

Authorization Through Creativity

FOR MANY CENTURIES women asserted their right to expression, their right to creativity, despite all constraints which thwarted and denied their talents. Female writers variously adapted to gender constraints, circumvented them or openly attacked them. Most of them found it quite impossible to ignore them. Yet there were women whose self-authorization was based solely on their confidence in their own creativity and who empowered themselves as writers and thinkers. Such women recognized that they had talent which enabled them to write and with their writings affect others. Acceptance of that talent as a gift of an almost mysterious nature enabled such women to disregard patriarchal constraints, gender-defined roles and the constant barrage of discouragement every intellectually active woman faced. The inner assurance and serenity that come with form-giving allowed such women to make their own place in the world and to stand by their talent, often in isolation, in loneliness and under the derision of contemporaries. And not a few of these women also advanced in their creative work toward feminist consciousness and its public expression. It is these women who concern us in this chapter.

Modern literary criticism has been much concerned with a debate on whether there is a separate literature of women and whether its existence, in case that can be shown, has a feminist or anti-feminist meaning. Is there a difference between a male and a female poet that can be discerned out of their poetry? The question is unanswerable, because different women have made vastly different choices.

Poets wishing to describe their female experience are quite explicit in their self-identification; they could not and did not wish to write about the male experience nor did they claim to be speaking of some universal female experience. They simply spoke out of their own lives. Others, disguising their feminine lives and not wishing to be judged by a lesser standard than men, adopted male pseudonyms or identities and wrote on presumably gender-free subjects. One can argue that the fact they did so proves more firmly than anything else the existence of a female voice and its denigration in the cultural world of the patriarchy. If the female voice were no different than the male or as acknowledged and honored as the male, there would be no need to abandon, deny or disguise it.

The mind of man or woman is located in a sexed body and that, I assume, would have to make some difference in its expression. The difference might be slight or unimportant, no more important let us say than the difference between a poet living with a frail body and one living with vigorous health, if it were not for the fact that in a patriarchal society sex is a significant marker of difference in power, rights and freedom. More important still, and for the purposes of this book essential to our discussion, is the fact that the male and the female poet live in a gendered society, that is, one in which the societal definitions of behavior and expectations appropriate to the sexes are embedded in every institution of society, in its thought, its language, its cultural product. If one surveys the literary product of Western civilization—books, poems, drama, biographies and auto-biographies, philosophy, religion and history—it becomes clear that the conditions under which the talent of men or women finds expression are and have been essentially different for the sexes. And finally, the male or female person of talent lives with a different relationship to history and historical process and that, inevitably, has to affect the form and mode of his or her thought. From this per-spective, female voice and female culture can be seen not as attri-butes of sex, but as products of gendered history.

Only a few examples need to be given of the genre of women's writing of their own experience. They wrote of their own lives, their griefs, their disappointments in love, their sorrow at the deaths of their children, their enjoyment of friendship, their awe and love of God. This is the oldest and most persistent form in which women's voices express themselves. Let us begin with an anonymous poem, which can serve as the prototype for many anonymous ballads and folksongs, all speaking to the plight of women spurned in love or betrayed by men they loved. The poem "Wife's Lament" is from the Exeter Book, an anthology of Anglo-Saxon poems presented to Exeter Cathedral by Leofric, Bishop of Exeter, in the 11th century. The first stanza reads:

> I sing of myself, a sorrowful woman,
> of my own unhap. All I have felt,
> since I grew up, of ill let me say,
> be it new or old—never more than now:
> I have borne the cross of my cares, always.

She describes her plight, her husband's absence, the conflict with her husband's kin.

> They drove me out to dwell in the woods
> under an oak tree, in that old stone-heap.
> Fallen is this house; I am filled with yearning.
> The dales are dim, the downs are high,
> the bitter yards with briars are grown,
> the seats are sorrowful. I am sick at heart,
> he is so far from me. . . .[1]

The theme of unrequited or betrayed love recurs through the centuries in women's poetry and song. Among the Languedoc "troubatrixes," the female troubadours, it sometimes gave rise to unusually frank expressions of the sexual power game. The Countess of Dia (b. *c.*1140), of whom little is known except that she was married and in love with another man, expressed herself with astonishing frankness:

> I've lately been in great distress
> over a knight who once was mine,
> and I want it known for all eternity
> how I loved him to excess.
> Now I see I've been betrayed
> because I wouldn't sleep with him;
> night and day my mind won't rest
> to think of the mistake I've made. . . .
>
> . . .
>
> Handsome friend, charming and kind,
> when shall I have you in my power?
> If only I could lie beside you for an hour
> and embrace you lovingly
> know this, that I'd give almost anything
> to have you in my husband's place,

> but only under the condition
> that you swear to do my bidding.[2]

The end phrase used in the original, "de far tot so qu'ieu volria" (to do whatever I wish), is even stronger than the phrase used in the translation. This distressed and betrayed lady has not lost her sense of self and of her own power. Women of later centuries were not as independent in actuality as were the noble women of the 12th century, nor were they as self-assertive; unrequited love was described by them as a shattering and devastating experience. Thus, the poet Louise Labé of Lyon (1525–66), a woman of the artisan classes who was married to a ropemaker and kept a cultural salon, wrote with great frankness in a series of remarkable poems of her adulterous love for a man who abandoned her:

> I live, I die. I burn myself and drown.
> I am extremely hot in suffering cold:
> my life is soft and hardness uncontrolled.
> When I am happy, then I ache and frown.
> Suddenly I am laughing while I cry
> and in my pleasure I endure deep grief:
> my joy remains and slips out like a thief.
> Suddenly I am blooming and turn dry.
> So Love inconstantly leads me in vain
> and when I think my sorrow has no end
> unthinkingly I find I have no pain.
> But when it seems that joy is in my reign
> and an ecstatic hour is mine to spend,
> He comes and I, in ancient grief, descend.[3]

In another of her poems Labé expressed not only her distress but anger at her lover's betrayal:

> What good is it to me if long ago
> you eloquently praised my golden hair,
> compared my eyes and beauty to the flare
> of two suns where, you say, love bent the bow,
> sending the darts that needled you with grief?
> Where are your tears that faded into the ground?
> Your death? by which your constant love is bound
> in oaths and honor now beyond belief?
> Your brutal goal was to make *me* a slave
> beneath the ruse of being served by you.
> Pardon me, friend, and for once hear me through:
> I am outraged with anger and I rave.

> Yet I am sure, wherever you have gone,
> your martyrdom is hard as my black dawn.[4]

Another theme relating to a common female experience, the grief of the widow, is beautifully expressed in one of Christine de Pizan's poems:

> I am a widow, robed in black, alone:
> my face is sad and I am plainly dressed.
> Dark is my daily life. I am distressed,
> for bitter mourning dries me to the bone.
>
> Of course I feel dejected, dead like stone,
> in tears, silenced, in every way depressed.
> I am a widow, robed in black, alone.
>
> For I have lost the one who makes me own
> the memory of pain with which I am obsessed.
> Gone are the days of joy I once possessed.
> With poison herbs my hard terrain is sewn.
> I am a widow, robed in black, alone.[5]

Poetry such as this comes to us through the centuries, speaking clearly and convincingly of the emotional life of women, of their endurance, forbearance and courage. In a somewhat different mode are works which speak of women's daily experiences in a tone that seemingly accepts male gender definitions and yet defies them or subtly subverts them.

Anne Bradstreet (1612?–1672), an Englishwoman who with her family arrived in Massachusetts in 1630 and combined a traditional life of Puritan domesticity with the inner life of a poet, the first American poet in fact, offers a good example of adaptation to gender constraints. She wrote:

> To sing of Wars, of Captaines, and of Kings,
> Of Cities founded, Common-wealths begun,
> For my mean Pen, are too superior things,
> And, how they all, or each, their dates have run:
> Let Poets, and Historians, set these forth,
> My obscure Verse, shal not so dim their worth.
>
> . . .
>
> I am obnoxious to each carping tongue
> Who sayes my hand a needle better fits,
> A Poet's Pen all scorn I should thus wrong;
> For such despight they cast on female wits:

> If what I doe prove well, it wo'nt advance,
> They'l say it's stolne, or else, it was by chance.
>
> . . .
>
> Let Greeks be Greeks, and Women what they are,
> Men have precendency, and still excel,
> It is but vaine unjustly to wage war;
> Men can doe best, and Women know it well;
> Preheminence in each and all is yours,
> Yet grant some small acknowledgement of ours.[6]

Bradstreet's sweet-tempered moderation can be read as ironic or conformist, but the significant fact is that she persisted all her life in working and publishing as a poet. At what cost to herself and her art can only be surmised. As Adrienne Rich observed: "To have written poems, the first good poems in America, while rearing eight children, lying frequently sick, keeping house at the edge of wilderness, was to have managed a poet's range and extension within confines as severe as any American poet has confronted."[7]

Anne Bradstreet ignored the "carping tongues" and assured herself and the world that she was writing mostly to her children and to praise God. Yet, in every generation, everywhere women were struggling for intellectual expression, some "carping tongue" reminded them of their female limitation, their female duty. Over and over again, we find women directed toward the loom, the shuttle, the distaff, the embroidery frame rather than the pen. Many of them heeded these calls: the artful textiles, the glorious quilts, the richly varied embroideries, the fancywork that decorated churches and homes, all testify to the flourishing creativity of women. And, as Alice Walker reminded us, the creation of gardens was, for many women, a form of art.[8] But the contested ground for men was that of literary creation, of definition. It was here they asserted their so-called prerogatives, claimed superiority of training and intellect, defined exclusionary standards, and used every form of psychological pressure possible to discourage women from claiming any of that terrain. Against such pressure only the strongest in character and motivation could hold their ground. As we have seen, those inspired by divine inspiration were amazingly steadfast. To cite just one example, the Mexican nun Sor Juana de la Cruz (see Chapter Two), when chastised by her confessor for her presumption in writing verse, replied that she could not help it and could not control her ability to do so; it came naturally to her and therefore must be a gift from God. From this she reasoned that she was entitled to write verse.

Women who were not that strongly motivated by religion nevertheless affirmed their talent. The recognition of such inborn talent and the ability to connect with readers through her writing had a powerful effect on the writer. A woman trained to be of service to others and to express her identity only through such service, would suddenly express quite different sentiments. She acknowledged that she wished to be remembered for her own work, her own writings. She wanted to have her authorship confirmed, her identity secured and her memory preserved. In short, she aspired to immortality. This desire and its expression runs totally counter to the studied avoidance of public attention to which women were indoctrinated. Thus, Marie de France (12th century), one of the medieval women best known in her own day, was quite precise in defining her authorship. She said:

> I'll give my name, for memory:
> I am from France, my name's Marie.[9]

In her book of *Lais* she identifies herself as "Marie, who in her time should not be forgotten."[10]

Fully five centuries later, Margaret Cavendish, Duchess of Newcastle (1623–74), ended her brief autobiography with an explanation for her unusual endeavor. She had intended this piece

> to tell the truth, lest after ages should mistake, in not knowing I was daughter to one Master Lucas of St. Johns, near Colchester, in Essex, second wife to the Lord Marquis of Newcastle; for my Lord having had two wives, I might easily have been mistaken, especially if I should die and my Lord marry again.[11]

Her self-definition as daughter and wife probably expresses the consciousness of women of her day quite accurately, but her fear of being mistaken for a preceding or succeeding wife of her "Lord" is remarkable. No matter how she tried to hide the consciousness of her autonomous personality, the hubris of one writing her life could not be fully repressed. It surfaced in another section of the same work when she expressed the hope that "my readers will not think me vain for writing my life, since there have been many that have done the like, as Caesar, Ovid, and many more, both men and women, and I know no reason I may not do so it as well as they."[12] Her self-confident assumption that she is a writer on a par with Caesar and Ovid soon falters. A few sentences later she defends herself against "the censuring readers" who will scornfully ask, "why hath this

Lady writ her own life" and answers: "It is true that 'tis no purpose to the readers, but it is to the authoress, because I write for my own sake, not theirs." Elsewhere in the autobiography she admits to being ambitious "to raise me to Fame's tower, which is to live by remembrance in afterages."[13]

The autobiography abounds in qualifications, explanations and apologies for such unseemly ambition, yet the Duchess's confession has the ring of truth. By her own words, then, the Duchess admits to writing from two motivations: in order to be remembered and for her own sake. The latter marks an important advance in feminist consciousness.

The Duchess of Newcastle was one among a number of women poets and writers who flourished in 17th-century England. Some based their work on their own experience and movingly drew on it for a more universal appeal. Aphra Behn (1640–89) was the first woman writing in English to earn her living by writing; the first woman to succeed as a dramatist (she wrote 14 plays) and the first one to challenge convention and tradition by frankly describing women's pleasure in sexual activities in her poems. In several of these poems the object of desire is a woman; Behn treats the subject without coyness or explanation. Late in her life, she published a series of prose-fiction works which pioneered the development of the novel. She withstood slander, ridicule and slights on her reputation and continued to write as a professional. Her life and struggles made possible the development of additional talented women as serious artists and professionals.

The 17th century also saw a proliferation of women poets emerge to brief notoriety and even fame in the German domain. This was due to the spread of female education and to the fact that the Reformation encouraged religious poetry and tracts as an outlet for female creativity. We have already mentioned the work of Anna Hoyers and of the poet Margaretha Suzanna von Kuntsch (Chapter Six). Although the newly popular literary societies generally excluded women, there were a few exceptions which offered a semi-public forum for creative women. The *"Palmorden"* in 1617 admitted the wife of its president to membership. Another such society, the *"Pegnesische Blumenorden"* in Nürnberg had nineteen female members. Yet even this limited opportunity for women writers led to vicious satirical attacks on women "scribblers." A young and talented poet, Sybilla Schwarz (1621–38), defended herself and other women against these attacks. In a poem entitled "Song Against Envy" she addressed

those who attacked women writers, suggesting that if they were up-
set by female writing, they should stop reading. She argued that the
seat of the Muses was as accessible to female as to male writers and
cited a list of female poets from Sappho to Anna Maria von Schurman to bolster her claim. She ended: "Give up your slander and
your envy. I know I can exist quite well without you, and dedicate
myself to poetry . . . I will not let you suppress me. . . . I will
trust the God who gave me my gifts and for whom I write and I tell
you, he who trusts in God in all matters will conquer world, envy
and death."[14] While her verse survived in posthumous publication,
she died in her teens.

Despite Sybilla Schwarz's defiant rebuttal, women continued to
be attacked for the act of writing. Nearly a hundred years after her
death another female German poet was both honored publicly and
savagely attacked. Christiana Mariana von Ziegler (1695–1760), twice
widowed and having lost both her children, ran a literary salon in
Leipzig, published a book of poetry, gave public lectures in defense
of women's education. She wrote the text of nine cantatas which
Johann Sebastian Bach put to music. Ziegler was the first woman
member ever admitted to the "German Society." She was also crowned
as a poet by the University of Leipzig in 1733. Yet she was attacked
in a number of satirical poems and mocked for her presumption. In
a poem "The Female Poet and the Muses" she expressed her anxiety
and defeat. She described how her inner urgings made her aspire to
reach Olympus because she knew that there the Muses, women like
herself, sang (worked as poets). But when she reached the sacred
mountain the Muses barred her entrance, fearing that Apollo might
prefer her to them.[15] Here, the despair over thwarted ambition is
turned into female self-hatred: this poet was not barred by hostile
men (as she was in reality) but by jealous females.

Yet, Sidonia Hedwig Zäunemann (1717–40) was so much influenced by Ziegler's fame that she embarked on a career as a writer.
"Her example heated up my blood," she wrote. She ignored the
usual "feminine" themes; instead she traveled widely by horse, often
in man's clothing and without chaperone and wrote of what she observed. One of her feats was to go underground in a mine and describe her impressions in a poem. In 1738 she was crowned "Imperial Poetess" by the University of Göttingen and after receiving this
honor she published her first volume of poems. Still, her success
exacted the usual price—in a long poem entitled "Virgin's Bliss" she
extolled the virtues of convent life. Virgins could live there in peace

and quiet, away from malicious gossip, while wives had to live in constant fear that a husband's kind words would only too soon turn to anger and blows. Presumably, Zäunemann explained her decision to forgo marriage in this poem, repeating a strategy for the avoidance of traditional gender-roles used by women for many centuries. Two years after the publication of her book, she died in an accident while traveling.

The harassment and disapproval of women writers was so commonplace an experience that it transcended national and ethnic boundaries. It is interesting to compare the experience of an 18th-century Jewish poet with those of the 17th-century German women we have just discussed. Rachel Morpurgo was that rarest of rarities, a female Jewish poet whose work has survived, who forcefully expressed the frustration at the conditions under which she had to work. Rachel Morpurgo (1790–1871) was born in Trieste into a family renowned for its learning. She was given an unusually good education for a girl, mastering Hebrew, the Bible, the Talmud and later Jewish literature. She refused an arranged marriage and married a man of her own choice. Writing in Hebrew, she won some renown as a poet.

> Woe is me, my soul says, how bitter is my fate,
> My spirit overweening aspired to be great.
> I hear a voice pronounce: your song deserves high state.
> What peers have you, Rachel, mistress of song?
>
> My spirit rebukes me: my virtue is held a sin,
> Exile after exile has withered my skin,
> My pungence is gone, my vineyard's cropped thin,
> Fearing disgrace, I can no longer sing.
>
> To the north I have turned, to south, east and west,
> "Woman's mind is frail," how can this one be best?
> After years if her memory's put to the test,
> Will it surpass a dead dog knowing province or town?
> Wherever you go, you will hear all around:
> The wisdom of woman to the distaff is bound.[16]

During the 18th century there appear a few women from the poorer classes who had acquired enough education to express themselves in verse and who managed to publish their poems. One of these is the Englishwoman Mary Collier (1689/90–after 1759). She was born in a poor family in Sussex and acquired her reading through her parents. She earned her living as a washer-woman, probably also as a domestic worker and seasonal agricultural laborer. In 1739 she responded angrily to a poem, "The Thresher's Labour" (1736), written by Stephen Duck who, echoing the prevailing attitudes toward women, casually denigrated the worth and effort of women field-workers. Mary Collier stated that on reading it she felt a "strong propensity to call an Army of Amazons to vindicate the injured Sex." She was encouraged by her employers to publish her long poem. In it she described the long day of field labor for the women and their double day:

> . . . when we home are come,
> We find again our Work but just begun;
> So many Things for our Attendance call,
> Had we ten Hands, we could employ them all.
> Our children put to Bed, with greatest Care
> We all Things for you coming home prepare:
> You sup, and go to Bed without Delay.
> And rest yourselves till the ensuing Day;
> While we, alas! but little Sleep can have,
> Because our froward [!] Children cry and rave;
> Yet, without fail, soon as Day-light does spring,
> We in the Field again our work begin.[17]

The poem continued to describe the unceasing toil of women domestic workers and washer-women in great detail, making the double burden of women's work a vividly felt experience.

Another example of a lower-class woman poet writing about her own experience is the German Anna Louisa Karsch (1722–91). Born into a poverty-stricken peasant family, she had a childhood of drudgery and barren of formal education. Yet she developed an astonishing talent for versifying, which she managed to turn into a source of livelihood by doing occasional verse for other villagers in exchange for food or small coin. Her proficiency enabled her to supplement the family income and help support her children in a marriage with an improvident, alcoholic husband who abused her and whom she divorced after eleven years of marriage. This woman's talents were brought to the attention of some local noble ladies, who made a sort of household pet of her and brought her and her children into educated society. Most of Karsch's literary production is quite conventional and devoid of interest. She was forced into the life of the "trained poodle" and managed to become self-supporting, even supporting another improvident husband and her seven children and relatives, by selling her poetic ability in the market. A collection of her poems appeared under the sponsorship of the poet Gleim, and she was introduced to Emperor Frederick II, who praised her abilities. Yet, in her later years she was reduced to begging noble ladies for financial help. In several poems she wrote for that purpose she offered a realistic description of her economic plight, describing the cold, the hunger, and the raggedness of her existence in spare language. In this particular poem she deals with her unhappy marriage:

> Oh, blasted holiness of marriage rack!
> I tremble when my mind starts looking back:
> How horrid was the state of being a slave . . .
> Covered with human skin, a hellish knave
> stood lordly over me, without restraint
> shouting his rage against my small complaint.
> Mocking my soft heart, for ten years
> he tore the pages holding my ideas.
> For this man, fallible through drink,
> my life's assassin, could not think.
> His walk, his word, his look were my bitter lot.
> Preserve and shelter me from such a man, oh God.[18]

Poets like Mary Collier and Anna Louisa Karsch add the voice of working-class women to the record of women's struggle for self-expression.

Late in the 18th century, writing became a means of earning a livelihood for a small number of Englishwomen. The emergence of middle-class women as professional writers was a product of many causes, all of them connected with modernization. Urbanization brought the emergence of daily newspapers and weekly or monthly magazines. The spread of education and of increased leisure for middle-class women led to the growth of female readership. The patronage system for the support of the arts began to give way to commercialism, and women began publishing books for profit. Sarah Fielding, Charlotte Smith and Susannah Rowson supported themselves and their families by their pens. The essayist Elizabeth Montagu, the historian Catharine Macaulay and Mary Wollstonecraft were among the women who earned their living by non-fiction writing.[19] In the United States, a changed environment for women of talent did not develop until the 19th century, when we see the flourishing of women fiction writers, biographers and compilers of notable women's biographies as well as journalists and magazine writers.

The women's novels of the 18th century began a genre that came to its fullest development in England, France, Germany and in America only in the 19th century. It is no accident that most of the great female novelists, Jane Austen, the Brontës, George Eliot, George Sand, Fanny Lewald, Annette Droste-Hülshoff, work in that period. Elizabeth Barrett Browning expanded the poetic form to give it novelistic dimensions in her widely read feminist verse-novel *Aurora Leigh*. Margaret Fuller, the African-American writer Frances Ellen Watkins Harper, Florence Nightingale and Helen Hunt Jackson are several among the many women writing non-fiction works which greatly influenced their contemporaries. With them, at last, the centuries-old struggle of women for the right to think and the right to define had come to fruition. These writers cast off the shackles of gender-definition and used their minds' potential, stretching to farther reaches than women had ever been able to reach.

WE HAVE SEEN throughout this book that women's autonomy had to be hard won before creativity could flourish. The cultural context for women's creativity was quite different from that of men. The absence of heroines and of Women's History crippled even the most talented women or deflected their talents into less ambitious or shorter forms: poems rather than drama cycles; letters and journals rather than works of philosophy. The social embarrassment connected with female authorship and publication created enormous tensions in women of talent, whose gifts, to be fully realized, demanded ambition, long-range goal-setting and a desire for fame. The social definitions of "femininity" and the unending familial obligations imposed on women made concentrated attention to professional writing difficult if not impossible for most women. Up until the middle of the 19th century it is rare to find a female writer who did not have to pay for her intellectual productivity with a distorted and unhappy life. Whether women had to forgo their sexual lives in order to have leisure and permission to think, imagine and create, whether they had to abandon marriage and motherhood in order to be free to concentrate on themselves and their intellectual product—they faced more obstacles than did their brothers in the pursuit of similar aims.

Beginning with Aphra Behn, there were also some women who defied societal taboos and led liberated or at least unconventional lives. They paid a heavy price for whatever happiness they derived from their lifestyles, and in a number of cases their work was repressed or denied a reading public because of the scandal they created. Mary Wollstonecraft is the best known example of this pattern: she was a writer reaching a wide reading public when, after her early death in childbirth, her life became a scandal. This was due to her husband's decision to publish a memoir of her life and a collection of her letters to her lover which made it apparent that she had had an illegitimate child and lived with two men outside of marriage. Thereafter, her life was paraded as an example of debauchery and of the linkage between feminism and deviance. This kind of attack on her was made all through the 19th century and was still being printed in the 1950s. It undoubtedly discouraged other women from having access to her work and from taking it seriously.

Frances Wright, a radical Scotswoman living in the United States in the 1820s and 30s, who was a follower of Robert Dale Owen and who formed a utopian colony of her own, was slandered in press and pulpit and lost most of her influence because of her advocacy of sexual freedom and racial intermarriage. Her name became an epithet, actually; to be a "Fanny Wrightist" was to be a deviant. These are just two examples of many others that could be cited from different countries. Women's lives and women's work were constantly in tension with patriarchal gender definitions.

THE DENIAL TO WOMEN of equal access to institutions of higher learning made it difficult for women writers to come into discourse with learned men. This may have been an actual advantage for the creative writers, since it freed them for innovation and creating works of the imagination. Most of the early great novelists, male or female, were not university-educated. But the absence of access to the universities deprived women of sheltered spaces for creative work and of a community of like-minded people on whom to test out their ideas. We will see in succeeding chapters how important the existence of such sheltered spaces and such communities were for the formation of women's consciousness.

We have seen in our discussion of the intellectual development of European women that their struggle for authorization was a necessary prerequisite for their empowerment as writers and thinkers. We have seen how some women achieved this by means of divine inspiration, mystic revelation or a sense of a special religious calling. Others were empowered by their role as mothers and educators of the young. Last, the women we discussed in this chapter were led to self-authorization by an acceptance of the demands of their talent. For women the assertion of their full humanity before God, of their full equality as human beings and of their autonomy as thinkers were truly revolutionary expressions. Individual women of talent made such statements of self-assertion as early as Hrosvitha of Gandersheim in the 8th century and, in the face of massive indifference, denial and denigration that statement had to be made over and over again. The Duchess of Newcastle assuring us that she was writing "for her own sake"; Anna Maria von Schurman asserting that women should be learned for the sake of learning—here were the roots of female cultural autonomy, arising in most unpropitious soil. It is fitting to close this chapter with Emily Dickinson, a woman who more than any of the creative women who preceded her was, in the words of one of her most recent interpreters, "the creator of her own discourse."[20] While her extreme mode of triumphing over conditions that threatened to thwart and deflect her talent belongs to an earlier time, she opened the path to the future and won the immortality she so boldly claimed by speaking as a free mind, a free soul and a woman. In this sense, Dickinson appears as the perfection and culmination of centuries of women's struggles for self-definition.

"I DWELL IN Possibility," wrote Emily Dickinson. That she was a genius is beyond doubt and that her genius was fully understood and protected by her is clearly evident both in her work and in her life. After a conventional childhood and adolescence she became in the last decades of her life a near-recluse in her father's house, seeing only her closest relatives and seldom leaving her room. She cultivated notable eccentricities, such as dressing only in white and speaking to even close friends only from behind a half-opened door. Her carefully calculated stance of the recluse and introvert freed her from unwanted social obligations, from the need to explain her refusal to get married and from many of the domestic obligations expected of young women of her class. It allowed her space and time to work and think. Her decision to live the life of a recluse can better be understood if she is placed along a continuum of women thinkers throughout the centuries, struggling to authorize themselves to creativity.

What first comes to mind is her proximity in life choice and style with several of the great women mystics—Hildegard of Bingen, Mechthild of Magdeburg, Christine Ebner, Julian of Norwich. Their power derived from their rejection of the "normal" life of women, from their chastity, their enclosure, their concentration on the inner self and its visions. Emily Dickinson referred to herself in several poems as a "nun" (#722 and #918), and in her work there are innumerable references to herself as serving mysteries beyond her own comprehension.[21]

Her retreat from public life did not mean a rejection of human contact and community, although the abbess and the cloistered nun had had a much greater involvement with public life than did the Amherst poet. As we have seen, Hildegard created a public role for the mystic visionary and exercised power in the widest possible public arena. Mechthild and Julian of Norwich rejected that kind of power and withdrew from it. The woman Dickinson most closely resembles in her choices is Isotta Nogarola, who deliberately decided to live a secluded life, in the company only of her mother, in order to maintain her ability to write. For Isotta that choice was less heroic than necessary; what makes Emily Dickinson's choice so puzzling is that it occurred 500 years after that of Nogarola. Dickinson lived in 19th-century America at a time when women were beginning to find communality in organizing for their rights. Other women coming out of environments not dissimilar to hers turned to club activity, to the struggle for women's higher education, to missionary work and to writing fiction for a readership of women. She, instead, chose seclusion and the life of a poet.[22]

That her choice was deliberate, carefully considered and repeatedly made is evident from a close study of her biography. She had alternatives and chose her life and did so not in bitterness and delusion but in ecstatic creativity and celebration of her hard-won powers. What she won and what she created was the conscious life of the mind, the world in which she was "Empress . . . Queen," the equal of the heroes of myth and literature, a soul free to argue with God and negotiate the terms of her dialogue. Like all great artists, she knew that such rewards come only after rigorous self-discipline and with great concentration of effort. Like all women artists, she knew that such gains cannot be made while performing traditional gender-defined services to a husband, to children, even to the community.

Emily Dickinson, one of the greatest poets in the English language, produced an awesome body of work—1,775 poems—of which fewer than twenty were published during her lifetime and most of these without her permission. This was not due to shyness or oversensitivity, as many of her interpreters have declared, but it was rather another deliberate choice she made, as we will see below.

Emily Dickinson (1830–86) grew up in Amherst, Massachusetts, the middle child in a closely knit family. Her father was a leading citizen and lawyer who served a term in the House of Representatives in Washington and one in the state legislature. He was a stern man, totally devoted to his work, authoritarian in his relationship with his wife and children. Emily saw him as a heroic and admirable figure. She wrote: "I never had a mother. I suppose a mother is one to whom you hurry when you are troubled." "I always ran home to AWE when a child, if anything befell me. He was an awful Mother, but I liked him better than none."[23] Yet her mother was always present in her life, an unhappy, shy woman whose ineffectuality and submissiveness provided no model for her brilliant daughter. "My Mother does not care for thought," Emily once wrote about her.[24] Still, she must have understood the causes of her mother's unhappiness, for she spent much of her time nursing her lovingly through years of invalidism, and she wrote with much affection about her.

Dickinson attended Amherst Academy for seven years. Her training in mathematics, astronomy and science was extraordinarily thorough for a young woman of her day, and her education during those years was equal to that of her brother. She was a brilliant student, had friendships with other students and visited in the homes of friends and neighbors. She liked to cook and excelled in baking, once winning second prize at the Agricultural Fair for her rye and Indian bread.

She attended Mt. Holyoke Academy for one year, but she had no desire to continue there. During the last years of her schooling several religious revivals took place in Amherst and at Mt. Holyoke, but she resisted these strenuously and with lonely defiance. Her ability to say "no" was already well developed at that time. During her twenties she lived much like her younger sister Lavinia—she played the piano, visited neighbors, entertained a number of suitors and took walks in the garden with them. Her father moved his family into "Homestead," the house on Main Street in Amherst which henceforth would be the place of residence for Emily. Years later, when her brother Austin was about to marry, the father built him a house on the adjoining lot.

While the outward events of her life were quite conventional during this time, her inner development was intense. The crisis over religion and her refusal to go the way of her family and friends by experiencing "conversion" were certainly momentous for her future work. Her "wrestle with God," as her biographer Cynthia Griffin Wolff described her lifelong struggle, began in this negative decision. In her religious battles she confronted a patriarchal God who had turned his face away from humankind and refused to reveal his meanings. Her deepest fears over abandonment and loss of love resonated in her poems as despair over the absence of God.[25]

We know that she began writing poetry in 1849, at age nineteen. In a valentine, written to her suitor George Gould and published anonymously in the student paper of the Academy, she wrote "I am Judith the heroine of the Apocrypha and you the orator of Ephesus. That's what they call metaphor in our country. Don't be afraid of it, sir, it won't bite."[26] In 1854 she wrote to her friend Jane Humphrey: "I have dared to do strange things—bold things, and have asked no advice from any."[27] She made clear in references in other letters that "the strange" and "bold things" were connected with her decision to live a poet's life. She experienced this decision as a momentous turning point, a new beginning, and above all empowerment. She wrote:

> They shut me up in Prose—
> As when a little Girl
> They put me in the Closet—
> Because they liked me "still"—
>
> Still! Could themself have peeped—
> And seen my Brain—go round—
> They might as wise have lodged a Bird
> For Treason—in the Pound—
>
> Himself has but to will
> And easy as a Star
> Look down upon Captivity—
> And laugh— No more have I—
> (#613, c. 1862, II, pp. 471–72)

The exultant sense of freedom she expressed here appears in a number of other poems, the strongest of which makes clear that she considered the commitment to her vocation a truly new beginning:

> I'm ceded— I've stopped being Theirs—
> The name They dropped upon my face
> With water, in the country church
> Is finished using, now,
> And They can put it with my Dolls,
> My childhood, and the string of spools,
> I've finished threading—too—

Baptized, before, without the choice,
But this time, consciously, of Grace—
Unto supremest name—
Called to my Full— The Crescent dropped—
Existence's whole Arc, filled up,
With one small Diadem.

My second Rank—- too small the first—
Crowned— Crowing— on my Father's breast—
A half unconscious Queen—
But this time— Adequate— Erect,
With Will to choose, or to reject,
And I choose, just a Crown— (#508, II, pp. 389–90)

She has ceased being her former self, no longer a creature defined by others and named by them. She has given up her baptismal name (role definition) which had not been her choice. But this time, conscious and "called to my Full" she is expressing her vocation, her search for the "one small Diadem." No longer the child on her father's breast, half-unconscious, *she* is now making the decisions, "Adequate—Erect/ With Will to choose, or to reject." The Crown she chooses, the "Diadem," is poetry. The poem has strong religious connotations; the moment described is "confirmation" or a "conversion experience," not based on emotional surrender but on rational grounds.

Sometime in 1862 she wrote:

I reckon— when I count at all—
First— Poets— Then the Sun—
Then Summer— then the Heaven of God—
And then— the List is done—

But, looking back— the First so seems
To Comprehend the Whole—
The Others look a needless Show—
So I write— Poets— All—
[poem continues 2 stanzas] (#569, c. 1862, II, p. 434)

In her reckoning, from here on out, poetry ranked above all other goals to be sought, it even included "the Heaven of God."

From the time of her acknowledgment of her vocation, Dickinson expressed her ambition and her pride in a language of assertiveness and strength no woman before her had ever used and few women since her have matched. Sometimes her own strength and hubris terrified her and she refered to herself as "a volcano," as "Vesuvius at Home":

> On my volcano grows the Grass
> A meditative spot—
> An acre for a Bird to choose
> Would be the General thought—
>
> How red the Fire rocks below—
> How insecure the sod
> Did I disclose
> Would populate with awe my solitude. (#1677, III, p. 1141)

How deceptive her meekness and her quiet conventional life. Beneath it rocks a fire which, if only she disclosed it, would fill the beholder with awe.

The critical and biographical literature on Emily Dickinson is very large. Much of it is formal analysis and criticism of the poems, yet both biographers and critics have been preoccupied with explaining her decision to live the life of a recluse. The earlier critics have sought to explain this decision as being based on unrequited love and much of the writing has consisted of more or less fanciful interpretations of selected references from the poems and letters to identify one or another candidate for her affections. Recently, feminist critics have added to this search by tracing her strong love relationships with one or more women through the poems and letters.[28] All of the evidence, while it remains somewhat mysterious and open to differing interpretations, shows that Dickinson wrote passionately erotic letters and poems throughout her lifetime to both men and women. Those to women are clearly identified as to their object; those to men are carefully disguised, except in the case of Judge Otis Lord, her last object of love, who offered her marriage after the death of his wife.

Dickinson herself refers repeatedly to a deep crisis which occurred somewhere between 1858 and 1862, which brought her close to madness, and from which she gradually recovered. The years following upon this period of her greatest suffering are the years of her most intense creativity. We can reconstruct the various elements which must have brought on the great crisis. First of all there was her disillusionment about her relationship with her father. Her father doted on her brother, whom he considered his primary heir, the promise for the future of the family, his intellectual equal and the source of his pride. Her father extravagantly praised his son's letters from college, considering them "altogether before Shakespeare" and promising to have them published, yet he never took the slightest notice of his daughter's writing. He had expressed himself strongly against the "literary wife" in a series of five articles he had published under a pseudonym in *The New England Inquirer*. In these articles he heaped ridicule and scorn on intellectual women and asserted in the confident voice of authority: "Modesty and sweetness of disposition, and patience and forbearance and fortitude, are the cardinal virtues of the female sex. . . . These will atone for the want of brilliant talents, or great attainments."[29] Surely, there was no want of brilliant female talent in Edward Dickinson's house, but he was blind to it. Emily doted on her father, and bitterly resented his so obvious preference for Austin. She slowly became convinced that her father would never give her what she most wanted from him: the recognition of her worth as an intellectual equal. Neither would her brother Austin.

Early in the 1850s Emily developed a passionate love relationship and friendship with Susan Gilbert, which continued while her brother Austin courted Susan. The fact that Susan turned away from Emily's love and married Austin was experienced by Emily as a betrayal and a devastating disappointment. In a sense it was a double loss, of her brother and of Susan as a lover. Her relationship with her brother never regained the intensity and intellectual sharpness it had had during her adolescence. But Susan Gilbert continued to be an important person in Emily's life and became a trusted friend, perceptive critic and supporter of her work as a poet.[30]

A second passionate love for a woman friend, Kate Anthon, also ended in rejection. The fact that Susan Gilbert and Kate Anthon remained close friends before and after that break might have rendered this disappointment even more bitter for Emily. Feminist critics have suggested the possibility that Dickinson's relationship with Kate Anthon made her realize her latent homosexuality and led to her poetic exploration of homoerotic love in a number of powerful poems.[31]

The strongest primary evidence that her painful rejection in love came from a man are the three unsigned and undated "Master" letters (written *c*.1858, 1861 and 1862) in which she addresses a male "Master," who has rejected her love, in the most abject and submissive way. Her biographers have variously focused on the Rev. Charles Wadsworth or on the editor Samuel Bowles as the object of these letters. Both were distinguished men, inaccessible because they were married, and both were men with whom she maintained lifelong friendship and to whom she sent many letters and poems. Both men had no understanding of her work and were far beneath her intellectually. There is, of course, the possibility that "Master" was a fictive character, a mental construct which enabled Dickinson to work out her ambiguous feelings about her "feminine" role, just as in the poems which concern the "marriage" of two women, two "Queens" alike and equal so that "Neither would be a Queen/Without the Other," she worked out an alternate model of loving and sharing.[32] The comment she made in a letter to Thomas Wentworth Higginson suggests her felt need for a "Master" in her life who could contain the frightening, dynamic forces which at that time seemed to threaten her sanity: "I have no Monarch in my life, and cannot rule myself, and when I try to organize—my little Force explodes—and leaves me bare and charred—."[33] The mystery remains.

Two additional conditions of her life may have helped to bring on the depression and crisis. Dickinson suffered from a visual impairment, which gradually worsened and which in 1862 made her fear she was going blind. She even abandoned her reclusive life in 1864 to spend several months in Boston for treatment of this eye ailment. Another factor was the steady deterioration of her mother's health, which made increasing demands on her time for nursing care.

It is possible a combination of several or some of these traumas produced the crisis Dickinson described as having nearly killed her and brought her to the brink of madness. Lacking the evidence, we will never know the actual causes. But there is no doubt that she saved herself and freed herself from what appears to have been obsession by writing some of the greatest poetry ever written by a woman. The sense of power and victory over fear she experienced after these struggles is reflected in her work:

> If your Nerve, deny you—
> Go above your Nerve—
> He can lean against the Grave,
> If he fear to swerve—
> (#292, I, p. 211.) Poem continues two more stanzas

> 'Tis so appalling—it exhilarates—
> So over Horror, it half Captivates—
> The Soul stares after it, secure—
> To know the worst, leaves no dread more—
> (#281, I, p. 200) Poem continues four more stanzas

In 1857 Dickinson had begun to create "packets" of her poems, arranging them in groups of up to twenty and sewing them neatly together. These may have been copied from earlier compositions, but they indicate a self-conscious effort on the part of the poet to select and create final versions of her work. Between 1858 and 1861 she composed fewer than a hundred poems a year. The next three years bring an astonishing outburst of creativity: 1862—366 poems; 1863—141 poems; 1864—174;1865—85 poems. Thereafter no single year produced more than fifty poems.[34]

Sometime late in the 1850s Dickinson began a number of attempts to get her poems published. She sent poems to Samuel Bowles, editor of the *Springfield Republican*, who finally published four of them. In 1862 she approached Higginson with several letters, asking for his support, his literary advice, his judgment upon her work. She wanted to be not just a poet, she wrote him, but to be a "Representative of the Verse."[35] This was, as she must have known, an impossible ambition for a woman in 19th-century America. Higginson responded with some encouragement, but advised her that her "gait . . . was spasmodic" and her "writing uncontrolled." Although he was an advocate of equal educational opportunities for women, and their literary friendship continued to the end of her life, Higginson did not appreciate her unique gifts. Dickinson must have understood that if a man like Higginson reacted in this way to her writing, she would have little chance of winning the approval of others. Her horror at the fact that the few poems she had submitted to friendly editors had been published with alterations in punctuation and words, fed into her decision to give up the quest for publication rather than to accommodate her style and craft to the demands of the market. With this ultimate refusal she freed herself to write as her talent dictated.

The period from 1866 to her death was the period of her most reclusive life. In 1869 she refused Higginson's invitation to Boston, stating that she no longer left "her father's grounds." She continued her active involvement with her family and with a few close friends and even encouraged new friendships, such as with Helen Hunt Jackson and Mabel Loomis Todd. Both of these women expressed their admiration for her work and Mabel Todd would be the driving force in arranging for posthumous publication of her poems. In the last decade of her life Emily Dickinson gave full and joyous expression to her love for Judge Otis Lord, an old family friend, who deeply reciprocated her feelings. There are indications that she had been in love with him for a long time, when several years after his wife's death he proposed marriage. She refused him. Her habit and practice of solitude was by then too deeply established for her to risk any change in it. The remaining years brought repeated and often shattering encounters with the deaths of loved ones. Emily Dickinson, after several years of illness, died in 1886.

By choice, she had moved her life into metaphor and through words discovered a power of control and creativity far beyond that reached by most writers, male or female. Her work is extraordinary both in form and content. Her wrenched syntax, elliptic language and intense metaphors confined within the smallest possible poetic space endow her work on the humblest subject matter—insects, bees, the movement of grass in the wind—with transcendent metaphysical and allegorical meaning. Like all great artists she created a world of her own, a secret and often mysterious alternate world in which she ruled freely and with total control. The common language of biblical metaphor, Christian myth and poetic reference allowed readers—or rather future readers—some foothold of entry, but Dickinson complicated both entry and participation by the way in which her language transformed the common symbols and gave them her own, quite specific meanings. No woman poet before her had ever probed the depths of her own feelings with such honesty or confronted her own passion, rage and despair with such surgical accuracy and cool detachment.[36]

But her work goes far beyond self-exploration. Dickinson's poems, read in their entirety and read along with her letters, reveal her as a major thinker who created a work of large scale. Like her predecessors, the medieval mystics, Dickinson was concerned with the large, metaphysical questions: man's relationship to God, to death and to Redemption. Unlike them, she was not sustained or supported by an institutional framework of explanation—she rejected both the Church and the Calvinist theology in which she was raised. In their place, she developed a loving and ultimately healing nature philosophy, and she wrote of love, friendship and nurturance, of rejection, betrayal and loss. She wrote of these themes as a woman, out of a consciousness grounded in a deep homoerotic and creative commitment to women.

She had taken loss, disappointment and abandonment through death and absence and turned them into renunciation, transforming them into sources of power. Her feat was subversive, in the best tradition of women's resistance to patriarchy. She turned the very "female virtues" into their opposites: passivity turned to watchfulness and the ability for concentrated listening to inner voices and signs; submissiveness turned into calculated withdrawal to the point of invisibility—I am so small, I disappear, like the mouse, like the bird ("I'm Nobody!"; #288). My weakness entitles my speech to heightened significance, not only because I am "God's trumpet" or a vessel for divine instruction, as Hildegard was, but because I am common, like household chores, like the dailyness of women's lives, like the humble bees and birds and meadow flowers. Renunciation of self was transformed into the immense discipline which could disdain what it could not gain and thus triumph over desire. It was out of this renunciation—which the mystics expressed through their chastity and their mortification of the flesh—that she could gain the arrogance of the God-wrestler, the divine Creator and the keeper of mysteries.

The questions we have asked of her life-choices—Were they necessary? Were they socially conditioned through patriarchal gender definitions? Were they the result of rejection by others?—are all essentially irrelevant. She found a way out of the conditions her life presented to her, and in so doing she dismantled the cage of restraints which patriarchal definition had placed on women of talent. She transformed "the house of her father," which she never physically left and to whose rules she so ostentatiously submitted, into a free temple of ungendered humanity, where the soul stood naked and unencumbered, open at last to all possibilities.

NINE

The Right to Learn, the Right to Teach, the Right to Define

FOR CENTURIES, WOMEN authorized themselves to think and write even though religion, custom and conventional wisdom informed them that these were not pursuits suitable to a woman. Each woman had to overcome her internalized sense of inferiority and empower herself to do what she was told was unseemly, improbable, if not impossible. Small wonder, then, that woman after thinking woman argued her way out of patriarchal confinement and constraints by asserting the intellectual equality of women. Granting men their special tasks and superior talents for leadership, courage and authority, women argued that nevertheless the capacity for reason and the intellectual potential of men and women were the same. It followed logically that the inequalities observable in society, the different rates of achievement, the different interests and activities of men and women were due to their sex-specific education. The systematic educational disadvantaging of women was the root cause of their perceived inferiority. According to this argument, which recurred century after century, the equalization of educational opportunities was the key to women's emancipation. Thus, it was through an argument for women's education that women thought their way towards a theory of women's emancipation, a feminist theory.

As she had in so many other ways, Christine de Pizan pioneered as an advocate of female education. In her work the argument for women's education is stated repeatedly, both explicitly and underlying all other arguments. Christine was bitter about having been denied a good education mostly at the insistence of her mother; she would rather have studied from books than played with dolls. But as a young widow she was able to overcome the deficiencies of her education by great effort, becoming a poet, a writer and a historian. The frontispiece illustrating her *Book of the City of the Ladies* shows two pictures side by side: in one Christine, looking up from reading a book, is in dialogue with the three ladies, Reason, Rectitude and Justice. In the accompanying illustration Christine helps one of the ladies lay the foundation stone for the City of the Ladies. Education gives women the ability to defend themselves and their sex and to found a liberating refuge for women. In thus presenting herself as a learned woman in the very opening of her book, Christine makes of herself an example of what educated women can achieve.[1] After listening to the three ladies explain the purpose of their appearance before her and having them explain the base motives of men who slander women, Christine asks what for her is a crucial question:

> Please enlighten me again, whether it has ever pleased this God, who has bestowed so many favors on women, to honor the feminine sex with the privilege of the virtue of high understanding and great learning, and whether women ever have a clever enough mind for this. I wish very much to know this because men maintain that the mind of women can learn only a little.
> She [Lady Reason] answered, My daughter . . . I tell you again . . . if it were customary to send daughters to school like sons, and if they were taught the natural sciences, they would learn as thoroughly and understand the subtleties of all the arts and sciences as well as men.[2]

Having thus affirmed woman's innate intellectual equality and ascribed to faulty education whatever differences there appear to be between men and women, Christine, probably using her own experience of self-education for comparison, wants to know why women don't learn more? Lady Reason explains that this is due to the constraints on women's activities. Women, confined to their domestic duties, are not challenged to know more and thus remain "simple-minded. All the same, there is no doubt that Nature provided them with the qualities of body and mind found in the wisest and most learned men."[3] Lady Reason then offers examples of the stories of learned women of Antiquity, including the poet Sappho. In response to Christine's inquiry whether any woman ever discovered by herself some new and unknown thing, the Lady reassures her by citing a long list of women from mythology and history: Nicostrata, who invented the Latin alphabet; Minerva, who invented Greek script and cloth-making; Ceres, who invented agriculture; Isis, who discovered the art of planting gardens. Christine, now utterly convinced, states: "It seems to me that neither in the teaching of Aristotle, which has been of great profit to human intelligence . . . nor in that of all the other philosophers who ever lived, could an equal benefit for the world to be found as that . . . [created] by these ladies."[4] The validity of the evidence, which may have been more convincing for the medieval than for the modern reader, is not what matters here. What matters is the strong argument for women's intellectual equality and the recognition that a reinterpretation of past mythology and history might yield a Women's History from which succeeding generations of women might draw inspiration and strength.

In her educational treatise, *Le Livre des trois vertus*, Christine outlined her plan for female education. As a pragmatist, she assumed that men and women have separate duties to perform, therefore the education of boys and girls must be different. Latin and speculative training would not be necessary for girls, but training in mathematics was as important for them as for boys. Girls must also be trained in sewing, knitting, embroidery and weaving. But the larger purposes of education, the development of the whole person into a virtuous and moral human being, must be the same for men and women. Drawing on her own experience as a young widow, she instructed women to prepare for the possibility of having to support themselves. Each woman must develop strength and resourcefulness, she must have "the heart of a man."[5] What she means by that phrase can be seen from her self-representation in another work, in which she describes a miraculous transformation she underwent with the help of the goddess Fortune who turned her into a man so that she might assume the responsibilities of head of household after her husband's death.[6] This extraordinary allegorical representation reflects both the recognition of the reality in which an independent woman became to be seen as a man and the Renaissance stereotype of the exceptional woman of strength, the *virago*. Christine, self-made, newly authorized by necessity, adopted the male virtues of courage, independence and strength and thus, symbolically, became a man. This seems, at first reading, as nothing more than her acceptance of traditional gender roles which forced her to give up her femininity in order to become a strong and active person. But Christine's insistence on the fact that women's intellect and moral judgment are equal to men's allowed her to make this transformation of self without losing her female identity. That redefinition of gender became a principle on which Christine based her concepts of education and her advice to women.

As we have seen, the debate known as the *querelle des femmes*, which Christine had initiated and which continued in the major countries of Europe and in England for a period of four hundred years, focused on questions pertaining to women's education: Were women fully human? Were women capable of absorbing education, exercising reason and controlling their feelings? And if the answer to the first two questions was positive and educational opportunities for women were equalized, what would be the effect on women's willingness to continue their sexual and maternal services to men and to families?

The "learned women" of the Renaissance, who usually were upper-class ladies connected with a particular court which fostered cultural pursuits, had mostly been single. If they married, they gave up their learned pursuits and instead established themselves as patrons of learning. Thus, the question of the effect of learning on woman's domesticity was not one they felt a need to address.[7]

By the beginning of the 16th century there appeared educated women of the urban middle class who expressed a love of learning. One of these is the poet Louise Labé, whose work we have discussed earlier. The wife of a ropemaker in Lyon she dedicated a book of her poetry to a noble lady, Mlle. Clemence de Bourges, and urged her to devote herself to learning and to writing. Women, she thought, should cultivate their minds for their own sake:

> The time having come, Mademoiselle, when the severe laws of men no longer keep women from applying themselves to the sciences and disciplines, it seems to me that those women, who have the means to do so, ought to use that excellent freedom which our sex desired so much formerly, to devote themselves to study.[8]

While Louise Labé's class background was unusual for an educated woman in the 16th century, her views of education were quite typical. Education was to be reserved for women of means, presumably because they were freer of domestic responsibilities than women of the lower orders, and education was to be seen as a means of self-improvement. This way of framing the problem avoided a direct challenge of gender definitions, while advancing an argument for women's education. Several other women used similar strategies.

Anna Maria von Schurman was the most celebrated of these scholarly women. In her Latin treatise *The Learned Maid or, Whether a Maid May Be Scholar* (1641) she advocated, as we have earlier discussed, the education of women for the glory of God and to promote their own salvation. She was quite specific in the restrictions she would put on educational opportunity: the woman must possess at least mediocre mental ability, she must be able to afford the means of instruction, she must have freedom from domestic cares. Schurman explicitly limited her advocacy of female education to single girls of well-to-do families. Yet she vigorously defended women against the various male objections to female education and challenged men to support women in their desire to learn:

> No one can properly judge our ability for study until he has first with the best of motives and with every possible support encouraged us to undertake serious study so that we may acquire a taste for the joys of it.[9]

Schurman's erudition and scholarly achievements did probably more than her writings to promote the idea that women could benefit from education and excel in it. She became during her lifetime the model and inspiration for other women throughout Europe and in England who aspired to intellectual emancipation. Schurman is unique in this respect; her name appears more frequently and more widely in the writings of other women than that of any previous woman. Her correspondence with men and women of many lands spread her influence. It had a different impact on her correspondents, depending on their sex: for men she became the prototype of the woman of genius, the grand exception to the generally accepted image of the intellectually inferior woman; to women she became a heroine and an example to be emulated.

A woman whose feminist tracts were known to Schurman and who may have influenced her was Marie le Jars de Gournay (1565–1645). Like Schurman she remained celibate all her life and thus avoided the conflict between domesticity and learning, but her argument is more openly feminist. She was the daughter of a nobleman who served at the court of King Charles IX of France. She grew up in Paris, but at her father's death, when she was fifteen, economic distress forced the family to move to their country estate. She taught herself Latin and Greek from books and pursued her interest in learning against her mother's wishes. At the age of eighteen she was deeply impressed by reading Michel de Montaigne's *Essais*. When her mother moved her family to Paris in order to present Marie at court, she contrived to meet the then 54-year-old Montaigne, who became her mentor and lifelong friend. He offered her the title "fille d'alliance," which implied the relationship of adopted daughter. The young woman hero-worshipped the statesman and author and he encouraged her literary career. They frequently visited until his death in 1592. Marie de Gournay, at the invitation of Montaigne's widow, became the editor of his work, which was issued in eight editions. She remained single until her death and frequently entered into literary controversy in defense of her mentor.

Her career was blighted by the mockery of her efforts as a serious scholar and by insinuations and slanders regarding her relationship with Montaigne. Later critics long neglected her own work in favor of her editorship. She was the subject of caricature as a *"précieuse"* and was alternately depicted as a failure for not becoming a "female Montaigne." Yet many male and female contemporaries regarded her highly. Schurman corresponded with her until her death and wrote an admiring poem in her honor.[10]

In addition to her editorial work and the translation in verse of the *Aeneid* into French, Gournay published many essays and poems, which were printed in a volume of over a thousand pages in 1626. Her two feminist treatises are of special interest here because of her radical position in favor of the unconditional equality of the sexes and because of her assumption that all differences between the sexes were due to unequal education.

In *Égalité des hommes et des femmes (1622)* she wrote: "If the ladies achieve a degree of excellence less frequently than the men that is entirely due to their lack of good education." She referred to it as a work in defense of the honor of women "oppressed by the tyranny of men," and cited the greatest men as her authorities, Socrates and Plato, Plutarch, Seneca and Montaigne. "The human animal is neither man nor woman. . . . Man and woman are so completely one that, if man is more than woman, then woman is more than man." As had others before her she cited biblical authority, "Man was created male and female . . . and the two are but one."[11]

Her treatise, when first published, did not have the desired impact and she wrote *Grief des Dames (1626)* in a sarcastic tone, upbraiding men for denying women the power of reasoning. Her bitterness was plain:

Happy are you, reader, if you do not belong to the sex to whom all good things are denied, since liberty is forbidden us as is also every virtue . . . and public office and functions. . . . Our only happiness is to rest on ignorance, servitude and the facility of playing the fool if that game pleases him.[12]

She ended by accusing men of ignorance and presumption, since they judged women's work without even bothering to read it.

WITH THE RELIGIOUS WARS of the Reformation, the flourishing of sects and the social experimentation on a grand scale which their appearance and existence brought about, the topic of education became more and more urgent and practical. Education was no longer only a necessity for economic and class advancement, it was now for Protestants the direct means for reaching salvation, a religious responsibility for the individual and for the community. This was reflected in the growth of public schooling in Protestant countries, in the commitment of the Puritan settlers in New England to the establishment of common schools, and in the arguments of Protestant reformers and educators of both sexes. But in order to quiet fears that women, once educated, would abandon their maternal and domestic duties, constraints on women's behavior became an accepted part of the argument for their intellectual emancipation. As we have seen earlier, women defending their sex in the 17th century argued that educated women would not only make better mothers, but better wives and helpmates.

The seeming opportunism and the acceptance of male-defined gender roles such an argument implies have made it unpalatable to modern readers and have obscured the transformative dynamic inherent in it. As long as social and economic conditions made the existence of self-supporting professional women impossible, no one could reason for alternative gender roles. But women could and did reason from their shared educational deprivation that they were a group with definable and collective grievances. Where the argument took this shape it at once became transformative. The individual woman with a wrong was transformed into a member of an aggrieved collectivity. By the end of the 17th century, women began to demand educational opportunities with a greater intensity and with a raised level of political consciousness.

These intellectual developments came, in England, out of a social setting in which educational opportunities for women were severely curtailed, ever since Henry VIII had broken with the Church of Rome and closed all convents and their schools in 1534. For Catholic girls this led to a severe restriction in schooling, and for nearly fifty years the only education available to them was through private tutors or unlicensed illegal schools. Teachers and parents sponsoring such schools were subject to persecution and severe penalties. At the same time there was no system of public education available for Protestant girls of the middle and lower classes. Charity schools for paupers educated girls of that class, but in much smaller numbers than boys.

It was against this background that Mary Ward (1585–1645) established her convent schools. Ward entered the convent of the Poor Clares as a lay sister in 1606 and in 1609 founded a religious community of women in France which ran a school for girls. This was followed by the founding of nearly a dozen communities in various European countries, each of which ran a school for English refugee boarding students, usually upper-class girls, and one for local day pupils, who were the children of the poor. The academic standards of the schools were unusually high, modeled on the schools for boys run by the Jesuits, and included the study of Latin and several foreign languages. From 1619 on Ward endeavored to establish similar schools in England and she sought recognition for her order from the Pope in 1629. Her congregations were suppressed in 1630 and 1631, but she continued to run such schools in England despite persecution. The English Civil War further eroded support for her endeavor, but in 1642 she set up a school in her native York which she directed until her death. It was forced to close shortly after, but the first convent school for girls, modeled on Ward's plan, was established and publicly recognized at York in 1686, after the Restoration.[13]

In the Catholic countries of Europe, the education of girls was mostly provided by Catholic orders. Angela Merici (1474–1540) founded the Ursuline order in Italy. It spread to France, Catholic Germany, Belgium and Holland and provided lower and secondary level education for rich and poor girls alike. Its emphasis was on preparing girls for Catholic motherhood and efficient homemaking. Other orders, such as the Sisters of Charity and the Sisters of Notre Dame of the Visitation offered health care and education to the poor. These religious schools supplemented the inadequate system of French *petites écoles*, local parish schools for both Protestant and Catholic children. By the end of the 18th century France and the territories of Germany offered widespread educational opportunities to urban girls, while such training lagged far behind in Italy and Spain.[14]

BY THE END OF THE 17th century in England, France and Holland some women had identified educational deprivation as the major cause of women's inferior status in society. They used a variety of pragmatic arguments to make their ideas acceptable to the men who had it in their power to actualize them.

In England the earliest female proponents of expanded educational opportunities for women were Bathsua Makin, Hannah Woolley and Mary Astell; all three were self-supporting women. Bathsua Pell Makin (1608?–74?) was orphaned at an early age, briefly married and then widowed. By 1640 she was reputed to be the most learned woman in England. She was tutor and governess of the children of Charles I and ran a school for young women sometime during her life. Her most celebrated pupils were the Princess Elizabeth, daughter of Charles I, who at age nine could read and write Greek, Latin, Hebrew, French and Italian, and Lucy Hastings, Countess of Huntingdon.

Makin's chief argument for women's education, *An Essay to Revive the Ancient Education of Gentlewomen,* was written anonymously. She assured the reader that her "intention is not to equalize Women to Men, much less to make them superior. They are the weaker Sex, yet capable of impressions of great things, something like the best of Men."[15] She stressed that women would derive benefits from education, including the "pleasure . . . founded in Knowledge" and the ability to exercise their minds, and that through education they would better be able to resist heresies. Answering every possible objection to her scheme, she assured men that educated women would make better wives and mothers.

> Had God intended women onely [!] as a finer sort of Cattle, he would not have made them reasonable. . . . God intended Woman as a help-meet to Man, in his constant conversation, and in the concerns of his Family and Estate, when he should most need, in sickness, weakness, absence, death, &c.[!] Whilst we neglect to fit them for these things, we renounce God's Blessing. . . . Married Persons, by vertue [!] of this Education, may be very useful to their Husbands in their Trades, as the Women are in *Holland.* . . . They may improve their Children in Learning, especially the Tongues; I mention it again, because it is a reason of so great weight, that it is sufficient (if there was nothing else) to turn the scale.

. . . None have so great an advantage of making most deep impression on their Children, as Mothers. . . .[16]

Makin proposed an innovative approach to the teaching of foreign languages: to teach English grammar for a year as the foundation for Latin; to begin intense foreign language study with students nine years of age; to start them on Latin, which could be learned in six months, so that they might proceed easily to learning French, which could be acquired in three months. She was able to point to her success with several of her illustrious students in using these methods.[17] But Makin also proposed to include in her curriculum "all things ordinarily taught in other schools," such as cooking, geography, music, singing, writing and keeping accounts.[18] It is interesting to note that in her argument she made extensive use of listing famous women worthies, including among them a large number of her contemporaries.[19]

Hannah Woolley (b.1623), an orphan, kept school from the age of fourteen and then became a governess. She married happily and, after being widowed, remarried and was again widowed. She supported herself by writing cookbooks and other advice books. Her sarcastic comments on women's education well reflect the climate of opinion out of which a more articulate and philosophical feminist argument could arise:

The right Education of the Female Sex, as it is in a manner every where neglected, so it ought to be generally lamented. Most of this depraved Age think a woman learned and wise enough if she can distinguish her husband's bed from another's.[20]

In addition to these three feminist educators, the century also produced a remarkable number of educated aristocratic ladies who through their writings in prose, poetry and drama created the prototype of the educated woman.

In mid-century, Marguerite Cavendish, Duchess of Newcastle, whom we have earlier encountered, gave expression to women's desire for education and to their longing for affirming female friendship. Poorly and haphazardly self-educated, the Duchess was a prolific, if not the most prolific, female writer of her century, having written five "scientific" treatises, published five collections of poetry, two of essays and letters and two volumes of plays. She was stinging in her description of the disabilities women suffered:

We live and Dye, as if we were produced from Beasts, rather than from Men; for, Men are happy, and we Women are miserable; they possess all the Ease, Rest, Pleasure, Wealth, Power, and Fame; whereas Women are Restless with Labour, Easeless with Pain, Melancholy for want of Pleasures, Helpless for want of Fame. Nevertheless, Men are so unconscionable and Cruel against us, that they endeavour to bar all of us of all sorts of Liberty, and will fain bury us in their houses or Beds, as in a Grave. The truth is we live like Batts, or Owls, labour like Beasts, and dye like Worms.[21]

In one of her plays, *The Convent of Pleasure* (1668), the heroine, a wealthy lady, founds a community for women. The heroine, Lady Happy, explains:

Men are the only troublers of Women. . . . they cause their pains, but not their pleasures. . . . Wherefore . . . I will take so many Noble persons of my own Sex, as my Estate will plentifully maintain, such whose Births are greater than their Fortunes, and are resolv'd to live a single life, and vow Virginity: with these I mean to live incloister'd with all the delights and pleasures that are allowable and lawful; my Cloister shall not be a Cloister of restraint, but a place for freedom, not to vex the Senses but to please them.[22]

This utopian vision of female community, printed in 1668, anticipated by a few years the vision of a women's community developed by Mary Astell. But there the similarity ends; the two women, although contemporaries and both concerned with the advancement of women's education, were vastly different in their style and thinking. The Duchess of Newcastle was wealthy, happily married and quite traditional in her thoughts about gender. We have seen how she translated her own ambitions into being the historian of her husband's life and how her incipient feminist sympathies found expressions in eccentricities of clothing and behavior which a woman of her rank could afford without loss of status.

Mary Astell was a gentlewoman of the merchant class; her father was a coal merchant in Newcastle. Orphaned at age twelve, she lived most of her life in genteel poverty supported by the beneficence of mostly female friends. She chose celibacy and rejoiced in the single state, creating for herself a respectable life as an independent writer in London. Her political and religious convictions were conservative; she was a Tory and High Church sympathizer and used her disciplined intelligence to engage in philosophical and political arguments with among others, John Locke.

Astell began her literary career by writing the Rev. John Norris, the Platonist philosopher, regarding several points in his book *Discourses*, with which she disagreed. In her letter she briefly dismissed the objections to learned women which others might raise, but not someone as "Equitable and ingenious" as Mr. Norris. "For though I can't pretend," she continued," to a Multitude of Books, Variety of Languages, the Advantages of Academical Education or any Helps but what my own Curiosity affords; yet *Thinking* is a Stock that no Rational Creature can want."[23] Her comments were so insightful and brilliant that he not only engaged in a lengthy correspondence with her, but insisted after nearly a year of it that they publish it. From the evidence of their published correspondence it appears that she was quite capable of winning a logical argument with this trained philosopher on his own ground. Astell agreed with Norris's precept that God was the cause of all thought and feeling and that "God should be the only object of our Love." But she found it difficult to attain such love. She had indeed "a strong propensity to friendly Love," but she confessed, "I have contracted such a Weakness . . . that it is a very difficult thing for me to love at all without something of a Desire." She made explicit that she was referring to her relationships with women. "I find an agreeable movement in my Soul toward her I love," she stated and continued: "Be pleased . . . to oblige me with a Remedy for this Disorder."[24]

John Norris answered with a generalization, the way he answered each of her questions, that there was a difference between movements of the Soul and of the Body and that "creatures" might be loved *"for* our good, but not loved *as* our Good."[25] But for Astell, this moral commandment was binding and furnished the religious basis for her lifelong dedication to celibacy and platonic friendships with women. Her major feminist work, *A serious Proposal to the Ladies, For the Advancement of their true and great Interest. By a Lover of Her Sex*, published a year before the publication of her correspondence with the Rev. John Norris, embodies this commitment and makes it the foundation for institutional reform.[26]

Like some of her predecessors, Astell was specifically concerned with the fate of single women who were, under then current conditions, forced into unwanted and disadvantageous marriages in order to find economic support. She proposed the founding of a boarding school and home for such women which would also serve as a refuge for those who wished to stay unmarried. Others, better educated as the result of having studied at this school, might be able to contract more favorable and honorable marriages. The tuition, she pointed out, would cost less than families now spent for a dowry. Astell envisioned that for the educated "the whole World is a single Lady's Family." Her appeal was grounded in a strong belief in the power of reason as expressed in the philosophy of Descartes. She encouraged women to think for themselves and to pay less attention to the judgment of others than to their own common sense.

This early work, although it had a great impact on her contemporaries, was far more moderate in its feminist expression than was her work on marriage. It is in this work that she defined most sharply the connection between the educational disadvantaging of women and their lack of power in society:

> Boys have much Time and Pains, Care and Cost bestow'd on their Education, Girls have little or none. The former are early initiated in the Sciences, are made acquainted with ancient and modern Discoveries, they study Books and Men have all imaginable Encouragement; not only Fame, a dry Reward nowadays, but also Title, Authority, Power, and Riches themselves, which Purchase all Things, are the Reward of their Improvement. The latter are restrain'd, frown'd upon, and beat, not *for*, but *from* the Muses; Laughter and Ridicule, that never-failing Scare-Crow, is set up to drive them from the Tree of Knowledge. But if, in spite of all Difficulties Nature prevails, and they can't be kept so ignorant as their Masters would have them, they are star'd upon as Monsters, censur'd, envied, and every way discouraged.
>
> Again, Men are possessed of all Places of Power, Trust and Profit, they make Laws and exercise the Magistracy, not only the sharpest Sword, but even all the Swords and Blunderbusses are theirs, which by the strongest Logick [!] in the World, gives them the best Title to every Thing they please to claim as their Prerogative: Who shall contend with them? Immemorial Prescription is on their Side in these Parts of the World, ancient [!] Tradition and modern Usage! Our Fathers, have all along, both taught and practised Superiority over the weaker Sex. . . .[27]

Astell's *Serious Proposal* was influential in her time; it won sufficient support among noble women so that it is reputed that a lady, possibly Princess Anne herself, offered the money necessary to establish such a school for women. She was dissuaded from the project by the arguments of Church officials, who feared that Astell's proposed "nunnery" would advance the "Popish" cause. Daniel Defoe took up Astell's idea and credited her with it in his *Essay upon Projects* (1697). Among the women who acknowledged the influence of her ideas upon them were Judith Drake, Lady Mary Chudleigh, Lady Mary Wortley Montagu and Elizabeth Elstob.

I have discussed Astell's religious feminist argument in Chapter Seven. In her *Reflections upon Marriage* Astell advanced over her predecessors in her criticism of the institution of marriage and in her advocacy of the single state. Although her indictment of marriage was straightforward and explicit, her political conservatism limited her analysis. She drew an analogy between marriage and the state, but since she did not believe in the right of the subject of the state to rebel even against unjust rule, she had to advise married women to submit as martyrs to unjust and unfair treatment. Her main thrust was therefore to advise women to enter marriage most cautiously or not to marry at all:

> A Woman has no mighty obligations to the Man who makes Love to her; she has no Reason to be fond of being a Wife, or to reckon it a Piece of Preferment when she is taken to be a Man's Upper-Servant; it is no Advantage to her in this World; if rightly manag'd it may prove one as to the next. For she who marries purely to do good, to educate Souls for Heaven, who can be so truly mortified as to lay aside her own Will and Desires, to pay such an intire [!] Submission for Life, to one whom she cannot be sure will always deserve it, does certainly perform a more Heroick [!] Action, than all the famous Masculine Heroes can boast of, she suffers a continual Martyrdom to bring Glory to GOD, and Benefit to Mankind; which Consideration, indeed, may carry her through all Difficulties, I know not what else can, and engage her to Love him who proves perhaps so much worse than a Brute, as to make this Condition yet more grievous than it needed to be. She has need of a strong Reason, of a truly Christian and well-temper'd Spirit, of all the Assistance the best Education can give her, and ought to have some good Assurance of her own Firmness and Vertue, [!] who ventures on such a Trial; and for this Reason 'tis less to be wonder'd at that Women marry off in haste, for perhaps if they took Time to consider and reflect upon it, they seldom would marry.
>
> 'Tis certainly no Arrogance in a Woman to conclude, that she was made for the Service of GOD, and that this is her End. Because GOD made all Things for Himself, and a rational Mind is too noble a Being to be made for the Sake and Service of any Creature. The Service she at any Time becomes oblig'd to pay to a Man, is only a Business by the Bye, just as it may be any Man's Business and Duty to keep Hogs; he was not Made for this, but if he Hires himself out to such and Employment, he ought conscientiously to perform it.[28]

Astell's logical argument for women's emancipation started with religion and with her assumption of the absolute and inherent equality of men and women. Education would elevate women, raise their consciousness of their own situation so that they might better protect themselves from abusive male power. And even those women who chose to get married would benefit from education because it would give them the support of philosophy and religion to bear their lot. Astell's conservative politics and her ascetic, religious commitment shaped her life: she reduced her wants and lived modestly, on the verge of poverty, but also she lived independently, in contact with the major intellectual movements of her time. Her dream of an intellectual women's community seemed utopian to her contemporaries, but in her own modest way she lived it in her later years in Chelsea. Struggling all her life against despondency over her loneliness, the last decade of her life found her surrounded by a caring and supportive circle of female friends. It was probably due to this life experience that she could more strongly than her predecessors project a woman-centered analysis and build a system of thought around it.

Following in her footsteps, other women kept sniping at the prevailing beliefs and mores and expressing disgust and anger at the sexual and societal prerogatives of men.

A sermon preached at a Dorsetshire wedding on May 11, 1699, produced a small pamphlet war in which women defended their sex and their right to education in a sprightly and witty manner. The Rev. John Sprint had used the occasion of the wedding to hold forth on the virtues of the good wife who must be pliant and yielding to her husband's desires. "Woman was made for the Comfort of Man," the minister asserted. "A good wife should be like a Mirror . . . which has no Image of its own, but receives its Stamp and Image from the Face that looks into it." He was answered quite sharply by "A Lady of Quality," who identified herself as "one that never yet came within the Clutches of a Husband."[29] She argued that woman was intended to be a "companion, a Person in whom a Man can confide . . . [not] a Slave sitting at his Footstool." Commenting sarcastically on the Rev. Mr. Sprint's advice that women ought to respect and love even cruel husbands, she charged him with encouraging wife-beating husbands: "He has inflam'd the domineering Temper and heightened the insulting Carriage of a many a barbarous husband."[30] Nothing is known about the anonymous author except her first name.

The same incident inspired another polemical defense of women from the pen of a well-known author. Lady Mary Chudleigh (1656–1710) published a volume of poems in 1703 and one of essays in 1710. She became famous for her poem "The Ladies Defence," which was occasioned by the Rev. Mr. Sprint's marriage sermon. In it she wittily attacked his views and argued for women's education. One of her male spokesmen summarized the masculine viewpoint in these words:

> Then blame us not if we our Interest Mind,
> And would have Knowledge to our selves confin'd.
> Since that alone Pre-eminence does give
> And rob'd of it we should unvalu'd live.
> While you are Ignorant, We are secure. . . .

To which the spokeswoman Melissa answered:

> 'T is hard we should be by the Men despis'd
> Yet kept from knowing what would make us priz'd.
> Debarr'd from Knowledge, banish'd from the Schools,
> And with the utmost Industry bred Fools.
> Laugh'd out of Reason, jested out of Sense,
> And nothing left but Native Innocence:
>
> . . .
>
> But spite of you, we'll to our selves be kind:
> Your Censures slight, your little Tricks despise,
> And make it our whole Business to be wise.
> The mean low trivial Cares of Life disdain, And read and Think,
> and Think and Read again,
> And on our Minds bestow the utmost Pain.[31]

In a remarkable introductory poem, addressed "To the Ladies," Chudleigh described marriage as veritable slavery, charging that "wife and servant are the same, but only differ in the Name." She likened wives to "Mutes, the Signs alone must make,/ and never any Freedom take," but still they must "be govern'd by a Nod,/ and fear her Husband as her God." Chudleigh concluded with this advice to women: "Value yourselves, and Men despise,/ You must be proud, if you'll be wise."[32]

Nearly two generations after Lady Mary Chudleigh's sprightly defense of women, there was another pamphlet war on the subject of women. An anonymous author who called herself "Sophia, a Person of Quality" published a pamphlet which sold for one shilling and bore the challenging title, *WOMAN Not Inferior to MAN or,*

A short and modest Vindication of the natural Right of the FAIR SEX to a perfect Equality of Power, Dignity, and Esteem, with the Men.[33]

Sophia's argument follows closely upon the arguments made by the most advanced feminist thinker of his century, the Frenchman François Poulain de la Barre. His book *De l'égalité des deux sexes* (1673) was published in England in translation in 1677.[34] Like Poulain de la Barre, Sophia argued that the difference in the sexes is only a difference in the body. But the soul has no sex, thus there can be no real difference between men and women. "All the diversity then must come from *education, exercise* and the *impressions* of those *external* objects which surround us in different Circumstances." Women would benefit from learning by developing "an exactness of thought, a propriety of speech, and a justness of actions" and the skill to regulate their passions. Sophia was quite explicit about the cause of women's educational disadvantaging: "Why are they [men] so industrious to debar us that learning we have an equal right to with themselves, but for our sharing with, and outshining them in, those public offices they fill so miserably."[35]

Building a forceful and logical argument, Sophia reasoned that women, since they were intelligent, courageous, virtuous, had the same rights as men to all employments in public life. "If we are not seen in *university chairs,* it cannot be attributed to some want of capacity to fill them, but to that violence with which men support their unjust intrusion into our plans."[36]

Poulain de la Barre had argued that women were capable of holding every office and employment in society, even that of military leaders, but he still assumed that motherhood was the most important task of all women. Sophia followed the first part of his argument but ignored the second. She cited the accomplishments of English queens and continued with admirable coolness:

> I cannot find how the oddity wou'd be greater, to see a lady with a truncheon in her hand, than with a crown on her head; or why it shou'd create more surprise, to see her preside in a council of war, than in a council of state. Why may she not be as capable of heading an army as a parliament; or of commanding at sea as of reigning at land? . . . . The military art has no mystery in it beyond others, which *Women* cannot attain to. A *Woman* is as capable as a *Man* of making herself, by means of a map, acquainted with the good and bad, the dangerous and safe passes, or the proper situations for encampment . . . *Women*

can shew as much eloquence, intrepidity, and warmth, where their honour is at stake, as is requisite to attack or defend a town. . . .

We neither want Spirit, strength, nor courage, to defend a Country,
nor prudence to rule it.[37]

In conclusion, she urged women to give up idle amusements and
to improve their minds. Sophia's argument, while not entirely original with her, is outstanding among those of other 17th-century
feminists for its self-confident and assertive tone.[38]

Despite the modest efforts Bathsua Makin, Mary Astell and Mary
Ward had made in founding schools, English girls had few educational institutions available to them at the end of the 17th century.
The pioneers of women's education had laid a theoretical foundation
for their enterprise and set up a few models, but they had not been
able to go much further. By the beginning of the 18th century the
major form of expression open to educated Englishwomen was in
the salons, where they could engage in intellectual conversations with
literary men and form informal networks of women with intellectual
aspirations. We will discuss this phenomenon more fully in Chapter
Ten.

We can summarize the situation of European intellectual women
at the beginning of the 18th century in saying that they had reached
the first three stages of feminist consciousness: authorization to speak;
inspired speech, and the right to learn and to teach.[39] Even then the
last right was won only by small numbers of women, and it included
only the most elementary levels of teaching; it would take two more
centuries before that right would encompass a majority of European
and American women.

One of the English "bluestockings," as the educated salonières
were derisively called, was Hannah More (1745–1833), a conservative thinker who wrote and worked for improved women's education. Her effort was part of the Sunday school movement which
aimed to elevate the morals of lower-class people by public education. In 1790 Hannah More and her sisters founded eleven village
schools after they had run the most successful girls' school of the
18th century in Bristol for many decades. The village schools were
held on Sunday after church, the only time the hard-working children of laborers and farmers were free. Hannah More won a wide
following for her educational ideas with her essays, novels and tracts.[40]

Despite the lack of progress in ameliorating women's education, discussion of this subject became the main instrument for the development of feminist ideas. For example, in France, the influential treatise by François de Salignac Fenelon *On the Education of Girls* (1686), written for the daughters of a French nobleman, expressed the Renaissance view on the nature of women and on their proper place. Fenelon thought that women's education should prepare them for their social role: noble women should know religion, the management of estates and servants and the economics of contract law. Fenelon's ideas were carried into practice by Mme. de Maintenon, mistress and later wife of King Louis XIV. Beginning in 1680, she founded several small boarding schools and finally St.-Cyr, the first state-supported school for girls in France, which in 1693 was closed by the revolutionary government. The educational plan of St.-Cyr became a model for many of the schools run by the Ursulines.[41]

Whereas Fenelon's educational principles reflected aristocratic and royalist ideas, the movement known as the Enlightenment initiated an intellectual revolution. Enlightenment thinkers, known as *philosophes*, put science in the place of religion and regarded the mind as man's most powerful tool for understanding himself, the world and the universe. Thought alone could help men to comprehend the laws of nature and those that governed the social world. Rejecting revelation, religion and authority, Enlightenment thinkers postulated a self-sufficient individual who derived knowledge from experience. With the proper education, all individuals could become useful and productive citizens in a society organized on the basis of rational principles. The rationalism of René Descartes had a liberating effect on women because it assumed that the mind, not the body, was the instrument for sensation and knowledge and that men and women had the same potential for understanding. Cartesianism denied that formal education was the road to higher insight; anyone could think and reason logically. The effect of these ideas was not only to inspire a number of women, such as Mary Astell, Lady Damaris Masham, Marie de Gournay, to enter philosophical discourse with the outstanding male thinkers of their time, but it also helped them to create a new form for such a discourse through personal correspondence.[42]

John Locke (1632–1704), the principal political theorist of his age, developed an optimistic, rational and secular political philosophy which influenced the founders and Constitution-makers of the United States of America and became the basis for political liberalism.

Locke postulated a benign state of nature without subordination or subjection, in which each individual is endowed with inalienable rights of life, liberty and property. To protect these rights, men enter upon a social contract and establish a state. But this state has no right to deprive individuals of their natural rights; therefore the state must be constitutional government based on the consent of the governed.[43] Locke did not ignore women in his theoretical model, but he separated them out of the social contract by asserting that woman's subordination to man within the family was natural and antedated organized society. Thus men had paternal power over women, but this "natural right" had, according to Locke, nothing to do with civil society—the problem of woman's status as a citizen simply dropped out of sight. Still, contract and natural rights theory provided theoretical weapons for all subordinate groups.[44]

The French philosopher Jean Jacques Rousseau applied Enlightenment ideas to education. One of the most radical thinkers of his day in regard to politics, Rousseau in his book *Émile* designed a scheme of education to form a citizen of the new idealized state. Émile would be educated to be self-reliant, autonomous, and rational. But in regard to women's education Rousseau was utterly conservative. In describing the education suitable for Sophie, Émile's future wife, he assumed that woman's purpose in life was to "tend him in manhood, to counsel and to console, to make his life pleasant and happy, these are the duties of Woman." Rousseau concluded, "Woman is framed particularly for the delight and pleasure of man."[45] Therefore, the purpose of woman's education should be to learn to love her duties toward men and to carry them out intelligently and cheerfully.

Mary Astell challenged Locke in her book *The Christian Religion* from the vantage point of a royalist and a believer in revealed religion.[46] Mary Wollstonecraft, herself a strong advocate of Enlightenment ideas, challenged Locke's neglect of women and claimed that women as well as men had natural rights. Unlike Astell, she accepted the Lockean philosophical and political argument but she expanded his ideas so as to encompass women. Similarly, she accepted Rousseau's ideas about the education of boys but rejected his conservative views of women's education.

While Wollstonecraft's work can no longer be regarded as the *first* full-fledged theoretical work of feminism, it is the first feminist theory to put the claims for women's rights and equality in the context of a broader liberationist theory for all of society and to separate such claims from the religious arguments which had hitherto been central to women's thought. In her major theoretical work, *The Vindication of the Rights of Women*, she reiterated most of the arguments made for the equal education of women since the 17th century, but she strongly challenged Rousseau's definition of women as permanent dependents with the flat statement, "What nonsense! . . . . If women are by nature inferior to men, their virtues must be the same . . . or virtue is a relative idea.[47]

She defined women as oppressed both by society and by men and explicitly reasoned for the solidarity of women. Yet she based her demands for women's rights on women's roles as wives and mothers:

> If children are to be educated to understand the true principle of patriotism, their mother must be a patriot. . . .
>
> As the care of children in their infancy is one of the grand duties annexed to the female character by nature, this duty would afford many forcible arguments for strengthening the female understanding, if it were properly considered. . . . To be a good mother—a woman must have sense, and that independence of mind which few women possess who are taught to depend entirely on their husbands. Meek wives are, in general, foolish mothers. . . .
>
> The conclusion which I wish to draw, is obvious; make women rational creatures, and free citizens, and they will quickly become good wives, and mothers; that is—if men do not neglect the duties of husbands and fathers.[48]

The theme of educated women as more effective and more virtuous mothers is here struck forcefully. It is this theme which will reappear with great force in the late 18th and early 19th century in France, in Germany and in America.

THE DEBATE ON women's education in the early American republic can serve as a prototype of similar debates in European countries. Women's active participation in the American Revolution through fund-raising, boycotts and petitions, their voluntary services in support of the troops, their indispensable economic role on the homefront, all had combined to give women a new sense of self, both in domestic and public roles. The debates around the writing and ratification of the Constitution and of the state constitutions inspired a radical republican ideology which inevitably led some members of groups omitted from the political debate to challenge its limits. An example of this is the debate between John and Abigail Adams we have earlier discussed (Chapter One). The playwright and first historian of the American Revolution, Mercy Otis Warren, created heroic women characters whose strength and dedication to freedom were intended to inspire her female contemporaries. But there was no willingness on the part of the leaders of the new republic to include women in their polity or to grant them a voice in the political debate. Even the concept of "learned women" was seen as dangerous to the unity of the home and with it the community.

Under such circumstances the definition of "Republican Motherhood" had both conservative and liberating aspects. It argued that a broad liberal education of the citizenry was essential for the functioning of republican government. An informed citizenry would guarantee that democratic rights would not be neglected or abused. Mothers would train their sons for republican citizenship and thereby they would perform an appropriate function as participants in the governance of the republic.[49]

The concept was publicly launched in an address given by Benjamin Rush at the opening of the Young Ladies' Academy in Philadelphia in 1787. Rush assumed that men and women would continue to function in separate spheres, but that in a republic the role of mothers would be elevated to a semi-public function. To perform such a function women would of necessity need to be well educated.

The remarkable spread of female academies between 1790 and 1820 shows that his message was expressive of an already established trend. The nature of the education offered in these academies clearly shows their limited concept of the range of women's education. At the Philadelphia Academy, for example, which was advanced for its day, girls were offered a curriculum of Reading, Writing, Arithmetic, English Grammar, Composition, Rhetoric and Geography plus the usual domestic skills. There was no intention to offer girls the same education as boys, rather they were to be educated as pleasing companions, helpers and supporters of middle-class men. The male-defined concept of women as mothers and educators of their children influencing the destiny of their nation, neatly combined an acceptance of gender-defined roles for women with a recognition of their actual and potential impact on political society. It did so in patriarchal terms: women's impact was to be indirect; it was to represent influence, not actual power, and it was to be exerted through others and for others. Above all, such political influence was defined as a secondary consequence of women's primary maternal role, an improvement in their situation and a recognition of their actual function, but not a right from which to mount further claims for equality. This was quite different from the feminist argument made much earlier by such men as Heinrich Cornelius Agrippa von Nettesheim and François Poulain de la Barre who had argued for the absolute equality of men and women on the grounds of religious, moral and natural rights.

Women, in most cases, defined "Republican Motherhood" somewhat differently. An example is a valedictory oration given by one Priscilla Mason at the same Young Ladies' Academy in Philadelphia two years after Rush's lecture. After duly apologizing for addressing "a promiscuous audience," which might be considered "a novelty," Miss Mason proceeded as follows:

> Our high and mighty Lords (thanks to their arbitrary constitutions) have denied us the means of knowledge, and then reproached us for the want of it. Being the stronger party, they early seized the sceptre and the sword . . . they denied women the advantage of a liberal education, forbid them to exercise their talents. . . . Happily a more liberal way of thinking begins to prevail.

She exhorted women in the audience to make the most of the new educational opportunities and asserted their right to employment in the churches and in the courts. Finally, she asked for the formation of a "senate of women . . . delegated from every part of the Union" to be formed as part of the federal government.[50]

A similar argument was made by Judith Sargent Murray in a pamphlet and later expanded in a series of articles. Murray warned young women "against a low estimation of self" which might propel them into hasty and ill-considered marriages, and urged them instead to become self-confident and self-reliant.[51] Eight years later, after having been widowed and having remarried, Murray developed her ideas into a fuller feminist argument in a series of magazine articles. She pointed out that young girls, by being taught contempt for "old maids," were being channeled into accepting any kind of marriage offer. Instead, she urged young women to "respect a single life and even to regard it as the *most eligible*. . . . I know that respectability, usefullness, [!] tranquility, independence, social enjoyments, and holy friendship, are to be found in a single life; and I am induced rationally to conclude, that if minds are not congenial . . . a state of celibacy is by far the most eligible." She urged women to prepare themselves for possible independence by learning "to administer by *their own efforts, to their own wants*."[52] It is noteworthy that she reinvented ideas and arguments earlier expressed by Mary Astell, of whose very existence she was ignorant.

The concept of "Republican Motherhood" was utilized to great advantage by a shrewd and determined educator who made a major contribution to the advancement of women's education in the United States. When in 1819 Emma Willard (1787–1870) presented the New York State legislature with her well-reasoned plan for a publicly supported institution of advanced learning for women, she intended to prove that girls were capable of absorbing the same academic subjects offered to boys. After detailing the inequities and educational disabilities under which women suffered, she argued:

> It is the duty of a government, to do all in its power to promote the present and future prosperity of the nation. . . . This prosperity will depend on the character of its citizens. The characters of these will be formed by their mothers. . . . It is the duty of our present legislators to begin now, to form the characters of the next generation, by controlling that of the females, who are to be their mothers . . . .[53]

Willard, who was not a feminist and would later oppose the organized woman's rights movement, stressed in her *Address* that she did not recommend a "masculine education" for women nor did she argue for women's right to education as citizens. Her plan, although it won some legislative support, was not implemented and she proceeded to found and finance her own school, the Troy Female Seminary, as a pioneering model which set the standards for quality higher education for girls. She ran it like a college preparatory school for boys, offering instruction in all subjects including Math, Science and Philosophy. Her students met formal curricular requirements and passed rigorous public examinations. Willard trained more than 12,000 students in her seminary between 1821 and 1870, many of whom became public school teachers. Others of her students became themselves the founders of schools, while she collaborated with the educator Henry Barnard in formulating his plans for public schools. Despite Willard's conservative stance, the students who had benefited from her rigorous training and moral indoctrination became a moving force for American feminism. Some, like Elizabeth Cady Stanton, would take direct and personal leadership of the woman's movement; others as professional teachers became models for a new definition of American womanhood.[54]

Other pioneers of female education in the United States used the same combination of Republican Motherhood ideology and shrewd pragmatism as had Emma Willard. Catharine Esther Beecher and Mary Lyon accomplished similar feats of institution-building and ideological indoctrination to create new careers for women and imbue them with a missionary zeal for promoting the education of their sex. Both women, like their earlier predecessor, firmly proclaimed themselves opposed to woman's rights advocacy, yet they, like Emma Willard, educated a significant cohort of community leaders, many of whom became feminists.

While the pragmatic institution-builders trained thousands of women professionals and helped to develop a new model of womanhood, a few thinkers broadened the argument for women's education and developed it into the foundation of a feminist world-view. In the American setting this intellectual advance was made by Frances Wright (1795–1852), a wealthy and well educated native of Scotland, who arrived in America in 1824 determined to support and improve American democracy. She was a talented writer and the founder of a short-lived utopian community in which she tried out her various unorthodox schemes for the improvement of society. She advocated a broad spectrum of reforms: the emancipation of slaves, birth control, liberal divorce laws, sexual freedom for both sexes, free public education for all children from age two upward in state-supported boarding schools. The last demand won the support of the first American working-class political party, the briefly successful New York Workingmen's Association. After 1829 she lectured in Ohio, Pennsylvania and New York, gaining some support and arousing much curiosity, hostility and vituperation. A true daughter of the Enlightenment, Frances Wright sought to advance rationalism and the spirit of free inquiry through the equal access of women to education. She said in one of her lectures:

> With regard to their sons, as to their daughters . . . they [parents] have only to consider them as *human beings*, and to ensure them the fair and thorough development of all the faculties, physical, mental and moral, which distinguish their nature. In like manner, as respects their daughters, they have nothing to do with the injustice of laws, nor the absurdities of society. Their duty is plain, evident, decided. In a daughter they have in charge a human being; in a son, the same. . . . Men will ever rise or fall to the level of the other sex. . . . Let them examine the relation in which the two sexes stand, and ever must stand, to each other. . . . Until power is annihilated on one side, fear and obedience on the other, and both restored to their birthright—equality. Let none think that affection can reign without it; or friendship, or

esteem. . . . Go then! and remove the evil first from the minds of women, then from their condition, and then from your laws.[55]

Frances Wright was limited in her effectiveness by her radical sexual ideas and her own lifestyle, which were seen as scandalous by her contemporaries. She was personally devastated by a divorce settlement which deprived her of not only all her property but also her only child. Yet within a decade of her appearance on the American scene, ideas similar to hers found forceful expression in the writings and lectures of Sarah and Angelina Grimké and in the writings of Margaret Fuller. In the 1840s the linkage between women's education and women's civil rights was firmly established both in theory and in the practice of thousands of women in their reform and antislavery organizations.

The argument that women had a right to equal educational opportunities, just as they had a right to legal and social equality and to the ballot became a founding concept of the newly organized woman's rights movement. In 1848 and 1850 that belief was incorporated in the basic charter of the fledgling woman's movement in the resolutions of the Seneca Falls (1848), the Ohio and the Worcester (Mass.) Woman's Rights conventions (1850).

The Ohio convention resolutions express the connection with particular force:

> Resolved, that all distinctions between men and women in regard to social, literary, pecuniary, religious or political customs and institutions, based on a distinction of sex, are contrary to the laws of Nature, are unjust, and destructive to the purity, elevation and progress in knowledge and goodness of the great human family, and ought to be at once and forever abolished. . . . Resolved, That the education of woman should be in accordance with responsibility in life, that she may acquire that self-reliance and true dignity so essential to the proper fulfillment of the important duties devolving on her.[56]

No longer was woman's right to education justified on religious and moral grounds or because of her motherly role. No longer was it argued on the grounds of her greater appeal as a wife, a companion to men or as a mother. Woman's right to education is a natural right; it is her right as a human being and she may use it for self-fulfillment or in pursuit of other goals, for independence or in the service of others. The decision is hers to make.

THE EDUCATIONAL opportunities for African-Americans were so severely limited in the pre-Civil War period that the issue of separate education for girls did not arise. Black boys and girls generally shared whatever inadequate educational facilities were available. Still, there were a few black women teachers in the early national period who founded and maintained schools for black children. In 1820, fifteen-year-old Maria Becraft opened the first boarding school for black girls in Washington, D.C. Two decades later the Institute for Colored Youth in Philadelphia became the training ground for a core of women teachers who significantly affected the development of black schools and whose training could match that of graduates of white female seminaries. Fannie Jackson Coppin (1837–1913), a former slave who in 1860 graduated from Oberlin College, headed the Institute's Female Department from 1869 on for over three decades. Like the other great teachers and founders of educational institutions who followed in her footsteps, her educational goal was first and foremost the elevation of her race and of its mothers.[57] In an adaptation of the ideology of Republican Motherhood the African-American pioneer educators developed an ideology which exalted black mothers as the emancipators of the race.

In one of the greatest social experiments in history, nearly a quarter-million black children, kept illiterate under slavery, were instructed in over 4300 schools within five years of the end of the Civil War. Some 45 percent of the teachers of the freedmen were women, many of them African-American. The movement of which they were a part laid the foundation for the establishment of public schools in the South.[58]

The great black educator Anna Julia Cooper, writing the first full-blown feminist argument in America made by an African-American woman, appealed to black men to "give the girls a chance. . . . Teach them that there is a race with special needs which they and only they can help; that the world needs and is already asking for their trained, efficient forces." And she described with great foresight the result of men's hegemony over ideas, concepts and theories:

So long as woman sat with bandaged eyes and manacled hands, fast bound in the clamps of ignorance and inaction, the world of thought moved in its orbit like the revolutions of the moon; with one face (the man's face) always out, so that the spectator could not distinguish whether it was a disc or a sphere. . . . I claim . . . that there is a feminine as well as a masculine side to truth; and that these are related not as inferior and superior, not as better or worse, not as weaker or stronger, but as complements—complements in one necessary and symmetric whole.[59]

With the beginning of the organized movement for woman's rights, male dominance over definitions and mental constructs was under continuous challenge. It would take another hundred years in the United States before women would gain equal access to all institutions of higher learning, but the trend and the outcome were inevitable. The world of thought would no longer reflect only the man's face. The other half of the human race had, after two millennia of struggle, found its voice and established its claims. At long last, a truly human edifice of human thought could and would be built, combining the male and the female vision and irrevocably altering our view of wholeness. Hereafter we, women and men, would know whether the moon is a disc or a sphere.

TEN

Female Clusters, Female Networks, Social Spaces

THE LONG AND SLOW ADVANCE of women intellectuals toward group consciousness and toward a liberating analysis of their situation proceeded in a spasmodic, uneven, and often repetitious manner. Marginalized from the male tradition and largely deprived of knowledge of a female tradition, individual women had to think their way out of patriarchal gender definitions and their constraining impact as though each of them were a lonely Robinson Crusoe on a desert island, reinventing civilization. Not for them the systematic story of progress, the methodical building of thesis, antithesis and synthesis by which succeeding generations of male thinkers grew taller by standing "on the shoulders of giants," each making his small or larger contribution to building a common heritage. As we have seen, women's creations sank soundlessly into the sea, leaving barely a ripple, and succeeding generations of women were left to cover the same ground others had already covered before them. How many generations of women had to "prove" that they were capable of using a full and rigorous education as well as their brothers, only for the next generation of women to undertake that useless, spiraling demonstration all over again . . .

Yet women thought their way out of patriarchy; stubbornly and persistently, like drops of water wearing out solid rock, they challenged patriarchal definitions, prescriptions and explanations. They insisted on their capacity for education and, when that argument seemed to have been won, they insisted on their right to education.

But their arguments and mental constructs remained abstract and utopian as long as they were not rooted in transformative social action. Only women organizing on behalf of women could generate truly liberating thought.

In this respect women as a group were no different from other subordinate groups. Liberating thought is always connected with liberating action in the public arena; thought and action represent two aspects of the same process by which social change is generated, with theory and practice always in complex tension and interaction.

The dialogue of the female mystics with God proved the essential equality of human beings before God, but it did not and could not lead to social change any more than could the artistic self-liberation of women of talent throughout the centuries. It was different with the utopian visions of religious sectarians, in whose lives personal experiences and communal expressions merged. The martyred victims of persecution, the public witnesses and the re-definers of religious world-views all shared the capacity to make their private ecstatic experiences part of the collective experience. As they transformed their consciousness, they went from the private to the public realm and acted in it, that is, they made their lives political.

Thinking women, like men, not only needed other thinkers against whom to argue in order to test out their ideas, but they needed audiences, whether private or public. Many of the women discussed in this book were in dialogue with a male mentor or antagonist. The women engaged in the various phases of the *querelle des femmes* argued with misogynist male predecessors, often sharpening their own thinking and arguments in rounds of rebuttals. The women in sectarian religious sects defined their own positions against the mentorship of male leaders and at times, as in the case of Margaret Fell and Johanna Petersen, they developed into female leaders working in collaboration with male co-equal leaders. A beautiful example of such collaboration and mutual reinforcement is to be found in the household of the Reformation humanist Conrad Peutinger, who wrote at one desk in his room, while his wife Margarete worked at the other. The husband described the scene to his friend Erasmus :

My wife and I were working at separate desks. She had before her your Latin translation of the New Testament and along with it an Old German version. She said to me,"I'm reading Matthew 20. I see that Erasmus has added something which is not in the German." . . . [It was a passage concerning baptism.] Then we looked it up in the Vulgate of St. Jerome and found that it is not there. We looked then at your *Annotations*, where you mention Origen and Chrysostom. My wife said, "Let's read them." We did and found there what you have added.[1]

Margarete Peutinger (1481–1552) was celebrated by German humanists as a learned wife, *uxor docta*. She must have also been a model mother, for her first child Juliana was proficient in Latin at age three and a year later gave a Latin welcoming address for the Emperor Maximilian. Margarete Peutinger also wrote jointly with her husband and was an enthusiastic advocate of a new kind of marriage, in which, she said, the woman no longer holds the candle for her husband, but by the light of the candle writes or studies by his side.[2]

A similar enlightened personal relationship of mutual support enabled Olimpia Morata (1526–55) to achieve more than most of the learned women of the Renaissance. While others, such as Isotta Nogarola and Laura Cereta, depended on the mentorship and intellectual guidance of enlightened men, she worked with a husband who fully appreciated her talents. She left Italy after her marriage to Andreas Grundler, a German Protestant physician, and shared the hardships of his early professional life in a period of religious warfare. Yet, unlike most of the learned women of the Renaissance, she continued writing on theology, philosophy and the education of women even after her marriage. Her reputation was such that she was in line for an appointment to a chair at the University of Heidelberg, where her husband had secured a professorship. Tragically, both husband and wife died in a cholera epidemic; thus the full outcome of such a relationship could not develop. Olimpia Morata was only twenty-nine years old at the time of her death and yet she was known among humanists as *poeta docta*, a learned female poet.[3] It needs to be observed that such heterosexual, mutually supportive relationships, while they do occur, are rare in the historical record.

There is a pattern of clustering in the appearance of European and American women intellectuals which seems to me to be more than accidental. I reason that all intellectual work is fostered and encouraged by institutional support and, despite the appearance of talented persons of genius of both sexes in a random scattering across the historical time lines, that there is a notable clustering of male intellectuals around certain institutions and places. For men, such institutions have been feudal courts and, most important, universities. From the 17th century onward, male intellectual support networks consisted also of alumni of universities banded together in associations, clubs or informal groupings, of urban political and religious movements, and of salons. The fact that women were excluded from universities between their founding in the 11th century to well into the late 19th century has significantly and adversely affected womens's intellectual development and productivity. For not only were women excluded from the training such institutions provided, but they were deprived of the informal networks of professionals arising out of such institutions of higher learning.

The "cultural prodding" provided by formal or informal clusters of readers, listeners or discussants is an essential element in the development of major thinkers. Certainly, it is possible for talented individuals to write in isolation and without the response of audiences, but intellectual development depends on response, encouragement, the ability to improve one's work by criticism and the testing out of ideas in social interaction. Here, as in other areas, women have been seriously disadvantaged by centuries of educational discrimination.

Women tried in various ways to compensate for these disadvantages, and we will try to trace some of them in this chapter. Most intellectually productive women had some male person to provide mentorship or encouragement. We have already mentioned the many learned women who depended for their intellectual empowerment on sympathetic fathers. Elizabeth Elstob was intellectually mentored and supported by her brother. In Protestant circles husbands sometimes provided that role of intellectual support, as in the cases of Margarete Peutinger and the wives of the German Pietists Zinsendorf and Petersen. There are the examples of the indulgent Duke of Newcastle, the Quaker husbands and those evangelicals in the United States whose wives turned to woman's rights. "How does it feel to be known as the husband of Mary Livermore?" was the snide question asked by a reporter of the Rev. Mr. Livermore, whose wife, a famous and popular writer, reformer and lecturer, often helped fill his pulpit and co-edited a periodical with him. Mr. Livermore responded with a charming smile: "Why, I'm very proud of it. You see, I'm the only man in the world who has that distinction." His reply is as notable for its good spirit as for its rarity.

Paradoxically, supportive mentoring males, fathers, brothers or husbands, also hampered their female charges' mental independence, even as they helped to foster their intellectual growth. There are very few happily married or mated women who helped to advance feminist thought and that should not be surprising. It is striking, as one looks over the lists of women from different countries, spanning over 1300 years, who have developed some aspects of feminist thought, how many of them lived what today we would call woman-focused lives. Whether by choice or for want of alternative, they removed themselves from the marriage-market and focused their most intense activity on abstract thought. Most of them did their significant work in the single state, either prior to marriage, during widowhood or as women who, by choice, remained single. And further, for most of them what mattered most was the existence of some female audiences or support network. This is true also for the exceptional married woman, like the Duchess of Newcastle or Mary Wollstonecraft, who besides having supportive husbands also had female friends and readers.

The horror stories were more frequent, like that of Louise Adelgunde Victorie Gottsched, b.Kulmus (1713–62), known to posterity only in the feminine version of her husband's name as *"die Gottschedin,"* a highly intelligent and well-educated woman. She married Johann Christoph Gottsched, a man considered the leader of the German Enlightenment movement and an advocate of women's education. Besides his major works as a theater and cultural critic, he edited several women's magazines, in which he wrote most of the articles, using female pseudonyms. His first female pupil, Christiana Mariana von Ziegler, was crowned as *poet laureate* at the University of Leipzig and did much to help promote Gottsched's reputation as writer and critic. He utilized his wife's considerable talents and erudition to avail himself of the French and English philosophical and dramatic literature of his day.

Although Louise Gottsched was childless, she played a traditional wifely role. According to her husband's testimony, "she carried on all her domestic work in kitchen, laundry and clothing meticulously. And oftentimes she carried on my literary correspondence in my name, and answered to many scientific inquiries when I was too busy to attend to them myself."[4]

Louise Gottsched seems to have been a woman possessed of prodigious energy, as a short survey of her literary activities will show. Between 1731 and 1759 she translated eight plays from the French and English, including Molière's *Le Misanthrope,* and translated six or more volumes of philosophy and literature. In a three-year period she translated 330 articles from Pierre Bayle's historical dictionary from the French, as well as many articles and scientific reports which were of interest to her husband. Her own production of poems, some articles and plays was spread out over three decades and quite obviously had to fit into the rare periods when she was not occupied with her husband's work. Her eight plays, most of which she published anonymously, revealed her talent for comedy and sharp characterization. After her death, her husband published a collection of her poems and her close friend Dorothea von Runckel published two years of her correspondence. This woman, who might have been an important playwright, but who instead spent most of her active life doing literary drudgery work for her husband, had a 30-year-long career behind her, when at age forty-nine she stated that her life had been a failure.[5]

There are a number of known historical examples of lovers who were also intellectual partners and did joint work, which, for one good reason or another, appeared in print under the man's name. One of the least controversial of these is the case of William Thompson and Anna Wheeler, both British Owenite Socialists, whose publication *Appeal of One-Half the Human Race* was an important and influential early feminist tract.[6] Thompson in a letter told how its arguments were conceived and developed both by him and Anna Wheeler. He referred to himself as "the interpreter and scribe" of her sentiments and called the book "their joint property." Yet, it appeared under his name only.[7]

Similarly, the American antislavery writer and organizer Theodore Weld produced a documentary study of slavery as an institution, based largely on the evidence of eyewitnesses. The book is considered the most important antislavery document prior to the publication of *Uncle Tom's Cabin*, and it sold over 100,000 copies in the first year.[8] It was published anonymously in 1839 by the American Antislavery Society, but an introductory note indicated that Theodore Dwight Weld was the editor, and subsequent editions have ascribed the work solely to him. Yet Weld himself stated in a private letter that for six months his wife Angelina Grimké and her sister Sarah had searched over 20,000 Southern newspapers for facts to be included in the work.[9] These factual citations, without any comment, make up half of the pamphlet. It is also clear from the evidence that the sisters contributed to the editing of the other half, which consisted of eyewitness reports, and that they contributed two articles of their own. Weld was a strong advocate of women's rights, and the suppression of the editorship of the two women was undoubtedly motivated by his desire to give the work greater authority and prestige by its having been authored by a man.

A similar motivation may have influenced Caroline Schlegel to insist that her name not be included as a translator of Shakespeare's plays into German. The translations of the plays, a much heralded achievement of German literary scholarship, were therefore entirely ascribed to her husband, August Wilhelm Schlegel, even though it is known that she collaborated on most of them and translated one play entirely on her own.

As a final example, the celebrated intellectual partnership of John Stuart Mill and Harriet Taylor Mill, which has often been considered an exemplary model of sexual equality, resulted in the publication of several works on which they collaborated under their separate authorship. But there remained their first joint effort, *Principles of Political Economy*, and the later *On Liberty*, both of which Mill acknowledged as having been the result of their collaboration, both credited to him as the author. Of the latter he wrote: "[It was] more directly and literally our joint production than anything else which bears my name, for there was not a sentence of it that was not several times gone through by us together."[10] In this case, one of the reasons his name may have appeared on the book was to avoid rumors about the couple's liaison while she was still married to John Taylor. What is worth noting in all the examples above is that the social situation in which women find themselves, their life situation, results in their authorship being obliterated, even when their co-authors are sympathetic and benevolent men.

Let us now examine some of the support networks of, for and by women in more detail and in historical sequence. Because of their isolation from intellectual life and because of the societal censure of learned women, such women were particularly dependent on finding supportive individuals or support networks. I have looked at the clusters of learned women, as they appear in the historical record, and tried to find what supported their existence. Learned women up until the Reformation appear in convents, in families which support learning and among noble families in which women are trained for sharing in governance. They also appear at certain courts, usually those courts in which a learned woman creates a social space supportive of cultural expression. Dissident or heretical religious movements also provide support and audiences for learned or inspired women. In the modern world, clusters of learned women continue in some courts, and they appear in the form of a supportive networks of female friends, which I will call "affinitive clusters." In the 17th and 18th centuries, female readership constitutes such affinitive clusters. I will discuss the development of "social spaces" and "feminist spaces" later in this chapter.

The earliest historical writing of women emerged from the abbeys and convents and took the form of biographies of abbesses written by nuns and the collective biographies of orders, known as the "sisterbooks," as we will discuss in the next chapter. Hrosvitha of Gandersheim honored her Abbess Gerberga as a major influence on her own development. The abbey of Helfta fostered the development of a number of learned women. These abbeys provided women not only with powerful female models but they provided a sheltered space in which discourse among women could flourish without challenge as to its validity.

There are clusters of learned women around certain Renaissance courts or families. Lucrezia Borgia, the Duchess of Ferrara, created a cultural center at her court. Similarly, Isabella d'Este attracted learned men and women from all over Europe to her court. An example of female learning as part of a family tradition is that of the family of Battista da Montefeltro Malatesta (1383–1450), the daughter of Antonio, Count of Urbino. Excellently educated before her marriage, she studied the literature of Classical Antiquity and corresponded with male humanists. In 1433 she greeted the Emperor Sigismund, as he passed through Urbino, with a Latin oration. In her widowhood she became a sister of the Franciscan Order of St. Clare. Her granddaughters, Cecilia Gonzaga and Constanza Varano, to whose education she contributed, were known as learned women. Cecilia Gonzaga (1425–51) was educated with her brothers in Vittorio da Feltre's school in Mantua. She mastered Greek at the age of eight. She resisted her father's efforts to marry her off, and after his death both she and her mother entered the Franciscan order. Constanza Varano (1426–47) was an accomplished Latinist who wrote orations, poems and letters. All her work ceased after her marriage to Alessandro Sforza, lord of Pesaro. She died shortly after giving birth to her second child. The most famous descendant of this family was a great-granddaughter, Vittoria Colonna (1490–1547). She became a famous poet and after the death of her husband, the center of a literary circle which included Michelangelo. This is one of the rare cases where we can trace a literary family tradition through the women of the family.[11]

From the beginning of the 15th century on a remarkable group of women on or near the throne of the kings of France served as models of the *femme forte*, as paragons of female learning and as women of power. The transitional figure, an illiterate woman of power deriving her authority from divine revelation and the tradition of medieval mystics and warrior women, was the peasant girl Jeanne d'Arc. In 1429 she roused the lethargic King Charles VII from defeat, led an army in his behalf to free Orléans from the English and the Burgundians. She saw the King triumphantly crowned at Reims, as her visions had predicted. Captured by the Burgundians, she was turned over to the English, with Charles VII abandoning her to her fate. She was burned as a heretic, but her life and deeds became a legend and a symbol of France's national pride. Inspired later in his life by his mistress Agnès Sorel, the King completed the expulsion of the English from French soil.

The tradition of strong women in or around the throne of France continued into the next generations. After the death of Charles VII's heir, his older daughter Anne de Beaujea (1441–1522) ruled France as a regent for her brother, then still a minor. She crushed a rebellion of nobles in 1485 and secured the attachment of Brittany to France by forcing the heiress of Brittany, Anne, to marry her brother Charles VIII. He assumed his majority in 1491 and ruled until his death in 1498, his various military adventures in Italy having failed. By contrast his able sister helped to develop the intellectual life of the court. She also influenced the education of Anne de Bretagne (Brittany) (1477–1514) and of Louise de Savoie (1476–1531), who later became the mother of Marguerite de Navarre and Francis I, future king of France.

Anne de Bretagne exerted power mostly in her role as queen through her successive marriages to Maximilian of Austria, Charles VIII of France and his successor Louis XII. Her impact on her daughter and granddaughter is of equal interest here. Her daughter, Claude de France, married Francis I, who succeeded Louis XII on the throne. Thus Francis I (1494–1547) was surrounded by a number of powerful, highly educated women who influenced him and his politics: his mother, Louise de Savoie, his wife Claude and his sister Marguerite de Navarre.

In her turn, Marguerite de Navarre (1492–1549), whom we discussed earlier as an author and theological thinker, educated and influenced Catherine de Medici, wife of Henry II and queen mother and regent for her son Charles IX. During her first marriage to the Duc d'Alençon, her brother, King Francis I, gave Marguerite the

Duchy of Berry, where she made the royal court a center of learning and humanism and helped to foster the growth of the University of Bourges. After her husband's death she married Henry d'Albret, King of Navarre. In Navarre, she once again attracted humanist scholars and artists to her court. As a Protestant married to a Catholic in a time of fierce religious warfare, her role was that of a peacemaker between Catholics and Protestants, and she protected the Protestant reformers at her court, often harboring them against her husband's will.

Marguerite de Navarre's daughter Jeanne, on her accession to the throne of Navarre, announced her adherence to Protestantism and made Navarre a haven for Huguenots.

In addition to educating her own daughter, Marguerite de Navarre also supervised the education of Renée de France, (1528–75), Duchess of Ferrara, and of her niece Marguerite de France (1523–74). The latter married the Duc de Savoie and became herself a recognized scholar and patron of poets. Both Renée de France and Marguerite de France were sympathetic to Protestantism, but remained Catholics as were their husbands.

We see in this "clustering" an inter-generational laying-on of hands by which the transmittal of knowledge to women becomes a family tradition. We also see three generations of learned and politically active women around the French throne. Quite similar clusters of powerful and learned women could be found by following the various Hapsburg and Tudor queens of the 15th and 16th centuries.

IN THE 17TH CENTURY we find the first affinity clusters, groups of women who shared an interest in literature, religion, philosophy and women's education. Two striking examples of such groups can be found in the one around Anna Maria von Schurman and another around Elizabeth Elstob.

The Dutch scholar Anna Maria von Schurman had a wide circle of friends and correspondents, which included some of the foremost intellectuals of her time. She corresponded with and was admired by Descartes, Cardinal Richelieu, the theologians Friedrich Spanheim and André Rivet, both of the University of Leyden. Among the women she inspired and influenced were Bathsua Makin, Dorothea Christiane Leporin, a vigorous advocate of education for women, Queen Christina of Sweden, Marie de Gournay and Lucretia Marinelli. She was a close friend of Princess Elizabeth of Bohemia, who was an important intellectual in her own right.[12] Unlike earlier pioneering women thinkers, Schurman was admired by and known to women of succeeding generations.

A similar affinity cluster sprang up in support of Elizabeth Elstob. Of the 260 subscribers who made it possible for her first scholarly work to be published nearly half were women.[13] Later, when she was poverty-stricken and cut off from all academic connections and support, it was through the efforts of a local bluestocking and clergyman's wife, Mrs. Sarah Chapone, that George Ballard first learned of her plight. Mrs. Chapone wrote a letter to the women of the local gentry urging support for Elstob. Among the women who helped to find a livelihood for her were the writer Mrs. Delaney [Mary Pendarves], Lady Elizabeth Hastings, Queen Caroline and the Duchess of Portland.[14] Inspired by Elizabeth Elstob's suggestion and the example of her life, George Ballard would later edit the important biographical encyclopedia, *Memoirs of Several Ladies of Great Britain. . . .*[15]

We have already mentioned the circle of women friends who gave intellectual, moral and financial support to Mary Astell which enabled her to lead an independent life and pursue her literary work. She, in turn, by virtually creating the role of the "bluestocking," influenced members of that group such as Lady Mary Chudleigh, Lady Mary Wortley Montagu, Mrs. Delaney and Mrs. Anne Dewes.[16]

The "bluestockings" represent another affinity group or support network for two generations of educated women. A circle of women held together by friendship, close association and frequent meetings in several country estates and London homes, they provided, in their salons, a social space in which men and women with intellectual interests could meet socially.[17] As was the case in the French and German salons, these gatherings fostered respectful intellectual friendships between educated men and women, mostly of the nobility. They set standards of behavior and taste for polite society and served as informal meeting grounds for prospective marriage partners of the nobility and the upper bourgeoisie. Members of the first group of bluestockings were Elizabeth Carter, Elizabeth Montagu, Catherine Talbot, Hester Chapone, Samuel Johnson, Samuel Pepys, George Berkeley, the Rev. Thomas Birch, Samuel Richardson. Women of this circle not only found encouragement for their writing in the exchange of letters and the serious recognition of their work by readings in their gatherings, but they also were encouraged to publish. For example, Elizabeth Carter's translation of the works of the Stoic philosopher Epictetus was published in 1758 after 1031 advance subscriptions had been secured from within the circle of the blue-stockings and their friends. A generation later, Fanny Burney's third novel, *Camilla, or Female Difficulties,* was published in 1796 on the basis of a subscription list gathered by members of the bluestocking circle, to which Hester Thrale and Hannah More also belonged.[18] While the first generation of bluestockings was ignorant of the work of the 17th-century feminists, they were familiar with some of their counterparts in France, such as Mme. de Sévigné, whose work was widely circulated in England.[19] The second generation of bluestockings benefited from the lives and experiences of the first by personal acquaintance or by reading their works.

One manifestation of the benefits of an inter-generational tradition is the creation of female audiences for the work of women writers. This happened through the establishment of libraries and popular magazines addressed to women which created a tradition of female readership.

Another way in which we can trace the existence of female audiences for the work of female writers is in looking at the persons to whom they dedicated their works. These, generally, fall into two categories: the works dedicated to reigning female monarchs or powerful aristocrats who might function as the author's protectress; and those works dedicated to women the author admired. In the first category falls the dedication by Elizabeth Elstob of *An English-Saxon Homily* . . . . She acknowledged and thanked her "encouragers . . . so many of the Ladies," then offered a remarkable list of *exempla* of early medieval women who contributed to the development of English culture, ending with her dedication to "the two greatest Monarchs that the World has known: for Wisdom and Piety, and constant Success in their Affairs, QUEEN ELIZABETH, and ANNE QUEEN OF GREAT BRITAIN."[20] In a similar spirit Mlle. de Gournay dedicated her essays *Égalité des femmes* to "Queen Anne d'Autriche," the wife of France's King Louis XIII. Bathsua Makin combined the two types of dedications when she dedicated her *Essay* to "all Ingenious and Vertuous Ladies" and in particular to Lady Mary, daughter of the Duke of York.[21]

Feminist literary critics have shown how in the 19th century women writers began to acknowledge women as their muses and their role models. Thus, George Eliot admired Harriet Beecher Stowe and was decisively influenced in her work by a thorough reading of the works of Jane Austen; Elizabeth Barrett Browning admired the work of George Sand and Mme. de Staël, while her work, in its turn, was an inspiration to Emily Dickinson. Margaret Fuller and Sarah Orne Jewett acknowledged their indebtedness to Mme. de Staël, the author of *Corinne*; and all of the American nineteenth-century woman's rights leaders considered Elizabeth Barrett Browning's *Aurora Leigh* an inspiration. The list could be indefinitely extended to show the almost desperate search of writing women for authoritative female predecessors.[22]

The creation of female audiences for the work of female authors depended, of course, on the development of women's magazines and cheap, readily accessible printed novels. This development proceeded from the early 18th century on in England and on the continent of Europe. In America it occurred only in the first half of the 19th century. The clustering of women writers occurs in direct relationship to the development of a female reading public. On the other hand, the existence of female readers did not necessarily lead to the development or to the spread of feminist consciousness. The relationship is complex: the existence of a female reading public enabled some female writers at last to make an independent living.[23] Some of those who did also developed an independent lifestyle, which may have led them to an increasingly feminist consciousness. Examples of this may be Aphra Behn, Mary Astell and Mary Wollstonecraft. On the other hand there are countless examples of female writers with vast female audiences who never developed any feminist consciousness; on the contrary many made their living by celebrating women's traditional maternal and nurturant functions or by fostering women's romantic focus on love and marriage.

The development of feminist consciousness depended on a variety of factors, most of which we have already discussed: the ability of a sizable group of women to live outside of marriage in economic independence; the demographic and medical changes which enabled larger groups of women to forgo reproductive activity or to limit the number of their children; women's access to equal education and last, the possibility of creating "women's spaces." It is the last factor we will need to discuss in some detail before we can trace the development of feminist consciousness. The historian Sara Evans has called attention to this phenomenon in her study of the development of the modern feminist movement in the United States. She listed among the preconditions for the development of "an insurgent collective identity . . . 1) social spaces within which members of an oppressed group can develop an independent sense of worth in contrast to their received definitions as second-class or inferior citizens; 2) role models of people breaking out of patterns of passivity; 3) an ideology that can explain the sources of oppression . . . ; 4) a threat to the new-found sense of self that forces a confrontation with the inherited cultural definitions . . . ; and finally 5) a communication or friend-ship network through which a new interpretation can spread, acti-vating the insurgent consciousness into a social movement."[24]

The first and the fifth conditions are of particular interest here. Social space has proven historically to be of particular importance in allowing women to move from one stage of consciousness to an-other. Whether this is so because of the pervasive effect of negative gender indoctrination on women's self-esteem and courage, which make a friendly environment a necessary precondition for their in-ner liberation, it is hard to say. Historically, men have also needed such social spaces to formulate liberating ideologies, but their insti-tutionalization in universities, trade unions or political parties has been readily available. For women, confined by gender restrictions to the domestic circle and discouraged from participation in the pub-lic sphere, such social spaces have had to be privately created. Since the locus of women's gender indoctrination has so often been the family, the social space necessary for liberating women has had to be a space outside the family.

We have throughout this book discussed the importance of role models for women and the deleterious effect of their absence on women's consciousness. Because the creation of social spaces for women always involves the participation and even leadership of women the process itself creates role models.

In 17th-century France and 18th-century England the salons pre-sided over by women created spaces for the exchange of ideas. One of the main conversational topics throughout the century was the definition of women's nature and their role in society, in essence a continuation of the ancient *querelle des femmes*. In these spaces, where intellectual men and women treated each other as equals, the inclination was to answer the questions raised by the centuries-old dispute in favor of the equality of women, at least, on an abstract, theoretical level. The practical outcome of these debates was much more ambiguous in its effect on women.

The first of the French salons was that of Mme. de Rambouillet in 1617, which exerted great influence on the country's cultural life and became the target of Molière's bitter satire in *Les Précieuses ridicules*. Mme. Madeleine de Scudèry's salon followed not long after; in it the discussion of the roles of men and women and of the pros and cons of marriage as an institution continued. In theses salons genuinely learned women mixed with *précieuses* whose superficial knowledge was merely an affectation, but there is little doubt that the existence of salons fostered women's intellectual development. By 1760 French salons had changed their function from that of intellectually representing courtly ideals to becoming what one historian has called "a highly developed community of discourse" for the thinkers of the Enlightenment.[25] Under the leadership of Mme. de Geoffrin, Mlle. de Lespinasse and Mme. Necker the salons became democratized, a working space in which people of the nobility and of the bourgeoisie mingled on equal footing and developed and spread the ideas of the Enlightenment. The women who led the Paris salons went through a period of apprenticeship in the salon of an older woman before establishing a salon of their own. Mme. de Geoffrin "apprenticed" in the salon of Mme. de Tencin for almost twenty years. Julie de Lespinasse, before opening her own salon, attended that of Mme. de Geoffrin and of Mme. du Deffand for twelve years. Hostesses in the salons prepared themselves seriously for the discussions of the evening, at times writing out themes and subjects in advance.[26] On another level, 17th-century French salons continued to be places in which potential marriage partners of different ranks could meet informally. Above all, salons were social spaces in which women could develop friendships with men and women based on common cultural interests.[27]

In England the earliest known salon is that held in the 16th century by Mary Herbert, Countess of Pembroke, sister of Sir Philip Sidney, where poets such as Spenser, Shakespeare and John Donne mingled with learned women, aristocrats and artists. In the British salons of the 18th century, the "bluestockings" continued women's patronage of the arts and literature, but they also provided a space for women to interact and support the work of other women, as we have discussed.

In the early 18th century there appears a cluster of German women intellectuals who encourage each other and read each other's work. Christiana Mariana von Ziegler (1695–1760) conducted a musical and literary salon in Leipzig. Her example inspired Sidonia Hedwig Zäunemann (1714–40) to pursue a literary career. Fifty years later similar circles existed in Darmstadt, Weimar and Berlin, as part of the early Romantic movement and they continued to flourish well into the middle of the 19th century.

It would take a separate volume to study in detail the effect of salons on the women who participated in them. Here I will examine only one example, that of the early Romantics of Germany. Johanna Schopenhauer (1766–1838), the mother of the philosopher Arthur Schopenhauer, moved to Weimar with her children after the suicide of her husband and there formed one of the first bourgeois salons in 1806. Since she was poor, she kept the refreshments simple, serving only tea, for which court society made her the butt of ridicule. Yet Goethe and his circle of friends frequented her salon, rather than the more aristocratic ones.[28] The important salons which were closely connected with the early Romantic movement were those in Jena of Sophie Mereau and Caroline Schlegel and in Berlin of Henriette Herz and Rahel Varnhagen. For the poets, philosophers, writers and historians of the early Romantic movement these salons were not only social and intellectual centers, but a supportive and highly interactive community which became a testing ground for their philosophical and political ideas. Members of the Jena circle, a group which formed around the publication of the literary journal *Das Athenaeum* (1798–1800) were: the philosopher Fichte; Ludwig Tieck and his wife Amalie, the poet Heinrich von Hardenberg, known as Novalis, and his fiancée Julie von Charpentier; August Wilhelm Schlegel and his wife Caroline; his brother Friedrich Schlegel and his mistress and future wife Dorothea. This circle was characterized by close intellectual affinity, shared work, familial interrelationships and a willingness to experiment with unusual sexual and household arrangements.

The early Romantics questioned not only the strictures and constraints of bourgeois society but thoroughly explored gender. Several of them were influenced by their reading of Oriental philosophies, their study of pre-Christian religions and mythologies. They redefined the concept of the "feminine" in a way which glorified and romanticized women. Friedrich Schlegel, in his essay "Über die Diotima" (1795) and his novel *Lucinde* (1799), developed the ideal of a new androgyny, which would be the combination of a gentle manhood and an independent womanhood. Women were welcomed into this new world of thought as partners, authors and lovers.[29] But as we will see, the patriarchal notion of woman as muse and helpmeet of the artist would in the end prevail.

The women of this circle were uniformly well educated, some of them extremely learned, charming, sparkling conversationalists, serious writers and thinkers in their own right and forerunners of the "free love" movements of the end of the 19th century in Great Britain and the United States.[30] As were the latter-day free-lovers, these women were committed to expressing their philosophical ideas and emancipatory convictions in unconventional lifestyles. Several of them had one or more divorces and some of them lived with their future husbands (or with other men) in free unions prior to their marriages. Caroline Schlegel-Schelling had an illegitimate child; Sophie Mereau, who later married Clemens Brentano, lived as a single mother for several years after her divorce. The 39-year-old divorced Dorothea Veit married Friedrich Schlegel, who was nine years younger than she, after living with him for several years. Rahel Levin married Carl Varnhagen von Ense, a man twelve years younger than herself, when she was forty-eight. Nearly all the women of this circle had a number of passionate love affairs in or out of marriage. They retained life-long friendships with former lovers and cultivated intellectual friendships with men outside their marriages. A few of the women, notably Bettina Brentano and Rahel Varnhagen, had passionate erotic and intellectual attachments to women.

Caroline Schlegel-Schelling (1763–1809) had the most remarkable life of all the women of this circle. The daughter of a famous Orientalist and theologian, she had the finest education then available. At age nineteen she entered an arranged marriage with a physician and lived for four unhappy years in a small town. She was pregnant with her third child when her husband suddenly died. One of her children had died as an infant and the widow with her two small children moved back to her family. It was during these years she met August Wilhelm Schlegel, who fell in love with her, but whom she rejected. Then another tragedy affected her life, the death of her three-year-old daughter. Caroline went to live with a childhood friend in Mainz, who herself was unhappy in her marriage. When the city was captured and occupied by Napoleon's armies, the friend left her husband and children to go off with a lover. Caroline stayed with the abandoned husband and took care of him and his children, but she had a brief affair with a young French officer of the occupying army, which led to her pregnancy. Her host's Jacobin sympathies and the rumor that she was his mistress led to her arrest. In jail she managed to hide the fact she was pregnant, but she was so desperate over the possibility of her pregnancy being discovered that she contemplated suicide. She was freed through the intervention of her brother, whereupon August Wilhelm Schlegel offered her shelter and a cover story until the birth of her son. She gave her son into foster care and he died at the age of two months. Thus

Caroline had lost three children in infancy, with only her daughter Auguste surviving.

August Wilhelm Schlegel proved to be a loyal and undemanding friend. His young brother Friedrich desperately fell in love with Caroline but did not press his suit, since he considered her engaged to his brother. Caroline, who was not in love with August Wilhelm but was immensely grateful for his friendship and support, agreed to a marriage with him which seemed to her to offer the only way out of social ostracism and poverty. She moved with her husband to Jena, where she became the central figure in the Jena circle, whose members gathered mostly in her home. Her position of social leadership among the Jena Romantics was marred only by bitter rivalry and conflict with the woman Friedrich Schlegel had married, Dorothea Veit.

Some years later, the philosopher Friedrich Wilhelm Schelling, then twenty-four, entered their circle. He developed a close friendship with Caroline, who was then nearly forty, and fell in love with her fourteen-year-old daughter. Caroline, already aware of her love for him, agreed to Schelling's engagement with her daughter, but the young girl died suddenly in 1800. Schelling and Caroline were devastated with grief and guilt and attempted to renounce each other. But their relationship resumed after a year's separation. In 1803, Caroline secured a divorce from August Wilhelm Schlegel and married Schelling. Thereafter her entire existence focused on her husband, with whom she lived happily until her death.

This extraordinary female life became paradigmatic for the Romantics and their followers as a woman's self-expression through love. But the other side of it also reveals the limitations of the Romantics' quest for a new sexual order. Caroline Schlegel-Schelling left only a slight literary inheritance—a few essays, some reviews, many letters and the beginning of an autobiography. Yet she had a full literary life as August Wilhelm Schlegel's collaborator in his translations of all of Shakespeare's plays. As mentioned earlier, at her own insistence her name did not appear in the printed books, which became for over a century the standard available German translations of Shakespeare. During her marriage to Schelling she devoted herself wholly to promoting her husband's career. The price Caroline Schlegel-Schelling paid for her self-expression through love was the abandonment of her existence as a writer.[31]

The limits of the autonomy of women Romantics are even more starkly illustrated in the case of Sophie Mereau Brentano (1770–

1806). Unhappily married to Professor F. E. K. Mereau in Jena, she began to write novels and poems. Two of her novels were published, one by Friedrich Schiller with his high praise, as were two volumes of her poetry. She was well established in her literary career when she divorced her husband. The poet Clemens Brentano, eight years younger than she, fell passionately in love with her and repeatedly proposed marriage. She resisted him for two years, while she made her living as an editor. After a stormy courtship she lived with him and was pregnant with his child when in 1803 she agreed to marry him. In the following two years she had two more pregnancies and died in 1806, after giving birth to her third child.

During the courtship Brentano wrote her a long, sarcastic letter in which he revealed his passion and his anger at her refusal of him. He expressed this in the form of a savage attack on women writers. Sophie Mereau answered tongue-in-cheek that his view of women writers very much affected her:

> Obviously, this [female writing] is not appropriate to our sex and only the extraordinary magnanimity of men has tolerated this abuse for so long. . . . In the future I will not waste my time in making verses, and if I should feel the urge to write, I will try only to write good and moral tracts or cookbooks. . . . [32]

Yet after her marriage she stopped her own writing and confined her literary work to doing translations from English and Italian.

Among the women of these circles perhaps the outstanding mind and most promising talent was Karoline von Günderrode (1780–1806). Excellently educated, she was early orphaned and after the age of seventeen lived in a home for Protestant women. Ascetic, highly self-controlled and brilliant, she had a charismatic personality and a large circle of learned friends. She was a serious student of theology, philosophy and history and a highly gifted poet. In 1804 she published a volume of prose and poetry under the male pseudonym Tian. Her poems were praised and ascribed to various well-known male writers. When Clemens Brentano challenged her to admit her authorship and questioned her on why she had decided to publish, she answered:

> I have always kept the longing alive and pure within me to express my life in a permanent form, to give it the shape which would dignify it to stand before the most excellent persons, to greet them and share in their community. Yes, I have always sought this collectivity, this is the church to which my spirit makes its pilgrimage here on earth. [33]

Brentano, behind her back, condemned her poems. She continued writing poetry, essays, short plays. Her feminist leanings were an essential part of her consciousness, despite the contradictions in her life. She had two passionate loves in her life, both unfulfilled. The writer and future statesman Friedrich Carl von Sevigny, with whom she had a lifelong intellectual friendship, after a long courtship of her, married Brentano's sister Kunigunde (Gunda), because he feared Karoline's "manly spirit." Sevigny, after his marriage, offered Karoline an intimate platonic friendship, to which she agreed. It worked much to Sevigny's advantage, for now he had a conventional wife and a brilliant intimate intellectual friend; for Karoline it only added to her misery, frustration and sense of being a freak. Interestingly, it was to Gunda Brentano that she expressed her most secret longings:

> I often had the unfeminine wish to die a hero's death, to throw myself into the wildness of battle, to die—why was I not born a man! I have no taste for female virtues and female bliss. Only what is wild, great, brilliant attracts me. This is an unhappy, but incorrigible misapprehension of my soul; thus it will and must remain, for I am a woman and have desires like a man, without the strength of a man.[34]

Her second passion was for the classical philologist Friedrich Creuzer, who was already married when she met him. He loved her, but was unwilling to leave his wife or get a divorce from her. She was greatly influenced intellectually by his studies of Oriental mythology and took a keen interest in the study of pre-patriarchal societies. Creuzer's major work influenced Johann J. Bachofen and through him later proponents of feminist matriarchal theories.[35] Günderrode wrote a volume of poems and essays in which she described her passionate love for him. Creuzer found a publisher for the volume, but before the actual publication he had decided to break off the relationship. The day she received that news from him, Karoline von Günderrode committed suicide by killing herself with a stiletto in her breast on the bank of the Rhine river. Creuzer thereupon decided that publication might reflect badly on his reputation and withdrew the manuscript from the publisher. It was first published nearly a hundred years later in 1906 in an edition of 400 copies. Günderrode has been rediscovered only recently by feminist literary critics.

Günderrode's feminist strivings ended in despair and suicide, yet in a strange way they had a formative impact on another woman writer of the Romantic circle. Bettina Brentano, sister of Clemens, became a close friend of Günderrode's a few years before her death, in a relationship which was passionately erotic on Bettina's part but that of a mentor/pupil on Karoline's. Bettina compared their friendship to that of Plato and Dionysius. The correspondence between the two women is fascinating in its richness, its intellectual and emotional intensity and in the way these two aspects of the self were merged for both women. Bettina, who read various philosophers at Karoline's suggestion and found them quite unpalatable, decided that the two of them should develop their own religion as a first step toward founding their own culture. Bettina wanted to combine self-development, rigorous mental discipline, with "the energies of desire" (*Sehnsuchtsenergien*), a concept by which she meant something akin to the 20th-century feminist concept of erotic power.[36] Bettina proposed that they call their new system a "floating religion" (*Schwebereligion*) to indicate its protean, structureless fluidity. Its first principle must be a rejection of formal education:

> That means no educated types, everyone is supposed to be curious about him- or herself and should attempt to mine the self as though it were a piece of metal to be brought up from the deep or a spring, all of education should be focused on letting the spirit come to light.[37]

This passage typifies their thinking in terms of a unity of knowledge, intuition and desire and the concept that an inner spirit, with its own form, is immanent in each person and can be found only through intuition and openness to feeling. In another of her letters to Günderrode, at whose recommendation Bettina had read the works of Fichte, Kant and Schelling, she offered a penetrating critique of the male mode of thought and the pretensions of academics:

> Do you know how I feel?—Dizzy . . . I'm embarrassed to have to attack the language with sledgehammer and axe in order to penetrate it . . . Don't you think philosophers are terribly arrogant. . . . Wisdom has to be natural, why should it need such disgusting paraphernalia in order to get into motion; it lives, after all? . . . It appears to me that the philosopher does not so much lie at the breast [of nature] and trust her . . . rather, that he is engaged in theft, to see what he can pry from her to digest in his secret factory. . . . and then he shows to his pupils how his perpetuum mobile works, and he is in a real sweat, and the pupils are astonished and end up feeling dumb.[38]

Had the collaboration and intellectual interchange between these two women continued, it might have led to a real advance in feminist consciousness. On the contrary, Günderrode broke off her intimacy with Bettina at the insistence of Creuzer, who disliked both Bettina and her brother. Still, Bettina was devastated by Günderrode's suicide and by her inability to read earlier signs of despair and depression in her friend. Many years later, she kept her memory alive in an epistolary novel *Die Günderode,* in which she rescued many of her friend's letters from oblivion.[39]

Bettina Brentano von Arnim (1785–1859) is the most interesting of the women of the German Romantic movement and the only one who can be said to have realized herself fully. After the death of both parents she went to live with her grandmother, Sophie de la Roche, a well-known writer, who encouraged Bettina's intellectual development and her independence. Bettina never felt suppressed and from childhood on cultivated a distinctive "personality," spontaneous, straightforward, impetuous and charming. Her family and friends considered her "odd" and worried about her unwillingness to conform to the social standards appropriate to her station in life. She was restless, both mentally and physically, and even into her old age friends would notice that she never sat still, but shifted from the seat of a chair to its arms or to sitting crosslegged on the floor.

After Günderrode's rejection of her, Bettina began a friendship with the mother of Goethe, which she would, in later years, use as the basis for her highly successful book, *Goethe's Briefwechsel mit einem Kinde* (Goethe's Correspondence with a Child). She met Achim von Arnim through her brother Clemens, whose best friend and collaborator he was, and married him in 1811.[40] For the next twenty years she lived the conventional life of rural domesticity, struggling to manage a country estate, keep up her literary and intellectual interests and raise seven children. Unlike the other women of her circle she never felt the need to submerge her talents to foster a man of genius; on the contrary, she encouraged Arnim's work while being fully conscious of his limitations and keeping up her own mental growth.

It was as a widow that she began a flourishing literary career. She moved to Berlin, where she not only became part of the literary circle of Rahel Varnhagen but established her own salon, which was more political than literary in its orientation. Her first book, mentioned above, published in 1835, was a free and imaginative account of her contacts and correspondence with Goethe, in which she cast herself as the admiring "child" to the great man. It is this book on which her literary reputation rests, yet today it emerges as less important than some of her other works. Her second publication, the memoir of Günderrode (published 1840), continued in the epistolary form of her first book and set a precedent for self-revelatory and autobiographical writing. Her third book was an adaptation of her correspondence with her brother Clemens, published in 1844.

Bettina von Arnim took a strong interest in social and political questions and, during a period when the men in her circle began to embrace conservative and reactionary causes, she became ever more radical. It began during the cholera epidemic in Berlin in 1831, when she physically nursed the poor and organized a vast relief effort in their behalf. While Clemens Brentano converted to Catholicism and set up residence next to a stigmatized nun in order to share in her sanctity, and her brother-in-law Carl von Sevigny became a Catholic-Conservative minister, Bettina collected documentary evidence in the slums of Berlin on the condition of the poor. Bettina published a persuasive political tract, *Dies Buch Gehört dem König* (This Book Is for the King, 1843), cast in the form of a Socratic dialogue of an older woman (presumably the highly respected Frau Rath, Goethe's mother) with various interlocutors. The books also contained sections of pure documentary description of the condition of the poor in the city, which had been collected by a Swiss man of Bettina's acquaintance. She argued powerfully for a change in social policy, addressing King Friedrich Wilhelm IV as though he were a king of the people. Her dedication to the King was a public challenge and proved to be a clever device for avoiding censorship. The book was widely read and reviewed and was printed in another edition.[41]

Bettina also supported the cause of the starving Silesian weavers, whose condition she documented in *Das Armenbuch* (The Book of the Poor). The book was at the printer when the weaver rebellion was brutally suppressed. Brentano-Arnim, who had already made herself politically suspect by her earlier book, feared persecution and withdrew the manuscript from the printer. Nevertheless, she was harassed by the government, which took the form of a lawsuit for slander filed against her by a Berlin magistrate in 1846. It followed upon her publication of her book *Dies Buch Gehört dem König* in a private publishing venture. The magistrate demanded that she apply for the rights of a citizen *(Bürgerrecht)*, apparently the right, as a person of the nobility, to engage in a bourgeois trade. Brentano-Arnim replied that she would be delighted to accept this right as a badge of honor, but that she would not buy it. She explained that she considered the right of the citizen higher than that of the nobility, but that she placed above both "the rights of the class of proletarians without whose character strength, survival skills in misery, self-denial and thrift the well-being of the whole could not exist."[42] These words formed the basis for the slander suit, for which the court sentenced her to the longest jail sentence it was possible to give a person of the nobility, two months. It was only through the intervention of Sevigny that the sentence was suspended.

Still, Bettina von Arnim continued to her death to embrace the cause of various groups of the oppressed: the poor, the criminal, the insane. She wrote public appeals in behalf of the Polish people, the ghetto Jews of Frankfurt, the political prisoners of the 1848 Revolution. Her incipient and thwarted feminism led her to become an advocate against all forms of oppression. Her strong advocacy of Jewish interests, both in her essays and her political writing is all the more remarkable in contrast to the overt anti-Semitism of her brother.[43]

It was characteristic of the male Romantics, many of them members of the nobility, that they mingled freely with wealthy Jewish women in the salons. In a sense both sides were members of marginal groups in the period of rising capitalism, and their intellectual encounters were full of tensions and mutual inspiration. But the relationships were one-sided in their effect: all of the Jewish women of this circle converted to Christianity, some because of true conversion, others because it was the sole condition of their marrying the men of their choice. Dorothea Veit-Schlegel was the daughter of the famous Jewish philosopher Moses Mendelsohn. Her marriage with Friedrich Schlegel took place only after her conversion to Protestantism, but her later conversion to Catholicism was the result of a serious spiritual quest. Some Jewish women who converted were nevertheless spurned by their aristocratic Christian admirers. Thus, Rebecca Friedländer divorced her Jewish husband, but the man she loved, Graf Egloffstein, had no intention of marrying a Jewish convert. Similarly Rahel Levin, despite her conversion, was spurned by Karl von Finkelstein. Her second aristocratic admirer, Karl Varnhagen von Ense, waited years to overcome the prejudices of his family before he married her in 1814. The historian Deborah Hertz has suggested that the preponderance of Jewish salon women who converted to Christianity was due to their desire for making hypergamous marriages, but she also shows that it represented a rebellion against the traditional Jewish upbringing in which they were denied education. Most of the Jewish salon women, in contrast to the noble women, were self-educated.[44]

Rahel Levin Varnhagen von Ense (1771–1833) is the last of the women of the Romantic movement whose life and career we should consider. Born in Berlin in a wealthy merchant family, she lived under financially strained circumstances after her father's death. Although she was a prolific writer, mostly of letters, she published little during her lifetime. She lived in an attic room in her mother's house in Berlin, where from 1806 on she conducted her celebrated salon. Her major impact on her contemporaries was as a brilliant conversationalist, whose ability to attract outstanding men from the realm of literature, philosophy, court life, art and politics to her circle made her a cultural leader. Her salon was frequented by the Romantic poets, the philosophers Hegel and Schleiermacher, the philologist Wilhelm von Humboldt and the brothers Jacob and Wilhelm Grimm. Her literary reputation was established only when her husband published her correspondence after her death. Her letters, which revealed a deeply searching, highly individualistic mind had enormous impact on generations of women. Fanny Lewald, an early German feminist, found in Rahel a forerunner of her quest for independence and autonomy. Ellen Key, who wrote Rahel's biography in 1907, considered her letters indispensable literature for women. In the 20th century her role as a vanguard feminist was recognized, even though her most famous biographer, Hannah Arendt, ignored that aspect of her thinking.[45]

Rahel Levin was early alienated from her Jewish religion and culture, probably through the bitter conflict with her harsh and authoritarian father. She suffered all her life from the slights, disparagement and discrimination she experienced as a Jew, yet she never felt or expressed a sense of solidarity with fellow Jews. For her, the decision to be baptized was an effort at finding acceptance in the community of intellectuals in which she lived; yet, once accomplished, her conversion did not lessen her feelings of isolation.

One can only surmise that her sense of being deviant, different and, despite the numerous affirmations given her of her popularity, of not being loved are more likely grounded in her being a woman of exceptional talent than in her being a Jew. She wrote about herself: "What can a woman do, if she is also human?"[46] And elsewhere:

I am as unique as the biggest appearance on this earth. The greatest artist, philosopher or poet does not rank above me. We consist of the same element. He who seeks to exclude the other, only excludes himself. But I was consigned to living; and I remained unrealized until my century and so I am, seen only from the outside, submerged.[47]

This perception of being stifled, choking, misunderstood is often expressed in her letters. Like the other women of the Romantic movement, she had several passionate loves for men who did not appreciate her and spurned her. Only Varnhagen offered her total admiration and acceptance. Like Bettina, Rahel also had passionate friendships with women, one with Regina Friedländer which lasted six years, another with Pauline Wiesel which was very intense and of long duration. Rahel wrote to her "Dearest beloved friend [using both the female and male version of the word "friend" in German] . . . You are alone, separated from me and I am alone separated from you. Only once could nature have made it possible for two creatures such as us to live at the same time. In this day and age . . . ." Is this merely loneliness and a general sense of alienation or is this an expression of a homoerotic love which frightened her? We will never know, for Karl Varnhagen edited out most of the correspondence of these women friends.

In comparison with other clusters of writing women, the women of the early Romantic movement were particularly privileged. The social space in which they moved or which they created was based on an acceptance of female intellectual equality and even leadership. The men in their lives were profoundly and sincerely devoted to deconstructing traditional gender definitions and several of them made theoretical contributions to that endeavor. All of these women were economically privileged, even when they were not rich, and most of them were not overburdened with domestic responsibilities. Like the learned women of the Renaissance, they were precocious and most of them had literary careers early in life. Unlike most of their predecessors they enjoyed intellectual discourse with and acceptance from the men in their circle, who were themselves men of great talent and accomplishments. Yet seen from a long-range perspective, where did it all lead?

The women lived amazingly autonomous, self-defined lives and they broke a great many conventions and sexual taboos. They anticipated the lifestyle of the free lovers of a much later period; in fragments and isolated expressions they revealed their authority as thinkers and their high ambitions. Of the ten or twelve women of that circle, six were writers. Of them one committed suicide at age twenty-six;

one married happily and died in childbirth at age thirty-six, having given up writing after her marriage; two devoted themselves entirely to their husbands' careers and gave up their own work; Rahel hardly published during her lifetime. Only Bettina Brentano achieved the impossible dream: to combine the life of a woman—love, friendship and children—with the life of the mind. Yet her achievements as a writer only occurred during her widowhood and old age.

THE CLUSTERING OF thinking women and the creation of audiences for their work did not necessarily lead to the development of feminist thought. This can be seen also by studying the lives and works of the women active in the 1848 revolutions in Germany and France, the American socialists and anarchists of the turn of the century and the women in the utopian communities. As the example of the women of the early Romantic movement shows, even the availability of social spaces in which men and women attempted to live with some semblance of equality and mutual respect did not lead women to advance feminist consciousness. It may even have had a contrary effect on them in that it encouraged them voluntarily to submerge their intellectual lives to those of the men with whom they lived.

Of the ingredients essential for the development of feminist thought and theory what was missing in all these social spaces was a knowledge of women's history and autonomous female organizations which might have tested women's thinking and experience in action. Women must organize for themselves and in their own interests before they can fully think their way out of patriarchy.

ELEVEN

The Search for Women's History

THE HISTORY OF WESTERN civilization, it is generally believed, began at Sumer, at the start of the second millennium B.C., as a direct consequence of the development of writing, which dates nearly a thousand years earlier. History, the preservation and collection of written documents and their constant reinterpretation by succeeding generations of specialists, is dependent on the literacy of at least an elite group and has, for most of these 4000 years in Western civilization, served the interests of ruling elites. This is to distinguish it from the process of historical development, which takes place regardless of the existence of literacy or interpretation and in which non-elite groups participate equally or perhaps even more significantly than elites. What I am concerned with here is the written History of literate societies and the way it has affected and treated men and women differently.

The first documents produced for the purposes of historical preservation and interpretation were the Sumerian and latter-day "king lists." The first such list starts with ten kings who presumably reigned before the Flood, and the next lists 19 kings who reigned after the Flood, and others down to the Third Dynasty of Ur. The length of each king's reign is given, amounting to fantastically long periods, such as 1500 or 1200 years each, a fact which presumably is to enhance the king's importance. Yet despite such unscientific elements, the Sumerian king lists have been at least partially validated by archaeological and other evidence, so that they can truly serve as the basis for historical documentation.[1] These lists of rulers, often including mythological figures as well as real persons from the past, were used to legitimate the claims of authority of existing rulers, many of them usurpers. By virtue of such lists a king of questionable authority could claim descent from a god or a goddess or trace his lineage to a recognized ruler of the past. Those included in the lists tended to become heroic, often mythologized figures, endowing the collectivity that claimed them, in most cases newly established city-states, with a legitimate and recognizable past. Thus the recording, historicizing and legitimating functions of these earliest manifestations of historical activity cannot be separated from their ideological function and their psychological impact. By way of the king lists, disparate groups of tribes, clans or villages could become linked through a common past and the promise of a common future into a not-yet existing statehood. The psychological impact of being able to identify with such illustrious and perhaps heroic predecessors functioned to impart pride of group adherence, regional identity and personal pride to even the humblest members of the group. This can be shown with particular force in the "king list" represented by the list of "begats" in the book of Genesis. The generations of Israelites there listed reach from the time of the Kingdom of David well into the dim and timeless past of the patriarchs, whose covenants with God legitimated the claims to dominance and authority of their heirs into future generations. Here male begat male without the intervention of women, and the male covenant community was extended to the beginning of time.

The next step in the development of written History comes when rulers engrave and preserve, on steles or monuments, a record of their victories or of the laws they enacted. The earliest such records in the Ancient Near East date from the second millennium B.C. From that period on, societies generated a vast store of "documents" of all kinds, from trade bills and inventory lists to ration lists, contracts, judicial decisions and agreements between states and their rulers. History through interpretation by an individual, who either bases his conclusions on his own observations or on the perusal of written documents, does not develop until more than a 1000 years later.

For nearly 3800 of the 4000 years of the recorded History of Western civilization the record mainly concerns the activities, experiences and achievements of men. Not of all men, either, but a narrow group of powerful elites. Women have participated in civilization-building equally with men, in a world dominated and defined by men. In the period when written History was being created, women already lived under conditions of patriarchy, their roles, their public behavior and their sexual and reproductive lives defined by men or male-dominated institutions. Women were then already educationally disadvantaged and did not significantly participate in the creation of the symbol system by which the world was explained and ordered. Current scholarship holds that women made no significant impact on the writing of History until the late 18th century. The single exception, frequently cited, is Christine de Pisan, whose solitary attempt at creating a Women's History sank into oblivion. I will show that while this generalization is true in its broadest outlines, there is a significant and almost constant effort on the part of women to create Women's History from the 7th century A.D. forward.

Women's effort at History-writing followed the same pattern men had much earlier created: the making of lists of notables and heroines; the documenting of individual lives and exploits; the documenting of the histories of communities; the interpretation of past documentation from a particular point of view and finally, in the 19th and 20th centuries, "scientific History."

Because of the particular conditions under which women's intellectual development took place, progression from one stage to another in this process did not go smoothly and in a pattern in which one generation built upon the achievements of another. Quite the contrary, it developed in a repetitive, circular pattern, with generation after generation of women repeating what others had done before them. Thus, women's progress into historical consciousness was doubly delayed—by educational disadvantaging and by a lack of knowledge of the work of their predecessors. As we have seen in the case of women's Bible criticism, women had to rediscover their history over and over again.

The documenting of individual lives by women writers first occurred in cloisters. One of the first known examples of this kind of historical biography is the *Life of St. Radegund* by the nun Baudovinia, written in the 7th century. Baudovinia identified herself in her work as a woman and a nun, yet her biography was disparaged by scholars in later centuries in comparison with the earlier biography of St. Radegund by Bishop Venantius Fortunatus. Baudovinia, writing at the abbey of Chelles in the period 609–14, intended to supplement her predecessor's work and to create in the *persona* of St. Radegund a heroic figure her fellow nuns could emulate. Radegund—the Thuringian princess whom we discussed in Chapter Two—was forced to marry the Merovingian King Chlotar, she endured an unhappy marriage and fled from it into monastic life. Baudovinia concentrated on the second half of Radegund's life, when she lived in a cell near the cloister she had built at Poitiers. Baudovinia depicted Radegund as an outgoing woman, nurturant and solicitous of her nuns and deeply concerned with her role as a peacemaker among warring kings.[2]

Another female historical biographer was a nun of Chelles who wrote the earliest version of the *vita* of St. Balthild, shortly after the Abbess's death in 670. At that time Chelles was still a female community, but during the reign of St. Balthild's successor Bertila (d.705) it was transformed into a double monastery. The biographer of St. Balthild must have known her well, for the story abounds in evidence of the Abbess's motherly kindness both in her earlier role as a reigning queen and in her later role as Abbess of Chelles. The medievalist Suzanne Wemple concludes that the appearance of the same themes of motherliness and peacefulness in both biographies is not due to imitation but rather represents a female viewpoint toward the two subjects.[3] Hugeburc (d. *c.*762), a well-educated Saxon nun who came to Germany with her relative Wynnebald, a co-worker of St. Boniface, joined the convent of Heidenheim, which Wynnebald had founded ten years earlier, and became its Abbess. She wrote two biographies, one of Bishop Wynnebald and another of his brother Willibald, describing the latter's seven-year pilgrimage to the Holy Land. This is not only a travel book but an account of the conversion to Christianity of Germans and Franks, thus, in a rudimentary way, a historical account. She indicated her authorship by a cryptogram of her name in the earliest extant manuscript.[4] The Carolingian Renaissance, which expanded educational opportunities mostly for men but also for female members of the royal family, did not lead to the fostering of women's authorship. While women continued to be well educated in nunneries as scribes, librarians and teachers, the Carolingian revival of learning was institutionalized in the court and in monastic schools. It was not until the 10th century that another female writer made a considerable contribution to the development of Women's History.

The nun Hrosvitha of Gandersheim (932–1002?) came from the high nobility, and possibly was a member of the royal family. She may have entered the convent early in her life, where she received an excellent education which included not only religious subjects but

Latin prosody, mathematics, astronomy and music. The convent's rich library may have helped to foster her education. At the time she was at Gandersheim this powerful abbey was freed both from Church and royal rule, with the Abbess having supreme authority. The Abbess of Gandersheim had her own court of law, sent the nobles on her lands to battle and had a seat in the Imperial Diet. Some of the nuns, presumably Hrosvitha among them, were actually canonesses. They had to take only vows of chastity and obedience, not vows of poverty and with permission were free to move in and out of the cloister. They could own books and some property and were permitted to have servants and receive visitors.[5]

Hrosvitha left a major body of work consisting of eight verse legends, six rhymed plays, a poem depicting scenes from the Apocalypse and two historical poems. She also wrote two *vitae* of the major patrons of Gandersheim—Anastasius and Innocentius—but the manuscripts have been lost.[6] The latest scholar who extensively analyzed her work, Peter Dronke, believes that there is good evidence that her plays were performed or at least read aloud at court during her lifetime.[7] What is of special interest here is not only her talent as a writer and her being the first known European female playwright but the fact that all of her work is concerned with history and especially the history of women. The legends are all historical, either in the sense of collecting past and present versions of legends about a certain figure or in the sense of dealing with a heroic saint of the past. The poem "Maria" belongs in the first category, the others all belong in the latter category. Five of the poems deal with Christian saints of the past and dramatize their miraculous salvation through the intercession of Christ or the Virgin. One poem, "Gongolf," describes the murder of a saintly Frankish king by his wife's lover and the swift punishment of the sinning pair. While the main themes which recur in Hrosvitha's plays concern miraculous salvation, the triumphs of martyred faithful even over death, and the powers of virginity, it is interesting to note that even in these earliest works the author seems to have a historical perspective and consciousness. In her Preface she explains the authenticity of each tale by giving its provenance, most of it coming from books available to her in the library of Gandersheim. In the single case of a poem about a contemporary, the poem "Pelagius," which describes the martyrdom of a Christian youth who repelled the lecherous advances of a Moorish tyrant and is miraculously delivered from death, the poet tells us that she heard the story from an eyewitness. "So if in either book I have included anything false in my composing, I have not misled of my own account," she explains, "but only by incautiously imitating misleading sources."[8] This rudimentary effort at documentation and source-critical analysis is quite remarkable in an age in which literature freely combined real stories, fabulous and miraculous events, legends, biblical sources and fantasy without distinction.

The six plays are patterned after plays of the Roman poet Terence, but they are turned into Christian morality plays. One of the main changes the medieval playwright makes is that in her plays the women are at the center of the action and their agency decides the outcome of the plot.[9] While the plots may seem preposterous to contemporary readers, the plays are well crafted, the dialogue is lively, and in some of the plays tragedy and burlesque humor mix effectively. For our purposes the plays *Dulcitius*, *Callimachus* and *Sapientia* are most interesting, for in them Hrosvitha comes closest to expounding her views about the power of women.

Dulcitius deals with the martyrdom of three virgins who are brought before the Emperor Diocletian, who orders that they be married. But the young girls resist, explaining they have vowed to live as virgins. They are turned over to Governor Dulcitius and imprisoned by him. Threatened with rape by the Governor, they are saved by a miracle; he mistakes the pots and pans in the kitchen for the objects of his passion and attacks them until his face and body are covered with soot, while the girls watch him through a crack in the wall and laugh at him. He then hands the maidens to Sisinnius, who is charged with administering punishment to them because they refuse to worship the Roman gods; but he too becomes the victim of delusions. Still he succeeds in getting two of them burnt and the third shot to death with arrows. Here, Hrosvitha stresses two of her major themes: the power of chastity over male power, and salvation through martyrdom. Yet the source of her play is historical; the play is based on edicts of the Emperor Diocletian as taken from *The Acts of Christian Martyrs*.

The play *Callimachus* also deals with rape. Callimachus tells Drusiana he loves her, but she refuses him not only because she is already married but because she has taken the vow of chastity. He threatens her with rape and she asks Christ to help her die. Her wish is granted, thus creating another illustration of the theme of women's power to be sanctified through martyrdom. But Callimachus enters her tomb to rape her corpse. Before he can carry out this evil design he is killed by a snake. He and Drusiana are later resurrected and he is converted to her beliefs. Again, the theme is woman's power, not only of petition and steadfast resistance but also of effecting miraculous conversions. Hrosvitha's depiction of the rapist in one play as a ludicrous fool whose power is illusionary and in the other as a perverse monster is certainly a remarkable evidence of feminist consciousness at this early period.

The play *Sapientia* also deals with the martyrdom of three holy virgins who are put to death in the presence of their mother Sapientia. The mother encourages them to bear their sufferings and after their death she embalms their bodies and buries them. Forty days later, while she is praying at her children's grave, her spirit is borne to heaven. The moral here is the strength of chastity, which gives pious women the power to overcome the earthly might of men, even emperors, and to lead women to salvation.

The first of Hrosvitha's purely historical works, *Gesta Ottonis*, was undertaken at the command of her Abbess Gerberga. Apparently the author was somewhat reluctant to undertake this work, as she explains in her Dedication to Gerberga:

> Thou hast indeed imposed upon me the difficult task of narrating in verse the achievement of an august emperor, which thou art well aware was impossible to gather abundantly from hearsay. . . . There are things of which I could find no written record, nor could I elicit information from anyone sufficiently reliable. I was like a stranger wandering without a guide through the depth of an unknown forest where every path was covered over and mantled with heavy snow.[10]

The fact that Hrosvitha had been given the assignment to celebrate the life and deeds of her sovereign Otto I, who also was the uncle of her superior, the Abbess Gerberga, speaks to the great reputation she had established by the age of thirty, as a result of her plays and poems. Such an assignment was expected of court poets or poets laureate; Hrosvitha was, however, quite uneasy with it and cut short her account of the civil war among members of the royal Saxon family. The poem, which was written between 965 and 968, ends when Otto I was at the height of his power as a king but before he became emperor. As she states in the quote above, she did cut her account short because she felt uneasy about the availability of neutral, reliable sources, which speaks strongly for her consciousness of herself as a historian obliged to provide a balanced account. But the task was also difficult for her because of her sex. "I do not think it fitting for a frail woman abiding in the enclosure of a peaceful monastery to speak of war, with which she ought not even to be acquainted. These matters should be reserved for the toil of qualified men. . . ."[11] This concession to gender and female weakness, the "humility *topos*," may in fact be no more than a convenient excuse by which a by then self-confident author faced with an unpleasant task reserved her right to control her own material.

Hrosvitha reacted quite differently when faced with the request to write a history of the abbey of Gandersheim, which was for her a labor of love. She composed this poem, the last of her known works, in 973, or slightly later. It is the only one of her works that has no Preface. The poem opens with two serene lines:

> Behold, my spirit, lowly and submissive,
> breaks forth to tell the origins of blissful Gandersheim.[12]

She tells of a miraculous event which caused Duke Liudolf, the reigning monarch, and his wife Oda to found the monastery in 856. A group of swineherds lodged in a little farm amidst the dark forest saw many bright lights sparkling in the woods "with a strange radiance." The vision was repeated for the owner of the farm and for the Duke, who interpreted it as a command to build a shrine. "All affirmed that this spot should be made holy, / in the service of him who had filled it with such light."[13] The parallel of this vision to the vision of the shepherds at the birth of Christ is striking. In a perceptive interpretation Peter Dronke suggests that Hrosvitha, who always referred to herself as the lowliest of those who lived at Gandersheim, also intended to celebrate the special vision of the lowly, the shepherds, the swineherds and herself, "the strong voice of Gandersheim," as she elsewhere called herself.[14] The increasingly confident references she makes to her work in the progression of Prefaces speaks to such an interpretation. In her historical account of her cloister, *Primordia Coenobii Gandeshemensis*, she shows no hesitation about bringing the story up to her own time. She also, perhaps not incidentally, celebrates the lives of three great women she admired, the succeeding abbesses, including her mentor and friend Gerberga.

Although Hrosvitha's works fell into oblivion for several centuries after her death, they were revived at the end of the 15th century when the Renaissance humanist Conrad Celtis found an early and incomplete manuscript of her works and published it in 1501, referring to her as the "German Sappho." Ever since, her poetic and dramatic talents have been recognized and celebrated, but her role as a pioneering historian of women should also be acknowledged.

The chronicling of the lives of women religious by other nuns continued for many centuries. A special, later, category of such historical work comprises the autobiographies of mystics and saints, many of which I have discussed in earlier chapters. Such autobiographical writings, while they may have been initially inspired by the desire to spread a religious message or to give credence to a mystic's visions by putting them into the context of her life, should also be seen as efforts of historical documentation. Women like Hildegard of Bingen, Dorothea of Montau, Margery Kempe and later St. Catherine of Siena and St. Teresa of Avila may have had a firm sense of the significance of their remarkable lives as models for future generations of women. The fact that some of these saints refer to other women saints as their predecessor speaks to this interpretation.

"Sister books," which represent a special category of historical writing by nuns, appear in the German-speaking domains in the 14th and 15th centuries in Dominican convents. The nun Katherine von Gebersweiler was the author of the oldest of these histories, one documenting the history of the convent at Unterlinden. Her work consists of eight chapters describing the daily life of the convent, and 47 *vitae*, of which only five are of her contemporaries.[15] A near contemporary, the nun Elisabeth von Kirchberg, wrote a work of the same genre, the "Kirchberger Schwesternbuch," which documented the lives of the nuns of her convent. She also wrote the so-called "Irmegard-Vita," which describes the life and ecstatic visions of a Sister Irmegard. This *vita* was first written in secret by Elisabeth, but when Irmegard found out about it, she helped in the composition, resulting in two additional versions. In the same convent another such work was found, which may have been authored by the same nun, concerning the Dominican cloister at Ulm. It is interesting to note that she identified herself as "Sister Elisabeth . . . whom God took from the Jews." Since she entered the convent at the age of four, she cannot have been a converted Jew. More likely, she was given to the convent by her parents to escape one of the massacres of Jews that took place in the area during the 13th and 14th centuries.[16]

Anna von Muenziger, prioress of the Dominican convent in Adelshausen, wrote a chronicle of this convent in 1318, describing the lives and mystical experiences of thirty-four nuns. Other such convent histories were written and preserved in the convent of St. Katherine in Thurgau, Switzerland, and in the convents in Töss, Ötenbach and Weiler.[17] Since most of the "sister books" were written by women about women, this can be considered an early instance of Women's History-writing.

The tradition of convent histories or the histories of outstanding women religious continued for many centuries. In the 16th century Caritas Pirkheimer—sister of the humanist Willibald Pirkheimer—a woman renowned for her learning, wrote the history of her convent of St. Clara in Nürnberg. Other convent histories were written in the 17th century for the Ursulines and the Order of the Visitation in France.[18]

THE MAKING OF LISTS of famous women as heroines, role models and as arguments for women's potential for achievement occupied both men and women for six centuries. It figures prominently in the various *querelles des femmes,* in which both feminist and antifeminist writers constructed their arguments around *exempla.* Antifeminist writers made lists of women with negative characteristics or those who follow gender stereotypes. Feminist writers were more inclusive and tended to stress women of achievement or heroic women. Since the practice is so pervasive and the listing of illustrious women occurs with such regularity on the part of feminist writers, one can perhaps view this as a repeated effort to counteract the ill effects on women of the denial of the existence of a history of women. As we will see, some authors are quite explicit about such an aim, others imply it or say nothing about it. I will examine these lists on a comparative basis, first, as to their inclusiveness and the criteria of selection used and, second, to see what they can tell us about the transmission of ideas about women's past.

One of the first of the lists of famous women was compiled by a man, Giovanni Boccaccio, between 1355 and 1359 and published during this period.[19] Boccaccio, a celebrated Renaissance humanist who had previously anthologized the biographies of famous men, collected the lives of 104 women of Antiquity with a specific didactic purpose. He wished to show that the secular wisdom of the ancients was equal in importance to the Christian writings and myths and that among the ancients could be found persons of moral strength performing heroic deeds. He had shown this previously in his biographies of famous men, working under the assumption that illustrious deeds deserved to be preserved for posterity. But, as he stated in his Preface to *De claris mulieribus:*

> I have been quite astonished that women have had so little attention from writers . . . that they have gained no recognition in any work devoted especially to them, although it can be clearly seen . . . that some women have acted with as much strength as valor. If men should be praised whenever they perform great deeds (with strength which Nature has given them), how much more should women be extolled (almost all of whom are endowed with tenderness, frail bodies, and sluggish minds by Nature), if they have acquired a manly spirit and if with keen intelligence and remarkable fortitude they have dared undertake and have accomplished even the most difficult deeds?[20]

Boccaccio here expresses the Renaissance concepts of women as by nature weaker, gentler and of inferior intellect, which coexist with the stereotype of the "manly woman," the woman of strength and valor. By setting up this contradictory set of definitions for women, it was possible to account for the heroic, "the exceptional," the learned woman, without seeing patriarchal gender definitions as problematic. We have already seen that many women also accepted this set of definitions and tried to fit their argument into it.

Boccaccio's list includes mythological and allegorical figures, such as the Muses, Ceres, Circe, Isis. The list also includes evil women such as Medea, Medusa and Sempronia. Boccaccio explains in his Preface that he wished to include not only those famous for their virtues but those "who have become renowned to the world through any sort of deed."[21] He comments that in most historical accounts about men, those renowned for splendid deeds are often included with men like the Gracchi, Hannibal and Crassus, men of bad character and known for evil deeds. He also deliberately excluded all Christian women, because they had been frequently honored and their deeds of virtue, virginity and saintliness had been well celebrated, while the deeds of pagan women had not been previously collected and celebrated.

Boccaccio's descriptions of these women are neither historically nor mythologically accurate. His sources are mostly Latin authors of Antiquity, and he uses them without particular respect, discarding information they provide or adding invented material to theirs. He aims to tell an entertaining story and include "some pleasant exhortations to virtue and add inducements to avoid and detest wickedness, so that by adding pleasure to these stories their value would enter the mind by stealth."[22] The desire to entertain and at the same time to serve a moralistic didactic purpose was evident also in other of Boccaccio's works, such as the *Decameron*, but the quality may have predominated in *Of Famous Women* because he spoke to an audience of women, who, he believed, both deserved to know of their famous predecessors and to be morally instructed in the process.

Boccaccio's list was the starting point and model for others for many centuries. The first woman to follow his model was Christine de Pizan, who in 1405 published *Le Livre de la Cité des Dames [The Book of the City of the Ladies]*, a spirited and broad-ranging attempt at a defense of women and at a universal History of women.[23] Christine used Boccaccio as a source for nearly three-quarters of her list of women. But she did not use all of his list, and she significantly departed from his text in her comments about the women. She also imposed a totally different ordering on her list, which flows from her conceptual framework and her differing aims.

Christine had experience in doing historical work by having earlier written a History of the reign of Charles V of France, which had been commissioned by the King's brother, based on written evidence and the testimony of informants.[24] While the book was written entirely in praise of the King, she did cover his military exploits, his domestic policies and his moral leadership. By the time she began her work on *The Book of the City of the Ladies* she had written and published several books of verse and had developed her views on women in the exchange of letters regarding the *Roman de la rose*. She had also written a prose work of more than a hundred short narratives. Thus she was well prepared both as a writer and a historian for her major work.

She began the book with a marvelous account of her own transformation of consciousness. Sitting in her study reading one of the many misogynist tracts of the day, she began to wonder "how it happened that so many different men . . . are so inclined to express . . . so many wicked insults about women . . . It seems that they all speak from one and the same mouth." She examined herself and her experience and could find no evidence to support the claims of these men. Yet, she bowed to the authority of the male experts. "And so I relied more on the judgement of others than on what I myself felt and knew."[25] Here, for the first time in the written record, we have a woman defining the tension every thinking woman has experienced—between male authority denying her equality as a person and her own experience. Christine was deeply depressed by this recognition, when, as in a vision, three ladies appeared to her to comfort her and to bring her out of the ignorance which had blinded her intellect. Lady Reason explained to her that she had been selected to "vanquish from the world the same error into which you had fallen" and that she was entrusted with the task of building a city of ladies in which all valiant women might find refuge from attacks and slander.[26] The other two ladies, Rectitude and Justice, would help her in this task. Awed and elated, Christine asked the three women to explain to her why men had so universally attacked and slandered women. The ladies offered various explanations: men were motivated by greed, envy, impotence and thwarted desire. The ensuing long dialogue with the three spiritual guides allowed Christine de Pizan to develop her historical argument and to illustrate by *exempla* the virtues of women.

This allegorical framework, which assumes that the patriarchal explanatory system is built on error, structures the book. It determines also the way in which she uses her sources. Where Boccaccio, with a few exceptions, followed a roughly chronological outline, Christine de Pizan arranged her list to follow a series of themes and arguments. She also used different criteria of selection. She wished to write a universal History of women and their achievements, therefore she included women of Antiquity, the Christian era and even her contemporaries. She reinterpreted the lives of the women on her list in a significant way, since her aim was different from that of Boccaccio, who simply wanted to prove that there had been illustrious women in Antiquity. Christine de Pizan wrote in defense of women against what she considered the misogynist attacks of men, and she wrote from an entirely woman-centered point of view. In revising Boccaccio's list therefore not only did she exclude all evil women, but she often reinterpreted the stories of women with a bad reputation so as to present them in a positive light. This is most obvious in her treatment of Medea, who is cited under the heading "The Faithfulness of Women in Love" without any reference to her murdering her children. Boccaccio's story of Medea abounds in condemnation of her treachery, her witchcraft, her cruelty. He described her murder of her brother, her theft of her father's wealth, her winning of Jason by sorcery and finally her murder of his children out of jealousy. Christine ignored all these crimes. Instead, she credited Medea with the wisdom and magic skill which she used to help Jason win the Golden Fleece on the condition that he would make her his wife and be faithful to her. "However, Jason lied about his promise, for after everything went just as he wanted, he left Medea, for another woman."[27] At this, Christine tells us, Medea turned despondent, and thus she ends Medea's story.

Another such example is the treatment of the Roman Sempronia. Boccaccio first listed her considerable accomplishments, her extraordinary beauty, her excellent memory, her ability to learn Latin and Greek and compose poetry, her charm, her eloquence and good humor. He devoted two paragraphs to her virtues, then continued for four more paragraphs to list her vices, her excessive and overt sexuality, her greed for money, her immoderateness and finally her participation in the Catiline conspiracy. Christine took his first two paragraphs, greatly elaborated on them and presented Sempronia as a model of intelligence and ingenuity, then ignored the rest.[28]

Neither Boccacio nor Christine could meet the standards of objectivity demanded of professional historians nearly 600 years later, and one cannot expect that they should. The changing of evidence to make a point or impart a didactic message was a well-established convention in the Middle Ages. What is remarkable is Christine's consistent insistence on her right, as a woman, to interpret the past from a point of view sympathetic to women, and her speaking as their advocate.

After questioning the truth of the historical tradition by pointing out the male bias of selection, Christine attempted to answer every commonplace prejudice voiced against women. Men had charged that women governed unwisely when they had power. Christine refuted this argument by citing a long list of *exempla* of women who governed wisely and well. She answered the charge of women's intellectual inferiority by citing a long list of women who excelled in learning, in poetry, in science and in philosophy. Here, as elsewhere, she freely mixed historical figures with allegorical and mythological persons. She also attempted to show female superiority in sensibility and caring by citing a long list of virtuous wives and mothers, chaste virgins and self-sacrificing women. All of this material evidence allegorically built the city of the ladies. When it was finished, the Queen of Heaven was invited to be its first inhabitant, attended by a large number of female saints.

Having thus completed the city, Christine dedicated it to "ladies from the past as well as from the present and future," urged all ladies to take refuge in it and to defend and guard it against enemies and assailants. She explicitly defined men "who accuse you of so many vices in everything" as the enemies and urged women to flee from male slanders and entrapment, "to cultivate virtue, to increase and multiply our City, and to rejoice and act well."[29]

The allegorical city of the ladies, filled with heroines of worth and valor, represents the first consistent effort by a woman at constructing Women's History as a means of creating collective consciousness. Her attempt at creating a unifying ideology is deliberately broadly based; she speaks at various points of "all women—whether noble, bourgeois, or lower-class," and even her seeming distinction between the virtuous and others is not to be taken too seriously since in her various lists she manages freely to include wicked and even sinful women.[30] Her essential contribution was not only to attempt to rebut misogynist arguments by means of historical evidence but to insist that patriarchal generalizations and *dicta* would have to be evaluated and tested in light of the female experience, past and present. What Christine de Pizan had to offer to women was the insight that women must look to other women for their defense and that the collective past of women could be a source of strength to them in their struggle for justice.

Christine de Pizan was one of the few medieval women whose works were widely read, translated and distributed during her lifetime and for centuries after. Two male feminist writers, publishing a century after her death, show acquaintance with her work. The German Heinrich Cornelius Agrippa von Nettesheim (1529), in his wide-ranging and explicitly feminist argument, used the same explanation as Christine did for women's superiority: namely, that they had been created in paradise like the angels and made of superior matter. He did not credit Christine as his source. On the other hand François de Billon in a similar essay proclaiming the superiority of women and using Christine's arguments for it, listed her as among the outstanding female *exempla*, together with Hélisenne de Crenne.[31]

Yet Christine de Pizan's most important feminist insights found no echo among women for many centuries to come. In the absence of social organization and of communities of women who could have carried her ideas forward, these ideas, new and revolutionary for their time, fell like seeds on rocky ground. As we will see, in analyzing the lists of notable women made by feminists in ensuing centuries, most of them did not even know of Christine's work or existence. Women's History could not be created as an intellectual pursuit in the absence of a social movement of women.

A few decades after Christine de Pizan's death the first clusters of learned women living outside of cloisters appeared in the Renaissance courts of Italy. Some of them were related by kinship or marriage; others had learned by reputation of the existence of such women. One cannot characterize this kind of minimal contact as a female network, yet this is the earliest time in which we can trace a rudimentary transmission of knowledge among women. Laura Cereta (1469–99) studied with her father, Silvestro Cereta, a member of Brescia's ruling elite and established a literary career before her marriage at age fifteen. Unlike most women of her time, she was able to keep up her studies during the three years of her marriage and the years of widowhood. Yet, like most of the educated women of her time, she was suspected of having copied and presented as her own the work of a male relative, in this case her father. In writing to defend herself against this false accusation, Cereta claimed that she must defend her entire sex and cited a list of learned women from Antiquity up to her own time. They mostly derived from Boccaccio with a few added from Diogenes Laertius. What is of greatest interest here is her inclusion of several contemporaries, namely, Isotta Nogarola, Cassandre Fedele and Nicolosa Sanuto of Bologna. In a letter to a male detractor Cereta also echoed a biblical argument developed by Isotta Nogarola. Clearly then, she knew and had read at least some of her female contemporaries' work.[32]

Another spirited defense of women's intellectual capacities and of their long history of achievement appeared in Italy in 1600 from the pen of one Lucretia Marinella.[33] Her long list of notable women included many of the women cited by her predecessors, but it was clearly not a case of simply copying Boccaccio. Marinella cited a broad range of authors other than Boccaccio as her authorities, even for those women listed in Boccaccio. She seems to have been widely read, and she skillfully wove among the usual names listed from Antiquity and from Christian sources the names of female rulers and medieval religious. She cited Elisabeth of Schönau, Hrosvitha of Gandersheim, Hildegard of Bingen and a number of learned women of the Renaissance. Yet her main appeal is to the authority of profeminist males. One gets the impression that she was well read in male sources but knew the female sources only by reputation. Like Christine de Pizan before her, Marinella argued for the superiority of women, but she also devoted a large section of her argument to giving *exempla* for the defects and faults of men.

In the first half of the 17th century learned women in England were engaged in the pamphlet war we earlier discussed as the *querelle des femmes*. One of the feminist pamphleteers, writing under the pseudonym Ester Sowernam, bolstered her argument with a list of "women worthies," which in some respects goes beyond those of earlier defenders of the sex. Her list of biblical women did not derive from Boccaccio but clearly shows her own biblical study, for she cited chapter and verse for each entry. In addition to the usual listing of the wives of the biblical patriarchs, the prophetess Deborah, the heroic Jael and Judith, she cited the nameless women who performed worthy deeds, Michal and Abigail as wise counselors, and chaste Susanna. The descriptions of the deeds of these heroines are original and idiosyncratic. She did a similar close reading of the New Testament to arrive at her own list of heroines. She also added to a short list of women of Antiquity a list of English queens up to and including Elizabeth I.[34] Although we know that Rachel Speght knew Sowernam's pamphlet, there is no reference to Speght in Sowernam's work. And neither of them referred to any woman writer before her.[35]

The debate in Europe over women's education led to a number of pamphlets in which lists of "women worthies" were used to bolster the main argument. One of the earliest and the most cited male defender of women was Heinrich Cornelius Agrippa von Nettesheim, whose book appeared first in 1529 in Antwerp and then in five other language editions within fifty years. It was followed by the defense of women by François Poulain de la Barre in 1555. Both men were frequently cited as authorities by suceeding writers on the same subject.[36] In Germany, one Johann Frauenlob in 1631 published a lengthy annotated list of women of distinction, which he derived not only from Boccaccio but from Coelius, Angelo Politiano and a number of Roman sources.[37] While he listed Christine de Pizan, he made no use of her list from *The Book of the City of the Ladies*. It is interesting to note that not only did his list contribute a large number of names of German women to the notables, but that he accurately listed most of the important learned women of the Italian Renaissance. One can assume that by the middle of the 17th century the list of famous learned women of Europe was known to educated men in Europe. The startling and dismaying fact is that it was not so known to women.

The argument for female education was further fostered by a pamphlet written collaboratively by a professor at Coburg, Johannes Sauerbrei, and one Jacob Thomasius, a teacher at Leibniz. The pamphlet, which appeared in 1671, was much cited and was reprinted in 1676.[38] Its argument for women's education is bolstered by a long list of "women worthies" which includes most of the women cited by Frauenlob.[39] However, Thomasius/Sauerbrei cited many male authorities for the information they list, among them five humanists, starting with Boccaccio and including Agrippa von Nettesheim. Again, no women were used as sources or authorities.

The German Christian Franz Paullini listed 270 German learned women in his defense of women's education, published in 1705.[40] The list includes "curiosities," such as deformed and handicapped women. A more scholarly work, which gives sources for its large list of learned woman was published a year later by Johann Eberti.[41]

The custom of listing women of achievement thus developed into a distinct literary genre. It represented a rudimentary attempt at creating Women's History and was, as we have seen, a byproduct of debates over the place of women in society and over their education. The practice took on a new life and meaning, chiefly in the 18th and 19th centuries, when both women and men created large, sometimes multi-volume works celebrating women's achievements as literary entertainment for a growing audience of women. A forerunner of this type in England was the work of Thomas Heywood, who made an effort at representativeness by including three Jews and three Gentiles in his *The Exemplary Lives and Memorable Acts of the Most Worthy Women of the World*.[42] A more overtly feminist orientation pervaded the work of George Ballard, a staymaker and amateur antiquarian, who not only listed women celebrated for their writings and their skill in languages, but attempted to give fairly comprehensive biographies and listings of their works. His work was based on original research and the information he offered is generally accurate.[43] It is worth noting that Ballard was inspired in this work by Elizabeth Elstob who had suggested the project to him. Elstob herself had much earlier begun to research notable women and had made entries on forty of them in her notebooks, but had done nothing further.[44]

Similar volumes of biographical compilation appeared in France and other European countries. I will cite just one such example because of its unusual form, *Les Femmes illustres* by Madeleine de Scudéry. The author, best known as a salonière and one of the most prolific novelists of the 17th century, here combined fictionalized speeches, supposedly spoken by the featured women, and biography. She presented forty women, primarily from Antiquity, but singled out as her heroine the poet Sappho, who declared that the only way a woman could be known to posterity is through her writing.[45]

In England the effort of the compilers continued with the publication of works by several women. In response to the publication of John Duncombe's poem *The Feminead* (1754), Mary Scott, objecting to his including only 25 women poets in his list, published a poem called *The Female Advocate . . .* , in which she listed 49 female English poets.[46] Interestingly, her list includes Phillis Wheatley, the American slave, whose book of poetry had recently reached England. Mary Hays's, *Female Biography or Memoirs of Illustrious and Celebrated Women of All Ages and Countries*, which is based largely on Ballard, attempted to be comprehensive and took six volumes, while Mary Roberts, *Select Female Biography: Comprising Memoirs of Eminent British Ladies*, chose to be highly selective.[47]

Biographies of eminent women designed to appeal to literate women readers became a popular genre in the 19th century in England and in other European countries.[48]

In the United States this genre is represented by a two-volume *History of Women* by Lydia Maria Child.[49] The first volume is a collection of ethnographic, anecdotal and cultural information about women of continents other than Europe and North America. In the second volume Child chronologically and by region lists women of achievement and renown. She uses prior compilations, including Boccaccio, and other authors as sources. The only female sources she uses are travel writers and Phillis Wheatley. Her omissions are more interesting than her inclusions; for example, under "Vindications of Women" she lists Marguerite de Navarre but neither Christine de Pizan nor Mary Wollstonecraft. Frances Wright, who shortly before the publication of Child's book had given widely publicized and highly controversial public lectures in the Eastern seaboard cities advocating women's rights and sexual freedom, was dismissed by Child in a passing reference as a modern disciple of "the infidels of the French revolution."[50] Child's attempt at a cultural and societal discussion of the "condition" of women is innovative, but her list is quite traditional.

Another example of the genre is a selection of biographies by Harriet Beecher Stowe, *Woman in Sacred History: A Series of Sketches Drawn from Scriptural, Historical and Legendary Sources*, which uses the Old and the New Testament as its source.[51] The sketches are prettified literary versions of the biblical tales, the only interpretive feature being the author's conviction that Christianity was a liberating force for women. The same conviction motivated Phebe A. Hanaford in her *Daughters of America, or Women of the Century.*[52] In her discussion of women of the Old Testament she stressed that "heathens" treated their women poorly. She combined the concept of Christian superiority with the claim that women's highest potential would be realized in America. A similarly celebratory and patriotic tone is evident in a number of other such anthologies printed in the last decades of the 19th century, all characterized by a strong Protestant, white and Anglo-Saxon bias.[53]

Sarah J. Hale, editor of *Godey's Lady's Book,* in her Introduction refers to a dozen such books which had appeared within just three years before her own publication. She considered her own work to be an aid and incentive for the educational progress of women and claimed to have gathered "from the records of the world the names and histories of all distinguished women," amounting to 2500 names. In line with her purpose she dedicated the work to "the Men of America who show, in their laws and customs respecting women, ideas more just and feelings more noble than were ever evinced by men of any other nation. . . ."[54] Hale stated firmly that she was not in sympathy with those advocating woman's rights, and she considered equality for women a foolish goal. But she considered woman "God's appointed agent of *morality,* the teacher and inspirer of . . . the virtues of humanity."[55] Her list is far more inclusive than any other previously published. Still, she omitted any woman she considered not quite respectable, such as Wollstonecraft or Frances Wright; she included no abolitionists and none connected with the advocacy of woman's rights. Her allotment of space further reveals her bias: the first and second "era" of her history contain 53 names, which are allotted 149 pages of text. The third era, 1500 to 1820, she considers remarkable because it features the genius and development of Anglo-Saxon women. This section contains 104 names in 412 pages. The last section comprises merely 30 years, 1820–50, but it contains 57 names in 266 pages. Hale considered her contemporaries so important that in this section she frequently printed selections from the women's writings. Typically, Hale's entry on Christine de Pizan contains a full biography, with lengthy emphasis on the men in her life, a list of her historical writings and no mention of *The Book of the City of the Ladies.*

The feminist compilers were no less present-minded. The most ambitious work from their ranks was published in 1893 by Frances E. Willard, president of the Women's Christian Temperance Union, and Mary A. Livermore, a reformer and woman's rights leader. *A Woman of the Century . . .* consists of 1470 biographical sketches with photographs of "Leading American Women in All Walks of Life."[56] The editors considered the 19th century to be the century of opportunities for women and set out to compile "this rosary of nineteenth century achievement."[57] They arranged their entries alphabetically with standard-length biographies and citations of authors' titles. The book has a professional look about it and is patterned after the *National Cyclopedia* and other biographical dictionaries. Still, the self-conscious celebratory tone of the essays and the selection of persons to be included reveal the authors' didactic intent. This volume celebrates women active in religious, welfare and educational work, the kind of women honored in the cultural programs of the women's clubs then springing up in every community in the United States. The omissions are equally telling: there is not one African-American woman listed, and all the famous women to whom any touch of "scandal," such as a divorce, adhered were excluded. Frances Wright, Ernestine Rose, Frances Kemble, Margaret Fuller did not pass the "respectability" test and were omitted.

The lists of women of achievement, like all efforts at compensatory History, reveal the biases of their compilers and serve their educational purposes. That is not surprising nor does it diminish the significance of their endeavor and the need for heroines that it expresses. On a more local scale we find innumerable compilations of such women made on the basis of their regional significance or of their special roles as educators, missionaries or women pioneering in one or another of the professions.[58] A special effort of this kind was the pioneering list of African-American women of achievement assembled within a book of essays and poems by Gertrude E. H. Mossell. It named and celebrated the work of African-American women in education, churches, mission and welfare organizations.[59] Like its counterparts written by white women, this book was inspired by and directed at the black women's club movement and fed the interests of an ever-widening circle of female readers.

As women struggled to gain access to higher education they countered arguments of their incapacity for learning by showing the achievements of educated women of the past. One can argue that they continued the centuries-old *querelle des femmes* in a more concentrated and intense fashion, but always in ignorance of the work and the arguments of their female predecessors. None of the compilers I have seen and cited had any knowledge of the women of past centuries who argued and fought for women's rights except for a few of the pioneers of women's education. As we have seen, the list-makers relied on male sources and did not know or did not use the work of women who had published before them. Thus, the impulse for creating Women's History took a form which we have earlier discussed in regard to feminist Bible criticism: women, ignorant of their history, had to reinvent the wheel over and over again.

Another aspect of women's History-making continued the medieval tradition: the writing by women of biographies of women. This activity can be found in every country, from the 18th century onward. While there are some isolated instances of biographical writings earlier, there is a dramatic increase in such writings after 1850, when a large female readership could provide financial success for such work.[60]

But toward the end of the 19th century we can discern a new approach in the effort at History-making by American women. They are no longer solely concerned with creating reference lists of women they and their daughters might seek to emulate. They are now concerned with collecting the raw materials for Women's History and with recording and preserving the record of their own achievements in educational and reform institutions, in churches, in women's clubs and in specific communities. It is from this period we can date the voluminous collections of Women's History sources which today are listed in the state-by-state directory of archival holdings on the subject, *Women's History Sources Survey*.[61] The self-consciousness of women as a group, their awareness of the value of their work in communities and organizations, found expression in a new and different attitude toward documentation. No longer are women solely concentrating on "outstanding" figures and on the celebration of leadership. What they are now preserving is the record of daily activities, the immense community-building work of ordinary women.[62] Whether they know it or not, this effort links them with the anonymous nuns writing "sister books" to record the history of their orders and with the long line of list-makers who tried to tease the existence of a History of women out of the scraps available to them from the History of educated men.

The most self-consciously feminist effort of this kind was represented in the six-volume *History of Woman Suffrage*, compiled by Elizabeth Cady Stanton, Susan B. Anthony and Matilda Joslyn Gage with contributions from women in every state.[63] The feminists engaged in this effort were already conscious of what the absence of

Women's History had meant to women as a group and they realized, however dimly, that the first need for those creating History is the existence of sources. They were aware of the danger that their movement, which combined with the woman's club movement was the biggest mass organization and the biggest coalition built in that century, might fall into oblivion if its records were lost. The effort to preserve the record was uppermost in the minds of the editors. Their somewhat haphazard assemblage of the documents they could find and preserve was an immense contribution, despite obvious and blatant failings.

The *HWS* is an incomplete, flawed and heavily biased assemblage of sources. It distorts the origins of the movement by ignoring or downplaying the role of many activists and antecedent activists in favor of stressing the leadership of a few women. The strongly secular bias of its editors and their disenchantment with the organized churches in regard to the struggle of women for their emancipation are reflected in the way they defined the movement as mostly political and constitutional, disregarding the important feminist struggles in the various churches during the century.[64] It is also factionally biased in its downplaying of the role of the women who in 1869 split with Stanton and Anthony, a distortion which is particularly striking in regard to the role of Lucy Stone. Yet these volumes have provided the basis for over a hundred years of historiography on the subject and, in what Mary Beard called "the long history of women," represent a milestone.

The woman's rights and suffrage advocates were concerned with their place in History and showed it by writing each other's biographies, by writing autobiographies and by preserving their correspondences.[65] The impulse represented by *HWS* was also manifest in the first efforts at writing narrative Women's History, the history of women's organizational activities and in an early attempt at a theoretical exploration of women's status in different societies throughout historical time.[66]

Yet by the end of the 19th century, at the very time when a mass movement of women laid the foundations for collecting Women's History sources and interpreting them, the academy, in its textbooks, monographs and teaching denied the existence of such a history. In the 1880s the development of modern American universities and the professionalization of History as a discipline coincided. Sex discrimination was institutionalized more firmly with the development of graduate schools from which women were by and large excluded and to which they had to gain access through prolonged struggles. Academic History produced by academically trained historians confirmed and solidified the already existing marginalization of women in the historical text. And it made the gap between the informal attempts at creating Women's History and the History developed and taught by professional historians ever wider.

The small group of female professional historians then active participated in the professionalization of History, but their employment opportunities were marginal, the majority confined to employment in women's colleges. Only one of nine academically trained women historians in the Progressive period studied by Kathryn Sklar taught in a coeducational college—Mary Barnes at Stanford for the last five years of her career.[67] Even as these professionally trained historians gained a foothold in the academy, they did it by exceling in traditional fields. Only two of them wrote Women's History. Dr. Kate Hurd-Mead, a medical doctor turned historian at the end of her distinguished career, wrote a history of women in science. Helen Sumner, a labor historian, focused on the history of working women in a pioneering study which was widely distributed in a government pamphlet and remains an authoritative source on the topic.[68]

Even in the 20th century, when women trained and fully qualified in historical scholarship began to raise the issue of women's marginalization in the cultural product, their own work was either marginalized or ignored. Like their forerunners, the second generation of professionally trained women historians had to struggle, inch by inch and step by step, for access to equal job opportunities, for research support and for representation in professional journals and at professional conventions. The small group of pioneers who in 1929 formed the first professional association of women historians and, starting in 1934, met annually as the Berkshire History Conference, in order to give a voice and offer support to women in the profession, understood that without the existence of a female support network they would not be able to survive within the confines of a centuries-old male academic tradition.

Out of this generation of women historians came the small handful who in the late 1930s produced monographs in colonial and Southern Women's History and in the History of Women's Education that pointed the way to the future development of the field.[69]

Meanwhile, non-academic women intellectuals continued the quest for the establishment of Women's History. The few works in Women's History produced in the first half of the 20th century were mostly written by women outside of the academy and remained generally unnoticed by professional historians.[70]

The most important of these works, Mary Beard's *Woman as Force in History*, was ridiculed by academic reviewers and otherwise ignored.[71] Yet it was Mary Beard who, reaching back to the 15th century, took up the theme Christine de Pizan had raised and which had for so long seemingly vanished in the consciousness of women. Writing as a well-trained historian who deliberately chose not to be part of the academy, Beard asserted boldly that women always were and always had been a force in history. Women were central to the historical process and History, to be true to life, would have to be written so that their world-view, their vantage point, would be as fully represented in it as that of men. "Woman *is* and *makes* history," she asserted and devoted her life to winning recognition for that fact.[72]

Mary Beard was herself an activist in the labor and feminist movement of the 1920s. She, together with a remarkable group of older suffragists, spent years in the struggle to create a World Center for Women's Archives, which was to serve as a repository of the sources of Women's History and was "to encourage recognition of women as co-makers of history."[73] Their effort failed for lack of support in the 1940s, but it did not fail entirely, for out of this struggle came the creation of one of the major Women's History archives in the United States—the Schlesinger Library Archives at Radcliffe College, as well as, eventually, the Miriam Holden collection, now housed at Princeton University.[74] Mary Beard not only conceptualized Women's History as an academic topic, she wrote four pioneering works on the subject and showed in her collaborative works with her husband, the historian Charles Beard, how the shifting focus provided by attention to women would transform the historical narrative.[75]

When one reads historical works covering long spans of time there are no more traces of our [women's] names to be found than there are traces to be found of a vessel crossing the ocean."[76]

Thus, Anna Maria von Schurman in a letter written in 1638 deplored the constraints on women's intellectual development and the effect it had on the writing of History. For 1200 years, in sporadic, intermittent and often pathetically ineffective ways, women struggled to counteract that.trend and to leave, as did men, traces of their names and actions in the historical record. Yet, in face of the patriarchal hegemony over culture, the leaving of "traces" and even the collection of sources was utterly insufficient to affect the way History was being written and being taught. Autobiographical and biographical works, even though produced with increasing frequency, enriched the source record but did not provide a coherent conceptualization of the past of women. And, as can be seen from the story of the U.S. 20th-century pioneers of Women's History who had a coherent concept of its shape and scope, even their efforts resulted only in disappointment and failure. This was so because they lacked what their predecessors had lacked most of the time, the support of a strong and viable women's movement.

History shows that for women the right to learn, to teach and to define has always come as the result of political struggle. The structuring of society in such a way that women were for millennia excluded from the creation of the cultural product has more decisively disadvantaged women in their economic and political rights than any other factor. Unlike for men, whose intellectual advancement on the part of men of genius were supported and furthered by institutions, the advances made by individual women of great talent, even in those cases where they were not entirely thwarted and buried without trace, did not translate into advances for the entire sex. Women as-a-group have made intellectual and educational advances only as a result of organized struggle.

Thus, despite the centuries of pioneering effort on the part of individuals and small groups of educated women, it was not until the rise of the second wave of the modern women's movement in the 1960s that the latest phase in the struggle for Women's History began. Then, for the first time in history, the existence of highly trained groups of women located strategically in institutions of higher education coincided with the emergence of a dynamic women's movement. In 1969, when the newly formed caucus of women's historians, the Coordinating Committee of Women in the Historical Profession, was organized with the avowed purpose of advancing the status of women in the profession and developing the field of Women's History, the two purposes fused.[77] The new group was part of an intellectual movement for redefining the content of the major fields of knowledge in such a way as to make women as central to the definition of the field as were men.

This new movement for Women's Studies and the integration of women into the curriculum have made spectacular advances in the United States and in the world in the past twenty years. While the development is uneven, depending as it does on the existence of women's movements, it is also irreversible. Once the basic fallacy of patriarchal thought—the assumption that a half of humankind can adequately represent the whole—has been exposed and explained, it can no more be undone than was the insight that the earth is round, not flat.

TWELVE

Conclusion

FEMINIST CONSCIOUSNESS consists (1) of the awareness of women that they belong to a subordinate group and that, as members of such a group, they have suffered wrongs; (2) the recognition that their condition of subordination is not natural, but societally determined; (3) the development of a sense of sisterhood; (4) the autonomous definition by women of their goals and strategies for changing their condition; and (5) the development of an alternate vision of the future.

Because of the way women have been structured into patriarchal institutions, because of their long history of educational deprivation and of their economic dependence on males, women have had to overcome many obstacles before this process of coming-into-consciousness could be achieved. As we have seen, they first had to overcome their internalized feelings of mental and spiritual inferiority. In order to think and write at all, they had to prove to themselves and to each other that they were equal creatures before God, that they were able to communicate with God without male mediation and to conceptualize the Divine in their own way. This was the great contribution to women's thought made by the long line of women mystics whose work we have examined. Other groups of women authorized themselves to write because they were mothers. For centuries women conceptualized their group coherence on the basis of their actual experience of or their capacity for motherhood. Maternal thinking and responsibility gave them a special role in so-

ciety and empowered them to resist certain aspects of patriarchal
thought and practice. The experience of motherhood as empowering
and as embodying specialized knowledge enabled women to subvert
patriarchal religious ideas by insisting on a female aspect of the Divine. This could take the form of giving female characteristics to
Jesus or of elevating the Virgin Mary to a position near to equality
with the Trinity. It could lead to the various efforts we have traced
by which women rewrote the story of the Redemption to make
women's role essential in it. The patriarchal "glorification of motherhood," which began in the 18th century and culminated in the
19th-century glorification of women's role in the domestic sphere,
led increasing numbers of women to the recognition that their collectivity needed to be defined not by their maternal role but by their
personhood. This kind of reasoning contributed to the definition of
"sisterhood" as the collective entity of women.

For over a thousand years women reinterpreted the biblical texts
in a massive feminist critique, yet their marginalization in the formation of religious and philosophical thought prevented this critique
from ever engaging the minds of the men who had appointed themselves as the definers of divine truth and revelation. Women's Bible
criticism not only did not alter the patriarchal paradigm but also
failed to spur the advancement of women's thought in a feminist
direction, for women did not know that other women before them
had already engaged in this enterprise of re-thinking and re-vision.
It helped individual women to authorize themselves and in some
cases to create important works of lasting impact. But what we need
to note is the discontinuity in the story of women's intellectual effort. Endlessly, generation after generation of Penelopes rewove the
unraveled fabric only to unravel it again.

A different group of women authorized themselves to think and
write by reliance on and an appeal to the gift of their special talent.
Creativity became the instrument by which these women emancipated themselves intellectually to a level from which they could think
their way out of patriarchy. There is a long history of these extraordinary women, which we have traced in this book. Their individual
achievements are awesome and inspire respect, yet it must be noted
that their individual effort could not lead to a collective advancement
in consciousness. The women of talent existed, they struggled val-
iantly, they achieved—and they were forgotten. The women coming
after them had to start all over again, repeating the process.

The awareness of a wrong is, as we have seen, something women developed over 1500 years from within patriarchal training and culture. Many women reasoned their way to an understanding that their condition was societally determined. This point was, in fact, the major insight provided by the generations of feminist Bible critics. The achievement of the next stage of awareness—namely, that they must join with other women to remedy the wrongs they suffered—was much harder to accomplish.

Crucial to the development of feminist consciousness are societal changes which allow substantial numbers of women to live in economic independence. We have earlier discussed these preconditions, most of them connected with industrialization, such as the decline in infant mortality and maternal death rates and the increase in life span. These are the developments that enable substantial numbers of women to choose not to be reproducers or, at the very least, to limit the number of years of their life span they devote to maternal work. Fully developed feminist consciousness rests on the precondition that women must have an economic alternative for survival other than marriage and that there exist large groups of single, self-supporting women. Only with such preconditions can women conceptualize alternatives to the patriarchal state; only with such preconditions can women elevate sisterhood to a unifying ideal. In order for women to verify the adequacy, even the power, of their own thinking they needed cultural affirmation, exactly as men did. The mystics and women religious could find such affirmation in their actual or spiritual communities. Secular women attempted to and sometimes did find it in women's clusters or networks. Beginning with the 17th century, women were able to find it in the response of female readers of their books and audiences for their dramas.

But as long as the vast majority of women depended for their economic existence and that of their children on the support of a man, the formation of such female support networks was the privilege of a tiny minority of upper-class women. All positions of economic, legal and political power were in the hands of men, thus even the intellectually most emancipated women, those hoping to make changes in society, could not conceive of the process other than doing so with the help of powerful men. The learned women of the Reformation aimed no further than achieving a respectful dialogue with the men of their circles. The women in the left-wing sects of the Protestant Reformation saw themselves, at best, as equal partners with men in redefining religious belief and practice.

From the 17th century on, the main issue for religious and secular women on which they focused their strivings for equality was education. From Astell to Wollstonecraft to Catharine Beecher, women correctly defined the wrong they suffered as educational discrimination and defined their goal as equal access. But the arguments they used for a long time were focused on gaining male support and thus defined the issue in a way that still rested largely on patriarchal gender definitions. Because women were mothers and had responsibility for educating the young, they needed to be granted better education. Because they were the mothers of the Republic, their citizenship could best be expressed by their raising loyal [male] citizens and to do so, they needed to be better educated themselves.

Yet, again starting in the 17th century, the same advocacy for women's equal education took a different form, often originating with women who had also used the earlier arguments. Bathsua Makin, with the support of a network of women, founded women's schools. Mary Astell advocated a sex-segregated institution for the education of women, again with the support of other women. In the 19th-century United States, Emma Willard, Mary Lyon and Catharine Beecher, using the most traditional arguments for women's right to education, each set up sex-segregated educational institutions. To do so, they created female networks which quickly began to take on a life of their own. Female sponsors and alumnae of these institutions began to see their roles in society in a new light and many of them formed the core of activists who created the 19th-century woman's rights movement. The development of the British, French and German woman's rights movements was also connected with the growth and development of women's education.

Similar to the situation in the 1840s and 1850s in the United States, when voting rights for white men were being expanded, women in Great Britain petitioned to have voting rights for women included in the electoral reform legislation of 1832. Their petitions went unheeded, and the women put their energy into other channels. In the 1850s they formed organizations to press for educational reforms, the right of divorce, a Married Women's Property Bill (passed in 1855), and greater employment opportunities for women. Out of these clusters of women active in reforms *for women*, arose the first woman's rights organization, the National Society for Women's Suffrage in 1867.[1]

In France, women had actively participated in the great revolutionary movements of 1792, 1848 and 1870, in each case forming sex-segregated organizations which made quite advanced feminist demands. These organization were short-lived and ineffective; they were destroyed by repressive regimes and a conservative backlash. The *Code Napoléon*, backed by the Catholic Church and enacted in 1804, classified married women with children, the insane and criminals as politicaly incompetent; restricted women's legal and civil rights; made married women economically and legally subject to their husbands and declared that they belonged to the family, not to public life. The *Code* forbade women to attend political meetings or to wear trousers.

In the 1848 revolution against the monarchy, women played an active part. They established several feminist clubs and newspapers, took part in revolutionary battles and street actions, petitioned the provisional government for the vote, and even attempted to run female candidates. Working-class women raised economic demands specific to their own interests. But all of these efforts proved fruitless. Universal male suffrage, which was enacted in 1848, excluded women; a school reform bill setting up primary education for girls put these schools under the control of the Catholic Church. Several women who had participated in the Revolution were sent to prison or exile. The feminist organizations died in the wake of the general repression.

A similar sequence of events occurred during and after the Paris Commune in 1871. Its defeat devastated a tiny feminist movement and the few radical women who had participated in the Commune. It was not until 1883 that a feminist organization, *Société du Suffrage des Femmes* (Women's Suffrage Society), was formed. French women did not receive legal recognition of their personhood and voting rights until 1938.[2]

In Germany, women's feminist consciousness was affected by the development of German nationalism. The journalist Louise Otto edited a feminist newspaper from 1849 to 1850 in Saxony as a result of her disappointment with the debates over a constitution for the future unified nation. "They think in their deliberations only about half the human race only about men," she commented. "When they speak of the people, they do not include the women."[3] She and the other women who participated in the 1848 revolutions gained this basic insight over and over again. As fighters on the barricades they were subject to the same persecution and prison sentences as the male revolutionaries, but when they advanced a program for the full equality of women, they met male indifference and resistance.[4] The reaction following the defeat of the revolution set back all organizational efforts. In most German states legislation enacted in 1850 forbade women and minors from attending any political meetings and joining political organizations. Yet in the 1850s autonomous women's organizations arose in many German cities out of welfare organizations for the victims of the defeated revolution. In Hamburg a woman's organization, set up to improve the discourse between Protestant and Jewish women, succeeded in developing plans for the establishment of a university for women, but their efforts, like those of other feminist groups, succumbed to the repression of all grassroots organizations after 1850. Adapting to this climate of repression, the *Allgemeiner Deutscher Frauenverein* (General Geman Women's Association), led by Louise Otto in the 1860s and 70s, limited itself to conservative demands and tactics. German national unification and statehood in 1870 under Prussia's leadership did not promote democracy. Nationalism, militarism and the most traditionalist emphasis on women's domestic role continued unchallenged. It was not until 1902 that it was possible for German women to form a major woman's suffrage association.

What emerges from this brief overview is that women's participation in general revolutionary movements did not bring them closer to advancing their own rights and interests. Time and time again, their sacrifices and contributions were appreciated, but their male colleagues and comrades considered their demands at best marginal and secondary and did not act on them. Interestingly, conservative political groups always considered the threat of feminism a central issue and made the repression of women's organizations an inevitable and essential feature of their political program. What also becomes clear is the necessary connection between women's work in sex-segregated groups under their own leadership and the advancement of feminist organizations.

Sex-segregated social space became the terrain in which women could confirm their own ideas and test them against the knowledge and experience of other women. Here, they could also, for the first time in history, test their theories in social practice. Unlike the social spaces in which women could have equal or nearly equal leadership roles, but in which the hegemony of men remained unchallenged— such as the salons, the utopian communities, the socialist and anarchist parties—these all-female spaces could help women to advance from a simple analysis of their condition to the level of theory formation. Or, in other words, to the level of providing not only their own autonomous definitions of their goals but an alternate vision of societal organization—a feminist world-view.

The sex-segregated institutions and organizations formed in the 19th century in the United States, England and on the European continent were usually driven by necessity. Women founded girls' academies because society did not adequately provide for the education of women. Women formed women's medical colleges, hospitals, nursing training institutions, because male-dominated schools and institutions excluded them. The earliest women's clubs in America, both those of white and of African-American women, were formed to counteract discriminatory practices by male clubs. The founders intended merely to right a wrong, to redress a grievance, to win limited equity and/or access. But the process of reaching that goal, the resistance they met, the struggles to overcome that resistance, all enhanced the process of consciousness-formation. It was this dynamic which enabled them to develop a sense of sisterhood and separate forms of women's culture, institutions and modes of living.

A similar development took place in social welfare and in religious organizations. In the United States throughout the 19th century we find women organizing first to help others, then to help themselves. In the social struggles they engaged in they experienced resistance to their efforts by men and by male-dominated institutions, ranging from universities to the state. It was only then, when they began not only to think of themselves as a coherent group, but when they began to act in society as such a group, that the concept of sisterhood could be more than a rhetorical term.

Throughout historical time, women have been discriminated against and disadvantaged economically, politically, legally and sexually. They have, depending on their class, race and ethnic affiliations with men also participated in discriminating against, disadvantaging and exploiting men and women different from themselves by race and class and religion. In short, they have, while being victimized by patriarchy, continued to support the system and helped to perpetuate it. They have done so because their consciousness of their own situation could not develop in a manner commensurate with their advancement in other aspects of their lives. Thus, the systematic educational disadvantaging of women and their definition as being persons "out of history" have been truly the most oppressive aspect of women's condition under patriarchy.

I have argued in this book that women's marginalization in the process of History-making has set them back intellectually and has kept them for far longer than was necessary from developing a consciousness of their collectivity in sisterhood, not motherhood. The cruel repetitiousness by which individual women have struggled to a higher level of consciousness, repeating an effort made a number of times by other women in previous centuries, is not only a symbol of women's oppression but is its actual manifestation. Thus, even the most advanced feminist thinkers, up to and including those in the early 20th century, have been in dialogue with the "great men" before them and have been unable to verify, test and improve their ideas by being in dialogue with the women thinkers before them. Mary Wollstonecraft argued with Burke and Rousseau, when arguing with Makin, Astell and Margaret Fell might have sharpened her thought and radicalized her. Emma Goldman argued for free love and a new sort of communal life against the models of Marx and Bakunin; a dialogue with the Owenite feminists Anna Wheeler and Emma Martin might have redirected her thinking and kept her from inventing "solutions" which had already proven unworkable fifty years earlier. Simone de Beauvoir, in a passionate dialogue with Marx, Freud, Sartre and Camus, could go as far with a feminist critique of patriarchal values and institutions as it was possible to go when the thinker was male-centered. Had she truly engaged with Mary Wollstonecraft's thought, the works of Mary Astell, the Quaker feminists of the early 19th century, the mystical revisioners among the black spiritualists and the feminism of Anna Cooper, her analysis might have become woman-centered and therefore capable of projecting alternatives to the basic mental constructs of patriarchal thought. Her erroneous assertion that, "They [women] have no past, no history, no religion of their own," was not just an oversight and a flaw, but a manifestation of the basic limitations which have for millennia limited the power and effectiveness of women's thought.[5]

Human beings have always used history in order to find their direction toward the future: to repeat the past or to depart from it. Lacking knowledge of their own history, women thinkers did not have the self-knowledge from which to project a desired future. Therefore, women have, up until very recently, not been able to create a social theory appropriate to their needs. Feminist consciousness is a prerequisite for the formulation of the kind of abstract thought needed to conceptualize a society in which differences do not connote dominance.

The hegemony of patriarchal thought in Western civilization is not due to its superiority in content, form and achievement over all other thought; it is built upon the systematic silencing of other voices. Women of all classes, men of different races or religious beliefs from those of the dominant, those defined as deviants by them—all these had to be discouraged, ridiculed, silenced. Above all they had to be kept from being part of the intellectual discourse. Patriarchal thinkers constructed their edifice the way patriarchal statesmen contructed their states: by defining who was to be kept out. The definition of those to be kept out was usually not even made explicit, for to have made it explicit would have meant to acknowledge that there was a process of exclusion going on. Those to be kept out were simply obliterated from sight, marginalized out of existence. When the great system of European universities secularized learning and made it more widely accessible, the very nature of the university was so defined as to exclude all women from it. In the 19th century, throughout Europe and in the United States, professions redefined their purposes, restructured their organizations, licensed and upgraded their services and enhanced their status in the societies in which they operated. All of this was based on the tacit assumption that women were to be excluded from these professions. It took nearly 150 years of organized struggle for women to make this assumption visible and, at least partially, reverse it.

An equally devastating pattern can be seen in the connection of advances in political democracy with contractions in the political/legal rights of women. I began this book by calling attention to this connection in the case of the democratic *polis* of ancient Greece and the democratic Constitution of the United States of America. The pattern becomes obvious when we contemplate the restrictions on the freedoms of noble women as a result of the Renaissance; the increase in witchhunts and persecution of heretics combined with the educational advancement of women after the Reformation; the backlash resulting in misogynist legislation after women's activism in the revolutions of the 18th and 19th centuries, such as the *Code Napoléon* after the French Revolution, the constraints on women's legal rights following the revolutions in Germany and in France in 1848; the inclusion of the word "male" as qualification for voting in the "liberalized" constitutions of the United States, the Netherlands and France in the 19th century. The pattern alters and begins to crack by the end of l9th century, directly as the result of women's raised feminist consciousness and their militant organizing. It is worth recollecting, even as a historical artifact, because the achievements of women as thinkers and creators of ideas cannot be really appreciated unless we know the obstacles against which they had to struggle.

It appears then, that there were women as great as the greatest male thinkers and writers, but their significance and their work have been marginalized and obscured. It appears most likely also that there were many others of equal potential who have been totally silenced and remain forgotten in the long forward march of male dominance over Western civilization. Most important, the female questions, the woman's point of view, the paradigm which would include the female experience has, until very recently, never entered the common discourse.

But now, the period of patriarchal hegemony over culture has come to an end. Even though in most places in the world and even in the Western democracies male dominance in major cultural institutions persists, the intellectual emancipation of women has shattered the solid monopoly men have held so long over theory and definition. Women do not as yet have power over institutions, over the state, over the law. But the theoretical insights modern feminist scholarship has already achieved have the power to shatter the patriarchal paradigm. Marginalization, ridicule, name-calling, budget-cutting and other devices designed to halt the process of redefining the mental constructs of Western civilization will all, in the long run, have to fail. They can temporarily retard the ongoing process of intellectual transformation, but they cannot stop it. As Galileo on his death-bed, long after the power of the Inquisition had forced him to recant his heretical theories, said, *"E pure si muove"* (And still, it moves).

More than thirteen hundred years of individual struggles, disappointments and persistence have brought women to the historic moment when we can reclaim the freedom of our minds as we reclaim our past. The millennia of women's pre-history are at an end. We stand at the beginning of a new epoch in the history of humankind's thought, as we recognize that sex is irrelevant to thought, that gender is a social construct and that woman, like man, makes and defines history.

Notes

ONE *Introduction*

1. An excellent discussion of the philosophical inadequacies of the patriarchal system of ideas, which corroborates my thinking, can be found in Elizabeth Kamarck Minnich, *Transforming Knowledge* (Philadelphia: Temple University Press, 1990).

2. Aristotle, *Politica* (tr. Benjamin Jowett), in W.D. Ross (ed.), *The Works of Aristotle* (Oxford: Clarendon Press, 1921), I, 2, 1254b, 4–6, 12–16.

3. *Ibid.*, 1254b, 24–26; 1255a, 2–5.

4. J.A. Smith and W.D. Ross (tr.), *The Works of Aristotle* (Oxford: Clarendon Press, 1912), "De Generatione Animalium," II, 3, 729a, 26–31.

5. See Linda Kerber, *Women of the Republic: Intellect and Ideology in Revolutionary America* (Chapel Hill: University of North Carolina Press, 1980) and Mary Beth Norton, *Liberty's Daughters: The Revolutionary Experience of American Women, 1750–1800* (Boston: Little, Brown, 1980).

6. Kerber, *Women of the Republic*, p. 82.

7. L.H. Butterfield *et al.* (eds.), *The Book of Abigail and John: Selected Letters of the Adams Family, 1762–1784* (Cambridge: Harvard University Press, 1975). First quote, Abigail Adams to John Adams, Braintree, March 31, 1776, p. 121; second quote, John Adams to Abigail Adams, April 14, 1776, p. 123.

8. *Ibid.*

9. The concept "feminist consciousness" is derived from and parallels the concept "class consciousness" as a means of defining the awareness of a group of its own oppression and of its struggle against that oppression. Deriving as it does from a Marxist conceptual framework, it assumes an "oppression" model, which in the case of women does not adequately describe the complex way they function in society and are structured into it. The use of this term tends to obscure the way women are simultaneously "oppressed" and may be themselves oppressors of other groups.

Another built-in limitation of the term is that it does not adequately reflect the positive definition of feminine values which were, for many women, implicit in their recognition of belonging to a group with distinct characteristics and interests. What we generally call "women's culture" was part of feminist consciousness, at least for some women. I hope to be able to show the complexity and richness of feminist consciousness as it developed historically and discuss its specific meanings for specific cases. There simply is no better term currently available.

10. For the 17th-century feminists, see Moira Ferguson, "Introduction" in M. Ferguson (ed.), *First Feminists: British Women Writers, 1578–1799* (Bloomington: Indiana University Press, 1985) and Hilda Smith, *Reason's Disciples: Seventeenth-Century English Feminists* (Urbana: University of Illinois Press, 1982). For Christine de Pizan as the forerunner of feminism, see Joan Kelly, "Early Feminist Theory and the *Querelle des Femmes*," in J. Kelly, *Women, History and Theory* (Chicago: University of Chicago Press, 1984), pp. 65–109.

TWO   *The Educational Disadvantaging of Women*

1. The argument for women's emancipation is in Sarah Moore Grimké, *Letters on the Equality of the Sexes and the Condition of Woman; Addressed to Mary Parker, President of the Boston Female Anti-Slavery Society* (Boston: Isaac Knapp, 1838). The quote is from Letter, Sarah Grimké to Harriot Hunt, Dec. 31, 1852, Theodore Dwight Weld Collection, William L. Clements Library, University of Michigan, Ann Arbor.

2. Sarah Moore Grimké (Notebook), "Education of Women," Weld Papers, Box 21. The sentence beginning with "Had I received the education" and ending with "of the helpless" appears in this notebook fragment. It is also cited, as an excerpt from Sarah Grimké's Diary in Catherine H. Birney, *The Grimké Sisters: Sarah and Angelina Grimké; The First American Women Advocates of Abolition and Woman's Rights* (Boston: Lee & Shepard, 1885), p. 38. This suggests that Sarah Grimké incorporated that earlier diary quote in the essay on education she was attempting to write in the 1850s.

3. My generalizations on women in the Middle Ages are drawn from my reading of primary sources, which are footnoted elsewhere, and on the following secondary sources: Angela M. Lucas, *Women in the Middle Ages: Religion, Marriage and Letters* (Brighton, Sussex: Harvester Press, 1983); Shulamith Shahar, *Die Frau im Mittelalter* (Königstein: Athenaeum Verlag, 1981); Peter Dronke, *Women Writers of the Middle Ages: A Critical Study of Texts from Perpetua (202) to Marguerite Porète (1310)*, (Cambridge: Cambridge University Press, 1984); Douglas Radcliff-Umstead (ed.), *The Roles and Images of Women in the Middle Ages and the Renaissance* (Pittsburgh: K&S Enterprises for the Center of Medieval and Renaissance Studies, University of Pittsburgh, 1975); Doris Mary Stenton, *The English Woman in History* (London: George Allen & Unwin, 1957); Phyllis H. Stock, *Better Than Rubies: A History of Women's Education* (New York: G.P. Putnam's Sons, 1978); Patricia H. Labalme (ed.), *Beyond Their Sex: Learned Women of the European Past* (New York: New York University Press, 1980); Penny Schine Gold, *The Lady and the Virgin: Image, Attitude and Experience in Twelfth-Century France* (Chicago: University of Chicago Press, 1985); Suzanne Fonay Wemple, *Women in Frankish Society: Marriage and the Cloister; 500–900* (Philadelphia: University of Pennsylvania Press, 1985).

4. Jane Tibbetts Schulenburg, "Women's Monastic Communities, 500–1000: Pat-

terns of Expansion and Decline," *SIGNS; Journal of Women in Culture and Society*, 14, # 2 (Winter 1989), 261–92, 266.

5. Wemple, *Women in Frankish Society*, pp. 158–67.

6. *Ibid.*, p. 182.

7. Sr. Mary P. Heinrich, *The Canonesses and Education in the Early Middle Ages* (Washington, D.C.: Catholic University, 1924), pp. 82–83.

8. *Ibid.*, pp. 45, 146.

9. Joan M. Ferrante, "The Education of Women in the Middle Ages in Theory, Fact and Fantasy," in Labalme (ed.), *Beyond Their Sex*, pp. 13–14.

10. *Ibid.*, p. 11.

11. William Harrison Woodward, *Studies in Education During the Age of the Renaissance; 1400–1600* (Cambridge: Cambridge University Press, 1924), p. 207.

12. Ursula Liebertz-Grün, "Höfische Autorinnen von der karolingischen Kulturreform bis zum Humanismus," in Gisela Brinker-Gabler (ed.), *Deutsche Literatur von Frauen*, Erster Band: *Vom Mittelalter bis zum Ende des 18. Jahrhunderts* (München: Verlag C. H. Beck, 1988), p. 39. See also Susan Groag Bell, "Medieval Women Book Owners: Arbiters of Lay Piety and Ambassadors of Culture," *SIGNS*, 7, # 4 (Summer 1982), 742–68.

13. The material on the Jewish women is in Sandra Henry and Emily Taitz, *Written Out of History: Our Jewish Foremothers* (Sunnyside, N.Y.: Biblio Press, 1988), pp. 88–101.

14. In contrast to men who are deemed "learned" only for extraordinary productivity or quality of thought, women are considered "learned" simply for achieving proficient levels of skills in subjects considered appropriate for men, such as Latin, Greek, Hebrew and a knowledge of ancient literature. If one examines closely the skills for which most learned women of the Renaissance were praised, one finds only a handful who produced original work. In most, the ability to compose a poem in Latin or Greek or to translate from ancient languages was celebrated as an astonishing feat. This is known today as the "dancing poodle" effect. It highlights the educational disadvantaging of women in a rather dramatic way.

15. I base these figures on the numbers of learned women I have been able to identify from the sources used in writing this book. I have included any women mentioned as "learned" by the authors who cite them, regardless of what such learning actually consisted. While these figures are, of necessity, impressionistic and are probably low because so few historians have studied the subject in detail, they illustrate the extent of the educational disadvantaging of women. I have no doubt that there existed many more learned women than those identified by historians, but that is precisely the point.

I find particularly noteworthy that the fact often cited as illustrative of women's advancement, namely, the existence of the learned women of the Renaissance is based on such slim evidence. A history of women's education encompassing at least Western Europe, Great Britain and the United States is badly needed to substantiate better what we now know mostly from negative evidence.

See Margaret L. King and Albert Rabil, Jr. *Her Immaculate Hand: Selected Work By and About the Women Humanists of Quattrocento Italy* (Binghamton, N.Y.: Medieval and Renaissance Texts and Studies, 1983), pp. 16–25; Roland H. Bainton, *Women of the Reformation in Germany and Italy* (Minneapolis: Augsburg Publishing House, 1971); Roland H. Bainton, *Women of the Reformation in France and England* (Minneapolis: Augsburg Publishing House, 1973); Roland H. Bainton, *Women of the Refor-mation: From Spain to Scandinavia* (Minneapolis: Augsburg Publishing House, 1977).

16. R. S. Schofield, "The Measurement of Literacy in Pre-industrial England," as cited in Jack Goody, *Literacy in Traditional Society* (Cambridge: Cambridge University Press, 1968), pp. 310–25; quote from fn 1, p. 313.

17. As cited in Liebertz-Grün, in Brinker-Gabler (see n. 12 above), p. 48.

18. Quoted from Eugenius Abel, *Isotae Nogarolae veronensis opera quae supersunt omnia,* 2 vols. (Vienna: apud Gerold et socios; Budapest: apud Fridericum Kilian, 1886), vol. I, pp. 79–82 (tr. M. King), as cited in Margaret King, "Book-Lined Cells: Women and Humanism in the Early Italian Renaissance," in Labalme (ed.), *Beyond Their Sex,* pp. 72–73.

A full bibliography on Isotta Nogarola is to be found in the "Appendix" to Margaret L. King, "The Religious Retreat of Isotta Nogarola (1418–1466): Sexism and Its Conse-quences in the Fifteenth Century," *SIGNS,* 3, # 4 (Summer 1978), 807–22, Appendix, 820–22. See also Margaret L. King, "Thwarted Ambitions: Six Learned Women of the Italian Renaissance," *Soundings: An Interdisciplinary Journal,* 59 (1976), 280–304.

19. Cited in King, *SIGNS* (1978), p. 809.

20. The single exception to this generalization might have been Olimpia Morata (1526–55), had she not died so prematurely as a result of wartime hardship. Morata was happily married to a supportive man and produced significant work after her marriage. But she became a Protestant and as such fits much better into the group of Protestant women thinkers than she does into the learned women of the Renaissance.

21. Lowell Green, "The Education of Women in the Reformation," *History of Ed-ucation Quarterly,* 19 (Spring 1979), 93–116; reference p. 106.

22. Elfrieda T. Dubois, "The Education of Women in Seventeenth-Century France," *French Studies,* 32, # 1 (Jan. 1978), 1–19.

23. As cited in A. A. Ward amd A. R. Waller (eds.), *Cambridge History of English Literature* (New York: G.P. Putnam & Sons, 1908), vol. IX, p. 449.

24. For Sor Juana I have drawn on the following sources: Alan S. Trueblood (tr.), *A Sor Juana Anthology* (Cambridge: Harvard University Press, 1988); [Sor Juana Ines de la Cruz,] Margaret Sayers Peden (ed. and Introd.), *A Woman of Genius: The Intel-lectual Autobiography of Sor Juana Ines de la Cruz* (Salisbury, Conn.: Lime Rock Press, 1982); Octavio Paz, *Sor Juana: or the Traps of Faith,* tr. Margaret Peden (Cambridge: Harvard University Press, 1988); Janis L. Pallister, "A Note on Sor Juana de la Cruz," *Women and Literature,* VII, #2 (Spring 1979), 42–46; Marilynn I. Ward, "The Feminist Crisis of Sor Juana Ines de La Cruz," *International Journal of Women's Studies,* I (1978), 475–81; quote p. 477.

25. Nina M. Scott, " 'If you are not pleased to favor me, put me out of your mind . . .': Gender and Authority in Sor Juana Ines de La Cruz," *Women's Studies Inter-national Forum,* II, # 5 (1988), 429–37; quote pp. 435–36.

The authenticity of this letter by Sor Juana to her confessor, written ten years before her "Reply to Sor Philotea" has been accepted by most Sor Juana scholars, including Octavio Paz. The article anticipates many of the arguments Sor Juana makes ten years later in the "Reply."

26. As quoted in Peden, *A Woman of Genius,* p. 3.

27. See Paz, *Sor Juana,* pp. 400–463.

28. Gerard Flynn, "Sor Juana Ines de la Cruz: Mexico's Tenth Muse," in J.R. Brink,

Female Scholars: A Tradition of Learned Women Before 1800 (Montreal: Eden Press, Women's Publications, 1980), pp. 119–36.

29. This anecdote is drawn from Leslie Stephen, "Elstob, Elizabeth," *Dictionary of National Biography*, Leslie Stephen (ed.), 63 vols (London: Smith, Elder, 1889–1900), vol. 17 (1889), pp. 334–35; and from biographical notes in Ada Wallas, *Before the Bluestockings* (London: Allen & Unwin, 1929), pp. 134–35.

For information about Elstob I have drawn on the following: George Ballard, *Memoirs of Several Ladies of Great Britain* (Oxford: W. Jackson, 1752); Ruth Perry, "Introduction," in R. Perry (ed.), George Ballard, *Memoirs of Several Ladies of Great Britain who have been Celebrated for Their Writings or Skill in the Learned Languages, Arts and Sciences* (Detroit: Wayne State University Press, 1985), pp. 12–48.; Myra Reynolds, *The Learned Lady in England, 1650–1760* (Boston: Houghton Mifflin, 1920), pp. 173–85; and "Elizabeth Elstob, the Saxon Nymph," in J.R. Brink (ed.), *Female Scholars*, pp. 137–60.

30. Elizabeth Elstob, *An Anglo-Saxon Homily, on the birth-day of St. Gregory: Anciently used in the English Saxon Church Giving an Account of the Conversion of the English from Paganism to Christianity*, Translated into English, with Notes. etc. (London: W. Bowyer, 1709). Also Perry, "Introduction," p. 22.

31. Elstob, *Homily*, Preface, as cited in Reynolds, *The Learned Lady in England*, p. 175. Author's spelling retained.

32. Elizabeth Elstob, *The Rudiments of Grammar for the English-Saxon Tongue, first given in English, with an Apology for the Study of Northern Antiquities* (London: W. Bowyer and C. King, 1715).

33. For further discussion of Ballard's work, see Chapter Eleven below.

34. As cited in Reynolds, *The Learned Lady in England*, p. 184.

35. Helen Sullivan, "Literacy and Illiteracy," in Edwin R. Seligman (ed.), *Encyclopedia of the Social Sciences* (New York: Macmillan, 1935), vol. IX, pp. 511–23; reference p. 513.

For background on the subject of literacy I have read: Hilda H. Golden, "Literacy," in David L. Sills (ed.), *International Encyclopedia of the Social Sciences* (New York: Macmillan, 1968), vol. IX, pp. 412–17; Jack Goody (ed.), *Literacy in Traditional Societies* (Cambridge: Cambridge University Press, 1968); Harvey J. Graff (ed.), *Literacy and Social Development in the West* (Cambridge: Cambridge University Press, 1982); Carl M. Cipolla, *Literacy and Development in the West* (Harmondsworth: Penguin Books, 1969); M. T. Clanchy, *From Memory to Written Record: England, 1066–1307* (Cambridge: Harvard University Press, 1979); Lawrence Stone, "Literacy and Education in England, 1640–1900," *Past & Present*, XLII (Feb. 1969), 69–139; D. P. Resnick and L. B. Resnick, "The Nature of Literacy: An Historical Exploration," *Harvard Educational Review*, XLVII, #3 (Aug. 1977), 370–85; Carl F. Kaestle, "The History of Literacy and the History of Readers," in Edmund W. Gordon, *Review of Research in Education*, XII (Washington, D.C.: American Educational Research Association, 1985).

36. Clanchy, *Written Record*, pp. 175–91; Herbert Grundmann, "*Litteratus-illitteratus: Der Wandel einer Bildungsnorm vom Altertum zum Mittelalter*," *Archiv für Kulturgeschichte*, vol. 40, #1, pp. 1–65.

32. Sullivan in Seligman, *Encyclopedia of the Social Sciences*, vol. IX, p. 515.

38. The meaning of illiteracy in predominantly rural societies was, of course, quite different from what it was in urban and later industrializing societies. Up until the 18th century a strong oral tradition continued side by side with a literary tradition, and the

ordinary person could lead a contented and fulfilling life without being able to read and write. Yet, even then, literacy was the prerequisite for acquiring formal higher education. It is for this reason that widespread female illiteracy is a good indicator of discrimination in education against women. David Cressy, "The Environment for Literacy: Accomplishment and Context in 17th-Century England and New England," in D. P. Resnick, *Literacy in Historical Perspective* (Washington, D.C.: Library of Congress, 1983), pp. 23–42.

39. David Cressy, "Levels of Illiteracy in England, 1530–1730," *The Historical Journal*, 20, #1 (1977), 1–24.

40. Rab Houston, "Illiteracy in Scotland, 1630–1760," *Past & Present*, #96 (Aug. 1982), 81–102; reference p. 93. Also, by the same author, "Literacy and Society in the West, 1500–1850," *Social History*, VIII, #3 (Oct. 1983), 269–89.

41. As cited in Margaret Spufford, "First Steps in Literacy: The Reading and Writing Experiences of the Humblest 17th-century Spiritual Autobiographers," *Journal of Social History*, IV, #3 (Oct. 1979), pp. 407–54. This study illustrates one of the methodological difficulties in discussing literacy—because of the greater availability of such sources, most studies are based on the ability to sign, which may underestimate people's ability to read. One author states that early 19th-century evidence suggests that half again as many people as had the ability to sign may have had basic reading ability. Further, that the ability to sign may have corresponded with the ability to read fluently. See R. S. Schofield, "Dimensions of Illiteracy, 1750–1850," *Explorations in Economic History*, X, #4, 2nd series (Summer 1973), 437–54; reference p. 40.

42. T.C. Smout, "Born Again at Cambuslang: New Evidence on Popular Religion and Literacy in 18th-Century Scotland," *Past & Present: A Journal of Historical Studies*, # 97 (Nov. 1982), 114–27; reference p. 127.

43. Sullivan in Seligman, *Encyclopedia of the Social Sciences*, vol. IX, p. 517.

44. Schofield, "Dimensions of Illiteracy, 1750–1850," 437–54, reference pp. 445–47.

45. *Ibid.*, pp. 443–53.

46. The figures are from Sullivan in Seligman, *Encyclopedia of the Social Sciences*, vol. IX, p. 521. Because they are based on a small and young age group, these figures show a far higher literacy rate than existed in the entire population.

UNESCO figures of 1979 show an overall illiteracy rate of 0.2%, the same for men and women. *UNESCO Statistical Yearbook, 1986* (Printed in Belgium, 1986), pp. 1–27.

47. *Ibid.*, Table 1.2, "Illiteracy population 15 years of age and over and percentage of illiteracy, by age group and by sex," pp. 1–15 to 1–29.

48. For background information on the development of U.S. education and literacy I have read the following: Thomas Woody, *History of Women's Education in the United States* (New York: Octagon Books, 1966, reprint of 1929 ed.), 2 vols.; Bernard Bailyn, *Education in the Forming of American Society* (Chapel Hill: University of North Carolina Press, 1970; reprint of 1960 ed.); Lawrence A. Cremin, *American Education: The National Experience, 1738–1876* (New York: Harper & Row, 1980); Barbara Cross, *The Educated Woman in America* (New York: Teachers College Press, 1965); Willystine Goodsell, *The Education of Women: Its Social Background and Its Problems* (New York: Macmillan, 1923); Mabel Newcomer, *A Century of Higher Education for American Women* (Washington, D.C.: Zenger Pub., 1976, reprint of 1959 ed.); Nancy Hoffman, *Women's True Profession* (New York: Feminist Press, 1981); Anne Louise Kuhn, *The Mother's Role in Childhood Education: New England Concepts, 1830–1860* (New Haven:

Yale University Press, 1947); Barbara Miller Solomon, *In the Company of Educated Women: A History of Women and Higher Education in America* (New Haven: Yale University Press, 1985); U. S. Congress, House Special Subcommittee on Education, *Hearings on Discrimination Against Women* (Washington, D.C.: U. S. Government Printing Office, 1970), 2 vols.; Carl F. Kaestle, *Pillars of the Republic: Common Schools and American Society, 1780–1860* (New York: Hill & Wang, 1983); L. Soltow and E. Stevens, *The Rise of Literacy and the Common School in the United States: A Socio-economic Analysis to 1870* (Chicago: University of Chicago Press, 1981).

49. Kenneth A. Lockridge, *Literacy in Colonial New England: An Enquiry into the Social Context of Literacy in the Early Modern West* (New York: W. W. Norton, 1974), p. 128,n.4, pp. 13, 38–42.

Lockridge's sample of females was quite small, representing less than 15% of his total sample. As has been pointed out by many experts on the subject, at a time when people were not forced to sign, but could instead make a mark, there may have been many psychological and other reasons for not signing. Elderly women, making their wills, even if they had the ability to write, may have been physically unable to do so. Further, as was discussed earlier, many people making a mark instead of signing, may nevertheless have been able to read.

50. These figures undoubtedly reflect the self-selection of a group of signers of deeds who would be likely to come from a propertied residential group and thus exclude poorer women and servants. We must therefore assume that the figures in the Auwers study show a larger signing ability rate than would those for the general population.

51. Linda Auwers, "Reading the Marks of the Past: Exploring Female Literacy in Colonial Windsor, Connecticut," *Historical Methods*, XIII (1980), 204–14; figures from pp. 204–5.

52. E. Jennifer Monaghan, "Literacy Instruction and Gender in Colonial New England," *American Quarterly*, 40, #1 (March 1988), 18–41; quotes on pp. 26, 27.

53. The information on Dedham comes from Nancy Cott, *The Bonds of Womanhood: "Woman's Sphere" in New England, 1780–1835* (New Haven: Yale University Press, 1977), p. 103, n.5. Information on the other towns is from Kaestle, *Pillars of the Republic*, p. 28.

54. Linda Kerber, *Women of the Republic: Intellect and Ideology in Revolutionary America* (Chapel Hill: University of North Carolina Press, 1980), chap. 7; Mary Beth Norton, *Liberty's Daughters: The Revolutionary Experience of American Women, 1750–1800* (Boston: Little, Brown, 1980), chap. 9.

55. Keith Melder, "Mask of Oppression: The Female Seminary Movement in the United States," *New York History*, LV (July 1974), 261–79.

56. Alma Lutz, *Emma Willard: Pioneer Educator of American Women* (Boston: Beacon Press, 1964). See also Anne Firor Scott, "What, Then Is the American: This New Woman?" and "The Ever-Widening Circle: The Diffusion of Feminist Values from the Troy Female Seminary, 1822–72," both in her *Making the Invisible Woman Visible* (Urbana: University of Illinois Press, 1984), pp. 37–88; Mrs. A. W. Fairbanks (ed.), *Mrs. Emma Willard and Her Pupils, or Fifty Years of Troy Female Seminary, 1822–1872* (New York, 1898).

57. Mae Harveson, *Catharine Beecher: Pioneer Educator* (Philadelphia: Science Press, 1932); Kathryn Kish Sklar, *Catharine Beecher: A Study in American Domesticity* (New Haven: Yale University Press, 1973); Mary Lyon, *The Power of Christian Benevolence Illustrated in the Life and Labors of Mary Lyon* (New York: American Tract Society,

1858). See also Eleanor Flexner, *Century of Struggle: The Woman's Rights Movement in the United States* (Cambridge: Belknap Press, 1975, revised 1959 ed.).

58. Mary Beth Norton uses the biographies in Edward James, Janet James, and Paul Boyer (eds.), *Notable American Women, 1670–1950: A Biographical Dictionary* (Cambridge: Harvard University Press, 1971), to measure the impact of educational reform on women. The percentage of American women who received advanced education remained fairly constant at 22% to about 1775, then climbed steeply to 63% of those born in the 1780–90 decade and leveled off at 74% of those born 1800–1809. Advanced education here means the academy level, either at school or by tutor. The group from which this generalization is made is, of course, exceptional, since it represents women of outstanding achievement, but the increase in educational opportunity is clearly evident. See Norton, *Liberty's Daughters*, pp. 287–89.

59. L. Soltow and Stevens, *The Rise of Literacy . . . .* , pp. 156, 189.

60. Patricia Albjerg Graham, "Expansion and Exclusion: A History of Women in American Higher Education," *SIGNS; Journal of Women in Culture and Society*, III, # 4 (Summer 1978), 759–72; quotes from pp. 764–66.

61. See E. Wilbur Bock, " 'Farmer's Daughter Effect': The Case of the Negro Female Professionals," *Phylon*, XXX (Spring 1969), 17–26. Bock first observed this phenomenon and coined the phrase "a sex loophole in race discrimination" to describe it. See Gerda Lerner, "Black Women in the United States," in Lerner, *The Majority Finds Its Past: Placing Women in History* (New York: Oxford University Press, 1979), chap. 5.

THREE *Self-authorization*

1. Suzanne Fonay Wemple, *Women in Frankish Society: Marriage and the Cloister: 500–900* (Philadelphia: University of Pennsylvania Press, 1985), pp. 19–26, 75–88. The reference to the execution of the nun Gerberga, apparently falsely accused as a witch, appears on p. 95. Wemple calls this "the first known instance in the Latin West of witchcraft being used as a legal ground for the execution of a woman."

2. There is a considerable body of scholarly work in literature on this subject. I have drawn particularly on the work of Sandra M. Gilbert and Susan Gubar, *The Madwoman in the Attic: The Woman Writer and the Nineteenth-Century Literary Imagination* (New Haven: Yale University Press, 1979); Ellen Moers, *Literary Women* (Garden City, N.Y.: Doubleday, 1976); Elaine Showalter, *A Literature of Their Own* (Princeton: Princeton University Press, 1977); Catharine R. Stimpson, "Ad/d Feminam: Women, Literature, and Society," in *Where the Meanings Are: Feminism and Cultural Spaces* (New York: Methuen, 1988), pp. 84–96; Mary G. Mason, "The Other Voice: Autobiographies of Women Writers," in James Olney (ed.), *Autobiography: Essays Theoretical and Critical* (Princeton: Princeton University Press, 1980).

3. As cited in Peter Dronke, *Women Writers of the Middle Ages: A Critical Study of Texts from Perpetua (d.203) to Marguerite Porète (d. 1310)* (Cambridge: Cambridge University Press, 1984), p. 65. Tr. P. Dronke. Styling retained as per Dronke.

4. As cited *ibid.*, pp. 73–74.

5. *Ibid.*, p. 74.

6. The controversy over the authenticity of Hildegard's medical writings is discussed

in Joan Cadden, "It Takes All Kinds: Sexuality and Gender Differences in Hildegard of Bingen's 'Book of Compound Medicine'," *Traditio*, 40 (1984), 149–74; fn. 1, p. 149.

7. J.F. Benton "A Reconsideration of the Authenticity of the Correspondence of Abelard and Héloïse," *Trier 1980*, p. 50, and its refutation in Dronke, *Women Writers*, pp. 108, 140–43.

8. Meg Bogin, *The Women Troubadours* (Scarborough, Eng.: Paddington Press, 1976) is the latest and most complete work on the subject, containing 23 poems by *trobairitzes*. For reference to the male ascriptions of authorship, see Dronke, *Women Writers*, pp. 97–98.

9. As cited in and translated by Harriet Spiegel, Marie de France, *Fables* (Toronto: University of Toronto Press, 1987), p. 4.

10. Christine de Pizan, *L'Avision*, as cited in Charity Cannon Willard, *Christine de Pizan: Her Life and Works* (New York: Persea Books, 1984), p. 160.

11. Margaret L. King and Albert Rabil, Jr.(eds.), *Her Immaculate Hand: Selected Works By and About the Women Humanists of Quattrocento Italy* (Binghamton, N.Y.: Medieval & Renaissance Texts and Studies, 1983), pp. 23–25, 77–86.

12. [Margaret Cavendish, Duchess of Newcastle] *A True Relation of the Birth, Breeding, and Life of Margaret Cavendish written by herself with critical Preface by Sir Egerton Brydges*, M.P. (Kent: Johnson and Warwick, 1814), pp. 8–9.

13. *Ibid.*, p. 178.

14. [No author] *Poems by Eminent Ladies . . . ,* vol. 1 (London: R. Baldwin, 1755), no page numbers.

15. Wolfgang Riehle, *Studien zur englischen Mystik des Mittelalters unter besonderer Berücksichtigung ihrer Metaphorik* (Heidelberg: Carl Winter Universitätsverlag, 1977), p. 52.

16. As cited in Dronke, *Women Writers*, p. 34.

17. For biographical information I have drawn on the following: Adelgundis Führkötter, *Hildegard von Bingen* (Salzburg: Otto Müller Verlag, 1972); J. Schmelzeis, *Das Leben und Wirken der heiligen Hildegardis nach den Quellen dargestellt . . . nebst einem Anhang Hildegardischer Lieder mit ihren Melodien* (Freiburg, 1879); Walter Pagel, "Hildegard von Bingen" in *Dictionary of Scientific Biography*, ed. Charles Coulston Gillespie (New York: Charles Scribner's Sons, 1972), vol. VI, pp. 396–98; Dronke, *Women Writers*, chap. 6. Marianne Schrader, *Die Herkunft der heiligen Hildegard*, neu bearbeitet by Adelgundis Führkötter (Mainz: Selbstverlag d. Gesellschaft für Mittelrheinische Kirchengeschichte, 1981). Barbara Newman, *Sister of Wisdom: St. Hildegard's Theology of the Feminine* (Berkeley: University of California Press, 1987) is the latest and most definitive study of Hildegard.

18. Whenever Hildegard resisted her visions and failed to carry out a command contained in them, she became seriously ill, usually with some kind of paralysis of parts of her body. She also describes states of blindness and voicelessness. These illnesses disappeared when she obeyed the instructions of the divine voice.

19. Führkötter, *Hildegard von Bingen*, pp. 14–15; tr. Gerda Lerner. Also Sarah Roche-Mahdi, "The Sybil of the Rhine" (review of Hildegard von Bingen, *Scivias/Know the Ways*, tr. Bruce Hozeski, in *Women's Review of Books*, 4, #2 (Nov. l986), 14–15; tr. Roche-Mahdi).

20. Maria David-Windstosser (ed.), *Deutsche Mystiker*, Band V, *Frauenmystik im Mittelalter* (Kempten und München: Verlag Kösleschen Buchhandlung, 1919); Donald

Weinstein and Rudolph Bell, *Saints and Society: The Two Worlds of Western Christendom, 1000–1700* (Chicago: University of Chicago Press, 1982).

21. This view of her knowledge is sustained by a number of the authors writing about her and her work, among others Barbara Newman, *Sister of Wisdom*, pp. 43–37, and Hans Liebeschütz, *Das allegorische Weltbild der Heiligen Hildegard von Bingen* (Leipzig: Studien der Bibliothek Warburg 16, 1930), pp. 6, 8, 167.

22. Letter, Hildegard of Bingen to Guibert of Gembloux (1175), as cited in Katharina Wilson, *Medieval Women Writers* (Athens: University of Georgia Press, 1984).

23. Between 1158 and 1161 she traveled to Mainz, Würzburg, Bamberg and several smaller cities, where she preached. Her second tour as a preacher brought her to Trier and the Rhineland in 1160. A third preaching tour in the Rhineland (1161–63) included a public sermon before clergy and a large crowd of worshippers in Köln. In 1163 she traveled to Mainz to attend the Imperial Diet *(Hoftag)*. On this occasion Emperor Frederick Barbarossa issued an edict for the protection of her Rupertsberg convent. Her last preaching tour in 1170–71 took her to the Rhineland and Swabia.

Adelgundis Führkötter, O.S.B., *Das Leben der Heiligen Hildegard von Bingen* (Düsseldorf: Patmos Verlag, 1968), pp. 132–34. See also Bernhard W. Scholz, "Hildegard von Bingen on the Nature of Woman," *American Benedictine Review*, 31 (1980), 361–83; the information on her travels and preaching is on p. 363.

24. I have read the following editions of her works: *Scivias*, Illuminated Manuscript, copy of Rupertsberg Codex, Abbey St. Hildegard, Rüdesheim-Eibingen. Also Hildegard von Bingen, *Wisse die Wege: Scivias* (Salzburg: Otto Müller Verlag, 1954); Hildegard von Bingen, *Wisse die Wege, Scivias*, tr. and ed. Maura Böckeler (Salzburg: Otto Müller Verlag, 1954); *Scivias by Hildegard of Bingen*, tr. Bruce Hozeski (Santa Fe, N. M.: Bear & Co., 1986); Hildegard von Bingen, *Heilkunde*, ed. Heinrich Schipperges (Salzburg: Otto Müller Verlag, 1957); *Hildegard von Bingen: Welt und Mensch, Das Buch De Operatione Dei*, ed. Heinrich Schipperges (Salzburg: Otto Müller Verlag, 1965); *Hildegard von Bingen, Naturkunde: Das Buch von dem inneren Wesen der verschiedenen Naturen in der Schoepfung*, tr. Peter Riethe (Salzburg: Otto Müller Verlag, 1959); Peter Riethe (tr.), *Hildegard von Bingen, Das Buch von den Steinen*, (Salzburg: Otto Müller Verlag, 1979); Hildegard von Bingen, *Illuminations of Hildegard von Bingen* with commentary by Matthew Fox (Santa Fe, N.M.: Bear & Co., 1985); Hildegard von Bingen, *Briefwechsel*, tr. Adelgundis Führkötter (Salzburg: Otto Müller Verlag, 1965). See also M. Schrader and A. Führkötter, *Die Echtheit des Schrifttums der hl. Hildegard von Bingen* (Köln, 1956); Werner Lauter, *Hildegard-Bibliography: Wegweiser zur Hildegard-Literatur* (Alzey: Verlag der Rheinischen Druckwerkstätte, 1970).

25. Führkötter (tr.) [H. Von Bingen] *Briefwechsel*; Bertha Widmer, *Heilsordnung und Zeitgeschehen in der Mystik Hildegards von Bingen* (Basler Beitraege zur Geschichtswissenschaft, Band 52 (Basel: Verlag von Helbing und Lichtenhahn, 1955), discusses the authenticity of the letters and concludes that while some of the letters are copies made by later editors and others are falsely assigned, the answers to Hildegard are authentic. Thus, the fact of her vast correspondence with prominent people is confirmed.

26. As cited in Dronke, *Women Writers*, p. 154; tr. Dronke.

27. As cited, *ibid.*, p. 197.

28. *Ibid.*, p. 144.

29. Pagel, "Hildegard of Bingen."

30. Both quotes, excerpts from her *Vita*, as cited in Dronke, *Women Writers*, pp. 150–51.

31. The historian Sara Evans discusses this concept in *Personal Politics: The Roots of Women's Liberation in the Civil Rights Movement and the New Left* (New York: Knopf, 1979), pp. 219–20. See also my discussion in Chapter Ten.

32. Dronke, *Women Writers*, pp. 165–67.

33. See reference in Hildegard, *Vita Sanctae Hildegardis*, autoribus Godefrido et theoderico monachis, Lib. II, 19. I am indebted for the information in this paragraph to Sr. Angela Carlevaris, O.S.B., Abbey St. Hildegard, Rüdesheim-Eibingen, who has made a lifelong study of the Hildegard manuscripts. Personal conversation November 1991.

34. Böckeler, *Wisse die Wege*, pp. 15–87, for illustrations; pp. 390–91, for discussion of sources. Also Fox, *Illuminations, passim*.

35. Schipperges, *Heilkunde*, VI, p. 124.

36. Hildegard von Bingen, *Causae et curae*, ed. Paul Kaiser (Leipzig, 1903), p. 46, as cited in Cadden, "It Takes All Kinds . . . ," p. 153.

37. *Ibid.*, pp. 154–55, for a summary of Hildegard's views. I have read the original text in German translation in Schipperges, *Heilkunde*, VI, pp. 124–27, and XII, 204–9. Note by contrast Thomas Aquinas' sexual doctrine in which the wife is merely an "adjunct" to the man's leading role in procreation. She is a thing *(res)*, a possession *(possesio)* and an instrument *(instrumentum)*. The child's well-being depends entirely on the physical contribution of the father.

38. Schipperges, *Heilkunde*, XII, p. 204 (tr. Gerda Lerner).

39. *Scivias*, I,2. For an interpretation similar to mine, see Margaret R. Miles, *Carnal Knowledge: Female Nakedness and Religious Meaning in the Christian West* (New York: Vintage Books, 1991), pp. 99–101.

40. Ernest W. McDonnell, *The Beguines and Begherds in Medieval Culture, with Special Emphasis on the Belgian Scene* (New Brunswick: Rutgers University Press, 1954), pp. 575–86. The author particularly describes the Sophia-mystic of Heinrich Seuse, Jacob Böhme and Johann George Gichtel. For a more recent feminist interpretation of the cultural ideal of the virginal woman, embodying both Sophia and Mary, see Rosemary Radford Ruether, "Misogynism and Virginal Feminism in the Fathers of the Church," in *Religion and Sexism: Images of Woman in the Jewish and Christian Traditions*, ed. Rosemary Radford Ruether (New York: Simon & Schuster, 1974), pp. 178–79; Rosemary Radford Ruether, *Sexism and God-Talk: Toward a Feminist Theology* (Boston: Beacon Press, 1983), chap. 2; for a definitive analysis of Hildegard's sapiental theology see Newman, *Sister of Wisdom*.

41. Böckeler, *Wisse die Wege*, II, #3, p. 160.

42. *Ibid.*, pp. 162, 163.

43. *Ibid.*, II, 5th vision, p. 175. (tr. Gerda Lerner).

44. Newman, *Sister of Wisdom*, pp. 47, 58.

45. *Ibid.*, p. 64.

46. The likeness in design of her illuminations to *mandalas* and other symbols of Eastern iconography is striking. A possible explanation for the origins of these Eastern cultural influences is her contact with members of the rabbbinical schools in the Rhineland. Jewish scholars connected with Jewish centers of learning in the Islamic world brought the knowledge of Eastern religions and even of Far Eastern concepts and designs to Europe. Hildegard may through these contacts have seen or heard of these works and

traditions. I am indebted for this suggestions to Sr. Angela Carlevaris, O.S.B., Abbey St. Hildegard, Rüdesheim-Eibingen. Personal conversation and correspondence.

For reference to the rabbinical schools in the Rhineland, see Ismar Elbogen and Eleonore Sterling, *Die Geschichte der Juden in Deutschland* (Frankfurt am Main: Athenaeum Verlag, 1988), p. 24.

47. For my interpretation of her medical and scientific writings I have drawn on Dronke, *Women Writers*; Cadden, "It Takes All Kinds . . . ," pp. 149–74; and Lynn Thorndike, *A History of Magic and Experimental Science I-II: During the First Thirteen Centuries of Our Era* (New York: Columbia University Press, 1929), vol. II.

48. Hildegard, *De Operatione Dei*, vision 2; visions 3 and 4 as reproduced in Fox, *Illuminations*, pp. 39, 42, 46. Three centuries later Christine de Pisan will appear in a similar pose in the illustrations of one of her books.

FOUR *The Way of the Mystics-1*

1. My generalizations about mysticism are based on the following sources: Ernst Benz, *Die Vision: Erfahrungensformen und Bilderwelt* (Stuttgart: Ernst Klett, 1969); Walter Holden Capps and Wendy M. Wright, *Silent Fire: An Invitation to Western Mysticism* (New York: Harper & Row, 1978); Richard Kieckhefer, *Unquiet Souls: Fourteenth-Century Saints and Their Religious Milieu* (Chicago: University of Chicago Press, 1984); Ernest W. McDonnell, *The Beguines and Begherds in Medieval Culture, with Special Emphasis on the Belgian Scene* (New Brunswick: Rutgers University Press, 1954); Elizabeth Alvilda Petroff, *Medieval Women's Visionary Literature* (New York: Oxford University Press, 1986); Wolfgang Riehle, *Studien zur englischen Mystik des Mittelalters unter besonderer Berücksichtigung ihrer Metaphorik* (Heidelberg: Carl Winter Universitätsverlag, 1977); Gershom G. Scholem, *Major Trends in Jewish Mysticism* (1941; New York: Schocken Books, 1978); Gordon S. Wakefield, *The Westminster Dictionary of Spirituality* (Philadelphia: Westminster Press, 1983); Donald Weinstein and Rudolph Bell, *Saints and Society: The Two Worlds of Western Christendom, 1000–1700* (Chicago: University of Chicago Press, 1982); Maria David Windstösser (ed.), *Deutsche Mystiker*, Band V: *Frauenmystik im Mittelalter* (Verlag Köselschen Buchhandlung, 1919). See also John Chapman, O.S.B., "Mysticism," in *Encyclopedia of Religion and Ethics*, James Hastings (ed.), 13 vols. (New York: Charles Scribner's Sons, 1955–58), vol. IX (1955), pp. 90–101.

2. The first citation (Hildegard) is from Adelgundis Führkötter (tr.) [Hildegard von Bingen] *Briefwechsel* (Otto Müller Verlag, Salzburg, 1965), Letter "Hildegard an Wibert von Gembloux," pp. 226–28, quote on p. 227. The English version is from Peter Dronke, *Women Writers of the Middle Ages: A Critical Study of Texts from Perpetua (d.203) to Marguerite Porète (d.1310)* (Cambridge: Cambridge University Press, 1984), p. 168. Second citation: J.O. Plassmann (ed. and tr.), *Die Werke der Hadewych* (Hannover: Orient-Buchhandlung Heinz Lafaire, 1923), Letter 20, pp. 41–42; translated from German to English by Gerda Lerner. See also, for an English version of this letter, Sr. M. Columba Hart, O.S.B.: "Hadewijch of Brabant," *American Benedictine Review*, vol. 13, #1 (1962), 1–24.

3. Dr. Wilhelm Öhl (tr.), *Mechthild von Magdeburg, Das fliessende Licht der Gottheit*, *Deutsche Mystiker*, Band 2 (Kempten und München: Verlag der Jos. Köselschen Buch-

handlung, 1922), p. 87 (tr. Gerda Lerner). Also seen: Gall Morel (ed.), *Offenbarungen der Schwester Mechtild of Magdeburg oder Das Fliessende Licht der Gottheit* (Darmstadt: Wissenschafliche Buchgesellschaft, 1963); and Lucy Menzies (tr.), *The Revelations of Mechthild of Magdeburg (1210–1297) or The Flowing Light of the Godhead* (London: Longmans, Green, 1953).

4. Letter 17 in Sr. M. Columba Hart, p. 14.

5. Mechthild, *Licht*, p. 89.

6. Sanford B. Meech and Hope Emily Allen (eds.), *The Book of Margery Kempe* (London: Oxford University Press, 1961), p. 77.

7. Gottfried Arnold, *Unparteyische Kirchen- und Ketzerhistorie, vom Anfang des Neuen Testaments bis auf das Jahr Christi 1688* (Frankfurt am Main: T. Fritschens Erben, 1729), vol.3, pp. 150–57.

8. For a 20th-century mind, especially one of a rationalist and materialist inclination, the achievement of the mystics is difficult to comprehend, much less to appreciate. The tendency to regard them as pathological, psychopathic or fraudulent obstructs one's ability to understand them from within their own time and place. I have found it useful to look at them by historically verifiable criteria; that is, I consider those worthy of inclusion in the narrative who had the ability to make at least some of their contemporaries believe in the veracity and actuality of their visions. In historical perspective the factuality of what they reported is neither important nor verifiable, what is important is that they transformed their visions into public action.

9. Menzies (tr.), *Flowing Light of the Godhead*, pp. 58–59.

10. *Ibid.*, Fifth Part: 12, pp. 135–36.

11. Caroline Walker Bynum, *Jesus as Mother: Studies in the Spirituality of the High Middle Ages* (Berkeley: University of California Press, 1982), pp. 247–54; quote p. 250.

12. The "not me, Lord" theme recurs frequently in Christian history, especially in the accounts and *vitae* of male and female mystics. It appears that before mystics can accept their empowerment and the responsibility given them by their visions, they need divine reassurance of their capacity and worthiness.

13. Mrs. Julia A. J. Foote, "A Brand Plucked from the Fire: An Autobiographical Sketch" (Cleveland: Printed for the author by W. F. Schneider, 1879), in William L. Andrews (ed.), *Sisters of the Spirit: Three Black Women's Autobiographies of the Nineteenth Century* (Bloomington: Indiana University Press, 1986), first quote pp. 200–201; second pp. 202–3. All references to Mrs. Foote's story are based on this source.

14. Both quotes, *ibid.*, p. 209.

15. Weinstein and Bell, *Saints and Society*, p. 220. In the 11th century only one in twelve saints was a woman, but this proportion rose to more than one in ten in the 12th century. In the 13th century female saints were 22% of the total (1 in 5), while in the 14th and 15th centuries their numbers rose to 23% and 28% (1 in 4), even though the total number of saints in the 15th century declined by almost a half.

16. *Ibid.*, pp. 220–21, 229.

17. The Beguine movement flourished in the 12th and the 13th centuries, chiefly in Northern Europe. It was a movement of lay women who lived in all-female communities and practiced poverty, chastity and good works. See text, p. 77 ff.

18. Carolyn Walker Bynum, *Holy Feast and Holy Fast: The Religious Significance of Food to Medieval Women* (Berkeley: University of California Press, 1987), p. 83.

19. My generalizations on women in the religious developments of the 12th century

are based on the following sources: Bynum, *Jesus as Mother*; J. B. Bury (ed.), *The Cambridge Medieval History*, 8 vols. (Cambridge: Cambridge University Press, 1924–36), vol. 6; P. Dinzelbacher and Dieter R. Bauer (eds.), *Religiöse Frauenbewegung und mystische Frömmigkeit im Mittelalter* (Wien: Böhlau Verlag, 1988); Friedrich Heer, *The Medieval World: Europe, 1100–1350* (London: Weidenfeld & Nicolson, 1962), tr. George Weidenfeld and Nicolson, Ltd.; Robert E. Lerner, Standish Meacham, Edward McNall Burns, *Western Civilizations: Their History and Their Culture* (New York: W. W. Norton, 1988, 11th ed.); R. W. Southern, *The Making of the Middle Ages* (New Haven: Yale University Press, 1953); Petroff, *Medieval Women's Visionary Literature*; Eileen Power, *Medieval Women* (Cambridge: Cambridge University Press, 1975); Shulamith Shahar, *Die Frau im Mittelalter* (Königstein: Athenaeum Verlag, 1981).

20. Heer, *The Medieval World*, p. 43.

21. An indication of this is the growth of female orders. By 1250 there were more than 500 female religious foundations in Germany alone. Lionel Rothkrug, "Religious Practices and Collective Perceptions: Hidden Homologies in the Renaissance and Reformation," *Historical Reflections*, 7, no.1, (Spring 1980), 3–264; references pp. 91–92, 52.

22. For information on the Cathars I have drawn on James Hastings (ed.), *Encyclopedia of Religion and Ethics* (New York: Charles Scribner's Sons, 1955), vol. 6, pp. 618–22. Also Norman Cohn, *The Pursuit of the Millennium: Revolutionary Millenarians and Mystical Anarchists of the Middle Ages* (New York: Oxford University Press, 1957); Dronke, *Women Writers*; Gottfried Koch, *Frauenfrage und Ketzertum im Mittelalter: Die Frauenbewegung im Rahmen des Katharismus und des Waldensertums und ihre sozialen Wurzeln (12–14. Jahrhundert)* (Berlin: Akademie-Verlag, 1962); Emmanuel Leroy Ladurie, *Montaillou,the Promised Land of Error* (New York: Vintage Books, 1979).

Koch, *Frauenfrage*, chap. 2, traces similarities between the Bogomilian heresy of the 10th century and that of the Cathars. He points out that in the Bogomilian sects women were active, treated as equals and even exercised ministerial functions as deaconesses.

23. In a discussion of the role of women among Cathars, Richard Abels and Ellen Harrison reach the conclusion that few *perfectae* performed the ministerial functions theoretically open to them. Their study is based on a statistical analysis of three Inquisition manuscripts in the Languedoc. Their findings, at least for this sample, seem to contradict Koch's generalizations. See Richard Abels and Ellen Harrison, "The Participation of Women in Languedocian Catharism," in *Medieval Studies*, XLI (1979), 215–51.

24. Koch, *Frauenfrage*, pp. 25, 52.

25. *Ibid.*, pp. 56–57.

26. *Ibid.*, pp. 56, 64–70.

27. *Ibid.*, pp. 22–23.

28. The economic explanation is accepted by Weinstein and Bell. Carolyn Bynum argues for an explanation combining economic with religious reasons. See Bynum, *Holy Feast*, pp. 18–22. By 1250 there were thousands of Beguine communities in the Rhineland, Belgium and the Hansa region. See Petroff, *Medieval Women's Visionary Literature*, chap. 4.

29. The Beguines were associated by their detractors with the heresy of the Free Spirit, which made them subject to investigation by the Inquisition. See Robert E. Lerner, *The Heresy of the Free Spirit in the Later Middle Ages* (Berkeley: University of California Press, 1972).

30. For information on the mystics discussed, I have drawn on the following sources:

Kieckhefer, *Unquiet Souls, passim;* Mirca Eliade (ed.), *The Encyclopedia of Religion* (New York: Macmillan, 1987), biographical entries; Philipp Strauch, *Margaretha Ebner und Heinrich von Nördlingen; Ein Beitrag zur Geschichte der Deutschen Mystik* (Freiburg: Akademische Verlagsbuchandlung von J.C.B. Mohr, 1882); Margaretha Ebner, *Die Offenbarungen der Margaretha Ebner und der Adelheid Langmann* (tr. into German by Joseph Prestel) (Weimar: Verlag H. Böhlaus Nachfolger, 1939); *Ebner Christine, Der Nonne von Engelthal Büchlein von der Gnaden Überlast,* ed. Karl Schröder (Tübingen, 1871); Clarissa W. Atkinson, *The Oldest Vocation: Christian Motherhood in the Middle Ages* (Ithaca: Cornell University Press, 1991).

31. Marguerite Porète, *Le Miroir des simples âmes anienties et qui seulement demourent en vouloir et désir d'amour* (hereafter referred to as the *Miroir*). This manuscript is available only in Italian. See R. Guarnieri (ed.), "Il 'Miroir des simples âmes' di Margherita Porete," *Archivio italiano per la storia della pietà IV* (1965), pp. 501–635. See also Petroff, *Medieval Women's Visionary Literature,* Introduction and chap. 7, pp. 276–83.

32. Both quotes, Marguerite Porète, as cited in Lerner, *Heresy of the Free Spirit,* p. 77; background on Porète, pp. 68–78.

33. Porète, *Miroir,* as cited in Dronke, *Women Writers,* p. 222.

34. Porète, as cited in Lerner, *Heresy of the Free Spirit,* p. 77.

35. Dronke, *Women Writers,* p. 217.

36. Both quoted passages from *Miroir,* as cited in Dronke, *Women Writers,* pp. 224, 227.

37. Ulrich Heid,"Studien zu Marguerite Porète und ihrem 'Miroir des simples âmes'," in Dinzelbacher and Bauer (eds.), *Religiöse Frauenbewegung,* pp. 185–214; reference to the surviving copies of her book, p. 189. Heid says that no other medieval text was as widely distributed in Western Europe.

38. For a thorough discussion of the historiography of Margery Kempe, see Clarissa W. Atkinson, *Mystic and Pilgrim: The Book and the World of Margery Kempe* (Ithaca: Cornell University Press, 1983), chap.7. I am indebted to this work for some of my interpretations. I have also used the Meech/Allen translation of Kempe's autobiography; see fn. 6 above.

39. W. Butler-Bowdon (ed.), *The Book of Margery Kempe, 1436: A Modern Version* (London: Jonathan Cape, 1936), p. 31. All subsequent citations of Kempe are from this book.

40. *Ibid.,* pp. 47–48.

41. *Ibid.,* pp. 67–69.

42. *Ibid.,* p. 107.

43. *Ibid.,* p. 108.

44. *Ibid.* p. 189.

45. Julian of Norwich, as cited in Atkinson, *Mystic and Pilgrim,* p. 124.

FIVE   *The Way of the Mystics-2*

1. Caroline Bynum, ". . . 'And Woman her Humanity': Female Imagery in the Religious Writings of the Later Middle Ages," in Caroline Walker Bynum, Stevan Harrell and Paula Richman (eds.), *Gender and Religion: On the Complexity of Symbols* (Boston: Beacon Press, 1986), pp. 250–79. See also Caroline Walker Bynum, *Holy Feast*

and Holy Fast: The Religious Significance of Food to Medieval Women (Berkeley: University of California Press, 1987), chaps. 9 and 10.

An example of the use of maternal imagery for Christ is in Adelheid von Lindau, a nun in the convent in Töss, who wrote: "Ai, dear Lord, you are my father and my Mother and my sister and my brother; ah, Lord, you are my all that I desire, and your Mother is my playmate." As cited in Anne Marie Heiler (ed. and tr.), *Mystik deutscher Frauen im Mittelalter* (Berlin: Hochweg-Verlag, 1929), p. 186.

2. Caroline Walker Bynum, *Jesus as Mother: Studies in the Spirituality of the High Middle Ages* (Berkeley: University of California Press, 1982), pp. 147–52; and chap. 4, pp. 110–35. See also Eleanor McLaughlin, "Women, Power and the Pursuit of Holiness in Medieval Christianity," in Rosemary Ruether and Eleanor McLaughlin, *Women of Spirit: Female Leadership in the Jewish and Christian Traditions* (New York: Simon & Schuster, 1979), pp. 100–130; Kari Elisabeth Børressen, "God's Image, Man's Image? Female Metaphors Describing God in the Christian Tradition," *Temenos*, 19 (1983), 17–32.

As we will discuss below, the cult of the Virgin Mary developed most fully in the 12th and 13th centuries, when women's role in the Church was more strictly confined than it had been in the early Middle Ages.

3. *The Works of Hadewych* (tr. J.O. Plassmann) (Hannover: Orient-Buchhandlung Heinz Lafaire, 1923), Part II, pp. 85–87. Translated from the German by Gerda Lerner. See also Sr. M. Columba Hart, O.S.B. "Hadewijch of Brabant," *American Benectine Review*, 13, #1 (1962), 1–24.

4. Caroline Walker Bynum, *Holy Feast and Holy Fast*, pp. 57–69. See also Eleanor McLaughlin, " 'Christ My Mother': Feminine Naming and Metaphor in Medieval Spirituality," *Nashota Review*, 15, #3 (Fall 1975), 228–48.

5. The "theology of the feminine" as developed by Hildegard is fully discussed in Barbara Newman, *Sister of Wisdom: St. Hildegard's Theology of the Feminine*, (Berkeley: University of California Press, 1987), esp. chap. 2; quote p. xviii.

6. Edmund Colledge and James Walsh (eds.), *A Book of Showings to the Anchoress Julian of Norwich* (Toronto: Pontifical Institute of Medieval Studies, 1978), The Long Text, chap. 58, Revelation 14, lines 14–16, 55–59, 62–63, pp. 583–88. I have used the translation into modern English of this passage to be found in Katharina M. Wilson (ed.), *Medieval Women Writers* (Athens: University of Georgia Press, 1984), pp. 286–87. I have also used Dom Roger Hudleston (ed.), *Revelations of Divine Love Shewed to a devout Ankress, by name Julian of Norwich* (London: Burns Oates and Washbourne, 1927).

See also James McIlwain, "The 'bodelye syekness' of Julian of Norwich," *Journal of Medieval History*, 10, #3 (Sept. 1984), 167–80; Kari Elisabeth Børressen, "Christ Notre Mère, la Theologie de Julienne de Norwich," *Mitteilungen und Forschungsbeiträge der Cusanus-Gesellschaft*, XIII (1978), 320–29.

7. Colledge and Walsh, *A Book of Showings*, chap. 60, Revelation 14, lines 47–51; 58–59, pp. 598–600. Wilson, *Medieval Women Writers*, p. 289.

8. Luisa Muraro, *Vilemina and Manfreda: Die Geschichte einer feministischen Häresie*, tr. Martina Kemper (Freiburg im Breisgau: Kore, 1987). This volume contains the text of the Inquisition trial. Stephen E. Wessley, "The Thirteenth-Century Guglielmites: Salvation Through Women," in Derek Baker (ed.), *Medieval Women* (Oxford: Blackwell, 1978). I am indebted to Kari Børressen for confirmation of the sources and for additional data on Manfreda.

9. My information on Prous Boneta is based on personal communication with Kari Børressen, and on William Harold May, "The Confession of Prous Boneta: Heretic and Heresiarch," in John H. Mundy, Richard W. Emery, Benjamin N. Nelson (eds.), *Essays in Medieval Life and Thought* (Columbia University Press, 1955), pp. 3–30; Petroff, *Medieval Women's Visionary Literature*, pp. 276–77, 284–90.

10. Georg Wolfgang Karl Lochner (ed.), *Leben und Gesichte der Christina Ebnerin, Klosterfrau zu Engelthal* (Nürenberg: Schmid, 1872), p. 15.

11. The radical model of the *huiskerk* was developed by Anna Maria von Schurman, a celebrated learned woman of the Renaissance, who spent the last decades of her life as an active Pietist. The information on Pietist women is drawn from Jeannine Blackwell, "Heartfelt Conversations with God: Confessions of German Pietist Women in the 17th and 18th Centuries," in Gisela Brinker-Gabler (ed.), *Deutsche Literatur von Frauen*, Erster Band: *Vom Mittelalter bis zum Ende des 18. Jahrhunderts* (München: C.H. Beck Verlag, 1988), pp. 264–89; and on Gottfried Arnold, *Unparteyische Kirchen- und Ketzerhistorie, vom Anfang des Neuen Testaments bis auf das Jahr Christi 1688* (Frankfurt am Main: T. Fritschen's Erben, 1729), vol. 3.

12. Gottfried Arnold, as cited in Werner Mahrholz (ed.), *Der Deutsche Pietismus* (Berlin: Furche-Verlag, 1921), p. 78.

13. Arnold, *Unparteyische Kirchen- und Ketzerhistoire*, p. 273.

14. Arnold, as cited in Merholz, pp. 80–84.

15. Arnold, *Unparteyische* . . . , Book III, pp. 275–76; tr. Gerda Lerner.

16. *Ibid.*, p. 161; tr. Gerda Lerner.

17. *Ibid.*, p. 113.

18. For Beate Sturm, see Blackwell, "Heartfelt Conversations . . . , p. 289.

19. Johanna Eleonora Petersen's autobiography is reprinted in German in Mahrholz, *Der Deutsche Pietismus*, pp. 201–45; citations p. 245; tr. Gerda Lerner. An abridged version in English is now available: Jeannine Blackwell and Susanne Zantop, *Bitter Healing; German Women Writers, 1700–1830; An Anthology* (Lincoln: University of Nebraska Press, 1990), pp. 51–84. Introduction, bibliography and translation by Cornelia Niekus Moore.

20. When her husband was banished from Germany for ten years and traveled abroad, Erdmuth von Zinzendorf handled all the affairs of the Herrnhut community and did missionary work in Denmark.

21. My information about these gender conflicts among Pietists is based on Richard Critchfield, "Prophetin, Führerin, Organisatorin: Zur Rolle der Frau im Pietismus," in Barbara Becker-Cantarino (ed.), *Die Frau von der Reformation zur Romantik* (Bonn: Bouvier Verlag Herbert Grundmann, 1980), pp. 112–37.

22. Mary Dyer and her male companions deliberately challenged the Massachusetts commonwealth's law forbidding Quakers, as a "cursed sect of heretics," from entering the colony under pain of death. She refused the leniency the court was prepared to show her—if she would stay away under the "protection" of her husband—and suffered execution. In both England and the United States the long Quaker tradition of female leadership manifested itself in the early woman's rights movements, in which Quaker women were represented in disproportionately large numbers.

23. One Hester Biddle addressed the city of Oxford in a pamphlet written in the first person, in which the "I" identified her with God. "Woe to thee city of Oxford. . . . repent whilst thou has time, lest I consume thee with fire, as I have done. . . . Remember you are warned in your lifetime, and all left without excuse. Hester Biddle."

Biddle's text, as quoted in Elaine Hobby, *Virtue of Necessity: English Women's Writing, 1649–88* (Ann Arbor: University of Michigan, 1992), p. 41.

24. Margaret Fell, *Women's Speaking Justified, Proved and Allowed by Scripture* . . . (London, 1667).

25. *Ibid.*, pp. 5 and 12.

26. The quotes are from Edward Deming Andrews, *The People Called Shakers: A Search for the Perfect Society* (New York: Oxford University Press, 1953), pp. 8, 10. No source ascription in this text.

27. *Ibid.*, p. 11.

28. Calvin Green and Seth Y. Wells (eds.), *Summary View of the Millennial Church or United Society of Believers, Commonly Called Shakers* . . . (Albany: C. Van Benthuysen, 1848), pp. 17–18.

29. See also Alice Felt Tyler, *Freedom's Ferment: Phases of American Social History from the Colonial Period to the Outbreak of the Civil War* (New York: Harper & Brothers, 1944), pp. 140–66; [no author] *Testimonies of the Life, Character, Revelations and Doctrines of Mother Ann Lee and the Elders with Her* . . . (Albany, N.Y.: Weed, Parsons & Co., 1888).

30. My information on Jemima Wilkinson is based on Tyler, *Freedom's Ferment*, pp. 115–21; Herbert A. Wisbey, Jr., "Jemima Wilkinson," in *Notable American Women* (Cambridge, Mass: Belknap Press, 1971), vol. 3, pp. 609–10; Herbert A. Wisbey, Jr., *Pioneer Prophetess: Jemima Wilkinson, the Publick Universal Friend* (Ithaca: Cornell University Press, 1964); Rev. John Quincy Adams, "Jemima Wilkinson, the Universal Friend," *Journal of American History*, IX, no. 2 (April–July 1915), 249–63.

31. For information on Joanna Southcott I have drawn on the following sources: Alice Seymour, *The Express: Life and Divine Writings of Joanna Southcott*, 2 vols. (London: Simpkin, Marshall, Hamilton, Kent, 1909); James K. Hopkins, *A Woman to Deliver Her People: Joanna Southcott and English Millenarianism in an Era of Revolution* (Austin: University of Texas Press, 1982); James Hastings (ed.), *Encyclopedia of Religion and Ethics*, vol. 11 (New York: Scribner's, n.d.), p. 756; entry by W. T. Whitley, "Southcottians." The quote is Southcott as cited in Hopkins, *A Woman to Deliver*, p. xi.

32. Hopkins, *A Woman to Deliver*, pp. 83–84.

33. Southcott in Seymour, *The Express*, vol 1, p. 231.

34. Southcott in Hopkins, *A Woman to Deliver*, p. 199.

35. [Sojourner Truth] *Narrative of Sojourner Truth, a Northern Slave* . . . (Boston: Printed for the Author, 1850), pp. 60–70.

36. Frances D. Gage, "Reminiscences; Sojourner Truth," in Elizabeth Cady Stanton, Susan B. Anthony, Matilda Joslyn Gage, *History of Woman Suffrage*, 6 vols. (New York: Fowler & Wells, 1881–1922), vol. 1, pp. 115–17; quote p. 116. I have omitted the effort by Frances Gage to render Sojourner's speech in dialect and restored the spelling to standard English (G.L.).

37. Another black woman lecturer who defined herself as a black feminist was Maria W. Stewart, who briefly lectured in Boston in the 1830s. Her career as a public lecturer lasted only three years; she gave it up due to the opprobrium she received and lack of support. She continued as a political and religious writer and in 1834 published a volume of her collected works. See Marilyn Richardson (ed.), *Maria W. Stewart, America's First Black Woman Political Writer: Essays and Speeches* (Bloomington: Indiana University Press, 1987).

38. *Ibid.*, vol. 2, pp. 193–94.

39. I am grateful to Professor Nell Irvin Painter for sharing her work-in-progress on Sojourner Truth with me in manuscript. A part of it is N. Painter, "Sojourner Truth in Feminist Abolitionism: Difference, Slavery and Memory," in Jean Fagan Yellin and John C. Van Horne (eds.), *An Untrodden Path: Antislavery and Women's Political Culture* (Ithaca: Cornell University Press, 1992).

40. For background on the black spiritual autobiographers: William L. Andrews, *Sisters of the Spirit: Three Black Women's Autobiographies in the Nineteenth Century* (Bloomington: Indiana University Press, 1986); Nellie Y. McKay, "Nineteenth-Century Black Women's Spiritual Autobiographies: Religious Faith and Self-empowerment," Personal Narratives Group, Joy Webster Barbre *et al.*, *Interpreting Women's Lives: Feminist Theory and Personal Narratives* (Bloomington: Indiana University Press, 1989), pp. 139–54; Jean M. Humez, " 'My Spirit Eye': Some Functions of Spiritual and Visionary Experience in the Lives of Five Black Women Preachers, 1810–1880," in Barbara J. Harris and JoAnne McNamara (eds.), *Women and the Structure of Society* (Durham: Duke University Press, 1984), pp. 129–43.

See also Cheryl Townsend Gilkes, " 'Together and in Harness': Women's Traditions in the Sanctified Church," in Darlene Clark Hine (ed.), *Black Women in United States History*, 4 vols. (Brooklyn, N.Y.: Carlson Publishing Co., 1990), vol. 2, pp. 377–98. All my references to Rebecca Jackson's story and all quotes are drawn from Jean M. Humez, *Gifts of Power: The Writings of Rebecca Jackson, Black Visionary, Shaker Eldress* (n.p.: The University of Massachusetts Press, 1981), pp. 85–88.

41. *Ibid.*

42. *Ibid.*; the dreams are on pp. 99; 100; 119–21.

43. *Ibid.*, pp. 107–8.

44. *Ibid.*, p. 145.

45. *Ibid.*, pp. 21–22.

46. *Ibid.*, p. 203.

47. *Ibid.*, pp. 174–75.

48. *Ibid.*, pp. 29–37, 39–41.

49. My generalizations about Jewish women are based on the following sources: Charlotte Baum, Paula Hyman and Sonya Michel, *The Jewish Woman in America* (New York: Dial Press, 1976); Jacob R. Marcus, *The American Jewish Woman: A Documentary History* (New York: Ktec Publ. Co., 1981); Sondra Henry and Emily Taitz, *Written Out of History; Our Jewish Foremothers* (Fresh Meadows, N.Y.: Biblio Press, 1983); Chava Weissler, "Women in Paradise," *Tikkun*, II, #2 (April–May 1987), 43–46, 117–20.

See also Isidore Singer (ed.), *The Jewish Encyclopedia*, 12 vols. (New York: Funk & Wagnalls, 1901); Geoffrey Wigoder (ed.), *The New Standard Jewish Encyclopedia* (New York: .Doubleday, 1977); Aviva Cantor, *The Jewish Woman: 1900–1980: Bibliography* (Fresh Meadows, N.Y.: Biblio Press, 1981).

50. Chava Weissler, "The Traditional Piety of Ashkenazic Women," in Arthur Green (ed.), *Jewish Spirituality: From the Sixteenth-Century Revival to the Present; An Encyclopedic History of the Religious Quest* (New York, Crossroads, 1987), vol. 14, pp. 245–75; reference pp. 255–56.

51. *Ibid.*, p. 256.

52. Chava Weissler, "Images of the Matriarchs in Yiddish Supplicatory Prayers,"

Bulletin of the Center for the Study of World Religions, Harvard University, 14, #1 (1988), 44–51.

53. *Ibid.;* reference to Serel, pp. 47–50.

54. The references to the Horowitz prayer are based on a manuscript by Professor Chava Weissler, in my possession. I am greatly indebted to Professor Weissler for sharing her work in progress with me, especially the chapter devoted to Leah Horowitz. Her careful analysis and comparison of the three parts of Horowitz's prayer have influenced my interpretation. Cited by permission. See also Weissler "Images of the Matriarchs," pp. 45–46.

55. "Kabbalah." Wigoder (ed.), *The New Standard Jewish Encyclopedia,* pp. 1093–98.

56. Gershom G. Scholem, *Major Trends in Jewish Mysticism* (New York: Schocken Books, 1941); both quotes pp. 37–38.

57. Henry and Taitz, *Written Out of History,* p. 253.

58. Both examples cited in Henry M. Rabinowicz, *The World of Judaism* (London: Vallentine, Mitchel & Co., 1970), pp. 205–6.

59. Ada Rapoport-Albert, "On Women in Hasidism: S.A. Horodecky and the Maid of Ludomir Tradition," in Ada Rapoport-Albert and Steven J. Zipperstein (eds.), *Jewish History: Essays in Honour of Chimen Abramsky* (London: Peter Halban, 1988), p. 518, fn. 10.

60. Henry and Taitz, *Written Out of History,* pp. 182–83; Ada Rapoport-Albert, in *Jewish History,* p. 503. Horodecky claimed that women enjoyed a position of relative equality in Chassidism, but Rapoport-Albert disputes this. She distinguishes between informal influence, which these women had through the distinguished males with whom they were affiliated, and actual leadership and power. She also makes the point that most sources concerning the women *tsaddiks* are apocryphal second-hand accounts.

61. All three quotes are from the Journal of Marian Louise Moore. MSS in Western Reserve Historical Society, Cleveland, Ohio.

SIX *Authorization Through Motherhood*

1. The concept of motherhood is historically connected to the concept of childhood. Philippe Aries, in his landmark work *Centuries of Childhood: A Social History of Family Life* (New York: Random House, 1962), argues that childhood did not come to be regarded as a separate category until the 17th century.

For a discussion of religious women who abandoned their children, see Clarissa W. Atkinson, *The Oldest Vocation: Christian Motherhood in the Middle Ages* (Ithaca: Cornell University Press, 1991), chap. 5.

For a discussion of attitudes toward, and the ideology of, breastfeeding, see Ruth Perry, "Colonizing the Breast: Sexuality and Maternity in Eighteenth Century England," *Journal of the History of Sexuality,* 2, # 2 (1991), 204–34; Dorothy McLaren, "Marital Fertility and Lactation, 1570–1720," in Mary Prior (ed.), *Women in English Society, 1500–1800* (London: Methuen, 1985), pp. 22–53.

2. See Adrienne Rich, *Of Woman Born: Motherhood as Experience and Institution* (New York: W. W. Norton, 1976).

3. The suggestion that this was due to Bernard's involvement with another woman is made in Atkinson, *The Oldest Vocation*, p. 96.

4. Peter Dronke, *Women Writers of the Middle Ages: A Critical Study of Texts from Perpetua (d. 203) to Marguerite Porète (d. 1310)* (Cambridge: Cambridge University Press, 1984), as cited p. 40.

5. *Ibid.*, p. 42.

6. Friedrich Maurer (ed.), *Die Dichtungen der Frau Ava* (Tübingen: Max Niemyer Verlag, 1966). See also Edgar Papp, "Ava," in Wolfgang Stammler *et al.*, *Die deutsche Literatur des Mittelalters: Verfasserlexikon*, vol. I (Berlin: Walter de Gruyter, 1978), pp. 560–65.

7. Christine de Pisan's work will more fully be discussed in Chapter Seven.

8. Christine de Pisan, *Les Enseignments moraux*, str. 47, in M. Roy (ed.), *Oeuvres poètiques de Christine de Pisan* (Paris: Soc. Anc. Textes (Paris), 33, 1886), vol. III, p. 34.

9. See David Herlihy, "Life Expectancies for Women in Medieval Society," in Rosemarie Thee Morewedge (ed.), *The Role of Woman in the Middle Ages* (Albany: State University of New York Press, 1975), pp. 1–22; reference, p. 5.

Among the Alemanni the *wergeld*, the money to be paid in the case of death, for a female serf was three times that for an ordinary woman. *Ibid.*, p. 7. Suzanne Wemple reports that in general the *wergeld* for women was twice that for men of the same social class. See Suzanne Fonay Wemple, *Women in Frankish Society: Marriage and the Cloister, 500 to 900* (Philadelphia: University of Pennsylvania Press, 1985), p. 70.

10. The lines of distinction between slaves, serfs and free peasants vary with time and place and cannot always be sharply drawn. But the obligations owed to the lord of the manor were generally the same for all members of the peasant class. Slaves were owned bodily; serfs were and remained attached to the land; and peasants, while free in body, were held to the land by contractual obligations.

11. In many countries the lord's right of the first night—his privilege of sleeping with the bride of his serfs on their wedding night—was recognized by law and custom well into the 19th century. See Bonnie S. Anderson and Judith P. Zinsser, *A History of Their Own: Women in Europe from Prehistory to the Present*, 2 vols. (New York: Harper & Row, 1988), vol I, pp. 120–21.

12. For a thorough description of the lives of medieval women, see Wemple, *Women in Frankish Society*, chaps. 2 and 3.

13. Women in medieval and Renaissance Europe lived with constant warfare, which for them meant not only the possible loss of their husbands but rape and pillage by invading armies. Even cloistered nuns were threatened by and subjected to rape. See Jane Schulenburg, "The Heroics of Virginity: Brides of Christ and Sacrificial Mutilation," in Mary Beth Rose (ed.), *Women in the Middle Ages and the Renaissance: Literary and Historical Perspectives* (Syracuse: Syracuse University Press, 1986), pp. 29–72, *passim*.

14. My generalizations on peasant women are largely based on the excellent treatment of the subject in Anderson and Zinsser, *A History of Their Own*, vol. I, section II. One of the best means of exercising birth control was to delay the age of marriage; the numbers of single women fluctuated sharply in different periods and places.

15. Herlihy, "Life Expectancies . . . ," p. 13. The author is careful to call these figures "a gross calculation." More accurate calculations are not available, but for our purposes what is significant here is the slight shift in male-female sex ratios implied by

these figures and the short life expectancy of both sexes, compared with the modern world.

16. E. A. Wrigley, *Population and History* (New York: McGraw-Hill, 1973). See also Anderson and Zinsser, *A History of Their Own*, vol. I, p. 111.

17. One form of birth control was breastfeeding, which may have inhibited conception somewhat. Dorothy McLaren thinks that is one reason why poor women had fewer pregnancies than rich women. McLaren, "Marital Fertility and Lactation."

18. Demographic data based on Anderson and Zinsser, *A History of Their Own*, vol. I, pp. 134–40.

19. Stephan Beissel, *Geschichte der Verehrung Marias in Deutschland während des Mittelalters, Ein Beitrag zur Religion, Wissenschaft und Kunstgeschichte* (Freiburg im Breisgau: Herder, 1909), pp. 46–52, 151.

20. Pamela Berger, *The Goddess Obscured: Transformation of the Grain Protectress from Goddess to Saint* (Boston: Beacon Press, 1985), documents this transition. The reference to the account of Gregory of Tours, pp. 33–34; the reference to the grain miracle, pp. 90–96.

21. References to Hrosvitha, pp. 93–95; quotation from Rosvith, p. 93 (tr. Gerda Lerner). See also John A. Phillips, *Eve: The History of an Idea* (New York: Harper & Row, 1984).

22. Iraneus as quoted *ibid.*, p. 133.

23. Jerome, "Letter 22 to Eustochium," in Charles C. Mierow (tr.), *The Letters of St. Jerome* (Westminster, Md.: Newman Press, 1963), vol. I, p. 154.

24. See Atkinson, *Oldest Vocation*, p. 124; and Barbara Newman, *Sister of Wisdom: St. Hildegard's Theology of the Feminine* (Berkeley: University of California Press, 1987), chap. 5.

25. Penny Schine Gold, *The Lady and the Virgin: Image, Attitude and Experience in 12th-Century France* (Chicago: University of Chicago Press, 1985), pp. 45–55.

26. My discussion of the development of the cult of Mary is based on Geoffrey Ashe, *The Virgin* (London: Routledge & Kegan Paul, 1976); Marina Warner, *Alone of All Her Sex: The Myth and the Cult of the Virgin Mary* (New York: Vintage Books, 1983); Ann Matter, "Mary: A Goddess?" in Carl Olson (ed.), *The Book of the Goddess, Past and Present: An Introduction to Her Religion* (New York: Crossroad Publ. Co., 1985), pp. 80–96; quotation p. 86; and Phillips, *Eve*. See also Atkinson, *The Oldest Vocation*, chap. 4.

27. The anecdote on Chartres and Mary's veil appears in Matter, "Mary," p. 86.

28. Warner, *Alone of All Her Sex*, p. 276.

29. *Ibid.*, p. 280.

30. Marina Warner summarized these practices and traditions regarding Mary: "A pivotal contradiction therefore exists at the centre of the figure of the immaculately conceived Virgin because . . . she is, at the very moment of her most complete triumph over carnality, a goddess of vegetable and animal and human fertility." *Ibid.*, p. 269.

31. *Ibid.*, p. 262. The queenship of Mary was glorified in the popular 12th-century hymns "Regina Coeli" and "Salve Regina," which express her triumph over human evil through her virginity. Pope Pius XII officially proclaimed her Queen of Heaven in 1954.

32. Warner, *Alone of All Her Sex*, p. 304.

33. Atkinson, *The Oldest Vocation*, pp. 137–40.

34. In 1235 a mill in Fulda burned down and two children trapped inside perished in the flames. A group of crusaders present in the town circulated the story that Jews

had killed the children in order to collect their blood for medicinal use. In the ensuing pogrom 32 Jewish men and women were killed. See Ismar Elbogen and Leonore Sterling, *Die Geschichte der Juden in Deutschland* (Frankfurt am Main: Athenaeum Verlag, 1988), p. 39.

35. Lionel Rothkrug, "Religious Practices and Collective Perceptions: Hidden Homologies in the Renaissance and Reformation," *Historical Reflections*, 7, # 1 (Spring 1980), 3–263; reference to bleeding host, pp. 85–91.

36. Warner, *Alone of All Her Sex*, pp. 305, 314.

37. By Church doctrine the term "Immaculate Conception" refers to the conception of Mary by her mother. It was promulgated as a dogma by Pope Pius IX in 1854, This doctrine took a long time to develop and was the subject of much controversy. See S. G. F. Brandon, "Mary," in Richard Cavendish (ed.), *Man, Myth and Magic. The Illustrated Encyclopedia of Mythology, Religion and the Unknown* (New York: Marshall Cavendish, 1985), vol. VII, pp. 1747–52.

Duns Scotus (d. 1308) argued that Mary has been preserved from sin from the moment of her conception and then was saved like all other humans through Christ. The doctrinal battle between the Franciscans, who believed in this interpretation and the Dominicans who, following St. Augustine, believed that Mary was human and conceived in sin, actually helped to promote the cult of Mary. The Dominicans introduced and spread the organization of Confraternities of the Rosary, organizations of lay people, predominantly women, who regularly recited the rosary in order to win remission of sins. At least one historian has argued that the Dominican effort was designed to "control female religious life and to destroy unsupervised forms of organized lay piety." See Rothkrug, "Religious Practices," p. 82.

The fact that the man chiefly responsible for promoting the Confraternity of the Rosary in Germany was the Dominican Jacob Sprenger, author of the misogynist *Malleus Maleficarum*, published in 1486, supports this interpretation.

38. C.P. Ceroke, "Mary, Blessed Virgin, I," in [The Catholic University] *New Catholic Encyclopedia* (New York: McGraw-Hill, 1967), vol. 9, pp. 335–47.

39. Constantia Munda, "The Worming of a Mad Dogge . . ." (London: Lawrence Hayes, 1617). I have used the text reprinted in Katherine Usher Henderson and Barbara F. McManus, *Half Humankind: Contexts and Texts of the Controversy About Women in England, 1540–1640* (Urbana: University of Illinois Press, 1985), pp. 244–63.

40. Barbara Becker-Cantarino (ed.), *Anna Ovena Hoyers, Geistliche und Weltliche Poemata* (Tübingen: Niemeyer, 1986; reprint of Amsterdam: Elsevier, 1650), p. 245 (tr. Gerda Lerner).

41. *Ibid.*, pp. 216–19.

42. She follows the traditional question and answer form of the catechism, a dialogue between a minister and a child, but substitutes the mother for the minister.

43. Becker-Cantarino, *Anna Hoyers*, pp. 3–39.

44. *The Memoirs of Glückel of Hameln*, tr. by Marvin Lowenthal (New York, Schocken Books, 1932; reprint of 1932 ed. published by Harper). The book, written 1690–91, was not published until 1896, when it appeared in Judeo-German in Frankfurt am Main, edited from a manuscript copy by David Kaufmann.

45. *Ibid.*, p. 36.

46. *Ibid.*, p. 38.

47. See, above, Chapter 3, fn. 12.

48. As cited in *Poems by Eminent Ladies* . . . , Vol. 1 (London: R. Balwin, 1755), pp. 22–25.

49. Gisela Brinker-Gabler (ed.), *Deutsche Dichterinnen vom 16. Jahrhundert bis zur Gegenwart* (Frankfurt am Main: Fischer Taschenbuch, 1978), pp.104–5 (tr. Gerda Lerner).

50. Historians have offered differing interpretations of the causes and effects of these trends. For some representative views, see Lawrence Stone, *The Family, Sex and Marriage in England: 1500–1800* (New York: Harper & Row, 1977); Carl Degler, *At Odds: Women and the Family in America: 1776 to the Present* (New York: Oxford University Press, 1980); Perry, "Colonizing the Breast . . ."; Anna Davin,"Imperialism and Motherhood," *History Workshop*, # 5 (1978), 9–65.

51. Mary Wollstonecraft, *A Vindication of the Rights of Woman with Strictures on Political and Moral Subjects* (1792; reprint New York: Garland, 1974), p. 51.

52. *Ibid.*, p. 254.

53. Quote from Mary Wollstonecraft, *Mary: A Fiction*, reprint of the 1788 edition (New York: Schocken Books, 1977), p. 111. I have been influenced in my interpretation of Wollstonecraft's fiction by an unpublished M.A. essay by Kathleen Brown. University of Wisconsin-Madison.

SEVEN *One Thousand Years of Feminist Bible Criticism*

1. Madrid, Escorial MS, a II 9, f. 90 v., as cited in Joyce E. Salisbury, "Fruitful in Singleness," *Journal of Medieval History*, 8, no. 2 (June 1982), 97–106; p. 102.

2. Helmust Koester, *Einführung in das Neue Testament im Rahmen der Religionsgeschichte und Kulturgeschichte der hellenistischen und römischen Zeit* (Berlin: Walter de Gruyter, 1980), pp. 485–89.

For a thorough discussion of the issues of ascription and interpretation of Paulinist writings, see Wm. O. Walker, Jr., "The 'Theology of Woman's Place' and the 'Paulinist' Tradition," *Semeia: An Experimental Journal for Biblical Criticism*, 28 (1983), 101–12. Most scholars agree that Paul wrote only eight of the letters ascribed to him and that he did not write I or II Timothy or Titus 2.

3. Tertullian, *De Cultu Feminarum*, I, l, as cited in Rosemary Radford Ruether, "Misogynism and Virginal Feminism in the Fathers of the Church," in R.R. Ruether, ed., *Religions and Sexism: Images of Women in the Jewish and Christian Traditions* (New York: Simon & Schuster, 1974), pp. 150–83; quote p. 157.

4. Ambrose,"Paradise," 6.34, in *Fathers of the Church*, 312, as cited in Margaret R. Miles, *Carnal Knowing: Female Nakedness and Religious Meaning in the Christian West* (New York: Vintage Books, 1991), p. 91.

5. St. Augustine, "The Literal Meaning of Genesis 11.37," *Ancient Christian Writers*, 42, 171, as cited in Miles, *Carnal Knowing*, p. 96.

6. Augustine, *De trinitate*, 12.7.10 (PL 42.1003), as cited on p. 202 in Maryanne Cline Horowitz, "The Image of God in Man—Is Woman Included?," *Harvard Theological Review*, 72, # 3–4 (July–Oct. 1979), 175–206.

7. The interpretation that Augustine's views were androcentric and contributed to the misogynist interpretations of the Church is upheld by, among others, Ruether, "Misogynism." Horowitz, "The Image of God in Man," argues strongly for the allegor-

ical reading of the text and states that "The notion that woman was 'not in God's image' was a rare view within both the Jewish and the Christian traditions" (p. 204).

8. Thomas Aquinas, *Summa Theologica*, 3a, qu.31, art. 4. I am indebted to Professor Nancy Isenberg for referring me to this quotation.

9. My synthesis was influenced by my reading of the following secondary sources: John A. Phillips, *Eve: The History of an Idea* (San Francisco: Harper & Row, 1984); Phyllis Bird, "Images of Women in the Old Testament," in Ruether, ed., *Religion and Sexism*, pp. 41–88; Bernard P. Prusak, "Woman: Seductive Siren and Source of Sin?," *ibid.*, pp. 89–116; Ruether, "Misogynism," *ibid.*, pp.150–83; Eleanor Commo McLaughlin, "Equality of Souls, Inequality of Sexes: Woman in Medieval Theology," *ibid.*, pp. 213–66; Ian Maclean, *Woman Triumphant: Feminism in French Literature: 1610–1652* (Oxford: Clarendon Press, 1977), chap.1; Elaine Pagels, *Adam and Eve and the Serpent* (New York: Random House, 1988). For an innovative interpretation of the Genesis passage of Creation and the Fall based on a modern translation of the ancient Hebrew text, see Carol Meyers, *Discovering Eve: Ancient Israelite Women in Context* (New York: Oxford University Press, 1988). Meyers thinks that all the misogynist interpretations of Eve are Christian in origin.

10. As cited in David Greene and Frank O'Connor (eds. and trs.), *A Golden Treasury of Irish Poetry: 600–1200* (London: Macmillan 1967), p. 158.

11. Hildegard of Bingen, *De Operatione Dei*, I. 4. 100 PL 197:885 bc, as cited in Barbara Newman, *Sister of Wisdom: St. Hildegard's Theology of the Feminine* (Berkeley: University of California Press, 1987), p. 96.

12. See Hildegard, *Causae et Curae*, 136, as cited in Newman, *Sister of Wisdom*, p. 98.

13. *Ibid.*

14. Joan Cadden, "It Takes All Kinds: Sexuality and Gender Differences in Hildegard of Bingen's 'Book of Compound Medicine'," *Traditio*, 40 (1984), 149–74, quote pp. 154–55.

15. For background on Christine de Pizan, see Charity Cannon Willard, *Christine de Pizan: Her Life and Works* (New York: Persea Books, 1984); Susan Groag Bell, "Christine de Pizan (1364–1430): Humanism and the Problem of a Studious Woman," *Feminist Studies*, III, # 3/4 (Spring/Summer 1976), 173–84; Astrik L. Gabriel, "The Educational Ideas of Christine de Pisan," *Journal of the History of Ideas*, XIII, # 1 (Jan. 1955), 3–21; Sandra L. Hindman, *Christine de Pizan's "Epistre d'Othea": Paintings and Politics at the Court of Charles VI* (Toronto: Pontifical Institute of Medieval Studies, 1986); S. Hindman, "With Ink and Mortar: Christine de Pizan's *Cité des Dames* (An Art Essay)," *Feminist Studies*, X, #3 (Fall 1984), 457–77; Mary A. Ignatius, "A Look at the Feminism of Christine de Pizan," *Proceedings of the Pacific Northwest Conference on Foreign Languages*, 29, Pt. 2 (1978), 18–21; Therese Ballet Lynn, "The '*Ditie de Jeanne d'Arc*': Its Political, Feminist and Aesthetic Significance," *Fifteenth Century Studies*, I (1978), 149–57; Christine M. Reno, "Feminist Aspects of Christine de Pizan's *Epistre d'Othea à Hector*," *Studi Francesi*, 71 (1980), 271–76.

16. Christine de Pizan, *The Book of the City of Ladies*, tr. Earl Jeffrey Richards (New York: Persea Books, 1982), I. 9. 2; pp. 23–24.

17. Hugh of St.-Victor, *De Sacramentis Christianae Fidei*, Libri II, PL. CLXXVI, as cited in Angela M. Lucas, *Women in the Middle Ages: Religion, Marriage, and Letters* (Brighton, Sussex: Harvester Press, 1983), p. 8.

18. Although this argument seems to be original with Christine de Pizan, historians

credit it to the 16th-century male writer Heinrich Cornelius Agrippa von Nettesheim, whose important work *Declamatio de nobilitate et praecellentia foemine sexus* (1529) influenced both male and female writers after him. This is characteristic of the way female intellectual contributions are lost and forgotten. See Maclean, *Women Triumphant*, pp. 25–26.

19. Christine de Pizan, *City*, I. 9. 3; p. 24.

20. *Ibid.*, I. 10. 3; p. 27.

21. *Ibid.*, I. 10. 5; pp. 29–30.

22. The earliest treatment of this aspect of Christine de Pizan's work is in Joan Kelly, "Early Feminist Theory and the *Querelle des Femmes*," in Kelly, *Women, History and Theory: The Essays of Joan Kelly* (Chicago: University of Chicago Press, 1984), pp. 65–109.

23. Isotta Nogarola in Margaret L. King and Albert Rabil, Jr. (eds.), *Her Immaculate Hand: Selected Works By and About the Women Humanists of Quattrocento Italy* (Binghamton, N.Y.: Medieval & Renaissance Texts & Studies, 1983), pp. 57–68.

For background reading on Nogarola and other learned women, see also Margaret L. King, "The Religious Retreat of Isotta Nogarola (1418–1466): Sexism and Its Consequences in the Fifteenth Century," *SIGNS*, 3, #4 (Summer 1978), 807–22; King, "Thwarted Ambitions: Six Learned Women of the Italian Renaissance," *Soundings 59* (1976), 280–304; Patricia H. Labalme, *Beyond Their Sex: Learned Women of the European Past* (New York: New York University Press, 1980); Roland Bainton *Women of the Reformation in Germany and Italy* (Minneapolis: Augsburg Publishing House, 1971); Bainton, *Women of the Reformation from Spain to Scandinavia* (Minneapolis: Augsburg Publishing House, 1977); Mary Agnes Cannon, *The Education of Women During the Renaissance* (Washington, D.C.: National Capitol Press, 1916; reprint Hyperion, 1958).

24. Nogarola as cited in King and Rabil, *Her Immaculate Hand*, pp. 59–60.

25. *Ibid.*, pp. 64, 66.

26. *Ibid.*, p. 78.

27. Laura Cereta to Augustinius Aemilius, "Curse against the Ornamentation of Women," as cited in *Her Immaculate Hand*, pp. 77–80; quote p. 80.

28. Renja Salminen (ed.), *Le Miroir de l'âme pecheresse de Marguerite de Navarre* (Helsinki: Suomaleinen Tiedeaketemia, 1979), v. 10–12 (tr. Paula Sommers and cited in Sommers, "The Mirror and Its Reflections: Marguerite de Navarre's Biblical Feminism," *Tulsa Studies in Women's Literature*, V, #1 (Spring 1986), 31). See also J.R. Brink (ed.), *Female Scholars: A Tradition of Learned Women Before 1800* (Montreal: Eden Press, Women's Publications, 1980), pp. 39–50.

29. Marguerite de Navarre, *Miroir*, v. 941–42; 953–56, as cited in Sommers, "The Mirror . . . ," p. 33.

30. *Ibid.*, v. 248–50; 261–68, as cited in Sommers, pp. 32–33. See also [Marguerite de Navarre] *Marguerites de la Marguerite des Princesses, Trèsillustre Rayne de Navarre* (New York: Johnson Reprint Corp., 1970), from the edition of Jean de Tournes (Lyon, 1547), p. 25.

31. Elaine V. Beilin, "Anne Askew's Self-portrait in *Examinations 77–91*," in Margaret Patterson Hannay (ed.), *Silent but for the Word: Tudor Women as Patrons, Translators and Writers of Religious Works* (Kent, Ohio: Kent State University Press, 1985), p. 85.

32. *Ibid.*, pp. 87, 86.

33. The chief antifeminist tract in France was Alexis Trousset's *Alphabet de l'imperfection et malice des femmes* (1617). It was reprinted in full eighteen times between 1617 and 1650.

In England the controversy began with the publication of a pamphlet which satirized women and catalogued all their vices. [Anon] *Here begynneth a litle boke named the Schole house of women: wherin every man may rede a goodly prays of the condicyons of women* (n.pl.: T.Peyt, 1541). The book ran through four editions in the next decades. This was followed by the exiled Puritan John Knox's, *The First Blast against the monstruous regiment of Women* (Geneva: J. Crespin, 1558), which was an attack against the Catholic Queen Mary, but also a general attack on women. Several more rounds of pamphlets arguing for, but mostly against, women appeared in the next three decades. A major pamphlet war, in which women were involved erupted with the publication of Joseph Swetnam's misogynist pamphlet *The Araignment of lewd, idle, froward and unconstant women: Or the vanitie of them, choose you whether* (n.pl.: E. Allde for T. Archer, 1615), British Library. This pamphlet was frequently reprinted in the next fifty years, while the pamphlets in defense of women were not reprinted. See Katherine Usher Henderson and Barbara F. McManus (eds.), *Half Humankind: Contexts and Texts of the Controversy About Women in England, 1540–1640* (Urbana: University of Illinois Press, 1985), Part 1.

See also Maclean, *Woman Triumphant*, pp. 30–35; Lula McDowell Richardson, "The Forerunners of Feminism in French Literature of the Renaissance from Christine of Pisa to Marie de Gournay," *The Johns Hopkins Studies in Romance Literatures and Languages*, XII (Baltimore: Johns Hopkins University Press, 1929).

34. *Jane Anger, her Protection for Women. To defend them against the Scandalous Reportes of a late Surfeiting Lover, and all other Venerians that complaine so to be overcloyed with womens kindnesse* (n.pl.: R. Jones and T. Orwin,1589), reprinted in Henderson and McManus, *Half Humankind*, pp. 172–88. I have also drawn on Simon Shepherd (ed.), *The Women's Sharp Revenge: Five Women's Pamphlets from the Renaissance* (London: Fourth Estate, 1985), p. 30. Shepherd argues convincingly that Jane Anger is not a pseudonym, although her identity cannot be firmly established.

35. Anger, as cited in Henderson and McManus, *Half Humankind*, pp. 180–81.

36. *Ibid.*

37. Swetnam [pseud.], *Araignment*. Swetnam largely plagiarized from an earlier misogynist pamphlet by John Lyly, *Euphues his censure to Philautus*, which was the pamphlet Jane Anger had answered. See Shepherd, *Women's Sharp Revenge*, pp. 53–55. Swetnam's pamphlet provoked answers from Rachel Speght, Constantia Munda and Ester Sowernam. It also provoked a play in defense of women, *Swetnam the Womanhater arraigned by Women* (London: Richard Meighen, 1620), which was performed at the Red Bull Theatre in 1619. See Coryl Crandall "The Cultural Implications of the Swetnam Anti-feminist Controversy in the Seventeenth Century," *Journal of Popular Culture*, 2, # 1 (Summer 1968), 136–48.

38. Rachel Speght, *Mortalities Memorandum with a Dreame Prefixed . . .* (London: Edward Griffin, 1621).

39. Rachel Speght, "A Mouzell for Melastomus, The Cynical Bayter of, and foule mouthed Barker against Evah's Sex..." (London: Thomas Archer, 1617), British Library, p. 10.

40. *Ibid.*, as cited in Shepherd, *Women's Sharp Revenge*, p. 66.

41. *Ibid.*, p. 67.

42. St.Paul, I. Cor. 7. Speght, *ibid.,* pp. 67–68.

43. *Ibid.,* quote p. 69; pp. 69–73.

44. Ester Sowernam, *Esther hath hang'd Haman . . . ,* in Henderson and Mc-Manus, *Half Humankind,* quote pp. 224–25.

There is no biographical information available on the person using the pseudonym Ester Sowernam and historians have suggested the author may have been a man. The same issue was raised about Constantia Munda. Shepherd, in a convincing argument, reasons that both were women, citing the fact that Rachel Speght, a contemporary refers to both as women. See Shepherd, *Women's Sharp Revenge,* pp. 86–87; 126.

Elsewhere, Shepherd convincingly argues, mostly from internal, textual evidence, that the author of *The Women's Sharp Revenge,* another satirical pamphlet written in defense of women was a man, one John Taylor. He wrote a pamphlet in 1639, attacking female scolds and then wrote its rebuttal himself, under the pseudonyms "Mary Tattle-well and Joan Hit-him-home, spinsters." This kind of literary fraud speaks to the popularity of the debate on women and to the expected profits to be derived from writing such pamphlets, both pro and con. I have accepted Shepherd's position and therefore omitted the "Mary Tattle-well . . ." pamphlet from consideration in this connection. *Ibid.,* pp. 160–61.

45. Sowernam in Henderson and McManus, *Half Humankind,* p. 225.

46. Sarah Fyge [Field Egerton], *The Female Advocate, or, An Anwser to a Late Satyr against the Pride, Lust and Inconstancy, &c. of Woman,* as cited in Moira Ferguson (ed.), *First Feminists: British Women Writers, 1578–1799* (Bloomington: Indiana University Press, 1985), pp. 154–67; quotation p. 157.

47. Aemilia Lanyer, *Salve Deus Rex Judaeorum,* sig. f3v as cited in Hannay, *Silent But for the Word,* p. 213.

48. Lanyer, sts. 94.5–96; 102.6–105, as cited *ibid.*

49. Lanyer, st. 121, as cited *ibid.*

50. Anna Maria von Schurman, as cited in Joyce Irwin, "Anna Maria von Schurman: From Feminism to Pietism," *Church History,* 46 (1977), 48–62; quotations pp. 53, 54. See also Brink, *Female Scholars,* pp. 77–79.

51. Ute Brandes, "Studierstube, Dichterklub, Hofgesellschaft: Kreativität und kultureller Rahmen weiblicher Erzählkunst im Barock," in Gisela Brinker-Gabler (ed.), *Deutsche Literatur von Frauen;* Erster Band: *Vom Mittelalter bis zum Ende des 18. Jahrhunderts* (München: C.H. Beck Verlag, 1988), pp. 222–64.

52. Jeannine Blackwell, "Heartfelt Conversations with God: Confessions of German Pietist Women in the 17th and 18th Centuries." *ibid.,* pp. 264–89. See also F. Ernest Stöffler, "Pietism," in Mirca Eliade (ed.), *The Encyclopedia of Religion,* 16 vols. (New York: Macmillan, 1987), vol. 11, pp. 324–26.

53. Antoinette Bourignon, as cited in Gottfried Arnold, *Unparteyische Kirchen-und Ketzer-historie, vom Anfang des Neuen Testaments bis auf das Jahr Christi 1688* (Frankfurt am Main: T. Fritschens Erben, 1729), vol.3, pp. 150–57. (tr. Gerda Lerner).

54. Margaret Fell, *Woman's Speaking Justified, Proved and Allowed of by the Scriptures . . .* (London, 1667). Reprinted by Augustan Reprint Society, Publ.# 194 (Los Angeles: William A. Clark Memorial Library, University of California, 1979), p. 11.

55. The work of Mary Astell will be discussed more fully in Chapter Nine.

56. Mary Astell, *Some Reflections upon Marriage* (New York: Source Book Press, 1970, reprint of the 1730 edition; earliest edition of this work is 1700), p. 115.

57. *Ibid.*, pp. 103–4.

58. Judith Sargent Murray, "On the Equality of the Sexes" (1790), as cited in Alice S. Rossi (ed.), *The Feminist Papers from Adams to Beauvoir* (New York: Bantam Books, 1974), p. 23.

59. See the arguments about Bible translation made by Sarah M. Grimké in her *Letters on the Equality of the Sexes and the Condition of Woman* (Boston: Isaac Knapp, 1838). Sarah Grimké claims that "almost everything written on this subject [the sphere of women] has been the result of a misconception of the simple truths revealed in the Scriptures, in consequence of the false translation of many passages of Holy Writ" (p. 4). The two quotes from Julia Smith derive from [Julia Smith] *The Holy Bible containing the Old and New Testaments: Translated literally from the original Tongues* (Hartford, Conn.: American Publishing Co., 1876), Preface.

For a biography of Julia Smith see the entry "Smith, Abby Hadassah and Julia Evelina" by Elizabeth George Speare in Edward T. James, Janet Wilson James and Paul Boyer (eds.), *Notable American Women, 1607–1950: A Biographical Dictionary*, 3 vols. (Cambridge: Harvard University Press, 1971), vol. III, pp. 302–4. See also Addie Stancliffe Hale, "The Five Amazing Smith Sisters," *Hartford Daily Courant*, May 15, 1932.

60. See Nancy Isenberg, *The Co-Equality of Women . . .* , Dissertation, University of Wisconsin-Madison, 1990, for a discussion of the complex ideological, mostly religious antecedents of the woman's rights movement.

61. Sarah Moore Grimké, *Letters on the Equality of the Sexes and the Condition of Woman, Addressed to Mary Parker, President of the Boston Female Anti-Slavery Society* (Boston: Isaac Knapp, 1838). Sarah Grimké did this work in close collaboration with her sister Angelina Grimké, but it was printed under her name and bears the imprint of her style. Her earlier pamphlet, which is an anti-slavery appeal to the clergy based on biblical texts, is *An Epistle to the Clergy of the Southern States* (New York, 1836). Margaret Fuller, *Woman in the Nineteenth Century* (New York: W. W. Norton, 1971; reprint of 1855 ed.).

62. See Catherine Birney, *The Grimké Sisters: Sarah and Angelina Grimké: The First Women Advocates of Abolition and Woman's Rights* (Boston: Lee and Shepard, 1885); Gerda Lerner, *The Grimké Sisters from South Carolina: Rebels Against Slavery* (Boston: Houghton Mifflin, 1967).

63. Sarah Grimké, *Letters*, p. 4; emphasis by author.

64. Luther's statement reads: *"Gott helfe mir. Hier stehe ich; ich kann nicht anders"* (God Help me. Here I stand. I cannot do otherwise).

65. Sarah Grimké, *Letters*, p. 5; emphasis by author.

66. *Ibid.*, p. 7; emphasis by author.

67. *Ibid.*, pp. 10, 11.

68. Sarah Grimké's argument reflected a debate among religious dissenters in the Northeastern American states regarding the assumed authority of the Church over the spiritual conduct of its members. This debate found its fullest expression in the 1840s and 1850s in the formation of a large number of dissident religious sects. For a full discussion of these sects and of their impact see Isenberg, *The Co-Equality of Women*, chaps. 2 and 4.

My generalizations about the early woman's rights movement are based on extensive study of the relevant primary sources, especially the Proceedings of all the Woman's Rights Conventions prior to 1860, letters and diaries of their participants and the organizational records of female Anti-Slavery societies.

69. *Ibid.*, pp. 118–19; emphasis by author.

70. *Ibid.*, p. 60.

71. *Free Thought Magazine*, XVI, no.6 (June 1898), from folder MC 377 (49) Matilda Gage papers, Schlesinger Library, Radcliffe College, Cambridge, Mass.

72. Letter from Elizabeth Cady Stanton to Matilda J. Gage, reprinted in *The Liberal Thinker* (Syracuse, N.Y., 1890).

73. Program of Women's National Liberal Union Convention, Feb. 24–25, 1890, Washington, D.C.

74. Elizabeth Cady Stanton and Matilda J. Gage (eds.), *The Woman's Bible* (New York: European Publishing Co., 1895).

75. Grimké, *Letters*, p. 3.

76. For the Newton aphorism, see Robert K. Merton, *On the Shoulders of Giants: A Shandean Postscript* (San Diego: Harcourt Brace Jovanovich, 1985). In this brilliant, witty spoof on pedantic scholarship Merton argues quite seriously that scientific discoveries "emerge from the existing cultural base and consequently become, under conditions that can be reasonably well defined, practically inevitable." While the predictability and inevitability of non-scientific thought cannot be similarly argued, the social origin of the generation of ideas and knowledge is similar to that of scientific thought. It is here that I perceive the differences in the intellectual development of men and women most strongly.

EIGHT *Authorization Through Creativity*

1. [Anon.], "Wife's Lament" as cited in Carol Cosman, Joan Keefe, Kathleen Weaver (eds.), *The Penguin Book of Women Poets* (Middlesex, Eng.: Penguin Books, 1979), pp. 63–64.

2. As cited in Meg Bogin, *The Women Troubadours* (Scarborough, Eng.: Paddington Press, 1976), p. 89; tr. Meg Bogin.

3. Louise Labé, Sonnett VIII, as cited in Aliki Barnstone and Willis Barnstone (eds.), *A Book of Women Poets from Antiquity to Now* (New York: Schocken Books, 1980), p. 209 (tr. Willis Barnstone). I also consulted the modern French version in Gerard Guillot, *Louise Labé* (n.p.: Edition Seghers, 1962), p. 129.

4. Labé, Sonnet XXIII, cited in Barnstone and Barnstone, p. 216 (tr. Willis Barnstone). See in French in Guillot, *Louise Labé*, p. 138.

5. Christine de Pizan, [untitled] in Barnstone and Barnstone, p. 203 (tr. Willis Barnstone).

6. [Anne Bradstreet] *Correspondence from The Tenth Muse, Lately sprung up in America in Severall Poems, compiled with great variety of Wit . . . by a Gentlewoman in these parts* (London: Stephen Botwell, 1650). The Memorial Libraries, University of Wisconsin-Madison.

7. Adrienne Rich, "The Tensions of Anne Bradstreet," in Adrienne Rich, *On Lies, Secrets, and Silence: Selected Prose, 1966–1978* (New York: W.W. Norton, 1979), pp. 21–32; quote p. 31.

8. Alice Walker, "In Search of our Mothers' Garden," in A. Walker, *In Search of Our Mothers' Garden: Womanist Prose* (San Diego: Harcourt Brace Jovanovich, 1983), pp. 232–43.

9. "Epilogue," Marie de France, *Fables*, ed. and tr. by Harriet Spiegel (Toronto: University of Toronto Press, 1987), p. 257. Her recognition by contemporaries can be

judged from the fact that twenty-three manuscripts of Marie de France's *Fables* survive, dating from the 13th century to the 15th century, as do five manuscripts of her *Lais*. *Ibid.*, p. 3.

10. As cited *ibid.*, p. 4.

11. Margaret Cavendish, *A True Relation of My Birth, Breeding and Life*, Originally published in *Poems, and Fancies: Written by the Right Honourable, the Lady Margaret Countesse of Newcastle* (London: J. Martin, 1653). Reprinted in Margaret Cavendish, *The Life of William Cavendish* (London, 1667); quotes are from 1667 edition.

12. *Ibid.*, p. 178.

13. *Ibid.*, p. 178, both quotes.

14. Sybilla Schwarz. "A Song Against Envy" (tr. Gerda Lerner), as cited in Gisela Brinker-Gabler (ed.), *Deutsche Dichterinnen vom 16ten Jahrhundert bis zu Gegenwart* (Frankfurt am Main: Fischer Taschenbuch Verlag, 1978), pp. 87–89.

15. Christiana Mariana von Ziegler, in Brinker-Gabler, *ibid.*, p. 119 (tr. Gerda Lerner).

16. Morpurgo, as cited in Cosman, Keefe, Weaver (eds.), *The Penguin Book of Women Poets*, pp. 164–65.

17. Mary Collier, *Poems, on Several Occasions . . . with some remarks on her life* (Winchester: printed for the author, 1762, as cited in Moira Ferguson (ed.), *First Feminists: British Women Writers: 1578–1799* (Bloomington: Indiana University Press, 1985), p. 262.

18. E.L.V. Klenke, geb. Karschin (ed.), *Gedichte von Anna Louisa Karsch (in), geb. Dürbach* (Berlin: Friedrich Maurer, 1797), p. 313 (tr. Gerda Lerner).

19. Elizabeth Inchbald, who also wrote plays, was another self-supporting writer. Mary Wollstonecraft's two novels did not contribute to her earnings during her lifetime.

20. Paula Bennett, *Emily Dickinson: Woman Poet* (Iowa City: University of Iowa Press, 1990), p. 22.

21. The feminist literary critic Sandra M. Gilbert discusses with insight this aspect of Dickinson's self-created *persona* with emphasis on the symbolic meanings of her choice of white dress for the period of her self-chosen life as a recluse. See Sandra M. Gilbert, "The Wayward Nun Beneath the Hill: Emily Dickinson and the Mysteries of Womanhood," in Suzanne Juhasz (ed.), *Feminist Critics Read Emily Dickinson*, Bloomington: Indiana University Press, 1983), pp. 22–66. The subject was earlier explored (1960) by Louise Bogan, "A Mystical Poet," in Richard B. Sewall (ed.), *Emily Dickinson: A Collection of Critical Essays* (Englewood Cliffs, N.J.: Prentice-Hall, 1963), pp. 137–43.

22. For biographical information I have relied on Richard B. Sewall, *The Life of Emily Dickinson* (New York: Farrar, Straus and Giroux, 1974, 1980) and Cynthia Griffin Wolff, *Emily Dickinson* (New York: Knopf, 1987). Sandra M. Gilbert and Susan Gubar, *The Norton Anthology of Literature by Women: The Tradition in English* (New York: W.W. Norton, 1985), "Introduction," pp. 839–43. The poems cited are from Thomas H. Johnson (ed.), *The Poems of Emily Dickinson* (Cambridge: Harvard University Press, 1955); hereafter cited as *Poems*. The letters are from Thomas Johnson and Theodora Ward, *The Letters of Emily Dickinson*, 3 vols. (Cambridge: Harvard University Press, 1958); hereafter cited as *Letters*. I have also read Rebecca Patterson, *Emily Dickinson's Imagery*, edited and with an introduction by Margaret H. Freeman (Amherst: University of Massachusetts Press, 1979); Suzanne Juhasz, *The Undiscovered Continent: Emily*

Dickinson and the Space of the Mind (Bloomington: Indiana University Press, 1983); Inder Nath Kerr, *The Landscape of Absence: Emily Dickinson's Poetry* (New Haven: Yale University Press, 1974); David Porter, *Dickinson: The Modern Idiom* (Cambridge: Harvard University Press, 1981).

23. As cited in Sewall, *Life*, p. 74.
24. Letter to T. W. Higginson, 25 April, 1862, *Letters*, p. 404.
25. Wolff, *Dickinson*, Part Three, "Pugilist and Poet," pp. 161–366.
26. As cited in Sewall, *Life*, p. 420.
27. *Ibid.*, p. 394.
28. The various men who supposedly were the objects of Dickinson's love have been identified as Willie Dickinson, Henry Emmons, the Rev. Charles Wadsworth, Samuel Bowles and Thomas Wentworth Higginson. The last three appear to be the prime choices of later interpreters as the object of the "Master" letters. Finally Judge Otis Lord.

The first feminist critic to suggest a homoerotic reading of the poems addressed to Sue Gilbert was Rebecca Patterson in 1951. She was so savagely criticized for this interpretation that no one else ventured forth with it until 1971, when the psychiatrist John Cody endorsed it in his *After Great Pain: The Inner Life of Emily Dickinson* (Cambridge: Harvard University Press, 1971). Recently, feminist critics have pursued this theme more assertively. In addition to the work of Patterson and Suzanne Juhasz cited earlier, see also Lillian Faderman, "Emily Dickinson's Letters to Sue Gilbert," *The Massachusetts Review*, 18 (Summer 1977), 197–225; Juhasz (ed.), *Feminist Critics Read Emily Dickinson*; and Paula Bennett, *Dickinson*, esp. chap. 5. I have found the last work particularly persuasive.

29. Edward Dickinson, "Female Education," *New England Inquirer*, Jan. 5, 1827, as cited in Wolff, *Emily Dickinson*, p. 574. "Shakespeare" quote *ibid.*
30. Her relationship with Sue Gilbert lasted thirty-six years. There are 153 known letters and notes and 276 poems sent and addressed to her. This is more than twice the number sent to any other correspondent. Probably there were many more, since there is an unexplained gap in the correspondence between Dickinson and Gilbert in the two years following upon Sue and Austin Dickinson's marriage. Lillian Faderman explains this gap as indicating the destruction of letters after Emily Dickinson's death at the insistence of Austin, possibly because the letters were considered embarrassing. See Faderman, "Emily Dickinson's Letters," pp. 216–25.
31. Bennett, *Dickinson*, chap. 5; Adelaide Morris, " 'The Love of Thee—a Prism Be': Men and Women in the Love Poetry of Emily Dickinson," in Juhasz, *Feminist Critics Read Emily Dickinson*, pp. 98–113.
32. The possibility is discussed from different points of view in Morris, " 'The Love of Thee' " and Margaret Homans, " 'Oh, Vision of Language!': Dickinson's Poems of Love and Death," both in Juhasz, *Feminist Critics*, pp. 98–133.
33. To T. W. Higginson, Aug. 1862, *Letters*, vol. II, p. 414.
34. Wolff, *Emily Dickinson*, p. 5.
35. Letter to T. W. Higginson, July 1862, *Letters*, vol. II, p. 411.
36. Allen Tate expressed a similar view: "Her poetry is a magnificent personal confession, blasphemous, and, in its self-revelation, its honesty, almost obscene. It comes out of an intellectual life toward which it feels no moral responsibility. Cotton Mather would have burnt her for a witch." Allen Tate in Sewall (ed.), *Emily Dickinson: A Collection of Critical Essays*, p. 27.

NINE *The Right to Learn, the Right to Teach,*
the Right to Define

1. Christine de Pizan, *The Book of the City of Ladies,* tr. Earl Jeffrey Richards (New York: Persea Books, 1982), p. 2. See also Mary Ann Ignatius, "A Look at the Feminism of Christine de Pizan," *Proceedings of the Pacific Northwest Conference on Foreign Languages,* 29, pt. 2 (1978), 18–21; Astrik L. Gabriel, "The Educational Ideas of Christine de Pisan," *Journal of the History of Ideas,* 13, # 1 (Jan. 1955), 3–21.

2. Christine de Pizan, *City of Ladies,* p. 63.

3. *Ibid.,* p. 64.

4. *Ibid.,* p. 81.

5. M. Laigle, *Le Livre des Trois Vertus de Christine de Pisan* (Paris: Champion, 1912), p. 321.

6. Christine de Pizan, *Le Livre de la Mutacion de Fortune,* Suzanne Solente (ed.), 4 vols.

7. The exception is the case of Isotta Nogarola, which I discussed in detail in Chapter Two.

8. Enzo Giudici (ed.) *Louise Labé: Oeuvres Complètes* (Geneva: Droz, 1981), Preface, p. 17 (tr. Gerda Lerner). See also M. Leon Feugère, *Les Femmes Poètes au XVIᵉ siècle . . .* (Paris: Didier, 1860), "Louise Labé," pp. 4–21; Anne R. Larsen, "Louise Labé's *Débat de Folie and d'Amour*: Feminism and the Defense of Learning," *Tulsa Studies in Women's Literature,* 2, # 1 (Spring 1983), 43–55.

9. Anna Maria von Schurman as cited in Barbara Becker-Cantarino, "Women in the Religious Wars: Official Letters, Songs and Occasional Writings," in Gisela Brinker-Gabler (ed.), *Deutsche Literatur von Frauen*; Erster Band: *Vom Mittelalter bis zum Ende des 18.ten Jahrhunderts* (München: C.H. Beck Verlag, 1988); quote p. 195 (tr. Gerda Lerner).

10. Marie de Gournay, *Égalité des hommes et des femmes,* 1622 (Paris: Côte-femmes Editions, 1989); reprint, in French. Also contains the essay "Grief des dames"; M.L. Feugère, *Femmes Poètes,* "Mademoiselle de Gournay," pp. 127–232; Mario Schiff, *La Fille d'alliance de Montaigne, Marie de Gournay* (Paris: Champion, 1910); Marjorie Henry Ilsley, *A Daughter of the Renaissance: Marie le Jars de Gournay; Her Life and Works* (The Hague: Mouton & Co., 1963). See also Cecil Insdorf, *Montaigne and Feminism* (Chapel Hill: North Carolina Studies in the Romance Languages and Literatures, 1977); Pierre Michel, "Un apôtre du feminism au XVIIᵉ siècle: Mademoiselle de Gournay," *Bulletin de la Société des Amis de Montaigne,* Quatrième Serie, # 27 (Oct.–Dec. 1971), 55–58; and Jean Morand, "Marie le Jars de Gournay: 'La fille d'alliance' de Montaigne," *ibid.,* 45–54. I have been influenced in my interpretation of Gournay by Maryanne Cline Horowitz, "Marie de Gournay, Editor of the *Essais* of Michel de Montaigne: A Case-Study in Mentor-Protégée Friendship," *The Sixteenth Century Journal,* XVII, # 3 (Fall 1986), 271–84.

11. First citation from *Égalité,* pp. 52–53 (tr. Gerda Lerner). Original text: "Si donc les Dames arrivent moins souvent que les hommes aux degrés d'excellence; c'est merveille que ce defaut de bonne education. . . ." Second and third quotations as cited in Ilsley, *A Daughter of the Renaissance,* pp. 205 and 207.

12. "Grief des dames," pp. 108–9 (tr. Gerda Lerner). Original text: "Heureux es-tu, Lecteur, si tu ne'es point de ce sexe, qu'on interdit de tous les biens, le privant de la

liberté: qu'on interdit encore a peu près, de toutes les vertus, lui soustrayant des Chargés, les Offices et fonctions publiques: en un mot, lui retranchant le pouvoir, en la moderation duquel plupart des vertus se forment; afin de lui continuer pour seule félicité . . . l'ignorance, la servitude et la faculté de faire le sot si ce jeu lui plait."

13. Sr. Marion Norman, I.B.V.M., "A Woman for All Seasons: Mary Ward (1585–1645) Renaissance Pioneer of Women's Education," *Paedagogica Historia*, XXIII, # 1 (1983), 125–43.

14. Phyllis Stock, *Better Than Rubies: A History of Women's Education* (New York: G.P. Putnam's Sons, 1978), pp. 51–62.

15. [Bathsua Makin] *An Essay to Revive the Ancient Education of Gentlewomen*, Augustan Reprint Society, No. 202, 1973. Reprint (Los Angeles: Wm. Andrews Clark Memorial Library, 1980), p. 29. See also J. R. Brink, "Bathsua Makin: Scholar and Educator of the Seventeenth Century," *International Journal of Women's Studies* (1978), pp. 717–26.

16. *Ibid.*, pp. 23, 27, 28.

17. [Makin], *An Essay*, p. 37.

18. Mitzi Myers, "Domesticating Minerva: Bathsua Makin's 'Curious' Argument for Women's Education," *Studies in Eighteenth Century Culture*, American Society for Eighteenth Century Studies (Madison: University of Wisconsin Press, 1985), pp. 173–92; citation p. 179; quote from [Makin], *Essay*, p. 42.

19. Myers offers insightful commentary on the significance of Makin's listings; see *ibid.*, pp. 181–85. I will be discussing the subject in greater detail in Chapter Eleven.

20. Hannah Woolley in *Gentlewoman's Companion*, p. 1, as cited in Ada Wallas, *Before the Bluestockings* (London: Allen & Unwin, 1929), p. 44.

21. Margaret Cavendish, Duchess of Newcastle, in Hilda Smith, *Reason's Disciples: Seventeenth-Century English Feminists* (Urbana: University of Illinois Press, 1982), p. 82.

22. Margaret Cavendish, Duchess of Newcastle, in "The Convent of Pleasure," in *Playes Never Before Printed* (London: n.p., 1668), p. 7, as cited in Ruth Perry, *The Celebrated Mary Astell: An Early English Feminist* (Chicago: University of Chicago Press, 1986), p. 143.

23. Mary Astell and John Norris, *Letters Concerning the Love of God, Between the Author of the Proposal to the Ladies and Mr. John Norris* (London: John Norris, 1695), pp. 2–3. See also Ruth Perry, *The Celebrated Mary Astell*, pp. 74–86.

24. Norris and Astell, *Letters Concerning the Love of God*, pp. 49–51.

25. *Ibid.*, p. 75.

26. (London: R. Wilkin, 1694).

27. [Mary Astell] *Some Reflections upon Marriage* (London: Wm. Parker, 1730), pp. 172–73.

28. *Ibid.*, pp. 122–23; 99.

29. Both quotes from [Eugenia] *The Female Advocate . . . Reflections on a late Rude and Disingenuous Discourse delivered by Mr. John Sprint in a Sermon at a Wedding May 11th at Sherburn in Dorsetshire, 1699* (London: Andrew Bell, 1700).

30. *Ibid.*, p. 53.

31. [Lady Mary Chudleigh] *The Ladies Defence: or, The Bride-Woman's Counsellor Answered: A Poem in a Dialogue Between Sir John Brute, Sir Wm. Loveall, Melissa and a Parson* (London: Bernard Lintott, 1709), pp. xxi, xix, xxix.

32. *Ibid.*, p. 40.

33. [Sophia] *Woman not Inferior* . . . (London: Printed for John Hawkins, 1739), all quotations pp. 23–24.

34. François Poulain de la Barre, *De l'égalité des deux sexes* (Paris, 1673) was published in an English edition as *The Woman as Good as the Man* in 1677. It most likely influenced Mary Astell and certainly did "Sophia." Another work by a male feminist which exerted some influence in England was Jacques Du Bosc's *The Compleat Woman*, English translation by N.N. of *L'Honneste Femme* (London: T. Harper and R. Hodgkinson, 1639).

35. [Sophia] *Woman not Inferior* . . . , pp. 23–24.

36. *Ibid.*, p. 40.

37. *Ibid,*, pp. 49, 61.

38. An invective-laden pamphlet published in rebuttal to hers appeared a few years later, authored by "a Gentleman." Sophia answered it in *Women's Superior Excellence over Man or a Reply by Sophia. A Person of Quality* (London: J. Robinson, 1743). In this reply she added feminist Bible criticism to her previous arguments and compared women offered up in the marriage market to "*Negroes* bought and sold at a *West-India* fair" (p. 69).

39. My generalizations on 18th-century women are based on the following: Katherine M. Rogers, *Feminism in Eighteenth Century England* (Urbana: University of Illinois Press, 1982); Alice Brown, *The Eighteenth-Century Feminist Mind* (Brighton, Sussex: Harvester Press, 1987); Doris Mary Stenton, *The English Woman in History* (Brit. ed., 1957; New York: Schocken Books, 1977); Moira Ferguson, *British Women Writers, 1578–1799* (Bloomington: Indiana University Press, 1985); Sylvia Harcstark Myers, *The Bluestocking Circle: Women, Friendship, and the Life of the Mind in Eigteenth-Century England* (Oxford: Clarendon Press, 1990).

40. Hannah More, *Strictures on the Modern System of Female Education with a View to the Principles and Conduct Prevalent Among Women of Rank and Fortune* (Philadelphia: Thomas Dobson, 1800).

41. Stock, *Better Than Rubies*, pp. 72–77.

42. This point is made by Ruth Perry in her "Radical Doubt and the Liberation of Women," *Eighteenth Century Studies*, 18, #4 (Summer 1985), 472–93. I am grateful to Ruth Perry for bringing this article to my attention.

43. John Locke, *Two Treatises of Civil Government*, 2nd ed., ed. Peter Laslett (Cambridge: Cambridge University Press, 1967).

44. For a thorough discussion and feminist critique of contract theory see Carole Patnam, *The Sexual Contract* (Stanford: Stanford University Press, 1988). For a discussion of the implications of Enlightenment philosophy for women, see Linda Kerber, *Women of the Republic: Intellect and Ideology in Revolutionary America* (Chapel Hill: University of North Carolina Press, 1980), pp. 15–32.

45. Jean Jacques Rousseau, *Émile*, Barbara Foxley (tr.), 1763 (London: J.M. Dent, 1974), V, First quote, p. 328; second, p. 322.

46. Mary Astell, *The Christian Religion, As Profess'd by a Daughter of the Church of England* (London: R. Wilkin, 1705). See Perry, *Mary Astell*, pp. 90–97.

47. Mary Wollstonecraft, *A Vindication of the Rights of Woman with Strictures on Political and Moral Subjects*, 1792 (New York: Garland, 1974), p. 51. I have greatly benefited from reading in manuscript, Virginia Sapiro, *A Vindication of Political Virtue:*

The Political Theory of Mary Wollstonecraft (Chicago: University of Chicago Press, 1992).

48. *Ibid.*, Wollstonecraft, *Vindication*, p. viii, (1st par. of quotation); p. 265 (2nd par.); and p. 312 (last par.).

49. The concept and development of "Republican Motherhood" are discussed in Kerber, *Women of the Republic*, chaps. 7 and 8; L. Kerber, "The Republican Mother: Women and the Enlightenment—an American Perspective," *American Quarterly*, 28 (Summer 1976), 187–205; Mary Beth Norton, *Liberty's Daughters: The Revolutionary Experience of American Women, 1750–1800* (Boston: Little, Brown, 1980), pp. 243–55; Jeanne Boydston, *Home and Work: Housework, Wages, and the Ideology of Labor in the Early Republic* (New York: Oxford University Press, 1990), chap. 2.

50. *The Rise and Progress of the Young Ladies' Academy of Philadelphia . . .* (Philadelphia: Stewart and Cochran, 1794).

51. [Judith Sargent Murray] Constantia, "Desultory Thoughts upon the Utility of Encouraging a Degree of Self-Complacency, Especially in FEMALE BOSOMS," *The Gentleman and Lady's Town and Country Magazine* (Oct. 1784), pp. 251–53.

52. [Judith Sargent Murray] Constantia, *The Gleaner: A Miscellaneous Production in Three Volumes* (Boston: I. Thomas and E.T. Andrews, 1798), vol. I, pp. 168–79.

53. Emma Willard, *An Address to the Public; Particularly to the Members of the Legislature of New York, Proposing a Plan for Improving Female Education*, 2nd ed. (Middlebury, Vt.: S.W. Copeland, 1819).

54. On Emma Willard and the Troy Seminary, see Anne Firor Scott, "The Ever-widening Circle: The Diffusion of Feminist Values from the Troy Female Seminary, 1822–72" and "Almira Lincoln Phelps: The Self-made Woman in the Nineteenth Century," in Anne Firor Scott, ed., *Making the Invisible Woman Visible* (Urbana: University of Illinois Press, 1984), pp. 64–106. The major primary source is Mrs. A.W. Fairbanks (ed.), *Mrs. Emma Willard and Her Pupils, or Fifty Years of the Troy Female Seminary, 1822–1872* (New York: published by Mrs. Russell Sage, 1898).

55. Frances Wright [d'Arusmont], *Course of Popular Lectures with 3 Addresses* (London: James Watson, 1834), pp. 24–32.

56. Resolutions, Ohio Woman's Rights Convention, held April 19 and 20, 1850.

57. Fannie Jackson Coppin, *Reminiscences of School Life* (Philadelphia: African Methodist Episcopal Book Concern, 1913). See also Linda M. Perkins, "Heed Life's Demands: The Educational Philosophy of Fanny Jackson Coppin," in Darlene Clark Hine, *Black Women in United States History*, 4 vols. (Brooklyn, N.Y: Carlson Publ. Co., 1990), vol. 3, pp. 1039–48.

58. For information on the African-American teachers, freedmen teachers and school founders, see Gerda Lerner (ed.), *Black Women in White America: A Documentary History* (New York, Pantheon, 1972), chap. 2. See also Linda M. Perkins, "The Black Female American Missionary Association Teacher in the South, 1861–1870," in Hine, *Black Women*, vol. 3, pp. 1049–63; Ellen N. Lawson and Marlene Merrell, "Antebellum Black Coeds at Oberlin College," *ibid.*, pp. 847–68.

59. [Anna Julia Cooper] *A Voice from the South by a Black Woman from the South* (Xenia, Ohio: Aldine Printing House, 1892), pp. 78, 56, 60.

TEN *Female Clusters, Female Networks, Social Spaces*

1. Desiderius Erasmus, *Opus Epistolarum Des. Erasmi Roterodami*, P.S. Allen (ed.), vol. 4, letter 1247, pp. 608–9, as cited by Roland H. Bainton, "Learned Women in the Europe of the Sixteenth Century," in Patricia H. Labalme (ed.), *Beyond Their Sex: Learned Women of the European Past* (New York: New York University Press, 1984), pp. 117–20; quote p. 119.

2. Ursula Hess, "Latin Dialogue and Learned Partnership: Women as Humanist Models in Germany: 1500–1550," in Gisela Brinker-Gabler (ed.), *Deutsche Literatur von Frauen*, Erster Band: *Vom Mittelalter bis zum Ende des 18ten Jahrhunderts* (München: C.H. Beck Verlag, 1988), pp. 113–48; quote pp. 136–37.

3. *Ibid.*, p. 146.

4. Ruth H. Sanders, "A Little Detour: The Literary Creation of Luise Gottsched," in Barbara Becker-Cantarino (ed.), *Die Frau von der Reformation zur Romantik: Die Situation der Frau vor dem Hintergrund der Literatur- und Socialgeschichte* (Bonn: Bouvier, 1981), pp. 170–94; quote from Johann Gottsched, p. 176. See also Barbara Becker-Cantarino, *Der lange Weg zur Mündigkeit* (München: Deutscher Taschenbuch Verlag, 1989), pp. 259–76.

5. Sanders, "A Little Detour," pp. 170–82.

6. William Thompson, *Appeal of One-Half the Human Race, Women, against the Pretensions of the other Half, Men, to retain them in political and thence in civil and domestic Slavery: in Reply to a paragraph of Mr. Mill's celebrated "Article on Government"* (1825).

7. The modern historian who has studied the issue most closely concludes that he, indeed, did most of the work of turning their joint ideas into a book. For Thompson's comments and this viewpoint, see Barbara Taylor, *Eve and the New Jerusalem: Socialism and Feminism in the Nineteenth Century* (New York: Pantheon, 1983), pp. 22–23, fn. p. 22.

8. [Theodore Dwight Weld] *American Slavery as It Is: Testimony of a Thousand Witnesses* (New York: American Anti-Slavery Society, 1839).

9. Catherine H. Birney, *The Grimké Sisters, Sarah and Angelina Grimké: The First American Women Advocates of Abolition and Woman's Rights* (Boston: Lee and Shepard, 1885), pp. 258–59; Gerda Lerner, *The Grimké Sisters from South Carolina: Rebels Against Slavery* (Boston: Houghton Mifflin, 1967), pp. 261–68.

10. John Jacob Coss (ed.), *The Autobiography of John Stuart Mill* (New York: Columbia University Press, 1924), p. 174. For an extended consideration of the problem of the Mill/Taylor collaboration, see Alice Rossi (ed.), *Essays on Sex Equality: John Stuart Mill and Harriet Taylor Mill* (Chicago: University of Chicago Press, 1970), pp. 22–45.

11. Margaret L. King and Albert Rabil, Jr. (eds.), *Her Immaculate Hand: Selected Works By and About the Women Humanists of Quattrocento Italy* (Binghamton, N.Y.: Medieval & Renaissance Texts & Studies, 1983), pp. 16–28.

12. Elisabeth Gössmann, *Das Wohlgelahrte Frauenzimmer*, Archiv für Philosophiegeschichtliche Frauenforschung, Band 1 (München, Iudicium, 1984), chap. 3.

13. The subscription itself was organized by Elstob's male supporters and colleagues in the field of Saxon studies at Queens College, Oxford. See "Introduction," by Ruth Perry (ed.) to George Ballard's *Memoirs of Several Ladies of Great Britain . . .* (Detroit: Wayne State University Press, 1985), pp. 21–25. While the support Elstob received from male scholars is exceptional for a learned woman, the fact that 121 women subscribed to

her first book is equally remarkable. See Doris Stenton, *The English Woman in History*, 1957 (New York: Schocken Books, 1977), p. 241.

14. Myra Reynolds, *The Learned Lady in England: 1650–1750* (Boston: Houghton Mifflin, 1920), pp. 174–85. Mary Astell was active in Elstob's behalf, as can be seen from her soliciting a contribution from Lady Ann Coventry for the publication of Elstob's "Homily." Mary Astell to Lady Ann Coventry, probably June or July 1714, reprinted in Ruth Perry, *The Celebrated Mary Astell: An Early English Feminist* (Chicago: University of Chicago Press, 1986), pp. 366–67.

15. George Ballard, *Memoirs of Several Ladies of Great Britain Who Have Been Celebrated for Their Writings or Skills in the Learned Languages of Arts and Sciences* (Oxford: W. Jackson, 1752). I have also used the later edition (London: T. Evans, 1775).

16. Perry, *Mary Astell*, pp. 268–69.

17. For background on the bluestockings, see Sylvia Harcstark Myers, *The Bluestocking Circle: Women, Friendship, and the Life of the Mind in Eighteenth-Century England* (Oxford: Clarendon Press, 1990); Katherine M. Rogers, *Feminism in Eighteenth-Century England* (Urbana: University of Illinois Press, 1982); Alice Browne, *The Eighteenth Century Feminist Mind* (Brighton, Sussex: Harvester Press, 1987); Stenton, *The English Woman in History*, chap. 10; Elizabeth Fox-Genovese, "Women and the Enlightenment," in Renate Bridenthal, Claudia Koonz, Susan Stuard (eds.), *Becoming Visible: Women in European History* (Boston: Houghton Mifflin, 1987), pp. 251–77. The term "bluestocking" first appeared in 1756 in Elizabeth Montagu's correspondence and was then applied to both female and male members of the circle. By the late 1770s the term referred only to women and gradually became a term of opprobrium and ridicule for all educated women. Reference in Myers, *The Bluestocking Circle*, pp. 9–10 and fn. 5.

18. Myers, *The Bluestocking Circle*, pp. 168, 260.

19. *Ibid.*, pp. 153–55.

20. Elizabeth Elstob, *An English-Saxon Homily on the Birth-day of St. Gregory* (1709), Landsdowne Manuscripts, British Library, "Preface," pp. xiii and ix. A printed edition appeared in 1839 (Leicester: Wm. Pickering).

21. Bathsua Makin, *An Essay to Revive the Ancient Education of Gentlewomen*, Augustan Reprint Society, No. 202 (1673). Reprint (Los Angeles: William Andrews Clark Memorial Library, 1980), p. 3.

22. Ellen Moers, *Literary Women* (Garden City, N.Y.: Doubleday, 1976), pp. 43–44, 46–49 (G. Eliot); pp. 53–55, 172 (E.B. Browning); pp. 57–60 (E. Dickinson); p. 177 (M. Fuller). Elizabeth Barrett Browning, *Aurora Leigh: A Poem*, 1864 (Chicago: Academy Chicago Publishers, 1979).

23. Examples of British women making a living as writers abound in the late 18th century: Charlotte Smith (1749–1806), while providing for her ten children, wrote and published more than twenty novels and collections of poems; Charlotte Lennox wrote five novels and translated six works from the French to support herself, her husband and her children. She also edited an early magazine, *The Ladies' Museum* (1760–61). Sarah (Robinson) Scott, impoverished after a bad marriage and divorce, wrote five novels and three histories between 1750 and 1772. Other professional writers of this period are Elizabeth Inchbald, Eliza Haywood, Frances (Fanny) Burney.

24. Sara Evans, *Personal Politics: The Roots of Women's Liberation in the Civil Rights Movement and the New Left* (New York: A. Knopf, 1979), pp. 219–20.

25. Dena Goodman, "Enlightenment Salons: The Convergence of Female and Phil-

osophic Ambitions," *Eighteenth-Century Studies*, 22, #3 (Spring 1989), 329–50; reference p. 329.

26. *Ibid.*, pp. 333, 335–36.

27. Carolyn C. Lougee, *Le Paradis des Femmes: Women, Salons and Social Stratification in Seventeenth-Century France* (Princeton: Princeton University Press, 1976). In her analysis of the *salonières* as a group, Carolyn Lougee used as a data base the lists of illustrious women which are appended to the printed arguments of feminist writers who participated in debates on the roles of women. She found that in and around Paris over 250 women were listed as *salonières* and patronesses of learning. See also a particularly comprehensive list mentioned by Lougee in Antoine Baudeau, sieur de Somaize, *Le Grand Dictionnaire des Prétieuses, historique, poetique, geographique, cosmographique. chronologique et armoirique*. See also Angela McCourt Fritz, "The Novel Women: Origins of the Feminist Literary Tradition in England and France," in Dorothy McGuigan (ed.), *New Research on Women at the University of Michigan* (Ann Arbor: Center for Continuing Education, 1974), pp. 20–46; Fox-Genovese, "Women and the Enlightenment," pp. 256–57.

28. Günter Jäckel (ed.), *Das Volk braucht Licht: Frauen zur Zeit des Aufbruchs, 1790–1848, in ihren Briefen* (Darmstadt: Agora, 1970), pp. 343–45.

29. Gisela Dischner, *Bettina von Arnim: Eine weibliche Sozialbiographie aus dem 19ten Jahrhundert kommentiert und zusammengestellt aus Briefromanen und Dokumenten* (Berlin: Verlag Klaus Wagenbach, 1977), p. 69 and *passim*.

30. Earlier circles of "free-lovers" were the group of sympathizers with Enlightenment radicalism and with the French Revolution, which included Mary Wollstonecraft, Tom Paine, William Blake, William Godwin. Other such circles existed around Robert Owen in England and Robert Dale Owen in the United States. Frances Wright was a member of the latter circle.

31. Gisela Dischner, *Caroline und der Jenär Kreis: Ein Leben zwischen bürgerlicher Vereinzelung und romantischer Geselligkeit* (Berlin: Klaus Wagenbach, 1979). For additional biographical information, see Dischner, *Bettina* . . . ; Jäckel, *Das Volk*, pp. 248–49; Elke Frederiksen, "Die Frau als Autorin zur Zeit der Romantik: Anfänge einer weiblichen literarischen Tradition," in Marianne Burkhard, *Gestalt und Gestaltend: Frauen in der deutschen Literatur*, Amsterdamer Beiträge zur Neueren Germanistik, Band 10 (Amsterdam: Rodopi, 1980), pp. 83–153; Margarete Susman, *Frauen der Romantik* (Köln: Joseph Melzer Verlag, 1960).

32. Sophie Mereau to Clemens Brentano as cited in Dischner, *Caroline* . . . , p. 87.

33. Karoline von Günderrode to Clemens Brentano, no date, cited in Christa Wolf (ed.), *Karoline von Günderrode: Der Schatten eines Traumes; Gedichte, Prosa, Briefe, Zeugnisse von Zeitgenossen* (Darmstadt: Luchterhand, 1981), p. 193 (tr. from German by Gerda Lerner).

34. Karoline von Günderrode to Gunda Brentano, 29 August 1801, as cited *ibid.*, p. 138 (tr. Gerda Lerner).

35. Friedrich Creuzer, *Symbolik und Mythologie der Alten Völker*, 5 vols. (Leipzig, 1841). The work was published in 1810, after Günderrode's death, but he had shared his research with her. Johann J. Bachofen, *Das Mutterrecht. Eine Untersuchung ueber die Gynaikokratie der alten Welt nach ihrer religioesen und rechtlichen Natur* (Stuttgart, 1861). This work in turn influenced Friedrich Engels, *Der Ursprung der Familie, des Privateigentums und des Staates* (1884), reprinted in Karl Marx, Friedrich Engels, *Werke,*

vol. 21 (Berlin: Dietz Verlag, 1962) and Robert Briffault, *The Mothers: A Study of the Origins of Sentiments and Institutions,* 3 vols. (New York, 1927).

36. See, for example, Audre Lorde, "Uses of the Erotic: The Erotic as Power," in Audre Lorde, *Sister Outsider: Essays and Speeches* (New York: The Crossing Press, 1984), pp. 53–59.

37. As cited in Dischner, *Bettina . . .* , p. 76. The run-on sentence construction appears in the original and is typical of the author's style (tr. Gerda Lerner).

38. Bettina Brentano to Karoline von Günderrode, October 1805, as cited in Dischner, *Bettina . . .* , p. 93.

39. Gustav Konrad (ed.), Bettina von Arnim, *Werke und Briefe* (Frechen/Köln: Bartmann-Verlag, 1959–61), 5 vols. *Die Günderode,* in vol. 1, pp. 215–536. Bettina von Arnim spelled Günderrode's name with one r.

40. *Goethe's Briefwechsel mit einem Kinde,* in Bettina von Arnim, *Werke und Briefe,* vol. 2 (1959). Clemens Brentano and Achim von Arnim (eds.), *Des Knaben Wunderhorn* (1805). This is the primary collection of German folksongs and poems.

41. Bettina von Arnim, *Werke und Briefe,* vol. 3/4. See also "Anmerkungen" (remarks by the editor), pp. 445–76.

42. Dischner, *Bettina . . .* , as cited pp. 80–81.

43. See their 1802 correspondence in regard to her friendship with a Jewish embroidery worker. As cited *ibid,* pp. 165–66.

44. My treatment of the Berlin salons is influenced by Deborah Hertz, "Salonières and Literary Women in Late Eighteenth-Century Berlin," *New German Critique,* # 14 (Spring 1978), 97–108. The reference to the Jewish women's marriages is on pp. 106–7. Of the eight Jewish salon women in Berlin, the seven who converted were: Esther Gan, Rebecca Friedländer, Marianne Meyer, Sara Meyer, Dorothea Mendelsohn Veit-Schlegel, Henriette Herz, Rahel Levin Varnhagen. *Ibid.,* p. 105, fn. 32.

45. My information on and my interpretation of her life are based on the following sources: Karl Varnhagen von Ense, *Rahel: Ein Buch des Andenkens für ihre Freunde* (Berlin, 1833); Hannah Arendt, *Rahel Varnhagen: Lebensgeschichte einer deutschen Jüdin aus der Romantik* (Frankfurt: Ullstein, 1975 reprint); Susman, *Frauen der Romantik,* pp. 77–105; Kay Goodman, "The Impact of Rahel Varnhagen on Women in the 19th Century," in Burkhard, *Gestalt und Gestaltend,* pp. 125–53; Deborah Hertz, "Hannah Arendt's Rahel Varnhagen," in John C. Fout (ed.), *German Women in the Nineteenth Century* (New York: Holmes and Meier, 1984), pp. 72–87; and Ruth-Ellen Joeres, "Self-conscious Histories: Biographies of German Women in the Nineteenth Century," *ibid.,* pp. 172–96.

46. Friedrich Kemp (ed.), *Rahel Varnhagen im Umgang mit ihren Freunden* (München: Kösel Verlag, 1967), p. 19, as cited in Frederiksen, "Die Frau als Autorin . . . ," p. 95.

47. Varnhagen, *Rahel,* as cited p. 266 (1972 reprint ed.).

ELEVEN   *The Search for Women's History*

1. C. Leonard Woolley, *The Sumerians* (New York: W.W. Norton, 1965), pp. 21–34.

2. My information on the Merovingian nuns is drawn from Suzanne Foy Wemple,

Women in Frankish Society: Marriage and the Cloister; 500–900 (Philadelphia: University of Pennsylvania Press, 1985), pp. 181–88.

3. *Ibid.*, p. 185.

4. *Ibid.*, p. 181. See also Rudolf Schieffer, "Hugeburc," in Wolfgang Stammler *et al., Die deutsche Literatur der Mittelalters: Verfasserlexicon*, 7 vols. (Berlin: Walter de Gruyter, 1978), vol. 4, p. 221; Peter Dronke, *Women Writers of the Middle Ages: A Critical Study of Texts from Perpetua (d.203) to Marguerite Porète (d.1310)* (Cambridge: Cambridge University Press, 1984), pp. 33–35; Elizabeth Alvilda Petroff, *Medieval Women's Visionary Literature* (New York: Oxford University Press, 1986), pp. 86–89, 92–106.

5. Biographical information on Hrosvitha is based on Anne Lyon Haight (ed.), *Hroswitha of Gandersheim: Her Life, Times and Works, and a Comprehensive Bibliography* (New York: The Hroswitha Club, 1965), pp. 3–12; Dronke, *Women Writers*, pp. 55–83; and Petroff, *Medieval Women's Visionary Literature*, pp. 89–90 and 114–35. The spelling of Hrosvitha's name varies widely. Other forms are Hroswitha; Hrotsvitha; Hrotsvit.

6. The information about the lost manuscript comes from Fidel Rädle, "Hrotsvit von Gandersheim," in Stammler, *Die deutsche Literatur*, vol. 4, pp. 196–210.

7. Dronke, *Women Writers*, pp. 57–59.

8. Helena Homeyer (ed.), *Hrotsvithae Opera* (Paderborn, 1970), p. 227, as cited in Dronke, *Women Writers*, p. 68. A modern translation of this play by Katharina M. Wilson is available in Petroff, *Medieval Women's Visionary Literature*, pp. 114–23. See also Katharina M. Wilson, "The Saxon Cauoness: Hrotsvit of Gandersheim," in *Medieval Women Writers* (Athens: University of Georgia Press, 1983).

9. I owe this insight to Sue-Ellen Case, "Re-Viewing Hrotsvit," *Theatre Journal*, 35, # 4, (Dec. 1983), pp. 533–42.

10. As cited in Haight, *Hroswitha of Gandersheim*, pp. 9–10.

11. *Ibid.*, as cited p. 29.

12. As cited in Dronke, *Women Writers*, p. 80.

13. As cited *ibid.*, p. 81.

14. *Ibid.*, pp. 82–83.

15. Stammler, *Verfasserlexicon*, vol. 4. pp. 1073–75.

16. *Ibid.*, vol. 2, pp. 479–82.

17. All these are mentioned in Stammler. I have only studied the ones in the German language domain. Further research and compilation in other countries of these important sources for the lives of religious women should yield good results.

18. Natalie Zemon Davis, "Gender and Genre: Women as Historical Writers, 1400–1820," in Patricia H. Labalme (ed.), *Beyond Their Sex: Learned Women of the European Past* (New York: New York University Press, 1984), pp. 153–82; reference to French convent histories p. 161.

19. The first editions were partial; the one published by Mathias Apiarius in Berne in 1539 contained all the biographies of women written by Boccaccio.

20. As cited in Guido A. Guarino (tr.), Giovanni Boccaccio, *Concerning Famous Women* (New Brunswick: Rutgers University Press, 1963), p. xxxvii.

21. *Ibid.*, p. xxxviii.

22. *Ibid.*

23. I have used the following edition of this book for my work: Earl Jeffrey Richards

(tr.), Christine de Pizan, *The Book of the City of Ladies* (New York: Persea Books, 1982). Christine de Pizan's contributions to the development of feminist thought have been brilliantly explored in Joan Kelly's important essay, "Early Feminist Theory and the *Querelle des Femmes*," in J. Kelly, *Women, History and Theory: The Essays of Joan Kelly* (Chicago: University of Chicago Press, 1984), pp. 65–109.

Other references to Christine de Pizan's contributions to the *querelle des femmes* are: Lula McDowell Richardson, "The Forerunners of Feminism in French Literature of the Renaissance from Christine of Pisa to Marie de Gournay, " *Johns Hopkins Studies in Romance Literatures and Languages*, XII (Baltimore: Johns Hopkins University Press, 1929); Astrik L. Gabriel, "The Educational Ideas of Christine de Pisan," *Journal of the History of Ideas*, 16, #1 (Jan. 1955), 3–21; Mary Ann Ignatius, "A Look at the Feminism of Christine de Pizan," *Proceedings of the Pacific Northwest Conference on Foreign Languages*, 29, pt. 2 (1978), 18–21.

24. Christine de Pizan, *Le Livre des fais and bonnes moeurs du sage Roy Charles V*, ed. Suzanne Solente (Paris: Société de l'Histoire de France, 1936–40), 2 vols.

25. Both quotes, Christine de Pizan, I.1, as cited in *City of Ladies*, pp. 3–4.

26. *City of Ladies*, I.3.3. p. 10.

27. *Ibid.*, II.56.1, pp. 189–90.

28. For Boccaccio on Sempronia, see Boccaccio, *Concerning Famous Women*, pp. 173–75. For Christine de Pizan on the same subject, see *City of Ladies*, I.42.1, p. 86.

29. *Ibid.*, III.19.1, pp. 254–55, and III.19.6, p. 256.

30. Quote, *ibid.*, III.19.6, p. 256.

31. Heinrich Cornelius Agrippa von Nettesheim, *The Glory of Women*, tr. E. Fleetwood (London: printed for Robert Ibbitson, 1652) and François de Billon, *Le Fort inexpugnable de l'honneur du sexe feminin* (Paris: J. d'Allyer, 1555).

32. Laura Cereta to Bibulus Sempronius as cited in Margaret L. King and Albert Rabil, Jr., *Her Immaculate Hand: Selected Works By and About the Women Humanists of Quattrocento Italy* (Binghamton, N.Y.: Medieval and Renaissance Texts and Studies, 1983), vol. 20, pp. 81–84. Second reference to Letter by Laura Cereta to Augustinius Aemilius, as cited *ibid.*, pp. 77–80.

33. Lucretia Marinella, *La Nobilita et Excellenze delle Donne et I Diffetti e Mancamenti de gli Huomini* (1600/1608), as cited in Elisabeth Gössmann, *Eva, Gottes Meisterwerk*, Archiv für Philosophiegeschichtliche Frauenforschung, vol. 2 (München: Iudicium, 1985), pp. 34–41.

34. Ester Sowernam, *Ester hath hang'd Haman . . .* (London: Nicholas Bourne, 1617). British Library.

35. Rachel Speght, *A Moussell for Melastomus, the Cynical Baiter of, and foule mouthed Barker against Evahs Sex . . .* (London: N. Okes for T. Archer, 1617).

36. See note 31, above. Agrippa's book appeared in French, German, Italian, English and Polish. See also François Poulain de la Barre, *The Women as Good as the Men, or, the Equality of Both Sexes* (1673) (Detroit: Wayne State University Press, 1988).

37. Johann Frauenlob, "Die Lobwürdige Gesellschaft der Gelehrten Weiber," in Gössmann, vol. 2, *Eva, Gottes Meisterwerk*. One can assume that his name—women's praise—was a pseudonym.

Angelo Poliziano (1454–94) was a humanist poet and prolific writer, living under the protection of Lorenzo di Medici. He was admired as a great scholar and poet.

Rhodiginua Lodovico Coelius (1450–1520) studied law at Padua, lived for some years in Paris and was appointed professor of Greek and Latin Literature in Milan. His chief work is *Lectionum Antiquarium* Libri XXX, an encyclopedia on various subjects including ancient drama, literature, history and philosophy.

38. Jacobus Thomasius/Johannes Sauerbrei, *De foeminarum eruditione,* as cited in Gössmann, *Eva,* vol.1, chap. 7.

39. The term "women worthies" was popularized by Natalie Zemon Davis in her influential essay, " 'Women's History' in Transition: The European Case," *Feminist Studies,* 3, # 3/4 (1976), 83–103.

40. Christian Franz Paullini, *Das Hoch- und Wohlgelahrte Teutsche Frauenzimmer* [The highly learned German female] (Leipzig: J.C. Stösseln, 1705).

41. Johann Caspar Eberti, *Eröffnetes Cabinet des gelehrten Frauen-Zimmers* (Frankfurt, 1706).

42. (London: Richard Rayston, 1640).

43. George Ballard, *Memoirs of Several Ladies of Great Britain* (Oxford: printed by W. Jackson for the author, 1752). Ruth Perry (ed.), "Introduction" to George Ballard's *Memoirs of Several Ladies of Great Britain* (Detroit: Wayne State University Press, 1985) is the latest and most thorough scholarly account of Ballard's work.

There are a number of other volumes authored by men which feature catalogues of women worthies and short biographical sketches. Typical of these are: Charles Gerbier, *Elogium Heroinum: or, The Praise of Worthy Women* (1651) and John Shirley, *The Illustrious History of Women* (1686), which offers a broad survey. Theophilus Cibber, *An Account of the Lives of the Poets of Great Britain and Ireland,* 4 vols. (London: R. Griffiths, 1753), lists fourteen women. A popular compilation for the amusement "of the Fair Sex" was published by William Alexander, *The History of Women from the Earliest Antiquity* . . . , 2 vols. (London: W. Strahan & T. Cadell, 1779). For a detailed discussion of the treatment of English women in literary biographies, see Myra Reynolds, *The Learned Lady in England, 1650–1760* (Boston: Houghton Mifflin, 1920), pp. 421–25.

44. Perry (ed.), "Introduction," to Ballard, *Memoirs,* p. 25.

45. Madeleine de Scudèry, *Les Femmes illustres* (Paris: Antoine de Sommaville, 1642), as cited in Faith E. Beasley, *Revising Memory: Women's Fiction and Memoirs in Seventeenth-Century France* (New Brunswick: Rutgers University Press, 1990), pp. 53–56. Beasley also refers to another female compiler, whose catalogue of women appeared in 1668, Marguerite Buffet.

46. John Duncombe, *The Feminead, A Poem* (1754), The Augustan Reprint Society #207 (Los Angeles: William Andrews Clark Memorial Library,1981); Miss [Mary] Scott, *The Female Advocate; A Poem occasioned by reading Mr. Duncombe's Feminead* (London: Jos. Johnson, 1774), Augustan Reprint Society, #224 (Los Angeles: William Andrews Clark Memorial Library, 1984).

47. Hays (London: Richard Phillips, 1803) and Roberts (London: Harbey & Derton, 1829).

48. Cf. Louisa Stuart Costello, *Memoirs of Eminent Englishwomen,* 4 vols. (London: Bentley, 1844); Jane Williams, *The Literary Women of England* (London, 1861); Julia Kavanagh, *English Women of Letters,* 2 vols. (London, 1863); Georgiana Hill, *Women in English Life,* 2 vols. (London: Bentley & Son, 1896); and Elizabeth Casey, *Illustrious Irishwomen,* 2 vols. (1887).

For Germany: cf. [Christian August Wichmann], *Geschichte berühmter Frauenzimmer. Nach alphabetischer Ordnung aus alten und neuen in- und ausländischen Ge-*

schichtssammlungen und Wörterbuechern zusammen getragen, 3 vols. (Leipzig, 1772–75); Claire von Glümer, *Bibliothek für die deutsche Frauenwelt,* 6 vols. (Leipzig, 1856); Louise Otto, *Merkwürdige und geheimnisvolle Frauen* (Leipzig, 1868) and *Einflussreiche Frauen aus dem Volke* (Leipzig, 1869).

For France: Marguerite V. F. Bernier Briquet, *Dictionnaire historique, littéraire and bibliographique des françaises et des étrangères naturalisées en France* (Paris, 1804).

49. Lydia Maria Child, *Brief History of the Condition of Women in Various Ages and Nations,* Ladies Family Library, Vol. IV (Boston: John Allen & Co., 1835), 2 vols.

50. *Ibid.,* vol. 2, p. 211.

51. Stowe (New York: J.B. Ford & Co., 1874).

52. Hanaford (Augusta, Maine: True & Co., 1882).

53. Sarah Josepha Hale, *Woman's Record or Sketches of Distinguished Women from "the Beginning" till A.D. 1850* (New York: Harper and Bros., 1853); Sarah Knowles Bolton, *Famous Types of Womanhood* (New York: Thomas Y. Crowell, 1892).

54. Hale, *Woman's Record,* pp. viii–ix, v.

55. *Ibid.,* p. xxxv.

56. Frances E. Willard and Mary A. Livermore (eds.), *A Woman of the Century: Fourteen hundred-seventy Biographical Sketches accompanied by Portraits of Leading American Women in all Walks of Life* (Chicago: Charles Wells Moulton, 1893).

57. *Ibid.*

58. For a representative example of this genre, see Elizabeth Ellet, *Pioneer Women of the West* (New York: C. Scribner, 1852) and Mary O. Douthit, *The Souvenir of Western Women* (Portland, Maine: Anderson and Duniway, 1905).

59. Mrs. N.F. Mossell, *The Work of the Afro-American Woman* (Philadelphia: Geo.S. Ferguson Co., 1908). Mrs. Mossell used the initials of her husband's name, Nathan Francis. The work is available in a reprint edition (New York: Oxford University Press, 1988).

60. Julia Ward Howe, *Margaret Fuller, Marchesa Ossoli* (Boston, 1883); Helen S. Campbell, *Anne Bradstreet and Her Time* (Boston, 1891); Mary S. Porter, *Recollections of Louisa May Alcott . . .* (Boston, 1893); Annie A. Fields, *Life and Letters of Harriet Beecher Stowe* (Boston, 1897).

61. Andrea Hinding (ed.), *Women's History Sources: A Guide to Archives and Manuscript Collections in the United States,* 2 vols. (New York: R. R. Bowker, 1979).

62. Representative of this genre is Jane Cunningham Croly, *History of the Woman's Club Movement in America* (New York: H. G. Allen and Co., 1898).

63. Elizabeth C. Stanton, Susan B. Anthony, and Matilda J. Gage, *History of Woman Suffrage,* 6 vols. (New York: Fowler and Wells, 1881–1922); hereafter referred to as *HWS.*

64. For a critique and re-evaluation of *HWS,* see Nancy Isenberg, *The Co-Equality of the Sexes: The Feminist and Religious Discourse of the Nineteenth-Century Woman's Rights Movement: 1848–1860.* Dissertation, University of Wisconsin-Madison, 1990.

65. The autobiographies and editions of letters are numerous. Since many of them were collected and published in the 20th century only they fall beyond the scope of this study. For representative examples, see Catherine Birney *The Grimké Sisters: Sarah and Angelina Grimké, the First American Women Advocates of Abolition and Women's Rights* (Boston: Lee and Shepard, 1885); Anna D. Hallowell (ed.), *Life and Letters of James and Lucretia Mott* (Boston: Houghton Mifflin, 1884).

Examples of autobiographical writings are: Harriot K. Hunt, M.D., *Glances and*

Glimpses; or Fifty Years Social Including Twenty Years Professional Life (Boston: John P. Jewett Co., 1856); Frances Willard, *Glimpses of Fifty Years: The Autobiography of an American Woman* (Chicago: H. J. Smith & Co., 1889); Elizabeth Cady Stanton, *Eighty Years and More: 1815–1897* (London: T. Fisher Unwin, 1898); Mary A. Livermore, *My Story of the War: A Woman's Narrative of Four Years' Personal Experience* . . . (Hartford, Conn.: A. D. Worthington and Co., 1889).

66. The earliest efforts at narrative history about women written by women were the works of the literary scholar Elizabeth Ellet and the antiquarian and amateur historian Alice Earle. See Elizabeth Ellet, *The Women of the American Revolution*, 3 vols. (New York: Baker & Scribner, 1848–50); and *Domestic History of the American Revolution* (New York: Baker & Scribner, 1850); Alice Earle, *Colonial Dames and Good Wives* (Boston: Houghton Mifflin, 1895) and *Child Life in Colonial Days* (New York: Macmillan, 1899).

For a history of women's organizational activities, see Croly, *History of the Woman's Club Movement in America*; and Frances E. Willard, *Glimpses of Fifty Years*; Mary I. Wood, *History of the General Federation of Women's Clubs* (New York, 1912); and Mary Ritter Beard, *Woman's Work in Municipalities* (New York: D. Appleton, 1915). For a history of African-American club women's work, see Elizabeth Lindsay Davis, *Lifting as They Climb* (n.pl.: National Association of Colored Women, 1933).

For an interpretative women's history see Matilda Joslyn Gage, *Woman, Church and State: A Historical Account of the Status of Woman Through the Christian Ages; With Reminiscences* (New York: The Truthseeker Co., 1893; reprint ed. Watertown, Mass: Persephone Press, 1980).

67. For a discussion of the careers of the earliest U.S. women historians see Kathryn Kish Sklar, "American Female Historians in Context, 1770–1930," *Feminist Studies*, 3, # 1/2 (Fall 1975), 171–84.

68. Kate C. Hurd-Mead, *A History of Women in Medicine . . . from the Earliest Times to the Beginning of the Nineteenth Century* (Haddam, Conn.: Haddam Press, 1938); and Helen L. Sumner, *History of Women in Industry in the United States*, Vols. 9 and 10, in *Report on Condition of Woman and Child Wage-Earners in the United States*, U.S. Senate Document 645 (Washington, D.C.: U.S. Government Printing Office, 1911).

69. Mary S. Benson, *Women in Eighteenth-Century America: A Study of Opinion and Social Usage*, 1935 (New York: AMS Press, 1976); Elizabeth Anthony Dexter, *Colonial Women of Affairs: A Study of Women in Business and the Professions in America Before 1776* (Boston: Houghton Mifflin, 1924); Julia Cherry Spruill, *Women's Life and Work in the Southern Colonies*, 1938 (New York: W. W. Norton, 1972); Willystine Goodsell, *The Education of Women: Its Social Background and Its Problems* (New York: Macmillan, 1923).

70. Cf. Eugenie Andrews Leonard, *The Dear-Bought Heritage* (Philadelphia: University of Pennsylvania Press, 1965); Eleanor Flexner, *Century of Struggle: The Woman's Rights Movement in the United States* (Cambridge: Harvard University Press, 1959). The biographical works of Alma Lutz and Katherine Anthony also fall into this category.

71. Mary Ritter Beard, *Woman as Force in History: A Study in Traditions and Realities* (New York: Macmillan, 1946).

72. The quote is from Mary Beard, "The Direction of Women's Education," an address delivered at Mount Holyoke College in 1937, reprinted in Ann J. Lane, *Mary*

Ritter Beard: A Sourcebook (New York: Schocken Books, 1977), pp. 159–67; quote p. 167.

73. The text and quote come from a pamphlet issued by the World Center for Women's Archives in the author's possession. The women chiefly engaged in the effort to raise support for this project were Elizabeth Schlesinger, Miriam Holden, Eugenia Leonard and Mary Beard.

74. The third and oldest of these archives, the Sophia Smith collection at Smith College, was also strengthened by their massive collection effort.

75. Mary R. Beard, *Women's Work in Municipalities; On Understanding Women* (New York: Grosset & Dunlap, 1931); *Woman as Force in History; The Force of Women in Japanese History* (Washington, D.C.: Public Affairs Press, 1953). The jointly edited work which most clearly bears the imprint of her concepts is Charles A. Beard and Mary Ritter Beard, *The Rise of American Civilization*, 2 vols. (New York: Macmillan, 1927). She also edited two collections of sources: *America Through Women's Eyes* (New York: Macmillan, 1933) and (with Martha Bensley Bruere) *Laughing Their Way: Women's Humor in America* (New York: Macmillan, 1934).

Useful sources on Mary Beard are: Ann J. Lane (ed.), *Mary Ritter Beard: A Sourcebook*; Barbara Turoff, *Mary Ritter Beard as Force in History* (Dayton, Ohio: Wright State University Monograph Series, #3, 1979); Bonnie G. Smith, "Seeing Mary Beard," *Feminist Studies*, 10, no. 3 (Fall 1984), 399–416. I have greatly benefited from the work of Nancy Cott on Mary Beard, which she generously shared with me in draft form and in unpublished lectures and grant proposals. See Nancy Cott (ed.), *A Woman Making History: Mary Ritter Beard Through Her Letters* (New Haven: Yale University Press, 1991).

76. Anna Maria von Schurman to André Rivet, as cited in Elisabeth Gössman, *Das Wohlgelahrte Frauenzimmer*, Archiv für Philosophie- und Theologiegeschichtliche Frauenforschung (München: Iudicium, 1984), Vol. I, p. 44. Translated by Gerda Lerner.

77. For a more detailed discussion of the struggle of female professional historians for equality and the recognition of Women's History, see my article "A View from the Women's Side", *The Journal of American History*, 76, #2 (Sept. 1989), 446–56.

TWELVE *Conclusion*

1. Information on the formation of the suffrage movements in Britain, France and Germany is based on Richard J. Evans, *The Feminist: Women's Emancipation Movements in Europe, America and Australasia, 1840–1920* (New York: Barnes & Noble Books, 1977); Bonnie G. Smith, *Changing Lives: Women in European History Since 1700* (Lexington, Mass.: D.C. Heath, 1989); Bonnie S. Anderson and Judith P. Zinsser, *A History of Their Own: Women in Europe from Prehistory to the Present*, 2 vols. (New York: Harper & Row, 1988), vol. II; Margrit Twellman, *Die deutsche Frauenbewegung im Spiegel repräsentativer Frauenzeitschriften; ihre Anfänge und erste Entwicklung, 1843–1889* (Meisenheim am Glau: Anton Hain, 1972).

2. See Darlene Gay Levy, Harriet Branson Applewhite, Mary Durham Johnson, *Women in Revolutionary Paris, 1789–1795* (Urbana: University of Illinois Press, 1979); Claire Goldberg Moses, *French Feminism in the 19th Century* (Albany, N.Y.: SUNY Press, 1984).

3. *Frauen-Zeitung* 1 (1849), as cited in Karin Hausen (ed.), *Frauen suchen ihre*

Geschichte: Historische Studien zum 19.– und 20. Jahrhundert (München: C.H. Beck, 1983), p. 200 (tr. Gerda Lerner).

4. An article in the feminist paper stated: "You speak of *brotherhood* and yet you think nothing of denying your *sisters* membership in your organizations. Moreover, you deliberately exclude them from work, denying them the means of existence." *Frauen-Zeitung* 37 (1849) as cited in Hausen, *Frauen suchen,* p. 208 (tr. Gerda Lerner).

5. Simone de Beauvoir, *The Second Sex,* (1949), tr. and edited by H.M. Parshley, 1952 (New York: Bantam, 1970), p. xix. For a fuller discussion of this point see Gerda Lerner, "Women and History," in Elaine Marks (ed.), *Critical Essays on Simone de Beauvoir* (Boston: G.K. Hall, 1987), pp. 154–67.

Bibliography

*Anthologies and Reference Works are also to be found within other sections where appropriate.

I HISTORY and THEORY OF WOMEN'S HISTORY

1. Books

Anderson, Bonnie S., and Judith P. Zinsser. *A History of Their Own: Women in Europe from Prehistory to the Present.* 2 vols. New York: Harper & Row, 1988.

Aries, Philippe. *Centuries of Childhood: A Social History of Family Life.* New York: Random House, 1962.

[Aristotle.] *The Works of Aristotle.* W.D. Ross (ed.). Oxford: Oxford University Press, 1921.

Auerbach, Nina. *Communities of Women.* Cambridge: Harvard University Press, 1978.

Bachofen, Johann J. *Das Mutterrecht. Eine Untersuchung über die Gynaikokratie der alten Welt nach ihrer religiösen und rechtlichen Natur.* Stuttgart: Krais and Hoffman, 1861.

Beauvoir, Simone de. *The Second Sex* (1949). H.M. Parshley, trans. and ed. New York: Knopf, 1953; Bantam, 1970.

Boulding, Elise. *The Underside of History: A View of Women Through Time.* Boulder, Colo.: Westview Press, 1976.

Briffault, Robert. *The Mothers: A Study of the Origins of Sentiments and Institutions.* 3 vols. New York: Macmillan, 1927.

Degler, Carl. *At Odds: Women and the Family in America; 1776 to the Present.* New York: Oxford University Press, 1980.

DuBois, Ellen Carol, et al. *Feminist Scholarship: Kindling in the Groves of Academe.* Urbana and Chicago: University of Illinois Press, 1985.

Elbogen, Ismar, and Leonore Sterling. *Die Geschichte der Juden in Deutschland.* Frankfurt am Main: Athenaeum Verlag, 1988.

Engels, Friedrich. *Der Ursprung der Familie, des Privateigentums und des Staates* (1884). Reprinted in Karl Marx and Friedrich Engels. *Werke,* vol. 21. Berlin: Dietz Verlag, 1962.

Ezell, Margaret J. M. *The Patriarch's Wife: Literary Evidence and the History of the Family.* Chapel Hill and London: University of North Carolina Press, 1987.

Faderman, Lillian. *Surpassing the Love of Men: Romantic Friendship and Love Between Women from the Renaissance to the Present.* New York: Morrow, 1981.

Flexner, Eleanor. *Century of Struggle: The Woman's Rights Movement in the United States* (1959). Cambridge: Belknap Press of Harvard University, 1975.

Fox-Genovese, Elizabeth. *Feminism Without Illusions: A Critique of Individualism.* Chapel Hill and London: University of North Carolina Press, 1991.

Gilbert, Sandra M., and Susan Gubar. *The Madwoman in the Attic: The Woman Writer and the Nineteenth-Century Literary Imagination.* New Haven: Yale University Press, 1979.

Heilbrun, Carolyn G. *Writing a Woman's Life.* New York: W.W. Norton, 1988.

————. *Hamlet's Mother and Other Women.* New York: Ballantine Books, 1990.

Hurd-Mead, Kate C. *A History of Women in Medicine . . . from the Earliest Times to the Beginning of the Nineteenth Century.* Haddam, Conn.: Haddam Press, 1938.

Janssen-Jurreit, Marie-Louise. *Sexismus.* München: Carl Hauser Verlag, 1976.

Jellinek, Estelle C. *Women's Autobiography.* Bloomington: Indiana University Press, 1980.

Kelly, Joan. *Women, History and Theory.* Chicago: University of Chicago Press, 1984.

Kleinbaum, Abby Wettan. *The War Against the Amazons.* New York: McGraw-Hill, 1983.

Köster, Helmut. *Einführung in das Neue Testament im Rahmen der Religionsgeschichte und Kulturgeschichte der hellenistischen und römischen Zeit.* Berlin: Walter de Gruyter, 1980.

Lerner, Gerda. *The Majority Finds Its Past: Placing Women in History.* New York: Oxford University Press, 1979.

Lerner, Robert E., Standish Meacham and Edward McNall Burns. *Western Civilizations: Their History and Their Culture.* 11th ed. New York: W.W. Norton, 1988.

Lorde, Audre. *Sister Outsider: Essays and Speeches.* New York: The Crossing Press, 1984.

Merton, Robert K. *On the Shoulders of Giants: A Shandean Postscript.* San Diego: Harcourt Brace Jovanovich, 1985.

Meyers, Carol. *Discovering Eve: Ancient Israelite Women in Context.* New York: Oxford University Press, 1988.

Minnich, Elizabeth Kamarck. *Transforming Knowledge.* Philadelphia: Temple University Press, 1990.

Moers, Ellen. *Literary Women.* Garden City: Doubleday, 1976.

Pagels, Elaine. *Adam and Eve and the Serpent.* New York: Random House, 1988.

Pateman, Carole. *The Sexual Contract.* Stanford: Stanford University Press, 1988.

Phillips, John A. *Eve: The History of an Idea.* New York: Harper & Row, 1984.

Rabinowicz, Henry M. *The World of Judaism.* London: Vallentine, Mitchel, 1970.

Rendall, Ruth. *The Origins of Modern Feminism: Women in Britain, France and the United States, 1780–1860.* London: Macmillan, 1985.

Rich, Adrienne. *Of Woman Born: Motherhood as Experience and Institution.* New York: W.W. Norton, 1976.

———. *On Lies, Secrets, and Silence: Selected Prose, 1966–1978.* New York: W.W. Norton, 1979.

Rowbotham, Sheila. *Hidden from History: Rediscovering Women in History from the 17th Century to the Present.* New York: Random House, 1974.

Ruether, Rosemary Radford. *Sexism and God-Talk: Toward a Feminist Theology.* Boston: Beacon Press, 1983.

Sewell, Elizabeth. *The Human Metaphor.* University of Notre Dame Press, 1964.

Showalter, Elaine. *A Literature of Their Own.* Princeton: Princeton University Press, 1977.

Smith, Bonnie G. *Changing Lives: Women in European History since 1700.* Lexington, Mass: D. C. Heath, 1989.

Spacks, Patricia Meyer. *The Female Imagination.* New York: Knopf, 1975.

Spender, Dale. *Women of Ideas and What Men Have Done to Them: From Aphra Behn to Adrienne Rich.* London: Routledge and Kegan Paul, 1982.

Stenton, Doris Mary. *The English Woman in History* (1957). New York: Schocken Books, 1977.

Stimpson, Catharine R. *Where the Meanings Are: Feminism and Cultural Spaces.* New York: Methuen, 1988.

Thorndike, Lynn. *A History of Magic and Experimental Science During the First Thirteen Centuries of Our Era.* 2 vols. New York: Columbia University Press, 1929.

Todd, Janet M. *Women's Friendship in Literature.* New York: Columbia University Press, 1980.

Walker, Alice. *In Search of Our Mothers' Garden: Womanist Prose*. San Diego: Harcourt Brace Jovanovich, 1983.

Whitelock, Dorothy. *The Beginnings of English Society*. Paperback ed. London: Penguin Books, 1984.

Wooley, C. Leonard. *The Sumerians*. New York: W.W. Norton, 1965.

Woolf, Virginia. *Three Guineas*. London: Hogarth Press, 1938.

———. *A Room of One's Own*. New York: Harcourt Brace Jovanovich, 1929.

———. *Women and Writing*. Michelle Barrett (ed.) New York: Harcourt Brace Jovanovich, 1979.

Wrigley, E.A. *Population and History*. New York: McGraw-Hill, 1973.

2. Articles

Bird, Phyllis. "Images of Women in the Old Testament." In Ruether, *Sexism and God Talk*, pp.41–88.

Davin, Anna. "Imperialism and Motherhood." *History Workshop*, no. 5 (1978), 9–65.

Davis, Natalie Zemon. "Gender and Genre: Women as Historical Writers, 1400–1820." In *Beyond Their Sex: Learned Women of the European Past*. Patricia H. Labalme (ed.). New York: New York University Press, 1984, pp. 153–82.

———. " 'Women's History' in Transition: The European Case." *Feminist Studies*, vol. 3, nos. 3/4 (1976), 83–103.

Fox-Genovese, Elizabeth. "Culture and Consciousness in the Intellectual History of European Women." *SIGNS*, vol. 12, no. 3 (Spring 1987), 529–47.

Fritz, Angela McCourt. "The Novel Women: Origins of the Feminist Literary Tradition in England and France." In *New Research on Women at the University of Michigan*. Dorothy McGuigan (ed.). Ann Arbor, Mich.: Center for Continuing Education of Women, 1974, pp. 20–46.

Horowitz, Maryanne Cline. "The Image of God in Man—Is Woman Included?." *Harvard Theological Review*, vol. 72, nos. 3–4 (July-Oct. 1979), 175–206.

Hufton, Olwen. "Women in History: Early Modern Europe." *Past and Present*, vol. 101 (Nov. 1983), 125–41.

Kelly, Joan. "Early Feminist Theory and the *Querelle des Femmes*." In Kelly, *Women, History and Theory*, pp. 65–109.

Kolodny, Annette. "Some Notes on Defining a Feminist Literary Criticism." *Critical Inquiry*, vol. 2 (Autumn 1975), 75–92.

Lerner, Gerda. "A View from the Women's Side." *The Journal of American History*, vol. 76, no. 2 (Sept. 1989), 446–56.

———. "Black Women in the United States." In Lerner, *Majority*, chap. 5.

———. "Women and History." In *Critical Essays on Simone de Beauvoir*. Elaine Marks (ed.). Boston: G. K. Hall, 1987, pp. 154–67.

Mason, Mary G. "The Other Voice: Autobiographies of Women Writers." In *Autobiography: Essays Theoretical and Critical*. James Olney (ed.). Princeton: Princeton University Press, 1980.

McLaughlin, Eleanor Commo. "Equality of Souls, Inequality of Sexes: Woman in Medieval Theology." In Ruether, *Religion and Sexism*, pp. 213–66.

Offen, Karen. "Toward an Historical Definition of Feminism: The Contribution of France."

Crow Working Papers, no. 22, Center for Research on Women, Stanford University, 1985.

Prusak, Bernard P. "Woman: Seductive Siren and Source of Sin?." In Ruether, *Religion and Sexism*, pp. 89–116.

Richardson, Lula McDowell. "The Forerunners of Feminism in French Literature of the Renaissance from Christine of Pisa to Marie de Gournay." *The Johns Hopkins Studies in Romance Literatures and Languages*, vol. 12. Baltimore: Johns Hopkins University Press, 1929.

Robinson, Lillian S. "Treason Our Text: Feminist Challenges to the Literary Canon." *Tulsa Studies in Women's Literature* , vol. 2, no. 1 (Spring 1983), 83–98.

Ruether, Rosemary Radford. "Misogynism and Virginal Feminism in the Fathers of the Church." In Ruether, *Religion and Sexism*, pp. 150–83.

Scott, Joan Wallach. "Women in History: The Modern Period." *Past and Present*, no. 101 (Nov. 1983), 141–57.

Stimpson, Catharine R. "Ad/d Feminam: Women, Literature, and Society." In Stimpson, *Where the Meanings Are*, pp. 84–96.

Walker, Wm. O., Jr. "The 'Theology of Woman's Place' and the 'Paulinist' Tradition." *Semeia: An Experimental Journal for Biblical Criticism*, vol. 28 (1983), 101–12.

II ANTHOLOGIES

1. Anthologies of Primary Sources

[Anon.] *Poems by Eminent Ladies . . . .* London: R. Balwin, 1755.

Barnstone, Alike, and Willis Barnstone. *A Book of Women Poets from Antiquity to Now*. New York: Schocken Books, 1980.

Blackwell, Jeannine, and Susanne Zantop (eds.). *Bitter Healing; German Women Writers, 1700–1830; An Anthology*. Cornelia Niekus Moore (trans.). Lincoln: University of Nebraska Press, 1990,

Brinker-Gabler, Gisela (ed.). Deutsche Dichterinnen vom 16.ten Jahrhundert bis zur Gegenwart. Frankfurt am Main: Fischer Taschenbuch Verlag, 1978.

———— (ed.). Deutsche Literatur von Frauen; Erster Band: Vom Mittelalter bis zum Ende des 18.ten Jahrhunderts. München: C.H. Beck Verlag, 1988.

Cibber, Theophilus. *An Account of the Lives of the Poets of Great Britain and Ireland*. 4 vols. London: R. Griffiths, 1753.

Cosman, Carol, Joan Keefe and Kathleen Weaver (eds.). *The Penguin Book of Women Poets*. Middlesex, Eng.: Penguin Books, 1979.

Ferguson, Moira (ed.). *First Feminists: British Women Writers, 1578–1799*. Bloomington: Indiana University Press, 1985.

Gilbert, Sandra M., and Susan Gubar. *The Norton Anthology of Literature by Women: The Tradition in English*. New York: W.W. Norton, 1985.

Gössman, Elisabeth. *Das Wohlgelahrte Frauenzimmer*, Archiv für Philosophiegeschichtliche Frauenforschung, Band 1. München: Iudicium, 1984.

————. *Eva, Gottes Meisterwerk*, Archiv für Philosophie-geschichtliche Frauenforschung, Band 2. München: Iudicium, 1985.

Hannay, Margaret Patterson (ed.). *Silent But for the Word: Tudor Women as Patrons,*

Translators and Writers of Religious Works. Kent, Ohio: Kent State University Press, 1985.

Henderson, Katherine Usher, and Barbara F. McManus. *Half Humankind: Contexts and Texts of the Controversy About Women in England, 1540–1640.* Urbana: University of Illinois Press, 1985.

Lerner, Gerda (ed.). *Black Women in White America: A Documentary History.* New York, Pantheon, 1972.

Rossi, Alice (ed.). *The Feminist Papers from Adams to Beauvoir.* New York: Bantam Books, 1974.

2. Collections of Interpretive Essays

Becker-Cantarino, Barbara (ed.). *Die Frau von der Reformation zur Romantik: Die Situation der Frau vor dem Hintergrund der Literatur- und Sozialgeschichte.* Bonn: Bouvier, 1981.

Bridenthal, Renate, and Claudia Koonz (eds.). *Becoming Visible: Women in European History.* Boston: Houghton Mifflin, 1977.

Bridenthal, Renate, Claudia Koonz and Susan Stuard (eds.). *Becoming Visible: Women in European History* (1977). 2nd. ed. Boston: Houghton Mifflin, 1987.

Brink, J.R. (ed.). *Female Scholars: A Tradition of Learned Women Before 1800.* Montreal: Eden Press, Women's Publications, 1980.

Burkhard, Marianne (ed.). *Gestalt und Gestaltend: Frauen in der deutschen Literatur,* Amsterdamer Beiträge zur Neueren Germanistik, Band 10. Amsterdam: Rodopi, 1980.

Collins, Adela Yarbro (ed.). *Feminist Perspectives on Biblical Scholarship.* Society of Biblical Literature, Centennial Publications, no. 10. Chico, Calif.: Scholars Press, 1985.

Ecker, Gisela (ed.). *Feminist Aesthetics.* London: The Women's Press, 1985.

Hine, Darlene Clark (ed.). *Black Women in United States History.* 4 vols. Brooklyn, N.Y.: Carlson Publishing Co., 1990.

Labalme, Patricia H. (ed.). *Beyond Their Sex: Learned Women of the European Past.* New York: New York University Press, 1984.

McGuigan, Dorothy (ed.). *New Research on Women at the University of Michigan.* Ann Arbor: Center for Continuing Education, 1974.

Mahl, Mary R., and Helene Koon (eds.). *The Female Spectator: English Women Writers Before 1800.* Bloomington: Indiana University Press; Old Westbury, N.Y.: The Feminist Press, 1977.

Paulsen, Wolfgang (ed.). *Die Frau als Heldin und Autorin: Neue kritische Ansäetze zur deutschen Literatur.* Bern: Francke Verlag, 1979.

Rose, Mary Beth (ed.). *Women in the Middle Ages and the Renaissance: Literary and Historical Perspectives.* Syracuse: Syracuse University Press, 1986.

III   REFERENCE WORKS

[The Catholic University.] *New Catholic Encyclopedia.* 15 vols. New York: McGraw-Hill, 1967.

Cavendish, Richard (ed.). *Man, Myth and Magic. The Illustrated Encyclopedia of Mythology, Religion and the Unknown.* New York: Marshall Cavendish, 1985.

Cole, Helena, Jane Caplan and Hanna Schissler. *The History of Women in Germany from Medieval Times to the Present: Bibliography of English Language Publications.* Washington, D.C.: German Historical Institute, 1990.

Egan, Edward W., Constance B. Hintz and L. F. Wise (eds.). *Kings, Rulers and Statesmen.* New York: Sterling, 1976.

Eliade, Mirca (ed.). *The Encyclopedia of Religion.* 16 vols. New York: Macmillan, 1987.

Gillespie, Charles Coulston (ed.). *Dictionary of Scientific Biography.* New York: Charles Scribner's Sons, 1972.

Hastings, James (ed.). *Encyclopedia of Religion and Ethics.* 13 vols. New York: Charles Scribner's Sons, 1955–58.

Hinding, Andrea (ed.). *Women's History Sources: A Guide to Archives and Manuscript Collections in the United States.* 2 vols. New York: R. R. Bowker, 1979.

Holland, David T.(ed.). *The Encyclopedia Americana.* International ed. 30 vols. Danbury, Conn.: Grolier, 1990.

Jackson, Guida M. *Women Who Ruled.* Santa Barbara and Oxford: ABC-CLIO, 1990.

James, Edward T., Janet Wilson James and Paul Boyer (eds.). *Notable American Women, 1607–1950: A Biographical Dictionary.* 3 vols. Cambridge: Harvard University Press, 1971.

Seligman, Edwin R. A. (ed.). *Encyclopedia of the Social Sciences.* 15 vols. New York: Macmillan, 1930–35.

Sicherman, Barbara, and Carol Hurd Green (eds.). *Notable American Women: The Modern Period.* Cambridge: Harvard University Press, 1980.

Sills, David L. (ed.). *International Encyclopedia of the Social Sciences.* 19 vols. New York: Macmillan, 1968–91.

Singer, Isidore (ed.). *The Jewish Encyclopedia.* 12 vols. New York: Funk & Wagnalls, 1901.

UNESCO Statistical Yearbook, 1986. Belgium: UNESCO, 1986.

Wakefield, Gordon S. *The Westminster Dictionary of Spirituality.* Philadelphia: Westminster Press, 1983.

Ward, A. A., and A. R. Waller (eds.). *Cambridge History of English Literature.* 15 vols. New York: G. P. Putnam & Sons, 1907–33.

Wigoder, Geoffrey (ed.). *The New Standard Jewish Encyclopedia.* New York: Doubleday, 1977.

IV   EDUCATION

1. Primary Sources

[Anon.] *The Rise and Progress of the Young Ladies' Academy of Philadelphia.* Philadelphia: Stewart and Cochran, 1794.

Bucknell, Joanna Rooker, and Martha Elizabeth Bucknell Papers, Elizabeth and Arthur Schlesinger Library, Radcliffe College, Cambridge, Mass.

Dwight, Timothy. *Travels in New England and New York.* 4 vols. London: William Boynes & Son, 1823.

Fuller, Margaret. *The Great Lawsuit: Woman in the Nineteenth Century.* New York: Jewett, Proctor and Worthingon, 1845.

U.S. Congress, House Special Subcommittee on Education. *Hearings on Discrimination Against Women.* 2 vols. Washington, D.C.: U.S. Government Printing Office, 1970.

Willard, Emma. *An Address to the Public; Particularly to the Members of the Legislature of New York, Proposing a Plan for Improving Female Education.* Middlebury, Vt.: S. W. Copeland, 1819.

2. Anthologies and Reference Works

Abel, James F., and Norman Bond. *Illiteracy in the Several Countries of the World.* Washington, D.C.: U.S. Government Publications, 1929. Dept. of the Interior, Bureau of Eucation, Bulletin for 1929, no. 4.

Goody, Jack (ed.). *Literacy in Traditional Societies.* Cambridge: Cambridge University Press, 1968.

Graff, Harvey J. (ed.). *Literacy and Social Development in the West.* Cambridge: Cambridge University Press, 1982.

Resnick, Daniel P. (ed.). *Literacy in Historical Perspective.* Washington, D.C.: Library of Congress, 1983.

3. Secondary Sources

BOOKS

Bailyn, Bernard. *Education in the Forming of American Society.* Chapel Hill: University of North Carolina Press, 1970.

Cipolla, Carl M. *Literacy and Development in the West.* Harmondsworth: Penguin Books, 1969.

Clanchy, M.T. (ed.). *From Memory to Written Record: England, 1066–1307.* Cambridge: Harvard University Press, 1979.

Cremin, Lawrence A. *American Education: The National Experience. 1738–1876.* New York: Harper & Row, 1980.

Cressy, David. *Literacy and the Social Order: Reading and Writing in Tudor and Stuart England.* Cambridge: Cambridge University Press, 1980.

Cross, Barbara. *The Educated Woman in America.* New York: Teachers College Press, 1965.

Goodsell, Willystine. *The Education of Women: Its Social Background and Its Problems.* New York: Macmillan, 1923.

Hickson, Shirley Ann. *The Development of Higher Education for Women in the Antebellum South.* Ph.D. Dissertation, University of South Carolina, 1985.

Hoffman, Nancy. *Women's True Profession.* New York: Feminist Press, 1981.

Houle, Cyril O. *Patterns of Learning.* San Francisco: Jossey-Bass, 1984.

Kaestle, Carl F. *Pillars of the Republic: Common Schools and American Society, 1780–1860.* New York: Hill & Wang, 1983.

Kuhn, Anne Louise. *The Mother's Role in Childhood Education: New England Concepts, 1830–1860*. New Haven: Yale University Press, 1947.

Lagemann, Ellen Condliffe. *A Generation of Women: Education in the Lives of Progressive Reformers*. Cambridge: Harvard University Press, 1979.

Lockridge, Kenneth A. *Literacy in Colonial New England: An Enquiry into the Social Context of Literacy in the Early Modern West*. New York: W.W. Norton, 1974.

Logan, Robert K. *The Alphabet Effect: The Impact of the Phonetic Alphabet on the Development of Western Civilization*. New York: William Morrow, 1986.

Marr, Harriet W. *The Old New England Academies*. New York: Comet Press Books, 1959.

Newcomer, Mabel. *A Century of Higher Education for American Women* (1959). Washington, D.C.: Zenger Pub., 1976.

Moorhouse, A. C. *The Triumph of the Alphabet*. New York: Henry Schuman, 1953.

Orme, Nicholas. *From Childhood to Chivalry: The Education of the English Kings and Aristocracy, 1066–1530*. New York: Methuen, 1984.

Rudolph, Frederick. *The American College and University: A History*. New York: Knopf, 1962.

Solomon, Barbara Miller. *In the Company of Educated Women: A History of Women and Higher Education in America*. New Haven: Yale University Press, 1985.

Soltow, L., and E. Stevens. *The Rise of Literacy and the Common School in the United States: A Socioeconomic Analysis to 1870*. Chicago: University of Chicago Press, 1981.

Stock, Phyllis. *Better Than Rubies: A History of Women's Education*. New York: G.P. Putnam's Sons, 1978.

Thompson, Eleanor Wolf. *Education for Ladies, 1830–1860*. New York: King's Crown Press, 1947.

Woodward, William Harrison. *Studies in Education During the Age of the Renaissance; 1400–1600*. Cambridge: Cambridge University Press, 1924.

Woody, Thomas. *History of Women's Education in the United States* (1929). 2 vols. New York: Octagon Books, 1966.

ARTICLES

Adamson, J.W. "The Extent of Literacy in England in the Fifteenth and Sixteenth Centuries: Notes and Conjectures." *The Library*, 4th Series, vol. 10 (1929–30), 163–93.

Auwers, Linda. "Reading the Marks of the Past: Exploring Female Literacy in Colonial Windsor, Connecticut." *Historical Methods*, vol. 13 (1980), 204–14.

Bock, E. Wilbur. " 'Farmer's Daughter Effect': The Case of the Negro Female Professionals." *Phylon*, vol. 30 (Spring 1969), 17–16.

Burstyn, Joan N. "Education and Sex: The Medical Case Against Higher Education for Women in England, 1870–1900." *Proceedings of the American Philosophical Society*, vol. 117, no. 2 (April 1973), 79–89.

———. "Sources of Influence: Women as Teachers of Girls." *Proceedings of the 1984 Annual Conference of the History of Education Society of Great Britain*. June Purvis (ed.). London: History of Education Society, 1985, pp. 61–76.

Clanchy, M.T. "Literate and Illiterate." In *From Memory to Written Record, England*

1066–1307. Michael Clanchy (ed.). Cambridge: Harvard University Press, 1979, pp. 175–201.

Conway, Jill Kerr. "Perspectives on the History of Women's Education in the United States." *History of Education Quarterly,* vol. 14 (Spring 1974), 1–12.

Cressy, David. "The Environment for Literacy: Accomplishment and Context in 17th Century England and New England." In Resnick, *Literacy,* pp. 23–42.

———. "Levels of Illiteracy in England, 1530–1730." *The Historical Journal,* vol. 20, no. 1 (1977), 1–24.

Dubois, Elfrieda T. "The Education of Women in Seventeenth-Century France." *French Studies,* vol. 22, no.1 (Jan. 1978), 1–19.

Ferrante, Joan M. "The Education of Women in the Middle Ages in Theory, Fact and Fantasy." In Labalme, *Beyond Their Sex,* pp. 9–42.

Gawthrop, Richard, and Gerald Strauss. "Protestantism and Literacy in Early Modern Germany." *Past and Present: A Journal of Historical Studies,* vol. 57, no. 4 (Aug. 1984), 31–55.

Golden, Hilda H. "Literacy." *International Encyclopedia of the Social Sciences,* vol. 9, pp. 412–17.

Graham, Patricia Albjerg. "Expansion and Exclusion: A History of Women in American Higher Education." *SIGNS,* vol. 3, no. 4 (Summer 1978), 759–72.

Green, Lowell. "The Education of Women in the Reformation." *History of Education Quarterly,* vol. 19 (Spring 1979), 93–116.

Houston, Rab. "Illiteracy in Scotland, 1630–1760." *Past & Present,* vol. 55 (Aug. 1982), 81–102.

———. "Literacy and Society in the West, 1500–1850." *Social History,* vol. 8, no. 3 (Oct. 1983), 269–89.

Kaestle, Carl F. "The History of Literacy and the History of Readers." In Edmund W. Gordon. *Review of Research in Education,* vol. 12, Washington, D.C.: American Educational Research Association, 1985, pp. 11–53.

———. "Literacy and Mainstream Culture in American History." *Language Arts,* vol. 43, no. 2 (Feb. 1981), 207–18.

Liebertz-Grün, Ursula. "Höfische Autorinnen von der karolingischen Kulturreform bis zum Humanismus." In Brinker-Gabler. *Deutsche Literatur von Frauen.* Erster Band . . . , pp. 39–64.

Keith Melder. "Mask of Oppression: The Female Seminary Movement in the United States." *New York History,* vol. 40 (July 1974), 261–79.

E. Jennifer Monaghan. "Literacy Instruction and Gender in Colonial New England." *American Quarterly,* vol. 40, no. 1 (March 1988), 18–41.

Resnick, D.P., and L.B. Resnick. "The Nature of Literacy: An Historical Exploration." *Harvard Educational Review,* vol. 47, no. 3 (Aug. 1977), 370–85.

Schofield, R. S. "The Measurement of Literacy in Pre-industrial England," as cited in Goody, *Literacy in Traditional Society.*

———. "Dimensions of Illiteracy, 1750–1850." *Explorations in Economic History,* vol. 10, no. 4, 2nd series (Summer 1973), 437–54.

Schwager, Sally. "Educating Women in America." *SIGNS,* vol. 12, no. 2 (Winter 1987), 333–72.

Shank, Michael H. "A Female University Student in Late Medieval Krakow." *SIGNS,* vol. 12, no. 2 (Winter 1987), 373–80.

Sicherman, Barbara. "Sense and Sensibility: A Case Study of Women's Reading in Late-

Victorian America." In *Reading in America: Literature and Social History.* Cathy N. Davidson (ed.). Baltimore: Johns Hopkins University Press, 1989.

Smout, T.C. "Born Again at Cambuslang: New Evidence on Popular Religion and Literacy in 18th Century Scotland." *Past & Present,* vol. 55, no. 97 (Nov. 1982), 114–27.

Spufford, Margaret. "First Steps in Literacy: The Reading and Writing Eexperiences of the Humblest 17th Century Spiritual Autobiographers." *Journal of Social History,* vol. 4, no. 3 (Oct. 1979), 407–54.

Stone, Lawrence. "Literacy and Education in England, 1640–1900." *Past & Present,* vol. 42 (Feb. 1969), 69–139.

Sullivan, Helen. "Literacy and Illiteracy." *Encyclopedia of the Social Sciences,* vol. 9, pp. 511–23.

V   MIDDLE AGES

1. Reference Works and Anthologies

[Frau Ava.] *Die Dichtungen der Frau Ava.* Friedrich Maurer (ed.). Tübingen: Max Niemyer Verlag, 1966.

Baker, Derek (ed.). *Medieval Women,* Oxford: Blackwell, l978.

Bury, J.B. (ed.). *The Cambridge Medieval History.* 8 vols. Cambridge: Cambridge University Press, 1924–36.

Dinzelbacher, Peter, and Dieter R. Bauer. *Religiöse Frauenbewegung und mystische Frömmigkeit im Mittelalter.* Köln: Böhlau Verlag, 1988.

Erickson, Carolly, and Kathleen Casey. "Women in the Middle Ages: A Working Bibliography." *Medieval Studies,* vol. 37 (1975), 340–59.

Green, David, and Frank O'Connor (eds.). *A Golden Treasury of Irish Poetry, 600–1200.* London: Macmillan, 1967.

Heer, Friedrich. *The Medieval World: Europe, 1100–1350.* George Weidenfeld and Nicolson, Ltd.(tr.). London: Weidenfeld & Nicolson, 1962.

Kirshner, Julius, and Suzanne F. Wemple (eds.). *Women in the Medieval World.* Oxford: Blackwell, 1985.

Mundy, John H., Richard W. Emery and Benjamin N. Nelson (eds.). *Essays in Medieval Life and Thought.* New York: Columbia University Press, 1955.

Morewedge, Rosemarie Thee (ed.). *The Role of Woman in the Middle Ages.* Albany: State University of New York Press, 1975.

Olson, Carl (ed.). *The Book of the Goddess, Past and Present: An Introduction to Her Religion.* New York: Crossroad Publ.,1985.

Petroff, Elizabeth Avilda. *Medieval Women's Visionary Literature.* New York: Oxford University Press, 1986.

Radcliff-Umstead, Douglas (ed.). *The Roles and Images of Women in the Middle Ages and Renaissance.* Pittsburgh: Center for Medieval and Renaissance Studies, 1975.

Ruether, Rosemary Radford (ed.). *Religion and Sexism: Images of Women in Medieval Theology.* New York: Simon and Schuster, 1974.

—— and Eleanor McLaughlin (eds.). *Women of Spirit: Female Leadership in the Jewish and Christian Traditions.* New York: Simon and Schuster, 1979.

Stammler, Wolfgang *et al. Die deutsche Literatur des Mittelalters: Verfasserlexikon.* 7 vols. Berlin: Walter de Gruyter, 1978.

Strayer, Joseph (ed.). *Dictionary of the Middle Ages.* New York: Charles Scribner & Sons, 1982.

Stuard, Susan Mosher (ed.). *Women in Medieval Society.* Philadelphia: University of Pennsylvania Press, 1976.

Thiebaux, Marcelle (tr. and ed.). *The Writings of Medieval Women.* New York: Garland, 1987.

Wilson, Katharina. *Medieval Women Writers.* Athens: University of Georgia Press, 1984.

2. Books

Ashe, Geoffrey. *The Virgin.* London: Routledge & Kegan Paul, 1976.

Atkinson, Clarissa W. *The Oldest Vocation: Christian Motherhood in the Middle Ages.* Ithaca: Cornell University Press, 1991.

Beissel, Stephan. *Geschichte der Verehrung Marias in Deutschland während des Mittelalters, Ein Beitrag zur Religion, Wissenschaft und Kunstgeschichte.* Freiburg im Breisgau: Herder, 1909.

Bennett, H. S. *Six Medieval Men and Women.* New York: Atheneum, 1968.

Berger, Pamela. *The Goddess Obscured: Tranformation of the Grain Protectress from Goddess to Saint.* Boston: Beacon Press, 1985.

Bogin, Meg. *The Women Troubadours.* Scarborough, Eng.: Paddington Press, 1976.

Bynum, Carolyn Walker. *Holy Feast and Holy Fast: The Religious Significance of Food to Medieval Women.* Berkeley: University of California Press, 1987.

———. *Jesus as Mother: Studies in the Spirituality of the High Middle Ages.* Berkeley: University of California Press, 1982.

Chenu, Marc D. *Nature, Man and Society in the 12th Century.* Chicago: University of Chicago Press, 1968.

Cohn, Norman. *Europe's Inner Demons: An Enquiry Inspired by the Great Witch-Hunt.* New York: New American Library, 1975.

———. *The Pursuit of the Millennium: Revolutionary Millenarians and Mystical Anarchists of the Middle Ages.* New York: Oxford University Press, 1957.

Dronke, Peter. *Women Writers of the Middle Ages: A Critical Study of Texts from Perpetua (202) to Marguerite Porète (1310).* Cambridge: Cambridge University Press, 1984.

Eckenstein, Lina. *Woman Under Monasticism: Chapters on Saint-Lore and Convent Life between A.D. 500 and A.D. 1500.* Cambridge: Cambridge University Press, 1896.

Gies, Frances and Joseph. *Women in the Middle Ages.* New York: Harper & Row, 1980.

Gold, Penny Schine. *The Lady and the Virgin: Image, Attitude and Experience in 12th Century France.* Chicago: University of Chicago Press, 1985.

Harksen, Sibylle. *Women in the Middle Ages.* Marianne Herzfeld (tr.). New York: A. Schram, 1975.

Heinrich, Sr. Mary P. *The Canonesses and Education in the Early Middle Ages.* Ph.D. Dissertation. Catholic University of America. Washington, D.C., 1924.

Herlihy, David. *Cities and Society in Medieval Italy.* London: Variorum Reprints, 1980.

Huizinga, J. *The Waning of the Middle Ages.* Garden City, N.Y.: Doubleday, 1954.

[St. Jerome.] *The Letters of St. Jerome.* Charles C. Mierow (tr.). Westminster, Md.: Newman Press, 1963.

Koch, Gottfried. *Frauenfrage und Ketzertum im Mittelalter: Die Frauenbewegung im Rahmen des Katharismus und des Waldensertums und ihre sozialen Wurzeln (12–14. Jahrhundert).* Berlin: Akademie-Verlag, l962.

[Kottanner, Helene.] *Die Denkwürdigkeiten der Helene Kottannerin, 1439–1440.* Karl Molloy (ed.). Wien: Wiener Neudrucke, 1971.

Labarge, Margaret Wade. *A Small Sound of the Trumpet: Women in Medieval Life.* Boston: Beacon Press, 1986.

Ladurie, Emmanuel Leroy. *Montaillou, The Promised Land of Error.* New York: Vintage Books, 1979.

Le Goff, Jacques. *Time, Work, and Culture in the Middle Ages.* Arthur Gildhammer (tr.). Chicago: University of Chicago Press, 1980.

Lerner, Robert E. *The Heresy of the Free Spirit in the Later Middle Ages.* Berkeley: University of California Press, 1972.

Lewis, C. S. *The Allegory of Love: A Study in Medieval Tradition.* London: Oxford University Press, 1936.

Lucas, Angela M. *Women in the Middle Ages: Religion, Marriage, and Letters.* Brighton, Sussex: Harvester Press, 1983.

Marie de France. *Fables.* Harriet Spiegel (ed. and trans.). Toronto: University of Toronto Press, 1987.

McDonnell, Ernest W. *The Beguines and Begherds in Medieval Culture, with Special Emphasis on the Belgian Scene.* New Brunswick: Rutgers University Press, 1954.

Meade, Marion. *Eleanor of Aquitaine: A Biography.* New York: Hawthorne Books, 1977.

Miles, Margaret R. *Carnal Knowledge: Female Nakedness and Religious Meaning in the Christian West.* New York: Vintage Books, 1991.

———. *Image as Insight: Visual Understanding in Western Christianity and Secular Culture.* Boston: Beacon Press, 1985.

Muraro, Luisa. *Vilemina und Mayfreda: Die Geschichte einer Feministischen Häresie.* Freiburg im Breisgau: Kore, Verlag T. Hensch, 1987.

Otis, Leah L. *Prostitution in Medieval Society: The History of an Urban Institution in Languedoc.* Chicago: University of Chicago Press, 1986.

Petersen, Karen, and J. J. Wilson. *Women Artists: Recognition and Reappraisal, From the Early Middle Ages to the Twentieth Century.* New York: Harper & Row, 1976.

Power, Eileen. *Medieval Women.* Cambridge: Cambridge University Press, 1975.

———. *Medieval English Nunneries.* Cambridge: Cambridge University Press, 1922.

Shahar, Shulamith. *Die Frau im Mittelalter.* Königstein: Athenaeum Verlag, 1981.

Southern, R. W. *The Making of the Middle Ages.* New Haven: Yale University Press, 1953.

Strayer, Joseph R. *Western Europe in the Middle Ages: A Short History.* New York: Appleton-Century-Crofts, 1955.

Warner, Marina. *Alone of All Her Sex: The Myth and the Cult of the Virgin Mary.* New York: Vintage Books, 1983.

———. *Joan of Arc: The Image of Female Heroism.* New York: Knopf, 1981.

Weinstein, Donald, and Rudolph Bell. *Saints and Society: The Two Worlds of Western Christendom, 1000–1700.* Chicago: University of Chicago Press, l982.

Ward, Benedicta. *Miracles and the Medieval Mind: Theory, Record and Event; 1000–1215.* Philadelphia: University of Pennsylvania Press, 1982.

Wemple, Suzanne Fonay. *Women in Frankish Society: Marriage and the Cloister; 500–900.* Philadelphia: University of Pennsylvania Press, 1985.

3. Articles

Abels, Richard, and Ellen Harrison. "The Participation of Women in Languedocian Catharism." *Medieval Studies*, vol.41 (1979), 215–51.

Attreed, Lorraine C. "From Pearl Maiden to Tower Princes: Towards a New History of Medieval Childhood." *Journal of Medieval History*, vol.9, no. 1 (March 1983), 43–58.

Bandel, Betty. "English Chroniclers' Attitudes Toward Women." *Journal of the History of Ideas*, vol. 16 (1955), 113–18.

Benedek, Thomas G. "The Roles of Medieval Women in the Healing Arts." In Radcliff-Umstead, *Roles and Images*, pp.145–59.

Bell, Susan Groag. "Medieval Women Book Owners: Arbiters of Lay Piety and Ambassadors of Culture." *SIGNS*, vol. 7, no. 4 (Summer 1982), 742–68.

Børressen, Kari Elisabeth. "God's Image, Man's Image? Female Metaphors Describing God in the Christian Tradition." *Temenos*, vol. 19 (1983), 17–32.

Browne, Thea Lawrence. "Irish Attitudes Toward Women's Education and Learning in the Early Middle Ages." *Studies in Medieval Culture*, vol. 10 (1977), 27–32.

Bynum, Caroline. ". . .'And Woman her Humanity': Female Imagery in the Religious Writings of the Later Middle Ages." In *Gender and Religion: On the Complexity of Symbols*, Caroline Walker Bynum, Stevan Harrell and Paula Richman (eds.). Boston: Beacon Press, 1986, pp. 250–79.

Cross, George. "Heresy." In *Encyclopedia of Religion and Ethics*, vol. 6, pp. 618–22.

Dygo, Marian. "The Political Role of the Virgin Mary in Teutonic Prussia in the 14th and 15th Centuries." *Journal of Medieval History*, vol. 15, no. 1 (March 1989), 63–81.

Fiorenza, Elizabeth Schuessler. "Word, Spirit and Power: Women in Early Christian Communities." In *Women of Spirit, Female Leadership in the Jewish and Christian Traditions*. Ruether and McLaughlin (eds.), pp. 30–70.

Facinger, Marion F. "A Study of Medieval Queenship: Capetian France, 987–1237." In *Studies in Medieval and Renaissance History*. William M. Bowsky (ed.). Vol. 5. Lincoln: University of Nebraska Press, 1968, pp. 3–48.

Farmer, Sharon. "Persuasive Voices: Clerical Images of Medieval Wives." *Speculum*, vol. 41, no. 3 (July 1986), 517–43.

Fox, Charles. "Marie de France." *English Historical Review*, vol. 25 (1910), 303–6.

Grundmann, Herbert. "*Litteratus - illitteratus*: Der Wandel einer Bildungsnorm vom Altertum zum Mittelalter." *Archiv für Kulturgeschichte*, vol. 40, no. 1, pp. 1–65.

Hajdu, Robert. "The Position of Noblewomen in the *Pays des Coutumes*, 1100–1300." *Journal of Family History*, vol. 2 (Summer 1980), 122–44.

Heid, Ulrich. "Studien zu Marguerite Porète und ihrem 'Miroir des simples Ames'." In Dinzelbacher and Bauer, *Religiöse Frauenbewegung*, pp. 185–214.

Herlihy, David. "Life Expectancies for Women in Medieval Society." In Morewedge, *Role of Women*, pp. 1–22.

Klinck, Anne L. "Anglo-Saxon Women and the Law." *Journal of Medieval History*, vol. 8, no. 2 (June 1982), 107–21.

Kristeller, Paul Oskar. "The School of Salerno." *The Bulletin of the History of Medicine*, vol. 17, no. 1 (Jan. 1945), 138–94.

Langmuir, Gavin I. "Medieval Anti-Semitism." In *The Holocaust: Ideology, Bureaucracy, and Genocide*. Henry Friedlander and Sybil Milton (eds.). Millwood, N.Y.: Kraus International, 1980, pp. 27–36.

Lehrman, Sara. "The Education of Women in the Middle Ages." In Radcliff-Umstead, *Roles and Images*, pp. 133–44.

McNamara, Joann, and Suzanne Wemple. "Sanctity and Power: The Dual Pursuit of Medieval Women." In Bridenthal and Koonz, *Becoming Visible*, (1977), pp. 90–118.

McLaughlin, Eleanor Commo. "Women, Power and the Pursuit of Holiness in Medieval Christianity." In Ruether and McLaughlin, *Women of Spirit*, pp. 100–130.

———. " 'Christ My Mother': Feminine Naming and Metaphor in Medieval Spirituality." *Nashota Review*, vol. 15, no. 3 (Fall 1975), 228–48.

———. "Equality of Souls, Inequality of Sexes: Women in Medieval Theology." In Ruether, *Religion and Sexism*, pp. 213–66.

Malverne, Marjorie M. "Marie de France's Ingenious Uses of the Authorial Voice and Her Singular Contribution to Western Literature." *Tulsa Studies in Women's Literature*, vol. 2, no. 1 (Spring 1983), 21–42.

Matter, Ann. "Mary: A Goddess?." In Olson, *Book of the Goddess*, pp. 80–96.

May, William Harold. "The Confession of Prous Boneta: Heretic and Heresiarch." In *Essays in Medieval Life and Thought*. John H. Mundy, Richard W. Emery, Benjamin N. Nelson (eds.). New York: Columbia University Press, 1955, pp. 3–30.

Ross, Margaret C. "Concubinage in Anglo-Saxon England." *Past and Present*, no. 108 (Aug. 1985), 3–34.

Rothkrug, Lionel. "Religious Practices and Collective Perceptions: Hidden Homologies in the Renaissance and Reformation." *Historical Reflections*, vol. 7, no. 1 (Spring 1980), 3–264.

Runciman, W. G. "Accelerating Social Mobility: The Case of Anglo-Saxon England." *Past and Present*, no. 104 (Aug. 1984), 3–30.

Salisbury, Joyce E. "Fruitful in Singleness." *Journal of Medieval History*, vol. 8, no. 2 (June 1982), 97–106.

Schibanoff, Susan. "Medieval *Frauenlieder*: Anonymous Was a Man?." *Tulsa Studies in Women's Literature*, vol. 1, no. 2 (Fall 1982), 189–200.

Schulenburg, Jane Tibbetts. "The Heroics of Virginity: Brides of Christ and Sacrificial Mutilation." In Rose, *Women in the Middle Ages*, pp. 29–72.

———. "Women's Monastic Communities, 500–1100: Patterns of Expansion and Decline." *SIGNS*, vol. 14, no. 2 (Winter 1989), 261–92.

———. "Sexism and the Celestial Gynaceum from 500 to 1200." *Journal of Medieval History*, vol. 4, no. 2 (June 1978), 117–33.

Sheehan, Michael M., O.S.B. "The Influence of Canon Law on the Property Rights of Married Women in England." *Medieval Studies*, vol. 25 (1963), 109–24.

Wemple, Suzanne. "Sanctity and Power: The Dual Pursuit of Medieval Women." In Bridenthal *et al., Becoming Visible,* pp. 131–51.

Wessley, Stephen E. "The Thirteenth-Century Guglielmites: Salvation Through Women." In Baker, *Medieval Women,* pp. 289–303.

Wilkins, David. "Woman as Artist and Patron in the Middle Ages and the Renaissance." In Radcliff-Umstead, *Roles and Images,* pp. 107–31.

Wood, Charles T. "The Doctor's Dilemma: Sin, Salvation, and the Menstrual Cycle in Medieval Thought." *Speculum,* vol. 56, no. 4 (Oct. 1981), 710–27.

Wilson, Katharina M. *"Figmenta vs. Veritas:* Dame Alice and the Medieval Literary Depiction of Women by Women." *Tulsa Studies in Women's Literature,* vol. 4, no. 1 (Spring 1985), 17–32.

4. Christine de Pizan

OWN WORKS

Christine de Pisan. *Le Livre des fais and bonnes meurs du sage Roy Charles V.* Suzanne Solente (ed.). 2 vols. Paris: Société de l'Histoire de France, 1936–40.

———. *Le Livre de la Mutacion de Fortune.* Suzanne Solente (ed.). 4 vols. Paris: Société de l'Histoire de France, 1959–66.

———. *Le Livre des Trois Vertus de Christine de Pisan.* Mathilde Laigle (ed.), Paris: Champion, 1912.

———. *Oeuvres poètiques de Christine de Pisan.* M. Roy (ed.). Paris: Soc. Anc. Textes, 33, 1886.

———. *The Book of the City of Ladies.* Earl Jeffrey Richards (tr.). New York: Persea Books, 1982.

BOOKS

Hindman, Sandra L. *Christine de Pizan's "Epistre Othea": Paintings and Politics at the Court of Charles VI.* Toronto: Pontifical Institute of Medieval Studies, 1986.

Willard, Charity Cannon. *Christine de Pizan: Her Life and Works.* New York: Persea Books, 1984.

ARTICLES

Bell, Susan Groag. "Christine de Pizan (1364–1430): Humanism and the Problem of a Studious Woman." *Feminist Studies,* vol. 3, nos. 3/4 (Spring/Summer 1976), 173–84.

Gabriel, Astrik L. "The Educational Ideas of Christine de Pisan." *Journal of the History of Ideas,* vol. 13, no. 1 (Jan. 1955), 3–21.

Hindman, Sandra L. "With Ink and Mortar: Christine de Pizan's *Cité des Dames,* An Art Essay." *Feminist Studies,* vol. 10, no. 3 (Fall 1984), 457–77.

Ignatius, Mary Ann. "A Look at the Feminism of Christine de Pisan." *Proceedings of* the Pacific Northwest Conference on Foreign Languages, vol. 29, pt. 2 (1978), 18–21.

Lynn, Therese Ballet. "The *Ditie de Jeanne d'Arc:* Its Political, Feminist and Aesthetic Significance." *Fifteenth Century Studies,* vol. 1 (1978), 149–57.

Reno, Christine M. "Feminist Aspects of Christine de Pizan's *Epistre d'Othea à Hector.*" *Studi Francesi,* vol. 71 (1980), 271–76.

5. Hrosvitha of Gandersheim

Homeyer, Helena (ed.). *Hrotsvithae Opera.* Paderborn, 1970.

BOOKS

Haight, Anne Lyon (ed.). *Hroswitha of Gandersheim: Her Life, Times and Works, and a Comprehensive Bibliography.* New York: The Hroswitha Club, 1965.

ARTICLES

Case, Sue-Ellen. "Re-Viewing Hrotsvit." *Theatre Journal,* vol. 35, no. 4 (Dec. 1983), 533–42.

Kuhn, Hugo. "Hrotsviths von Gandersheim Dichterisches Programm." *Deutsche Vierteljahrsschrift für Literaturwissenschaft und Geistesgeschichte,* vol. 24 (1950), 181–96.

Wilson, Katharina M. "The Saxon Canoness: Hrotsvit of Gandersheim." In Wilson (ed.), *Medieval Women Writers,* pp. 30–63.

———. "The Old Hungarian Translation of Hrotsvit's Dulcitius: History and Analysis." *Tulsa Studies in Women's Literature,* vol. 1, no. 2 (Fall 1982), 177–87.

VI MYSTICISM AND SPIRITUALITY

1. Primary Sources

[no author.] *Testimonies of the Life, Character, Revelations and Doctrines of Mother Ann Lee and the Elders with her* . . . Albany, N.Y.: Weed, Parsons & Co., 1888.

Foote, Mrs. Julia A. J. "A Brand Plucked from the Fire: An Autobiographical Sketch" (1879). In *Sisters of the Spirit: Three Black Women's Autobiographies of the Nineteenth Century.* William L. Andrews (ed.). Bloomington: Indiana University Press, 1986.

Heiler, Anne Marie (ed. and tr.). *Mystik deutscher Frauen im Mittelalter.* Berlin: Hochweg-Verlag, 1929.

[Jackson, Rebecca.] *Gifts of Power: The Writings of Rebecca Jackson, Black Visionary,*

Shaker Eldress. Jean M. Humez (ed.). Boston: University of Massachusetts Press, 1981.

Lee, Jarena. *Religious Experience and Journal of Jarena Lee, A Coloured Lady, Giving an Account of her Call to Preach the Gospel* (1836). In William L. Andrews (ed.), *Sisters of the Spirit*, pp. 25–48.

Mahrholz, Werner (ed.). *Der Deutsche Pietismus.* Berlin: Furche-Verlag, 1921.

Mechthild of Hackeborn. *The Book of Gostlye Grace.* T.A. Halligan (ed.). Toronto, 1979.

[Maria W. Stewart.] *Maria W. Stewart, America's First Black Woman Political Writer: Essays and Speeches.* Marilyn Richardson (ed.). Bloomington: Indiana University Press, 1987.

[Truth, Sojourner.] *Narrative of Sojourner Truth, a Northern Slave. . . .* Boston: Printed for the Author, 1850.

——. Frances D. Gage. "Reminiscences; Sojourner Truth." In Elizabeth Cady Stanton, Susan B. Anthony, Matilda Joslyn Gage. *History of Woman Suffrage.* 6 vols. New York: Fowler & Wells, 1881–1922. I, pp. 115–17.

[Wilkinson, Jemima.] *Pioneer Prophetess: Jemima Wilkinson, the Publick Universal Friend.* Herbert A. Wisbey, Jr. (ed.). Ithaca: Cornell University Press, 1964.

Windstösser, Maria David (ed.). *Deutsche Mystiker.* Band V, *Frauenmystik im Mittelalter.* Kempten und München: Verlag Kösleschen Buchhandlung, 1919.

2. Books

Benz, Ernst. *Die Vision: Erfahrungensformen und Bilderwelt* (Stuttgart: Ernst Klett, 1969.

Braude, Ann. *Radical Spirits: Spiritualism and Women's Rights in Nineteenth-Century America.* Boston: Beacon Press, 1989.

Bynum, Caroline Walker, Stevan Harrell and Paula Richman. *Gender and Religion: On the Complexity of Symbols.* Boston: Beacon Press, 1986.

Capps, Walter Holden, and Wendy M. Wright. *Silent Fire: An Invitation to Western Mysticism.* New York: Harper & Row, 1978.

[Ebner, Christina.] *Ebner Christina, Der Nonne von Engelthal Büchlein von der Gnaden Überlast.* Karl Schröder (ed.). Tübingen, 1871.

[——.] *Leben und Gesichte der Christina Ebnerin, Klosterfrau zu Engelthal.* Georg Wolfgang Karl Lochner (ed.). Nürnberg: Schmid, 1872.

Ebner, Margaretha. *Die Offenbarungen der Margaretha Ebner und der Adelheid Langmann.* Joseph Prestel (tr.). Weimar: Verlag H. Böhlaus Nachfolger, 1939.

[——.] *Margaretha Ebner und Heinrich von Nördlingen; Ein Beitrag zur Geschichte der Deutschen Mystik.* Philip Strauch (ed.). Freiburg: Akademische Verlagsbuchhandlung von J.C.B. Mohr, 1882.

Kieckhefer, Richard. *Unquiet Souls: Fourteenth-Century Saints and Their Religious Milieu.* Chicago: University of Chicago Press, 1984.

Riehle, Wolfgang. *Studien zur englischen Mystik des Mittelalters unter besonderer Berücksichtigung ihrer Metaphorik.* Heidelberg: Carl Winter Universitätsverlag, 1977.

Scholem, Gershon M. *Major Trends in Jewish Mysticism* (1941). New York: Schocken Books, 1978.

3. Articles

Adams, Rev. John Quincy. "Jemima Wilkinson, the Universal Friend," *Journal of American History*, vol. 9, no. 2 (April-July 1915), 249–63.

Bynum, Caroline Walker. "Women Mystics and Eucharistic Devotion in the Thirteenth Century." *Women's Studies*, vol. 11, nos. 1 & 2 (1984), 179–214.

Chapman, John. "Mysticism (Christian, Roman, Catholic)." In *Encyclopedia of Religion and Ethics*. James Hastings (ed.). Vol. 9, pp. 90–101.

Critchfield, Richard. "Prophetin, Führerin, Organisatorin: Zur Rolle der Frau im Pietismus." In *Die Frau von der Reformation zur Romantik*. Barbara Becker-Cantarino (ed.). Bonn: Bouvier Verlag Herbert Grundmann, l980, pp. 112–37.

Foster, K. "St. Catherine of Siena." In *New Catholic Encyclopedia*. [The Catholic University.] New York: McGraw-Hill, 1967, vol. 3, pp. 258–60.

Gilkes, Cheryl Townsend. " 'Together and in Harness': Women's Traditions in the Sanctified Church." In *Black Women in United States History*. Darlene Clark Hine (ed.). 4 vols. Brooklyn, N.Y.: Carlson Publishing Co., 1990, vol. 2, pp. 377–98.

Hug, P.L. "St. Catherine of Genoa." In *New Catholic Encyclopedia*. [The Catholic University.] vol. 3, pp. 254–56.

Humez, Jean M. " 'My Spirit Eye': Some Functions of Spiritual and Visionary Experience in the Lives of Five Black Women Preachers, 1810–1880. " In *Women and the Structure of Society* . Barbara J. Harris and JoAnn McNamara (eds.). Durham: Duke University Press, 1984, pp. 129–43.

McKay, Nellie Y. "Nineteenth-Century Black Women's Spiritual Autobiographies: Religious Faith and Self-Empowerment." In Personal Narratives Group, Joy Webster Barbre *et al. Interpreting Women's Lives: Feminist Theory and Personal Narratives*. Bloomington: Indiana University Press, 1989, pp. 139–54.

McLaughlin, Eleanor. "The Heresy of the Free Spirit and Late Medieval Mysticism." In *Medievalia et Humanistica Studies in Medieval and Renaissance Culture*. Paul Maurice Clogan (ed.). New Series no. 4. Denton: North Texas State University Press, 1973.

McLaughlin, Mary Martin. "Peter Abelard amd the Dignity of Women: Twelfth Century Feminism in Theory and Practice." In *Pierre Abelard, Pierre le Venerable: Les courants philosophiques, litteraires et artistiques en occident au milieu du XIIe siècle*. Paris: C.N.R.S., 1975, pp. 287–334.

Painter, Nell Irvin. "Sojourner Truth in Feminist Abolitionism: Difference, Slavery and Memory." In *An Untrodden Path: Antislavery and Women's Political Culture*. Jean Fagan Yellin and John C. Van Horne (eds.). Ithaca: Cornell University Press, 1992.

Rohrbad, Peter. "St. Teresa of Avila." In *The Encyclopedia of Religion*. Mirca Eliade (ed.). vol. 14, pp. 405–6.

Stoeffler, F. Ernest. "Pietism." In *Encyclopedia of Religion*, vol. 14, pp. 324–26.

Underhill, Evelyn. "Medieval Mysticism." In *Cambridge Medieval History*. Cambridge, Eng., 1964, vol. 7, pp. 777–812.

Wessley, Stephen E. "The Thirteenth-Century Guglielmites: Salvation Through Women." In Baker, *Medieval Women*, pp. 289–303.

4. Hadewijch

Plassmann, J.O. (ed. and tr.). *Die Werke der Hadewych.* Hannover: Orient-Buchhandlung Heinz Lafaire, 1923.

Hart, Columba, O.S.B. "Hadewijch of Brabant." *American Benedictine Review*, vol. 13, no. 1, pp. 1–24.

5. Mechthild of Magdeburg

Oehl, Dr. Wilhelm (tr.). *Mechtild von Magdeburg, Das fliessende Licht der Gottheit, Deutsche Mystiker*, Band 2. Kempten u. München: Verlag der Jos. Kösel'schen Buchhandlung, 1922.

Morel, Gall (ed.). *Offenbarungen der Schwester Mechtild of Magdeburg oder Das Fliessende Licht der Gottheit.* Darmstadt: Wissenschaftliche Buchgesellschaft, 1963.

Menzies, Lucy (tr.). *The Revelations of Mechthild of Magdeburg (1210–1297) or The Flowing Light of the Godhead.* London: Longmans, Green, 1953.

6. Margery Kempe

Butler-Bowdon, W. (ed.). *The Book of Margery Kempe, 1436: A Modern Version.* London: Jonathan Cape, 1936.

Meech, Sanford B., and Hope Emily Allen (eds.). *The Book of Margery Kempe.* London: Oxford University Press, 1961.

Atkinson, Clarissa W. (ed.). *Mystic and Pilgrim: The Book and the World of Margery Kempe.* Ithaca: Cornell University Press, 1983.

7. Julian of Norwich

Colledge, Edmund, and James Walsh (eds.). *A Book of Showings to the Anchoress Julian of Norwich.* Toronto: Pontifical Institute of Medieval Studies, 1978.

Hudleston, Dom Roger (ed.). *Revelations of Divine Love Shewed to a devout Ankress, by name Julian of Norwich.* London: Burns Oates and Washbourne, 1927.

Børressen, Kari Elisabeth. "Christ Notre Mère, la theologie de Julienne de Norwich." *Mitteilungen und Forschungs-beiträge der Cusanus-Gesellschaft*, vol. 13 (1978), 320–29.

McIlwain, James. "The 'bodelye syekness' of Julian of Norwich." *Journal of Medieval History*, vol. 10, no. 3 (Sept. 1984), 167–80.

8. Hildegard of Bingen

OWN WORKS

Scivias. Illuminated manuscript copy of Rupertsberg Codex, Abbey St. Hildegard, Eibingen, Germany.

Hildegard von Bingen. *Briefwechsel*. Adelgundis Fürkötter (tr.). Salzburg: Otto Müeller Verlag, 1965.

Hildegard von Bingen. *Wisse die Wege: Scivias*. Maura Böckeler (tr.). Salzburg: Otto Müller Verlag, 1954.

Hildegard von Bingen. *Illuminations of Hildegard von Bingen*. With commentary by Matthew Fox. Santa Fe, N.M.: Bear & Co. 1985.

———. *Scivias by Hildegard of Bingen*. Bruce Hozeski (tr.). Santa Fe, N.M.: Bear & Co., 1986.

Hildegard von Bingen. *Heilkunde*. Heinrich Schipperges (ed.). Salzburg: Otto Müeller Verlag, 1957.

———. *Hildegard von Bingen: Welt und Mensch, Das Buch De Operatione Dei*. Salzburg: Otto Müeller Verlag, 1965.

Hildegard von Bingen, Naturkunde: Das Buch von dem inneren Wesen der verschiedenen Naturen in der Schöpfung. Peter Riethe, (tr.). Salzburg: Otto Müller Verlag, 1959.

———. *Hildegard von Bingen, Das Buch von den Steinen*. Salzburg: Otto Müller Verlag, 1979.

Letter, Hildegard of Bingen to Guibert of Gembloux (1175) as cited in Katharina Wilson. *Medieval Women Writers*. Athens: University of Georgia Press, 1984.

BOOKS

Führkötter, Adelgundis. *Hildegard von Bingen*. Salzburg: Otto Müller Verlag, 1972.

———. *Das Leben der Heiligen Hildegard von Bingen*. Düsseldorf: Patmos Verlag, 1968.

Lauter, Werner. *Hildegard-Bibliography: Wegweiser zur Hildegard-Literatur*. Alzey: Verlag der Rheinischen Druckwerkstätte, 1970.

Liebeschütz, Hans. *Das allegorische Weltbild der Heiligen Hildegard von Bingen*. Leipzig: Studien der Bibliothek Warburg 16, 1930.

Newman, Barbara. *Sister of Wisdom: St. Hildegard's Theology of the Feminine*. Berkeley: University of California Press, 1987.

Schmelzeis, J. *Das Leben und Wirken der heiligen Hildegardis nach den Quellen dargestellt . . . nebst einem Anhang Hildegardischer Lieder mit ihren Melodien.* Freiburg, 1879.

Schrader, Marianne. *Die Herkunft der heiligen Hildegard*. Neu bearbeitet von Adelgundis Führkötter. Mainz: Selbstverlag d. Gesellschaft für Mittelrheinische Kirchengeschichte, 1981.

——— and A. Führkötter. *Die Echtheit des Schrifttums der hl. Hildegard von Bingen*. Köln, 1956.

Widmer, Bertha. *Heilsordnung und Zeitgeschehen in der Mystik Hildegards von Bingen*. Basler Beiträge zur Geschichtswissenschaft, Band 52, Basel: Helbing und Lichtenhahn, 1955.

ARTICLES

Cadden, Joan. "It Takes All Kinds: Sexuality and Gender Differences in Hildegard of Bingen's 'Book of Compound Medicine.' " *Traditio*, vol. 40 (1984).

Pagel, Walter. "Hildegard von Bingen." In *Dictionary of Scientific Biography*. Charles Coulston Gillespie (ed.). New York: Charles Scribner's Sons, 1972, vol. 6, pp. 396–98.

Scholz, Bernhard W. "Hildegard von Bingen on the Nature of Woman." *American Benedictine Review*, vol. 31 (1980), 361–83.

9. Joanna Southcott

Seymour, Alice. *The Express: Life and Divine Writings of Joanna Southcott*. 2 vols. London: Simpkin, Marshall, Hamilton, Kent & Co., 1909.

Hopkins, James K. *A Woman to Deliver Her People: Joanna Southcott and English Millenarianism in an Era of Revolution*. Austin: University of Texas Press, 1982.

Whitley, W. T. "Southcottians." In *Encyclopedia of Religion and Ethics*, vol. 11, p. 756.

10. Shakers

PRIMARY SOURCES

Green, Calvin, and Seth Y. Wells (eds.). *A Summary View of the Millennial Church, or United Society of Believers, commonly called Shakers* . . . . Albany: C. Van Benthuysen, 1848.

[Lee, Ann.] *Testimonies of the Life, Character, Revelations of Mother Ann Lee, and the Elders with Her . . . collected from living Witnesses, in Union with the Church* (1888). New York: AMS Press, 1975.

SECONDARY SOURCES

Andrews, Edward D. *The People Called Shakers: A Search for the Perfect Society*. New York: Oxford University Press, 1953.

Melcher, Marguerite Fellows. *The Shaker Adventure*. Princeton: Princeton University Press, 1941.

Robinson, Charles Edson. *The Shakers and Their Homes: A Concise History of the United Society of Believers Called Shakers* (1893). Somerworth, N.H.: New Hampshire Publishing, 1976.

VII   RENAISSANCE AND REFORMATION

1. Primary Sources

[Agrippa] Nettesheim, Heinrich Agrippa Cornelius von. *The Glory of Women*. E. Fleetwood (trans). London: Printed for Robert Ibbitson, 1652.

[Anon.] *Here begynneth a litle boke named the Schole house of women: wherin every man may rede a goodly prays of the condicyons of women.* N.pl.: T. Peyt, 1541.

[Anger, Jane.] *Jane Anger, her Protection for Women. To defend them against the Scandalous Reportes of a late Surfeiting Lover, and all other Venerians that complaine so to be overcloyed with womens kindnesse.* N.pl.: R. Jones and T. Orwin, 1589. Reprinted in Katherine Usher Henderson and Barbara F. McManus (eds.). *Half Humankind: Contexts and Texts of the Controversy About Women in England,1540–1640.* Urbana: University of Illinois Press, 1985, pp. 172–88.

Billon, François de. *Le Fort inexpugnable de l'honneur du sexe feminin.* Paris: J. d'Allyer, 1555.

Foxe, John. *Acts and Monuments . . . of these latter and perillous dayes . . . [Foxe's Book of Martyrs].* London: John Day, 1563.

Knox, John. *The First Blast against the monstruous regiment of Women.* Geneva: J. Crespin, 1558.

Munda, Constantia. *The Worming of a Mad Dogge. . . .* London: Lawrence Hayes, 1617.

Sowernam, Ester. *Ester hath hang'd Haman . . . .* London: Nicholas Bourne, 1617. British Library.

Speght, Rachel. *A Mouzell for Melastomus, the Cynicall Bayter of, and foule mouthed Barker against Evah's Sex . . . .* London: N. Okes for T. Archer, 1617. British Library.

2. Secondary Sources

ANTHOLOGIES AND REFERENCE WORKS

Boxer, Marilyn, and Jean Quataert. *Connecting Spheres: Women in the Western World, 1500 to the Present.* New York: Oxford University Press, 1980.

Cocalis, Susan L. *The Defiant Muse: German Feminist Poems from the Middle Ages to the Present.* New York: Feminist Press, 1986.

Flores, Angel and Kate. *The Defiant Muse: Hispanic Feminist Poems from the Middle Ages to the Present.* New York: Feminist Press, 1986.

Hale, J. R. *A Concise Encyclopedia of the Italian Renaissance.* London: Thames and Hudson, 1981.

King, Margaret L., and Albert Rabil, Jr. *Her Immaculate Hand: Selected Work by and about the Women Humanists of Quattrocento Italy.* Binghamton, N.Y.: Medieval and Renaissance Texts and Studies, 1983.

Prior, Mary (ed.). *Women in English Society, 1500–1800.* London: Methuen, 1985.

Riemer, Eleanor S., and John C. Fout. *European Women: A Documentary History, 1789–1945.* New York: Schocken Books, 1980.

3. Books

Albistur, Maite, and Daniel Armogathe. *Histoire du feminism français du moyen âge à nos jours.* Paris: Des Femmes, 1977.

Bainton, Roland H. *Women of the Reformation in Germany and Italy*. Minneapolis: Augsburg Publishing House, 1971.

————. *Women of the Reformation in France and England*. Minneapolis: Augsburg Publishing House, 1973.

————. *Women of the Reformation: From Spain to Scandinavia*. Minneapolis: Augsburg Publishing House, 1977.

————. *The Age of the Reformation*. New York: Van Nostrand, 1956.

————. *The Reformation of the Sixteenth Century*. Boston: Beacon Press, 1952.

Boccaccio, Giovanni. *Concerning Famous Women*. Guido A. Guarino (tr.). New Brunswick: Rutgers University Press, 1963.

Brown, Judith C. *Immodest Acts: The Life of a Lesbian Nun in Renaissance Italy*. New York: Oxford University Press, 1986.

Burckhardt, Jacob. *The Civilization of the Renaissance in Italy* (1860). New York: New American Library, 1960.

[Calvin, John.] *Letters of John Calvin*. Jules Bonnet (ed.). Edinburgh: Thomas Constable, 1855.

Cannon, Mary Agnes. *The Education of Women During the Renaissance*. Washington, D.C.: National Capital Press, 1916.

Capellanus, Andreas. *The Art of Courtly Love*. Frederick W. Locke (ed.). New York: Frederick Ungar, 1957.

Castiglione, Baldassare. *The Book of the Courtier*. Charles Singleton (ed.). Garden City: Anchor Books, 1959.

Davis, Natalie Zemon. *Society and Culture in Early Modern France*. Stanford: Stanford University Press, 1965.

Ginzburg, Carlo. *The Cheese and the Worms: The Cosmos of a 16th Century Miller*. London: Henly, 1980.

[Helisenne de Crenne.] *A Renaissance Woman: Helisenne's Personal and Invective Letters*. Marianna M. Mustacchie and Paul J. Archambault (trs. and eds.). Syracuse: Syracuse University Press, 1986.

Irwin, Joyce L. *Womanhood in Radical Protestantism, 1525–1675*. New York: Edwin Mellen Press, 1979.

Jordan, Constance. *Renaissance Feminism: Literary Texts and Political Models*. Ithaca: Cornell University Press, 1990.

Kelso, Ruth. *Doctrine for the Lady of the Renaissance*. Urbana: University of Illinois Press, 1956.

[Kramer, Heinrich, and James Sprenger.] *The Malleus Maleficarum of Heinrich Kramer and James Sprenger* (1487). Montague Sommers (ed.). New York: Dover, 1971.

Kristeller, Paul Oskar. *Renaissance Thought: The Classic, Scholastic and Humanist Strains*. New York: Harper & Row, 1966.

Mattingly, Garrett. *Catherine of Aragon* (1941). New York: Vintage Books, 1960.

Ozment, Stephen. *When Fathers Ruled: Family Life in Reformation Europe*. Cambridge: Harvard University Press, 1983.

Powicke, Sir Maurice. *The Reformation in England*. London: Oxford University Press, 1941.

Putnam, Emily James. *The Lady*. Chicago: University of Chicago Press, 1970.

Richardson, Lula M. *The Forerunners of Feminism in French Literature of the Renaissance. Part I. From Christine de Pisan to Marie de Gournay*. Baltimore: Johns Hopkins University Press, 1929.

Shepherd, Simon (ed.). *The Women's Sharp Revenge: Five Women's Pamphlets from the Renaissance.* London: Fourth Estate, 1985.

Smith, Preserved. *The Social Background of the Reformation.* New York: Collier Books, 1962.

Stone, Lawrence. *The Family, Sex and Marriage in England, 1500–1800.* New York: Harper, 1977.

Woodward, William Harrison. *Studies in Education During the Age of the Renaissance: 1400–1600.* Cambridge: Cambridge University Press, 1924.

————. *Vittorino da Feltre and Other Humanist Educators.* New York: Teachers College Publications, 1963.

4. Articles

Bainton, Roland H. "Learned Women in the Europe of the Sixteenth Century." In Labalme, *Beyond Their Sex,* pp. 117–20.

Beilin, Elaine V. "Anne Askew's Self-Portrait in *Examinations 77–91.*" In Margaret Patterson Hannay (ed.). *Silent But for the Word: Tudor Women as Patrons, Translators and Writers of Religious Works.* Kent, Ohio: Kent State University Press, 1985.

De Tolnay, Charles. "Sofonisba Anguissola and Her Relations with Michelangelo." *Journal of the Walters Art Gallery,* no. 4 (1941), 115–19.

Green, Lowell C. "The Education of Women in the Reformation." *History of Education Quarterly,* vol. 19 (Spring 1979), 93–116.

Hess, Ursula. "Latin Dialogue and Learned Partnership: Women as Humanist Models in Germany: 1500–1550." In Brinker-Gabler, *Deutsche Literatur von Frauen,* Erster Band, pp. 113–48.

Horowitz, Maryanne Cline. "The Woman Question in Renaissance Texts." *History of European Ideas,* vol. 8, nos. 4/5 (1987), 587–95.

King, Margaret. "Book-lined Cells: Women and Humanism in the Early Italian Renaissance." In Labalme, *Beyond Their Sex,* pp. 72–73.

————. "The Religious Retreat of Isotta Nogarola (1418–66); Sexism and Its Consequences in the Fifteenth Century." *SIGNS,* vol. 3, no. 4 (Summer 1978), 807–22, 820–22.

————. "Thwarted Ambitions: Six Learned Women of the Italian Renaissance." *Soundings: An Interdisciplinary Journal,* vol. 59 (1976), 280–304.

Martines, Lauro. "A Way of Looking at Renaissance Florence." *Journal of Medieval and Renaissance Studies,* vol. 4, no. 1 (Spring 1974), 15–29.

Norman, Sr. Marion, I.B.V.M. "A Woman for All Seasons: Mary Ward (1585–1645), Renaissance Pioneer of Women's Education." *Paedagogica Historica,* vol. 23, no. 1 (1983), 125–43.

Potter, Mary. "Gender Equality and Gender Hierarchy in Calvin's Theology." *SIGNS,* vol. 11, no. 4 (Summer 1986), 725–39.

Travitsky, Betty. "The Lady Doth Protest: Protest in the Popular Writings of Renaissance Englishwomen." *English Literary Renaissance,* vol. 14 (Autumn 1984), 255–83.

5. Marguerite de Navarre

Marguerite de Navarre. *Marguerites de la Marguerite des Princesses, Trésillustre Rayne de Navarre* (1547). New York: Johnson Reprint, 1970.

――――. *The Heptameron of Margaret, Queen of Navarre*. 5 vols. Walter F. Kelly (ed. and tr.). London, no date.

Sommers, Paula. "The Mirror and Its Reflections: Marguerite de Navarre's Biblical Feminism." *Tulsa Studies in Women's Literature*, vol. 5, no. 1 (Spring 1986).

Wade, Claire Lynch. "Marguerite de Navarre, 'Les Prisons'." New York: Peter Lang, 1989, pp. i–xiii.

6. Louise Labé

[Labé, Louise.] *Louise Labé: Oeuvres Complètes*. Enzo Giudici (ed.). Geneva: Droz, 1981.

Guillot, Gerard. *Louise Labé*. Edition Seghers, 1962.

Feugère, M. Leon. *Les Femmes Poètes au XVIᵉ siècle*. . . . Paris: Didier et Cie, 1860.

Larsen, Anne R. "Louise Labé's *Debat de Folie and d'Amour:* Feminism and the Defense of Learning." *Tulsa Studies in Women's Literature*, vol. 2, no.1 (Spring 1983), 43–55.

VIII SEVENTEENTH CENTURY

1. Primary Sources

[Anon.] *Swetman: The Woman-hater* . . . . London: R. Meighen, 1620. British Library.

[Anon.] *La Femme généreuse*. . . . Paris: François Piot, 1643.

Arnold, Gottfried Arnold. *Unparteyische Kirchen- und Ketzerhistorie, vom Anfang des Neuen Testaments bis auf das Jahr Christi 1688*. Frankfurt am Main: T. Fritschens Erben, 1729.

Ballard, George. *Memoirs of Several Ladies of Great Britain*. Oxford: W. Jackson, 1752. British Library.

Behn, Aphra. *The Histories and Novels of the Late Ingenious Mrs. Behn: In One Volume*. London: S. Briscoe, 1696.

Du Bosc, Jacques. *The Compleat Woman*. N.N. (trans.). London: T. Harper and R. Hodgkinson, 1639.

[Eugenia]. *The Female Advocate* . . . *Reflections on a late Rude and Disingenuous Discourse delivered by Mr. John Sprint in a Sermon of a Wedding May 11, at Sherburn in Dorsetshire, 1699*. London: Andrew Bell, 1700.

Fell, Margaret. *Woman's Speaking Justified, Proved and Allowed of by the Scriptures* . . . (1667). The Augustan Reprint Society, No. 194. Los Angeles: William Andrews Clark Memorial Library, University of California, 1979.

Heywood, Thomas. *The Exemplary Lives and Memorable Acts of Nine of the Most Worthy Women of the World*. London: Richard Rayston, 1640.

Makin, Bathsua. *An Essay to Revive the Antient Education of Gentlewomen, in Reli-*

gion, Manners, Arts & Tongues . . . . (1673). Augustan Reprint Society, No. 202. Los Angeles: William Andrews Clark Memorial Library, 1980.

[Manley, Mary de La Riviere.] *Letters written by Mrs. Manley* . . . . London: London and Westminster, 1696.

Masham, Damaris. *A Discourse Concerning the Love of God.* London: Awnsham and John Churchill, 1696.

Poulain de la Barre, François. *De l'égalité des deux sexes.* Paris, 1673.

Speght, Rachel. *Mortalities Memorandum with a Dreame Prefixed* . . . . London: Edward Griffin, 1621. British Library.

———. *A Mouzell for Melastomus, the Cynicall Bayter of, and foule mouthed Barker against Evah's Sex* . . . . London: Thomas Archer, 1617. British Library.

Swetnam, Joseph. *The Araignment of lewd, idle, froward and unconstant women: Or the vanitie of them, choose you whether.* London: T. Archer, 1615. British Library.

Wolley, Hannah. *The Accomplished Lady's Delight* (1677).

2. Reference Works and Anthologies

Mahl, Mary R., and Helene Koon (eds.). *The Female Spectator: English Women Writers Before 1800.* Bloomington: Indiana University Press, 1977.

Marholz, Werner (ed.). *Der Deutsche Pietismus: Eine Auswahl von Zeugnissen, Urkunden und Bekenntnissen aus dem 17. 18. und 19. Jahrhundert.* Berlin: Furche-Verlag, 1921.

Spender, Dale, and Janet Todd. *British Women Writers: An Anthology from the Fourteenth Century to the Present.* New York: Peter Bedrick, 1989.

Tattlewell, Mary, and Joan Hit-him-home. *The Women's Sharp Revenge* (1640). In Henderson and McManus, *Half Humankind,* pp. 305–25.

Thomasius, Jacobus, and Johannes Sauerbrei. *De fœminarum eruditione* (1617–76). In *Das Wohlgelahrte Frauenzimmer.* Gössmann (ed.). Archiv für Philosophiegeschichtliche Frauenforschung, vol. 1. München: Iudicium, 1984, pp. 99–117.

Westerbrook, Arlen G. R., and Perry D. Westerbrook (eds.). *The Writing Women of New England, 1630–1900: An Anthology.* Metuchen, N.J.: Scarecrow Press, 1982.

3. Books

Becker-Cantarino, Barbara. *Der lange Weg zur Mündigkeit: Frauen und Literatur in Deutschland von 1500 bis 1800.* München: Deutscher Taschenbuch Verlag, 1989.

Behn, Aphra. *Works.* Montague Summers (ed.). 6 vols. London: William Heinemann, 1915.

Frauenlob, Johan. *Die Lobwuerdige Gesellschaft der Gelehrten Weiber* (1631–1633). In *Eva, Gottes Meisterwerk.* Gössman (ed.). Archive für Philosophiegeschichtliche Frauenforschung, vol. 2. München: Iudicium, 1985, pp. 52–83.

Fyge, Sarah Field Egerton. *The Female Advocate, or, An Answer to a Late Satyr against the Pride, Lust and Inconstancy, Etc. of Woman* (1687). As cited in Ferguson, *First Feminists,* pp. 154–55.

[Glückel of Hameln.] *The Memoirs of Glückel of Hameln*. Marvin Lowenthal (trans.). New York: Schocken Books, 1977.

Hobby, Elaine. *Virtue of Necessity: English Women's Writing, 1649–88*. Ann Arbor: University of Michigan, 1992.

[Hoyers, Anna Ovena.] *Anna Ovena Hoyers, Geistliche und Weltliche Poemata* (1650). Barbara Becker-Cantarino (ed.). Tübingen: Niemeyer, 1986.

Lanyer, Aemilia. *Salve Deus Rex Judaeorum*. As cited in Hannay, *Silent But for . . .* , pp. 94–96; 102–5, 213.

Locke, John. *Two Treatises of Civil Government*. 2nd ed. Peter Laslett (ed.). Cambridge: Cambridge University Press, 1967.

Lougee, Carolyn C. *Le Paradis des femmes: Women, Salons and Social Stratification in Seventeenth-Century France*. Princeton: Princeton University Press, 1976.

Maclean, Ian. *Woman Triumphant: Feminism in French Literature: 1610–1652*. Oxford: Clarendon Press, 1977.

Reynolds, Myra. *The Learned Lady in England, 1650–1760*. Boston: Houghton Mifflin, 1920.

Richards, S.A., M.A. *Feminist Writers of the Seventeenth Century*. London: David Nutt, 1914.

Rousseau, Jean Jacques. *Émile* (1763). Barbara Boxley (tr.). London: J.M.Dent, 1974.

Smith, Hilda. *Reason's Disciples: Seventeenth-Century English Feminists*. Urbana: University of Illinois Press, 1982.

Wallas, Ada. *Before the Bluestockings*. London: Allen & Unwin, 1929.

4. Articles

Becker-Cantarino, Barbara. "Women in the Religious Wars: Official Letters, Songs and Occasional Writings." In Brinker-Gabler. *Deutsche Literatur von Frauen; Erster Band*.

Blackwell, Jeannine. "Heartfelt Conversations with God: Confessions of German Pietist Women in the 17th and 18th Centuries." In Brinker-Gabler, *ibid.*, pp. 264–89.

Brandes, Ute. "Studierstube, Dichterklub, Hofgesellschaft: Kreativität und kultureller Rahmen weiblicher Erzählkunst im Barock." In Brinker-Gabler, *ibid.*, pp. 222–64.

Brink, J. R. "Bathsua Makin: Scholar and Educator of the Seventeenth Century." *International Journal of Women's Studies* (1978), 717–26.

Crandall, Coryl. "The Cultural Implications of the Swetnam Anti-Feminist Controversy in the Seventeenth Century." *Journal of Popular Culture*, vol. 2, no. 1 (Summer 1968), 136–48.

Gardiner, Judith Kegan. "Aphra Behn: Sexuality and Self-Respect." *Women's Studies*, vol. 7, nos. 1/2 (1980), 67–78.

Hageman, Elizabeth H., and Josephine A. Roberts. "Recent Studies in Women Writers of Tudor England." *English Literary Renaissance*, vol. 14 (Autumn 1984), 409–39.

Huber, Elaine C. " 'A Woman Must Not Speak': Quaker Women in the English Left Wing." In Ruether and McLaughlin, *Women of Spirit*, pp. 154–81.

Irwin, Joyce. "Anna Maria von Schurman: From Feminism to Pietism," *Church History*, vol. 46 (1977), 48–62.

Norman, Sr. Marion, I.B.V.M. "A Woman for All Seasons: Mary Ward (1585–1645), Renaissance Pioneer of Women's Education." *Paedagogica Historica*, vol. 23, no. 1 (1983), 125–43.

Notestein, Wallace. "The English Woman, 1580–1650." In *Studies in Social History*. J.H. Plumb (ed.). London: Longmans, Green, 1955.

Roodenburg, Herman W. "The Autobiography of Isabella De Moerloose: Sex, Child-rearing, and Popular Belief in Seventeeth Century Holland." *Journal of Social History*, vol. 18, no. 4 (Summer 1985), 517–40.

Sanders, Ruth H. "A Little Detour: The Literary Creation of Luise Gottsched." In Barbara Becker-Cantarino, *Die Frau . . .* , pp. 170–94.

Seidel, Michael. "Poulain de la Barre's *The Woman as Good as the Man*." *Journal of the History of Ideas*, vol. 35, no. 3 (July-Sept. 1974), 499–508.

Shapiro, Susan C. "Feminists in Elizabethan England." *History Today*, vol. 27 (Nov. 1977), 703–11.

Thomas, Keith. "Women and the Civil War Sects." *Past and Present*, vol. 13 (April 1958), 42–62.

5. Mary Astell

OWN WORKS

Astell, Mary. *Some Reflections upon Marriage*. London: Wm. Parker, 1730.

———. *The Christian Religion, As Profess'd by a Daughter of the Church of England*. London: R. Wilkin, 1705.

———. *A Serious Proposal to the Ladies*. London: R. Wilkin, 1694.

[———.] *The Christian Religion . . . .* London: R. Wilkin, 1705.

[———.] *An Essay in Defence of the Female Sex . . . .* London: Roger and Wilkinson, 1696.

———, and John Norris. *Letters Concerning the Love of God, Between the Author of the Proposal to the Ladies and Mr. John Norris*. London: John Norris, 1695.

BOOKS

Perry, Ruth. *The Celebrated Mary Astell: An Early English Feminist*. Chicago: University of Chicago Press, 1986.

6. Anne Bradstreet

Bradstreet, Anne. "To My Dear Children." In *The Works of Anne Bradstreet*. Jeannine Hensley (ed.). Cambridge, Mass.: Belknap Press, 1967.

[———.] *Correspondence from the Tenth Muse Lately Sprung up in America or Severall Poems, compiled with great Variety of Wit . . . By a Gentlewoman in those parts. . . .* London: Stephen Bowtell, 1650.

———. *The Works of Anne Bradstreet in Prose Verse*. John Harvard Ellis (ed.). Charlestown, Mass.: Abram E. Cutter, 1867.

————. *The Poems of Mrs. Anne Bradstreet Together with her Prose Remains* (1897). As cited in *The Writing Women of New England, 1630–1900: An Anthology.* Arlen G. R. Westerbrook and Perry D. Westerbrook (eds.). Metuchen, N.J.: Scarecrow Press, 1982.

Campbell, Helen S. *Anne Bradstreet and Her Time.* Boston, 1891.

7. Margaret Cavendish, Duchess of Newcastle

Cavendish, Margaret, Duchess of Newcastle. *A True Relation of My Birth, Breeding and Life.* Originally published in *Poems, and Fancies: Written by the Right Honourable, the Lady Margaret Countesse of Newcastle.* London: J. Martin, 1653.

————. *A True Relation of the Birth, Breeding, and Life of Margaret Cavendish written by herself with critical Preface by Sir Egerton Brydges, M.P.* Kent: Johnson and Warwick, 1814.

————. *Philosophical Letters . . . .* London, 1664.

————. *The Philosophical and Physical Opinions Written by her Excellency, the Lady Marchioness of Newcastle.* London: F. Martin and F. Aldestrye, 1655. British Library.

————. *The Life of William Cavendish . . . .* (1667). C.H. Firth (ed.). London: George Routledge and Sons, 1857.

Grant, Douglas. *Margaret the First: Biography of Margaret Cavendish, Duchess of Newcastle, 1623–1673.* London: Rupert Hart-Davis, 1957.

8. Mary Lee (Lady Chudleigh)

[Lady Chudleigh.] *The Ladies Defence: or, The Bride-Woman's Counsellor Answered: A Poem in a Dialogue between Sir John Brute, Sir Wm. Loveall, Melissa and a Parson.* London: Bernard Lintott, 1709.

————. *Poems on Several Occasions . . . .* London: Bernard Lintott, 1709.

9. Marie le Jars de Gournay

Gournay, Marie de. *Égalité des hommes et des femmes: 1622.* Paris: Côte-femmes editions, 1989.

BOOKS

Ilsley, Marjorie Henry. *A Daughter of the Renaissance: Marie le Jars de Gournay; Her Life and Works.* The Hague: Mouton, 1963.

Insdorf, Cecil. *Montaigne and Feminism.* Chapel Hill: Studies in the Romance Languages and Literatures, 1977.

Schiff, Mario. *La Fille d'alliance de Montaigne, Marie de Gournay.* Paris: Champion, 1910.

ARTICLES

Michel, Pierre. "Un apôtre du feminism au XVIIe siècle: Mademoiselle de Gournay." *Bulletin de la Société des Amis de Montaigne*, quatrième serie, no. 27 (Oct.-Dec. 1971), 55–58.

Morand, Jean. "Marie le Jars de Gournay: La fille d'alliance de Montaigne." *Bulletin de la Société des Amis de Montaigne*, quatrième serie, no. 27 (Oct.-Dec., 1971), 45–54.

Horowitz, Maryanne Cline. "Marie de Gournay, Editor of the *Essais* of Michel de Montaigne: A Case-Study in Mentor-Protégée Friendship." *The Sixteenth Century Journal*, vol. 17, no. 3 (Fall 1986), 271–84.

IX EIGHTEENTH CENTURY

1. Primary Sources

[Anon.] *The Rise and Progress of the Young Ladies' Academy of Philadelphia . . . .* Philadelphia: Stewart and Cochran, 1794.

Duncombe, John. *The Feminead, A Poem.* Augustan Reprint Society, No. 207. Los Angeles: William Andrews Clark Memorial Library, 1981.

More, Hannah. *Strictures on the Modern System of Female Education with a View to the Principles and Conduct Prevalent Among Women of Rank and Fortune.* Philadelphia: Thomas Dobson, 1800.

Scott, Mary. *The Female Advocate; A Poem. Occasioned by Reading Mr. Duncombe's Feminead* (1774). Augustan Reprint Society, No. 224. Los Angeles: William Andrews Clark Memorial Library, 1984.

[Sophia.] *Woman not Inferior . . . .* London: Printed for John Hawkins, 1739. British Library.

———. *Women's Superior Excellence Over Man or a Reply by Sophia. A Person of Quality.* London: J. Robinson, 1743. British Library.

2. Reference Works and Anthologies

Jacobs, Eva, *et al.* (eds.). *Woman and Society in Eighteenth-Century France: Essays in Honour of John Stephenson Spink.* London: Athlone Press, 1979.

Lonsdale, Roger (ed.). *Eighteenth-Century Women Poets.* Oxford and New York: Oxford University Press, 1989.

[Wichmann, Christian August.] *Geschichte berühmter Frauenzimmer. Nach alphabetischer Ordnung aus alten und neuen in- und ausländischen Geschichtssammlungen und Wörterbüchern zusammengetragen.* 3 vols. Leipzig, 1772–75.

3. Books

Austen, Jane. *Selected Letters, 1796–1817.* R.W. Chapman (ed.) and Marilyn Butler (intro.). Oxford: Oxford University Press, 1985.

Benson, Mary S. *Women in Eighteenth-Century America: A Study of Opinion and Social Usage* (1935). New York: AMS Press, 1976.

Brown, Alice. *The Eighteenth-Century Feminist Mind*. Brighton, Sussex: Harvester Press, 1987.

Butterfield, L.H., et al. (eds.). *The Book of Abigail and John: Selected Letters of the Adams Family, 1762–1784*. Cambridge: Harvard University Press, 1975.

Collier, Mary. *Poems, on Several Occasions*. Winchester: Printed for the author, 1762. As cited in Ferguson, *First Feminists*, pp. 258–65.

Dexter, Elizabeth Anthony. *Colonial Women of Affairs*. Boston: Houghton Mifflin, 1924.

Earle, Alice. *Child Life in Colonial Days*. New York: Macmillan, 1899.

———. *Colonial Dames and Good Wives*. Boston: Houghton Mifflin, 1895.

Ellet, Elizabeth. *Domestic History of the American Revolution*. New York: Baker & Scribner, 1850.

———. *The Women of the American Revolution*. 3 vols. New York: Baker & Scribner, 1848–50.

Halkett, Anne. *The Autobiography of Anne Lady Halkett*. John Gough Nichols (ed.). London: Camden Society, 1895.

[Hays, Mary.] *The Love-Letters of Mary Hays*. A.F. Wedd (ed.). London: Methuen, 1925.

Kerber, Linda. *Women of the Republic: Intellect and Ideology in Revolutionary America*. Chapel Hill: University of North Carolina Press, 1980.

Levy, Darline Gay, Harriet Branson Applewhite and Mary Durham Johnson. *Women in Revolutionary Paris, 1789–1795*. Urbana: University of Illinois Press, 1979.

Myers, Sylvia Harcstark. *The Bluestocking Circle: Women, Friendship, and the Life of the Mind in Eighteenth-Century England*. Oxford: Clarendon Press, 1990.

Norton, Mary Beth. *Liberty's Daughters: The Revolutionary Experience of American Women, 1750–1800*. Boston: Little, Brown, 1980.

Poovey, Mary. *The Proper Lady and the Woman Writer: Ideology as Style in the Works of Mary Wollstonecraft, Mary Shelley, and Jane Austen*. Chicago: University of Chicago Press, 1984.

Rogers, Katherine M. *Feminism in Eighteenth-Century England*. Urbana: University of Illinois Press, 1982.

Spruill, Julia Cherry. *Women's Life and Work in the Southern Colonies* (1938). New York: W.W. Norton, 1972.

Ulrich, Laurel Thatcher. *Good Wives: Images and Reality in the Lives of Women in Northern New England, 1650–1750*. New York: Oxford University Press, 1983.

4. Articles

Brown, Irene Q. "Domesticity, Feminism, and Friendship: Female Aristocratic Culture and Marriage in England, 1660–1760." *Journal of Family History* (Winter 1982), pp. 406–24.

Fox-Genovese, Elizabeth. "Women and the Enlightenment." In Bridenthal et al., *Becoming Visible*, pp. 251–77.

Goodman, Dena. "Enlightenment Salons: The Convergence of Female and Philosophic Ambitions." *Eighteenth-Century Studies*, vol. 22, no. 3 (Spring 1989), 329–50.

Goodman, Dena. "Governing the Republic of Letters: The Politics of Culture in the French Enlightenment." *History of European Ideas*, vol. 13, no. 3 (1991), 183–99.

Hertz, Deborah. "Salonières and Literary Women in Late Eighteenth-Century Berlin." *New German Critique*, no. 14 (Spring 1978), 97–108.

Kerber, Linda. "The Republican Mother: Women and the Enlightenment—an American Perspective." *American Quarterly*, vol. 28 (Summer 1976), 187–205.

Myers, Mitzi. "Domesticating Minerva: Bathsua Makin's 'Curious' Argument for Women's Education." *Studies in Eighteenth Century Culture*. American Society for Eighteenth Century Studies. Madison: University of Wisconsin Press, 1985, pp. 173–92.

Perry, Ruth. "Colonizing the Breast: Sexuality and Maternity in Eighteenth Century England." *Journal of the History of Sexuality*, vol. 2, no. 2 (1991), 204–34.

———. "Radical Doubt and the Liberation of Women." *Eighteenth Century Studies*, vol. 18, no. 4 (Summer 1985), pp. 472–93.

———. "Introduction." In Ruth Perry (ed.). George Ballard. *Memoirs of Several Ladies of Great Britain. . . .* Detroit: Wayne State University Press, 1985.

———. "George Ballard's Biographies of Learned Ladies." In *Biography in the Eighteenth Century*. J.D. Browning (ed.). New York: Garland Publishing, 1980, pp. 85–111.

5. Sor Juana de la Cruz

OWN WORKS

[Sor Juana de la Cruz.] *A Sor Juana Anthology*. Alan Trueblood (tr.). Cambridge: Harvard University Press, 1988.

[———.] *A Woman of Genius: The Intellectual Autobiography of Sor Juana Ines de la Cruz*. Margaret Sayers Peden (ed.). Salisbury, Conn.: Lime Rock Press, 1982.

[———.] In Mary Hays. *Female Biography*. London, 1803, pp. 440–43.

BOOKS

Paz, Octavio. *Sor Juana: or the Traps of Faith*. Margaret Peden (tr.). Cambridge: Harvard University Press, 1988.

ARTICLES

Flynn, Gerard. "Sor Juana Ines de la Cruz: Mexico's Tenth Muse." In Brink, *Female Scholars*, pp. 119–36.

Pallister, Janis L. "A Note on Sor Juana de la Cruz," *Women and Literature*. vol. 7, no. 2 (Spring 1979), 42–46.

Scott, Nina M. " 'If you are not pleased to favor me, put me out of your mind. . .': Gender and Authority in Sor Juana Ines de la Cruz." *Women's Studies International Forum*, vol. 2, no. 5 (1988), 429–37.

Ward, Marilynn I. "The Feminist Crisis of Sor Juana Ines de la Cruz." *International Journal of Women's Studies*, vol. 1 (1978), 475–81.

6. Elizabeth Elstob

OWN WORKS

Elstob, Elizabeth. *An English-Saxon Homily on the Birth-day of St. Gregory* (1709). Landsdowne Manuscripts, British Library. A printed edition appeared in 1839 (Leicester: Wm. Pickering).
————. *The Rudiments of Grammar for the English-Saxon Tongue.* London: W. Bowyer and C. King, 1715.

ARTICLES

Reynolds, Myra. "Elizabeth Elstob, the Saxon Nymph." In Brink, *Female Scholars*, pp. 137–60.

7. Anna Luisa Karsch

Karsch, Anna Luisa. *Auserlesene Gedichte* (1764). Stuttgart: J. B. Metzler, 1966.
Klenke, E.L.V., geb. Karschin (ed.). *Gedichte von Anna Louisa Karsch (in), geb. Duerbach.* Berlin: Friedrich Maurer, 1797.

8. Catharine Macaulay

Macaulay, Catharine. *Letters on Education, With Observations on Religious and Metaphysical Subjects* (1790). Gina Luria (ed.). New York: Garland, 1974.

ARTICLES

Donnelly, Lucy Martin. "The Celebrated Mrs. Macaulay." *William and Mary Quarterly*, 3rd. ser., vol. 6, no. 2 (April 1949), 174–207.
Hill, Bridget and Christopher. "Catharine Macaulay and the Seventeenth Century." *Welsh History Review*, nos. 3/4 (Dec. 1967), 381–402.
Withey, Lynne E. "Catharine Macaulay and the Uses of History: Ancient Rights, Perfectionism, and Propaganda." *Journal of British Studies*, vol. 16, no. 1 (Fall 1976), 59–83.

9. Judith Sargent Murray

[Judith Sargent Murray.] Constantia. "Desultory Thoughts upon the Utility of encouraging a degree of Self-Complacency, especially in FEMALE BOSOMS." *The Gentleman and Lady's Town and Country Magazine* (Oct. 1784), 251–53.

———. *The Gleaner: A Miscellaneous Production in Three Volumes.* Boston: I.Thomas and E. T. Andrews, 1798.

———. "On the Equality of the Sexes" (1790). As cited in *The Feminist Papers from Adams to Beauvoir.* Alice S. Rossi (ed.). New York: Bantam Books, 1974.

———. *Some Deductions from the System Promulgated in the Page of Divine Revelation . . . .* Portsmouth, N. H., 1782.

10. Mary Wollstonecraft

Wollstonecraft, Mary. *A Vindication of the Rights of Woman with Strictures on Political and Moral Subjects* (1792). New York: Garland, 1974.

———. *Mary: A Fiction* (1788). New York: Schocken Books, 1977.

BOOKS

Flexner, Eleanor, *Mary Wollstonecraft.* New York: Coward- McCann, 1972.

George, Margaret *One Woman's Situation: A Study of Mary Wollstonecraft.* Urbana: University of Illinois Press , 1970.

Sapiro, Virginia. *A Vindication of Political Virtue: The Political Theory of Mary Wollstonecraft.* Chicago: University of Chicago Press, 1992.

X NINETEENTH CENTURY

1. Primary Sources

MANUSCRIPTS AND RECORDS

Journal of Marian Louise Moore. Western Reserve Historical Society, Cleveland, Ohio.

Program of Women's National Liberal Union Convention. Feb. 24–25, 1890, Washington, D.C.

Resolutions, Ohio Woman's Rights Convention. Held April 19 and 20, 1850.

BOOKS

[Alcott, Louisa May.] *Louisa May Alcott: Her Life, Letters, and Journals.* Ednah D. Cheney (ed.). Boston: Roberts Brothers, 1889.

[———.] *Recollections of Louisa May Alcott . . . .* Mary S. Porter (ed.). Boston, 1893.

Andrews, William L. (ed.). *Sisters of the Spirit: Three Black Women's Autobiographies of the Nineteenth Century.* Bloomington: Indiana University Press, 1986.

[Anthony, Susan B.] Harper, Ida H. *The Life and Work of Susan B. Anthony.* 3 vols. Indianapolis: Hollenbeck Press, 1898–1908.

Arnim, Bettina von. *Werke und Briefe.* Gustav Konrad (ed.). 5 vols. Frechen/Köln: Bartmann-Verlag, 1959–61.

[———.] *Bettina von Arnim: Eine weibliche Sozialbiographie aus dem 19ten Jahrhundert kommentiert und zusammengestellt aus Briefromanen und Dokumenten.* Gisela Dischner (ed.). Berlin: Verlag Klaus Wagenbach, 1977.

Bolton, Sarah Knowles. *Famous Types of Womanhood.* New York: Thomas Y. Crowell, 1892.

Bradford, Sarah. *Harriet Tubman, the Moses of Her People* (1869). Secaucus, N.J.: Citadel Press, 1974.

[Brentano, Sophie Mereau.] *Briefwechsel zwischen Clemens Brentano und Sophie Mereau.* Heinz Amelung (ed.). Leipzig: Insel, 1908.

Browning, Elizabeth Barrett. *Aurora Leigh: A Poem* (1856). Chicago: Academy Chicago Publishers, 1979.

Child, Lydia Maria. *Brief History of the Condition of Women in Various Ages and Nations,* Ladies Family Library. Boston: John Allen & Co., 1835.

[Cooper, Anna Julia.] *A Voice from the South by a Black Woman from the South.* Xenia, Ohio: The Aldine Printing House, 1892.

Coppin, Fannie Jackson. *Reminiscences of School Life.* Philadelphia: African Methodist Episcopal Book Concern, 1913.

Croly, Jane Cunningham. *History of the Woman's Club Movement in America.* New York: H. G. Allen, 1898.

Ellet, Elizabeth. *Pioneer Women of the West.* New York: C. Scribner, 1852.

Fairbanks, Mrs. A. W. (ed.). *Mrs. Emma Willard and Her Pupils, or Fifty Years of the Troy Female Seminary, 1822–1872.* New York: Mrs. Russell Sage, 1898.

Gage, Matilda Joslyn. *Woman, Church and State: The Original Exposé of Male Collaboration Against the Female Sex* (1893). Sally Roesch Wagner (ed.). Watertown, Mass.: Persephone Press, 1980.

Grimké, Charlotte Forten. *The Journals of Charlotte Forten Grimké.* Brenda Stevenson (ed.). Schomburg Library of Nineteenth-Century Black Women Writers. New York: Oxford University Press, 1988.

[Günderrode, Karoline von.] *Karoline von Günderrode: Der Schatten eines Traumes; Gedichte, Prosa, Briefe, Zeugnisse von Zeitgenossen.* Christa Wolf (ed.). Darmstadt: Luchterhand, 1981.

Hale, Sarah Josepha. *Woman's Record or Sketches of Distinguished Women from "the Beginning" till A.D. 1850.* New York: Harper, 1853.

Hanaford, Phebe A. *Daughters of America, or Women of the Century.* Augusta, Maine: True, 1882.

Hays, Mary. *Female Biography or Memoirs of Illustrious and Celebrated Women of All Ages and Countries.* London: Richard Phillips, 1803.

Hill, Georgiana. *Women in English Life.* 2 vols. London: Bentley & Son, 1896.

Hunt, Harriot K., M.D. *Glances and Glimpses; or Fifty Years Social Including Twenty Years Professional Life.* Boston: John P. Jewett Co., 1856.

[Harriet A. Jacobs.] *Incidents in the Life of a Slave Girl Written by Herself* (1861). L.M. Child (ed.). Jean Fagan Yellin (ed.). Cambridge: Harvard University Press, 1987.

Jaeckel, Günter (ed.). *Das Volk Braucht Licht: Frauen zur Zeit des Aufbruchs, 1790–1848, in ihren Briefen.* Darmstadt: Agora, 1970.

Lyon, Mary. *The Power of Christian Benevolence Illustrated in the Life and Labors of Mary Lyon.* New York: American Tract Society, 1858.

[————.] *Recollections of Mary Lyon with Selections from Her Instructions to the Pupils of Mt. Holyoke Female Seminary.* Fidela Fiske (ed.). Boston: American Tract Society, 1866.

Livermore, Mary A. *My Story of the War: A Woman's Narrative of Four Years Personal Experience . . . .* Hartford, Conn.: A.D. Worthington, 1889.

[Mill, John Stuart.] *The Autobiography of John Stuart Mill.* John Jacob Coss (ed.). New York: Columbia University Press, 1924.

[————.] *Essays on Sex Equality: John Stuart Mill and Harriet Taylor Mill.* Alice Rossi (ed.). Chicago: University of Chicago Press, 1970.

[Mitchell, Maria.] *Maria Mitchell: Life, Letters and Journals.* Phebe M. Kendall (ed.). Boston: Lee and Shepard, 1896.

[Mott, James and Lucretia.] *Life and Letters of James and Lucretia Mott.* Anna D. Hallowell (ed.). Boston: Houghton Mifflin, 1884.

Norton, The Honorable Mrs. [Caroline Elizabeth]. *Lost and Saved.* 3 vols. London: Hurst and Blackett, 1863.

Otto, Louise. *Merkwürdige und geheimnisvolle Frauen.* Leipzig, 1868.

————. *Einflussreiche Frauen aus dem Volke.* Leipzig, 1869.

Roberts, Mary. *Select Female Biography: Comprising Memoirs of Eminent British Ladies.* London: Harvey & Darton, 1829.

[Smith, Julia.] *The Holy Bible Containing the Old and New Testaments: Translated Literally from the Original Tongues.* Hartford: American Publishing Co., 1876.

Stowe, Harriet Beecher. *Woman in Sacred History: A Series of Sketches Drawn from Scriptural, Historical and Legendary Sources.* New York: J.B. Ford, 1874.

————, *et al. Our Famous Women . . . .* Hartford, Conn.: A.D. Worthington, 1884.

[————.] *Life and Letters of Harriet Beecher Stowe.* Annie A. Fields (ed.). Boston, 1897.

Thompson, William. *Appeal of One-Half the Human Race, Women, against the Pretensions of the other Half, Men, to retain them in political and thence in civil and domestic Slavery: in Reply to a paragraph of Mr. Mill's celebrated "Article on Government"* (1825).

Trial: Norton v. Viscount Melbourne, for CRIM.CON. London: William Marshall, 1836.

Williams, Jane. *The Literary Women of England.* London, 1861.

Harriet E. Wilson. *Our Nig; or, Sketches from the Life of a Free Black . . .* (1859). New York: Vintage Books, 1983.

PERIODICALS

"Address of Anti-Slavery Women of Western New York." In *National Anti-Slavery Standard* (April 20, 1848).

Barmby, Goodwyn. "Document on Marriage in the New Common World." *The Educational Circular and Communist Apostle,* new ser., no. 1 (Nov. 1841).

Free Thought Magazine, vol. XVI, no. 6 (June 1898). Matilda Gage papers, Schlesinger Library, Radcliffe College, Cambridge, Mass.

La Roche, Sophie von. *Pomona für Teutschlands Tochter.* Jurgen Vorderstemann (ed.). 4 vols. München: K.G. Saur, 1987.

Stanton, Elizabeth Cady, to Matilda J. Gage. Letter reprinted in *The Liberal Thinker*, Syracuse, N.Y., 1890.

2. Reference Works and Anthologies

Bell, Susan Groag, and Karen M. Offen (eds.). *Women, the Family, and Freedom: The Debate in Documents*, vol. 1: 1750–1880. Stanford: Stanford University Press, 1983.

Briquet, Marguerite V. F. Bernier. *Dictionnaire historique, littéraire and bibliographique des françaises et des étrangères naturalisées en France*. Paris, 1804.

Glümer, Claire von. *Bibliothek für die deutsche Frauenwelt*. 6 vols. Leipzig, 1856.

Hausen, Karin (ed.). *Frauen suchen ihre Geschichte: Historische Studien zum 19. und 20. Jahrhundert*. München: C.H. Beck, 1983.

Hellerstein, Erna Olafson, *et al.* (eds.). *Victorian Women: A Documentary Account of Women's Lives in Nineteenth-Century England, France and the United States*. Stanford: Stanford University Press, 1981.

Twellman, Margrit (ed.). *Die deutsche Frauenbewegung im Spiegel repräsentativer Frauenzeitschriften; ihre Anfänge und erste Entwicklung, 1843–1889*. Meisenheim am Glau: Anton Hain, 1972.

3. Secondary Sources

BOOKS

Boydston, Jeanne. *Home and Work: Housework, Wages and the Ideology of Labor in the Early Republic*. New York: Oxford University Press, 1990.

Brittain, Vera. *Lady into Women: A History of Women from Victoria to Elizabeth II*. London: A. Deker, 1953.

Conrad, Earl. *Harriet Tubman: Negro Soldier and Abolitionist*. New York: International Publishers, 1942.

Conrad, Susan P. *Perish the Thought: Intellectual Women in Romantic America, 1830–1860*. New York: Oxford University Press, 1976.

Cott, Nancy. *The Bonds of Womanhood: "Woman's Sphere" in New England, 1780–1835*. New Haven: Yale University Press, 1977.

Dischner, Gisela (ed.). *Caroline und der Jenaer Kreis: Ein Leben zwischen bürgerlicher Vereinzelung und romantischer Geselligkeit*. Berlin: Klaus Wagenbach, 1979.

Douglas, Ann. *The Feminization of American Culture*. New York: Knopf, 1977.

DuBois, Ellen Carol. *Feminism and Suffrage: The Emergence of an Independent Women's Movement in America, 1848–1869*. Ithaca: Cornell University Press, 1978.

Evans, Richard J. *The Feminists: Women's Emancipation Movements in Europe, America and Australasia, 1840–1920*. New York: Barnes & Noble Books, 1977.

Gerin, Winifred. *Charlotte Brontë: The Evolution of Genius*. Oxford: Clarendon Press, 1967.

Hardesty, Nancy. *Women Called to Witness: Evangelical Feminism in the Nineteenth Century*. Nashville: Abingdon, 1984.

Harveson, Mae E. *Catharine Beecher: Pioneer Educator*. Philadelphia: Science Press, 1932.

Herold, J. Christopher. *Mistress to an Age: A Life of Madame de Staël*. New York: Bobbs-Merrill, 1958.

Hersh, Blanche Glassman. *The Slavery of Sex: Feminist Abolitionists in America*. Urbana: University of Illinois Press, 1978.

Marshall, Helen F. *Dorothea Dix* (1937). New York: Russell and Russell, 1967.

Moses, Claire Goldberg. *French Feminism in the 19th Century*. Albany, N.Y.: SUNY Press, 1984.

Perkins, A.J.G., and Theresa Wolfson. *Frances Wright: Free Enquirer*. Philadelphia: Porcupine Press, 1939.

Powell, David A. *George Sand*. Boston: Twayne, 1990.

Scott, Anne Firor. *Making the Invisible Woman Visible*. Urbana: University of Illinois Press, 1984.

Sklar, Kathryn Kish. *Catharine Beecher: A Study in American Domesticity*. New Haven: Yale University Press, 1973.

Susman, Margarete. *Frauen der Romantik*. Köln: Joseph Melzer Verlag, 1960.

Taylor, Barbara. *Eve and the New Jerusalem: Socialism and Feminism in the Nineteenth Century*. New York: Pantheon Books, 1983.

Tiffany, Frances. *The Life of Dorothea Lynde Dix* (1918). Detroit: Gale, 1971.

Tyler, Alice Felt. *Freedom's Ferment: Phases of American Social History from the Colonial Period to the Outbreak of the Civil War*. New York: Harper & Bros., 1944.

ARTICLES

Frederiksen, Elke. "Die Frau als Autorin zur Zeit der Romantik: Anfänge einer weiblichen literarischen Tradition." In Burkhard, *Gestalt und Gestaltend*, pp. 83–153.

Ginzberg, Lori. " 'Moral Suasion Is Moral Balderdash': Women, Politics, and Social Activism in the 1850s." *Journal of American History*, vol. 73, no. 3 (Dec. 1986), 601–22.

Hale, Addie Stancliffe. "The Five Amazing Smith Sisters," *Hartford Daily Courant*, May 15, 1932.

Lawson, Ellen N., and Marlene Merrell. "Antebellum Black Coeds at Oberlin College." In Hine, *Black Women*, vol. 3, pp. 847–68.

Offen, Karen. "Depopulation, Nationalism, and Feminism in Fin-de-siècle France." *American Historical Review*, vol. 89, no. 3 (June 1984), 648–76.

Perkins, Linda M. "Heed Life's Demands: The Educational Philosophy of Fanny Jackson Coppin." In Hine, *Black Women*, vol.3, pp. 1039–48.

———. "The Black Female American Missionary Association Teacher in the South, 1861–1870." In Hine, *Black Women*, vol.3, pp.1049–63.

Scott, Anne Firor. "The Ever-Widening Circle: The Diffusion of Feminist Values from the Troy Female Seminary, 1822–72." In Scott, *Making the Invisible Woman Visible*, pp. 64–88.

———. "Almira Lincoln Phelps: The Self-Made Woman in the Nineteenth Century." In Scott, *ibid.*, pp. 89–106.

Speare, Elizabeth George. "Smith, Abby Hadassah and Julia Evelina." In James, *Notable American Women*, vol. 3, pp. 302–4.

UNPUBLISHED MANUSCRIPTS

Isenberg, Nancy Gale. *The Co-Equality of the Sexes: The Feminist and Religious Discourse of the Nineteenth-Century Woman's Rights Movement: 1848–1860.* Dissertation, University of Wisconsin-Madison, 1990.

4. Emily Dickinson

OWN WORKS

[Emily Dickinson.] *The Poems of Emily Dickinson*. Thomas H. Johnson (ed.). Cambridge: Harvard University Press, 1955.

[———.] *Further Poems of Emily Dickinson Withheld from Publication by Her Sister Lavinia*. Edited by her niece Martha D. Bianchi and Alfred Leete Hampson. Boston: Little, Brown, 1929.

[———.] *The Letters of Emily Dickinson*. Thomas H. Johnson and Theodora Ward (eds.). 3 vols. Cambridge: Harvard University Press, 1958.

BOOKS

Bennett, Paula. *Emily Dickinson: Woman Poet*. Iowa City: University of Iowa Press, 1990.

Cody, John. *After Great Pain: The Inner Life of Emily Dickinson*. Cambridge: Harvard University Press, 1971.

Juhasz, Suzanne (ed.). *Feminist Critics Read Emily Dickinson*. Bloomington: Indiana University Press, 1983.

———. *The Undiscovered Continent: Emily Dickinson and the Space of the Mind*. Bloomington: Indiana University Press, 1983.

Kerr, Inder Nath. *The Landscape of Absence: Emily Dickinson's Poetry*. New Haven: Yale University Press, 1974.

Patterson, Rebecca. *Emily Dickinson's Imagery*. Margaret H. Freeman (ed.). Amherst: University of Massachusetts Press, 1979.

Porter, David. *Dickinson: The Modern Idiom*. Cambridge: Harvard University Press, 1981.

Sewall, Richard B. *The Life of Emily Dickinson*. New York: Farrar, Straus and Giroux, 1974, 1980.

——— (ed.). *Emily Dickinson: A Collection of Critical Essays*. Englewood Cliffs, N.J.: Prentice-Hall, 1963.

Wolff, Cynthia Griffin. *Emily Dickinson*. New York: Knopf, 1987.

ARTICLES

Bogan, Louise. "A Mystical Poet." In Sewall, *The Life of Emily Dickinson*, pp. 137–43.

Faderman, Lillian. "Emily Dickinson's Letters to Sue Gilbert." *The Massachusetts Review*, vol. 18 (Summer 1977), 197–225.

Gilbert, Sandra M. "The Wayward Nun Beneath the Hill: Emily Dickinson and the Mysteries of Womanhood." In Juhasz, *Feminist Critics*.

5. Margaret Fuller

OWN WORKS

Margaret Fuller, *Woman in the Nineteenth Century* (1845). New York: Norton, 1971.

[———.] *The Writings of Margaret Fuller*. Mason Wade (ed.). Fairfield. N.J.: A. Kelley, 1941.

BOOKS

Chevigny, Bell. *The Woman and the Myth: Margaret Fuller's Life and Writings*. Old Westbury, N.Y.: Feminist Press, 1976.

Deiss, Joseph Jay. *The Roman Years of Margaret Fuller*. New York: Crowell, 1969.

Howe, Julia Ward. *Margaret Fuller, Marchesa Ossoli* (1883). Westport, Conn.: Greenwood Press, 1970.

6. Angelina and Sarah Grimké

OWN WORK

Grimké, Angelina Emily. *Appeal to the Christian Women of the Southern States*. New York, 1836.

———. *An Appeal to the Christian Women of the Nominally Free States*. New York: W. S. Dorr, 1837.

———. *Letters to Catharine E. Beecher . . . .* Boston: Issac Knapp, 1838.

Grimké, Sarah Moore. *An Epistle to the Clergy of the Southern States*. New York, 1836.

———. *Letters on the Equality of the Sexes and the Condition of Woman; Addressed to Mary Parker, President of the Boston Female Anti-Slavery Society*. Boston: Isaac Knapp, 1838.

———. Letters, notebooks and diaries in Theodore Dwight Weld Collection, William L. Clements Library, University of Michigan, Ann Arbor.

[Weld, Theodore Dwight.] *American Slavery as It Is: Testimony of a Thousand Witnesses*. New York: American Anti-Slavery Society, 1839.

BOOKS

Birney, Catherine. *The Grimké Sisters: Sarah and Angelina Grimké: The First Women Advocates of Abolition and Woman's Rights.* Boston: Lee & Shepard, 1885.
Lerner, Gerda. *The Grimké Sisters from South Carolina: Rebels Against Slavery.* Boston: Houghton Mifflin, 1967.

7. Elizabeth Cady Stanton

Stanton, Elizabeth Cady. *Eighty Years and More: 1815–1897.* London: T. Fisher Unwin, 1898.
———, Susan B. Anthony and Matilda J. Gage (eds.). *A History of Woman Suffrage.* 6 vols. New York: Fowler and Wells, 1881–1922.
———, and Matilda J. Gage (eds.). *The Woman's Bible.* New York: European Publishing Co., 1895.

8. Rahel Varnhagen von Ense

OWN WORKS

[Varnhagen von Ense, Rahel.] *Rahel Varnhagen im Umgang mit ihren Freunden.* Friedrich Kemp (ed.). München: Kösel Verlag, 1967.
Varnhagen von Ense, Karl. *Rahel: Ein Buch des Andenkens für ihre Freunde* (1834). Neudruck Bern: Herbert Lang, 1972.

BOOKS

Arendt, Hannah. *Rahel Varnhagen: Lebensgeschichte einer deutschen Jüdin aus der Romantik.* Frankfurt: Ullstein, 1975.
Goodman, Kay. "The Impact of Rahel Varnhagen on Women in the 19th Century." In Burkhard, *Gestalt und Gestaltend,* pp. 125–53.
Hertz, Deborah. "Hannah Arendt's Rahel Varnhagen." In *German Women in the Nineteenth Century.* John C. Fout (ed.). New York: Holmes and Meier, 1984, pp. 72–87.
Joeres, Ruth-Ellen. "Self-Conscious Histories: Biographies of German Women in the Nineteenth Century." In Fout, *German Women,* pp. 172–96.

9. Frances Willard

OWN WORKS

Willard, Frances. *Glimpses of Fifty Years: The Autobiography of an American Woman.* Chicago: H. J. Smith, 1889.

Willard, Frances. *An Address to the Public; Particularly to the Members of the Legislature of New York, Proposing a Plan for Improving Female Education.* 2nd ed. Middlebury, Vt.: S. W. Copeland, 1819.

———, and Mary A. Livermore (eds.). *A Woman of the Century: Fourteen hundred-seventy Biographical Sketches Accompanied by Portraits of Leading American Women in All Walks of Life.* Chicago: Charles Wells Moulton, 1893.

BOOKS

Lutz, Alma. *Emma Willard: Pioneer Educator of American Women.* Boston: Beacon Press, 1964.

10. Frances Wright [D'Arusmont]

Wright, Frances [D'Arusmont.] *Course of Popular Lectures with 3 Addresses.* London: James Watson, 1834.

———. *Biography, Notes and Political Letters of Frances Wright D'Arusmont.* New York: J. Myles, 1844.

———. *Views of Society and Manners in America . . . By an Englishwoman.* New York: E. Bliss and E. White, 1821.

XI   TWENTIETH CENTURY

1. Primary Sources

Davis, Elizabeth Lindsay. *Lifting as They Climb.* National Association of Colored Women, 1933.

Douthit, Mary O. *The Souvenir of Western Women.* Portland, Maine: Anderson and Duniway, 1905.

Mossell, Mrs. N. F. *The Work of the Afro-American Woman.* Philadelphia: Geo. S. Ferguson, 1908.

Sumner, Helen L. *History of Women in Industry in the United States,* vols. 9 and 10 of *Report on Condition of Woman and Child Wage-Earners in the United States.* U.S. Senate Document 645. Washington, D.C.: U.S. Government Printing Office, 1911.

2. Secondary Sources

Evans, Sara. *Personal Politics: The Roots of Women's Liberation in the Civil Rights Movement and the New Left.* New York: Knopf, 1979.

Vicinus, Martha. *Independent Women: Work and Community for Single Women, 1850–1920.* Chicago and London: University of Chicago Press, 1985.

Wood, Mary I. *History of the General Federation of Women's Clubs.* New York, 1912.

Sklar, Kathryn Kish. "American Female Historians in Context, 1770–1930." *Feminist Studies*, vol.3, nos. 1/2 (Fall 1975), 171–84.

3. Mary Ritter Beard

OWN WORKS

Beard, Mary Ritter. *Woman's Work in Municipalities*. New York: D. Appleton, 1915.

———. *On Understanding Women*. New York: Grosset & Dunlap, 1931.

———. *America Through Women's Eyes*. New York: Macmillan, 1933.

———. *Woman as Force in History: A Study in Traditions and Realities*. New York: Macmillan, 1946.

———. *The Force of Women in Japanese History*. Washington, D.C.: Public Affairs Press, 1953.

——— with Martha Bensley Bruere. *Laughing Their Way: Women's Humor in America*. New York: Macmillan, 1934.

Beard, Charles A., and Mary Ritter Beard. *The Rise of American Civilization*. 2 vols. New York: Macmillan, 1927.

Cott, Nancy (ed.). *A Woman Making History: Mary Ritter Beard Through Her Letters*. New Haven: Yale University Press, 1991.

Lane, Ann J.(ed.). *Mary Ritter Beard: A Sourcebook*. New York: Schocken Books, 1977.

OTHER BOOKS

Turoff, Barbara. *Mary Ritter Beard as Force in History*. Dayton, Ohio: Wright State University Monograph Series, no. 3, 1979.

Smith, Bonnie G. "Seeing Mary Beard," *Feminist Studies*, vol. 10, no. 3 (Fall 1984), 399–416.

XII   JEWISH WOMEN

BOOKS

Baum, Charlotte, Paula Hyman and Sonya Michel. *The Jewish Woman in America*. New York: Dial Press, 1976.

Cantor, Aviva. *The Jewish Woman: 1900–1980: Bibliography*. Fresh Meadows, N.Y.: Biblio Press, 1981.

Henry, Sondra, and Emily Taitz. *Written Out of History: Our Jewish Foremothers*. Fresh Meadows, N.Y.: Biblio Press, 1983.

Heschel, Susannah (ed.). *On Being a Jewish Feminist*. New York: Schocken Books, 1983.

Marcus, Jacob R. *The American Jewish Woman: A Documentary History*. New York: Ktec, 1981.

Rabinowicz, Harry M. *The World of Hasidism*. London: Hartford House, 1970.

Spiegel, Marcia Cohn, and Deborah Lipton Kremsdorf (eds.). *Women Speak to God: The*

Prayers and Poems of Jewish Women. San Diego: Woman's Institute for Continuing Jewish Education, 1987.

ARTICLES

Kaplan, Marion. "Tradition and Transition: The Acculturation, Assimilation, and Integration of Jews in Imperial Germany—a Gender Analysis." *Leo Bäck Institute Yearbook,* vol. 27 (1982), 3–35.

Lerner, Elinor. "American Feminism and the Jewish Question, 1890–1940." In *Anti-Semitism in American History.* David A. Gerber (ed.). Urbana: University of Illinois Press, 1986.

[Morpurgo, Rachel.] "Rachel Morpurgo." *Encyclopedia Judaica,* Jerusalem: Keter, 1971, vol. 12, p. 349.

Rapoport-Albert, Ada. "On Women in Hasidism: S.A. Horodecky and the Maid of Ludmir Tradition." In *Jewish History: Essays in Honour of Chimen Abramsky.* Rapoport-Albert and Steven J. Zipperstein (eds.). London: Peter Halban, 1988.

Weissler, Chava. " 'For Women and for Men Who Are Like Women': The Construction of Gender in Yiddish Devotional Literature." *Journal of Feminist Studies in Religion,* vol. 5, no. 2 (Fall 1989), 7–24.

———. "Images of the Matriarchs in Yiddish Supplicatory Prayers." *Bulletin of the Center for the Study of World Religions, Harvard University,* vol. 14, no. 1 (1988), 44–51.

———. "The Religion of Traditional Ashkenazic Women: Some Methodological Issues." *AJS Review,* vol. 7, no. 1 (Spring 1987), 73–94.

———. "The Traditional Piety of Ashkenazic Women." In *Jewish Spirituality from the Sixteenth-Century Revival to the Present.* Arthur Green (ed.). New York: Crossroad, 1987.

———. "Women in Paradise." *Tikkun,* vol. 2, no. 2 (April-May 1987), 43–46, 117–20.

Index